# The Modern World

## Allan Todd

# OXFORD
### UNIVERSITY PRESS

Great Clarendon Street, Oxford OX2 6DP

Oxford University Press is a department of the University of Oxford.
It furthers the University's objective of excellence in research, scholarship,
and education by publishing worldwide in

Oxford  New York

Athens  Auckland  Bangkok  Bogotá  Buenos Aires  Cape Town  Chennai
Dar es Salaam  Delhi  Florence  Hong Kong  Istanbul  Karachi  Kolkata
Kuala Lumpur  Madrid  Melbourne  Mexico City  Mumbai  Nairobi  Paris
São Paulo  Shanghai  Singapore  Taipei  Tokyo  Toronto  Warsaw
with associated companies in Berlin  Ibadan

Oxford is a registered trade mark of Oxford University Press
in the UK and in certain other countries

British Library Cataloguing in Publication Data

Data available

ISBN 0 19 9134251

Printed by Butler and Tanner, UK.

Author's acknowledgements:

The author would like to thank the following people for their valuable
contributions to this project: Katharine Burn, Marion Cooper, and the Head of
History and History students of Years 10, 11 & 12 (2000-1) at Morton School,
Carlisle for evaluating draft materials.

Cover Photographs: London Illustrated News  Magnum  Corbis
Illustrations by Jeff Edwards, Picture research by Zooid

## Photograph Credits

6t Corbis UK Ltd.  6b Hulton Getty Picture Collection Ltd.  7 Mary Evans Picture Library
11 Western Mail and Echo Limited  12 Hulton Getty Picture Collection Ltd.  13t Mary Evans
Picture Library  13b Oxford University Press  14 Hulton-Deutsch Collection/Corbis UK Ltd.
15 Mary Evans Picture Library  17 Hulton Getty Picture Collection Ltd.  18 Hulton Getty Picture
Collection Ltd.  19 Hulton Getty Picture Collection Ltd.  22t Robert Hunt Library  22c Leonard
de Selva/Corbis UK Ltd.  22b Corbis UK Ltd.  23t Hulton-Deutsch Collection/Corbis UK Ltd.
23b Topham Picturepoint  29 Popperfoto  30t AKG - London  30b Hulton Getty Picture
Collection Ltd.  33t TRH Pictures (The Research House)  33b Hulton Getty Picture Collection
Ltd.  35t Hulton-Deutsch Collection/Corbis UK Ltd.  35b AKG - London  36 Mary Evans Picture
Library  37 Hulton Getty Picture Collection Ltd.  40 Mary Evans Picture Library  41 Hulton Getty
Picture Collection Ltd.  42 Bettmann/Corbis UK Ltd.  43 Hulton-Deutsch Collection/Corbis UK
Ltd.  45 Bettmann/Corbis UK Ltd.  49 Mary Evans Picture Library  50 Hulton Getty Picture
Collection Ltd.  51 Mary Evans Picture Library  52 Bettmann/Corbis UK Ltd.  54t Hulton-
Deutsch Collection/Corbis UK Ltd.  54b Wellcome Centre for Medical Science  56 A. Bruni/Mary
Evans Picture Library  60t Hulton-Deutsch Collection/Corbis UK Ltd.  60b Mary Evans Picture
Library  61 Mary Evans Picture Library  64 Hulton-Deutsch Collection/Corbis UK Ltd.  66 Sean
Sexton Collection/Corbis UK Ltd.  67 Hulton-Deutsch Collection/Corbis UK Ltd.
69 Bettmann/Corbis UK Ltd.  70 Hulton-Deutsch Collection/Corbis UK Ltd.  73 Hulton-Deutsch
Collection/Corbis UK Ltd.  75 National Museum of Ireland  76t David King Collection
76c David King Collection  76b David King Collection  77 David King Collection  78 David King
Collection  81 Bettmann/Corbis UK Ltd.  83 David King Collection  86 David King Collection

87 David King Collection  89 David King Collection  90 David King Collection  91 David King
Collection  93 David King Collection  94 David King Collection  97 Bettmann/Corbis UK Ltd.
101l David King Collection  101r David King Collection  102t Mary Evans Picture Library
102b Corbis UK Ltd.  103 AKG - London  104t Hulton-Deutsch Collection/Corbis UK Ltd.
104b AKG - London  107 Hulton Getty Picture Collection Ltd.  108 Austrian Archives/Corbis UK
Ltd.  109 AKG - London  110 Hulton Getty Picture Collection Ltd.  111 David King Collection
113 Hulton-Deutsch Collection/Corbis UK Ltd.  115 David Low/ Evening Standard/Centre for
Study of Cartoons and Caricatures  118 Mary Evans Picture Library  120 Hulton-Deutsch
Collection/Corbis UK Ltd.  122 Mary Evans Picture Library  123 AKG - London  125 Mary Evans
Picture Library  126t Dorothea Lange/AKG - London  126b Hulton Getty Picture Collection Ltd.
127t Bettmann/Corbis UK Ltd.  127b Bettmann/Corbis UK Ltd.  128 Peter Newark's American
Pictures  129 Hulton Getty Picture Collection Ltd.  131 Corbis UK Ltd.  135 Museum of History
& Industry/Corbis UK Ltd.  136 Corbis UK Ltd.  137 Bettmann/Corbis UK Ltd.  138 Mary Evans
Picture Library  139 Corbis UK Ltd.  145 Peter Newark's American Pictures  147 Hulton Getty
Picture Collection Ltd.  148t Bettmann Archive/Corbis UK Ltd.  148c Hulton Getty Picture
Collection Ltd.  148b Corbis UK Ltd.  149 Popperfoto  150 Walter Ballhause/AKG - London
152 Hulton Getty Picture Collection Ltd.  153 Mary Evans Picture Library  154t Mary Evans
Picture Library  154b Mary Evans Picture Library  155 Bettmann/Corbis UK Ltd.
156 Bettmann/Corbis UK Ltd.  158 Corbis UK Ltd.  159 AKG - London  160 David King
Collection  162 Hulton Getty Picture Collection Ltd.  163 Yevgeny Khaldei/Corbis UK Ltd.
164 Hulton Getty Picture Collection Ltd.  165 Hulton Getty Picture Collection Ltd.  166 Corbis
UK Ltd.  167 Bettmann/Corbis UK Ltd.  170bl AKG - London  170br Corbis UK Ltd.
170t Hulton Getty Picture Collection Ltd.  171 Hulton-Deutsch Collection/Corbis UK Ltd.
172 Corbis UK Ltd.  174 Hulton-Deutsch Collection/Corbis UK Ltd.  175 Corbis UK Ltd.
176 Hulton Getty Picture Collection Ltd.  177 Topham Picturepoint  179 Hulton Getty Picture
Collection Ltd.  182 Atlantic Syndication Partners  183 Hulton-Deutsch Collection/Corbis UK
Ltd.  185l Popperfoto  185r Advertising Archives  186bl Popperfoto  186br TRH Pictures (The
Research House)  186t Corbis UK Ltd.  188 Hulton-Deutsch Collection/Corbis UK Ltd.  191 AKG
- London  192 David King Collection  193 AKG - London  195 Bettmann/Corbis UK Ltd.
197 AKG - London  198 Mary Evans Picture Library  200 Bettmann/Corbis UK Ltd.
201 Bettmann/Corbis UK Ltd.  204 US Sgt. Ronald L. Haeberle/AKG - London
205 Bettmann/Corbis UK Ltd.  206 Bettmann/Corbis UK Ltd.  208 Hulton Getty Picture
Collection Ltd.  209 Hulton Getty Picture Collection Ltd.  210 Bettmann/Corbis UK Ltd.
211 Popperfoto  213 Bettmann/Corbis UK Ltd.  214 Rex Features  215 Bettmann/Corbis UK
Ltd.  216 Bettmann/Corbis UK Ltd.  221l Bettmann/Corbis UK Ltd.  221r Leif Skoogfors/Corbis
UK Ltd.  222 Hulton Getty Picture Collection Ltd.  223 Corbis UK Ltd.  227 AKG - London
233 Bettmann/Corbis UK Ltd.  234t Bettmann/Corbis UK Ltd.  234b Popperfoto
237 Popperfoto  239 Hulton-Deutsch Collection/Corbis UK Ltd.  240 Hulton Getty Picture
Collection Ltd.  241 Amar Amar/Rex Features  247t Hulton Getty Picture Collection Ltd.
247b Hulton-Deutsch Collection/Corbis UK Ltd.  248 Bettmann/Corbis UK Ltd.
249 Bettmann/Corbis UK Ltd.  250 Sipa Press/Rex Features  251 Hulton Getty Picture
Collection Ltd.  252 Bryn Colton; Assignments /Corbis UK Ltd.  253 Gary Hershorn/Popperfoto
255 Corbis UK Ltd.  256t Hulton Getty Picture Collection Ltd.  256c Hulton Getty Picture
Collection Ltd.  256b Hulton Getty Picture Collection Ltd.  257l Hulton Getty Picture Collection
Ltd.  257r Reuters/Corbis UK Ltd.  258 Popperfoto  259 AKG - London  263 Popperfoto
264 Bettmann/Corbis UK Ltd.  266 Hulton-Deutsch Collection/Corbis UK Ltd.  268t AKG -
London  268b AKG - London  269 Sipa Press/Rex Features  272t Rex Features  272c AKG -
London  272b Mary Evans Picture Library  273l David King Collection  273r Stuart
Franklin/Magnum Photos  276 Sipa Press/Rex Features  278 David King Collection  280 David
King Collection  282 Bettmann/Corbis UK Ltd.  285 Cauquelin/ Sipa Press/Rex Features
288 David King Collection  289 David King Collection  292t Bettmann/Corbis UK Ltd.
292b Bettmann/Corbis UK Ltd.  293l Rex Features  293r Peter Turnley/Corbis UK Ltd.
297 Bettmann/Corbis UK Ltd.  298 Bettmann/Corbis UK Ltd.  299t Bettmann/Corbis UK Ltd.
299b Benson/ Daily Express/Hulton Getty Picture Collection Ltd.

# Contents

# How to use this book

This book is designed so that all of the main aspects of a specification topic are dealt with in self-contained double-page spreads, which can then be used as the bases of individual lessons. Each chapter is opened by a double-page spread which introduces some of the key questions and topics to be covered in the chapter. Each sub-topic is then dealt with by the main narrative text, which contains enough information for C-grade answers. The margin text then gives further information, biographical details or explains key terms. The questions for each sub-topic are designed to test understanding or to give practice at answering exam-style questions based on the sources. Finally, each chapter ends with a brief summary of the main events and points covered, and specific tips on answering all of the principal types of examination questions.

## Citizenship, ICT, and key skills

All specifications are designed to provide opportunities for students to experience aspects of citizenship and ICT, and to develop certain key skills. Most specifications also offer specific suggestions as to where such opportunities would be possible. This book will help students to follow these up and to develop independent learning.

## Citizenship

- Students can use their work to help explain the ethnic and religious differences in the Middle East or Ireland.
- Human and citizens' rights in Nazi Germany, South Africa or the USA can be debated.
- Work on decision-making processes can be based on an examination of the operation of the League of Nations in the 1920s and 1930s.
- How individuals and groups bring about social and political change can be explored via events in South Africa or race relations in the USA.
- Students can work on understanding differing viewpoints by trying to express and defend views on anti-Semitism in Germany, the conflict in Ireland in the 1920s and the Middle East today, or the fairness of the Treaty of Versailles.

## ICT

- Database software, web-sites, graphs and charts can be used to study, for example, changing unemployment statistics in the USA or Germany in the 1930s, or the growing electoral success of the Nazi Party from 1928-33.
- CD-Roms and websites can be used to research the reasons for the failure of the League of Nations, the different causes of the Second World War or the effectiveness of appeasement.
- Students can use ICT-processed writing frames to produce, for example, a class presentation on the causes of the Cold War, the defeat of the USA in Vietnam or the collapse of communism in the USSR and eastern Europe.
- E-mail projects can be undertaken which involve contacting experts on conflict in the Middle East or the collapse of apartheid in South Africa.

## Key skills

- Communication - Students can present and debate the differing aims of the Big Three at the peace conferences, or use cartoons to explain the causes of the Second World War. Group work on, for example, assessing the seriousness of the Cuban Missile Crisis or the reasons behind the Soviet invasion of Hungary in 1956 can also be undertaken.

- Application of number – Comparison work on the casualties of different countries in the First World War, or examining the fluctuations and relationship between unemployment and votes in the USA or Germany during the Depression, would provide useful evidence of this skill, as would extracting information about the production increases under Stalin's Five-Year Plans.

- Information Technology - In addition to previous suggestions, students can be guided to websites where extra information can be extracted for the production of newspaper articles on, for example, Mao's policies, the wars in the Middle East, or the Russian Civil War.

- Working with others - Students can be asked to produce group reports or presentations on the peace treaties of 1919-20, or the failure of the League of Nations. Alternatively, they can be asked to produce a script for a TV show on the life of a key historical individual, such as Stalin, Hitler, Mao or Mandela.

By careful planning, all or most of these key skills can be developed, and evidence of achievement provided, within the same piece of work.

| | | EDEXCEL | AQA | OCR | WJEC (WALES) | CCEA (N.IRELAND) | SQA STANDARD (SCOTLAND) |
|---|---|---|---|---|---|---|---|
| 1 | Britain before the First World War | ■ | ■ | | | ■ | |
| 2 | The First World War | | | ■ | | | ■ |
| 3 | The peace treaties | | ■ | ■ | ■ | | ■ |
| 4 | The League of Nations, 1919-1929 | | ■ | ■ | ■ | | |
| 5 | Britain between the wars | ■ | | ■ | ■ | ■ | |
| 6 | Russia and the USSR, 1900-1941 | ■ | ■ | ■ | ■ | ■ | ■ |
| 7 | Germany, 1918-1945 | ■ | ■ | ■ | ■ | ■ | ■ |
| 8 | The USA, 1918-1941 | ■ | ■ | ■ | ■ | | ■ |
| 9 | The Second World War | ■ | ■ | | ■ | ■ | ■ |
| 10 | Britain and the Second World War | ■ | ■ | | ■ | ■ | |
| 11 | The Cold War, 1945-1961 | ■ | | ■ | ■ | | ■ |
| 12 | Cuba and Vietnam: Cold War 'hotspots', 1962-1975 | ■ | | ■ | ■ | | ■ |
| 13 | The USSR and eastern Europe, 1945-1991 | ■ | | ■ | | ■ | |
| 14 | Conflict in the Middle East | ■ | | ■ | | ■ | |
| 15 | South Africa | ■ | | | | ■ | |
| 16 | The rise of Communist China | | ■ | | | | |
| 17 | Race relations in the USA, 1945-1980 | ■ | ■ | ■ | | | |

# CHAPTER 1

## BRITAIN BEFORE THE FIRST WORLD WAR

*An advertising poster for the Titanic in 1912.*

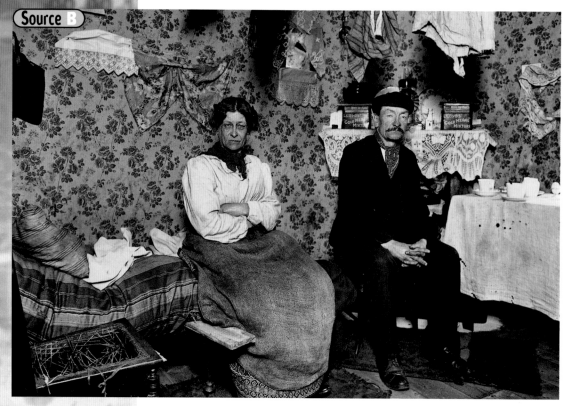

*Poverty in the East End of London in 1912.*

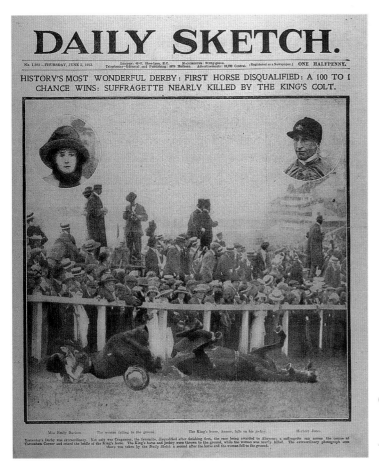

**DAILY SKETCH.**

No. 1,323—THURSDAY, JUNE 5, 1913. London: 45-47, Shoe-lane, E.C. Manchester: Withy-grove. ONE HALFPENNY.
Telephones—Editorial and Publishing: 5876 Holborn. Advertisements: 10,793 Central. (Registered as a Newspaper.)

HISTORY'S MOST WONDERFUL DERBY: FIRST HORSE DISQUALIFIED: A 100 TO 1
CHANCE WINS: SUFFRAGETTE NEARLY KILLED BY THE KING'S COLT.

Miss Emily Davison.   The woman falling to the ground.   The King's horse, Anmer, falls on his jockey.   Herbert Jones.

Yesterday's Derby was extraordinary. Not only was Craganour, the favourite, disqualified after finishing first, the race being awarded to Aboyeur; a suffragette ran across the course at Tattenham Corner and seized the bridle of the King's horse. The King's horse and jockey were thrown to the ground, while the woman was nearly killed. The extraordinary photograph seen above was taken by the *Daily Sketch* a second after the horse and the woman fell to the ground.

**Source C**

*Emily Davison's fatal suffragette protest at the 1913 Derby, reported in the* Daily Sketch.

**Key Questions**

**Why** did Britain in the early twentieth century contain such scenes of poverty as shown in **Source B**, when **Source A** shows it to have been a wealthy and industrially advanced country?

**Who** were the suffragettes referred to in **Source C**?

**Why** were so many women like Emily Davison prepared to break the law and even risk their lives in Britain before the start of the First World War?

These are some of the issues that we will cover in this chapter. The main focus of this chapter on Britain will be:

• The new Liberal government and its early reforms, 1906-09

• Opposition to the Liberals and their reforms, 1909-11

• The women's suffrage movement, and the suffragettes' campaign

• Growing tensions in Ireland

• The emergence of the Labour Party, and rising trade union militancy

• Continuing Liberal reforms, 1911-14

# Britain in 1900

*Imperialism is the process of conquering other countries for either economic gain, or for strategic and military reasons - or for both. The importance of economic considerations behind imperial expansion was seen in Britain's efforts to control southern Africa. This led to two wars in the period 1880-1902 against the two independent Boer republics which bordered the British territories of the Cape Colony and Natal and which contained rich deposits of gold and diamonds. In 1910, the whole of South Africa became part of the British Empire.*

## The British Empire

By the time Queen Victoria died in 1901, the British Empire covered about 11.5 million square miles (almost 20% of the land surface of the world) and contained over 400 million people from all the continents of the world. During the last quarter of the nineteenth century, British imperialism had concentrated on Africa. Explorations by David Livingstone and others had allowed Britain and other European countries to move into Africa and establish new colonies. In 1875, only about 10% of Africa had been colonised by European nations. By 1900, the figure was over 90%. This process, known as the 'Scramble for Africa', was intended to supply valuable raw materials, extra food and increased markets for British industrial goods.

**Source A**

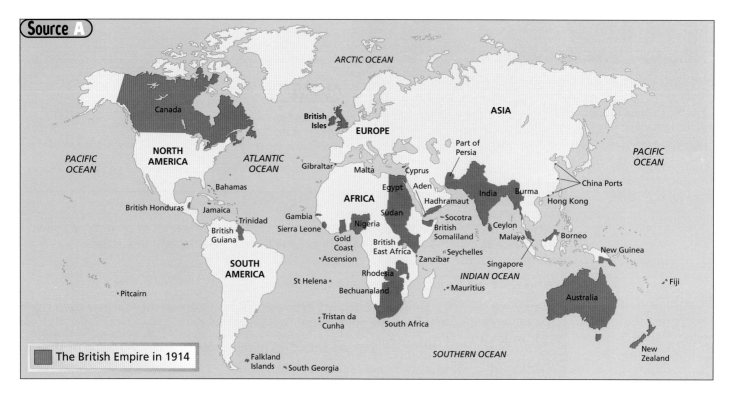

The British Empire in 1914

## Poverty in a land of plenty

On the surface, Britain in 1900 seemed to be the most wealthy and powerful country in the world. British industrial production and exports were high; the British Empire was still the largest in the world; and the British people as a whole seemed to be benefiting from increased world trade.

Yet, below the surface, there were already signs of problems and decline. Much of Britain's prosperity was based on 'old' industries such as shipbuilding, coal, iron, steel and textiles. These industries were beginning to slow down, and were coming under increased competition from countries such as Germany, Japan and the USA.

Although the possession of a large empire meant enormous sums of money flowed back to Britain, most of this was re-invested overseas rather than in modernising British industry and so improving its competitiveness.

The period from the death of Victoria in 1901 until the First World War broke out in 1914, is sometimes referred to as a 'Golden Age'. This is because Britain still appeared to be the world leader. Yet many of the industrial problems which had emerged in the past 25 years had still not been dealt with. In addition, very little of the Empire's vast surplus wealth 'trickled down' to the poor, and the health, welfare and education of many ordinary British people needed drastic improvement. The extent of the poverty and problems existing in many British towns and cities had been shown up by the Boer War (1899-1902). Many of the volunteers had had to be rejected as unfit for military service.

## Industrial relations

Although there was much poverty in Britain in 1900, real wages for many workers had been steadily if slowly improving since the late 1880s. This increase was partly the result of increased membership of trade unions - especially for the unskilled workers. This had happened because of changes to the law which gave legal protection to unions engaged in peaceful activities. There had also been important strikes in the years 1888-89, including the Matchgirls' Strike of 1888, and the Dockers' Strike of 1889. The success of these strikes encouraged the formation of several powerful unions for the unskilled and semi-skilled workers, such as the Miners' Federation of Great Britain and the General Railway Workers' Union.

Because of these successful strikes, many employers turned to Parliament and the courts to limit the ability of the unions to organise successful strikes. The unions were particularly worried by the Taff Vale Case in 1901, which seemed to rule out the right to strike in practice, as trade unions would soon be bankrupted. This situation worried many trade unionists as, during the period before 1914, prices began to rise more quickly than wages.

## The rise of Labour

As a result of these legal setbacks, the trade unions decided to turn to Parliament as a way of regaining their earlier rights. At first, many decided to help the Liberals, who promised to repeal the Taff Vale Judgement. In 1900, the Trades Union Congress (TUC) set up the Labour Representation Committee (LRC) to increase the number of working-class MPs. The rise of the LRC put pressure on the Liberals to promise to improve social welfare conditions and trade union rights.

**Source B**

Recruitment for the Boer War showed how physically unfit many of those who volunteered for military service were. Since most volunteers presumably thought themselves reasonably fit, they may have represented only the tip of the iceberg... Major-General Frederick Maurice concluded in 1903 'neither the unskilled labourer who has been tempted into the towns, nor the hereditary townsman who, after two or three generations, has deteriorated in physical vigour, will be able to rear a healthy family'.

*An extract from a history book published in 1997 about the long-term effects of malnutrition and poor living conditions.*

**Taff Vale Case**

*In 1901, the Taff Vale Railway Company in South Wales took the Amalgamated Society of Railway Servants to court for profits lost during a strike. The judge awarded the company £23 000 compensation, even though the strike had been legal and peaceful. The union appealed to the Conservative-dominated House of Lords but the Law Lords ruled that the union was liable and should pay the compensation.*

**Questions**

1 Why was imperialism seen as being important for maintaining Britain's position?

2 How useful is **Source B** for showing the social problems in Britain which were brought to light by the Boer War?

# CHAPTER 1

# The Liberals and reform, 1905-09

## From Conservative to Liberal rule

The Conservative Party had dominated British politics almost continuously since 1886, apart from 1892-95 when the Liberals had been in power. However, by 1905, the Conservatives had begun to lose support and, at the same time, suffered serious internal divisions. As a result of these problems, A.J. Balfour, the Conservative Prime Minister, resigned in December 1905.

At first, the Conservatives hoped the Liberals would be too inexperienced to form a lasting government. However, the Liberals won a massive majority in the January 1906 elections. They won 377 seats, which included 54 LRC MPs (about half of whom were 'Lib-Labs') and 83 Irish MPs who hoped to obtain Home Rule for Ireland at last. The new Liberal Prime Minister, Henry Campbell-Bannerman, was determined to push through a broad programme of significant social and political reforms.

Herbert Asquith was Chancellor of the Exchequer and David Lloyd George was President of the Board of Trade. In 1908, Campbell-Bannerman was replaced as Prime Minister by Asquith, while Lloyd George took over as Chancellor of the Exchequer. From 1906-09 this group of leading Liberals were able to get many acts through Parliament.

## Social reforms

A wide range of social reforms and laws were made in the years 1907-09. These included several to improve the welfare of children: the School Meals Act (1907), gave LEAs the power to provide free (though basic) school meals (breakfast and/or lunch) for children from poor families; while the Medical Inspection Act (1907), ordered LEAs to carry out medical inspections of younger children. Both these reforms were in part the result of the fact that many of the recruits for the Boer War (1899-1902) who were living in the poorer areas, had had to be rejected as medically unfit. Children were also helped by the Childrens' Charter of 1908. This was made up of two acts: the Childrens' Act made street begging and the purchase of alcohol and tobacco by children illegal, and outlawed entry into pubs; the Prevention of Crimes Act introduced the Borstal system for young offenders, so that they did not have to go to adult prisons. Special juvenile courts and the probation system were also begun by the Liberals.

The Housing and Town Planning Act (1909) gave the Local Government Board the power to force local authorities to demolish back-to-back housing, and allowed the authorities to purchase land for future housing development. Also in 1909, the Poor Law Report came out, but failed to give one overall recommendation.

**LRC**

*The Labour Representation Committee (LRC), set up by the Trades Union Congress in 1900, decided to form pacts with the Liberals in many working-class constituencies. This made sure that Independent Labour Party and Liberal candidates did not compete against each other – instead, there would be just one Lib-Lab candidate. This would avoid splitting the anti-Conservative vote.*

**David Lloyd George**

*Born in 1863, his family moved to Wales in 1864. He became a Liberal MP in 1890, and was on its more radical wing. He was particularly opposed to hereditary privileges and the English landowning upper classes. From 1908-15, he was Chancellor of the Exchequer. In 1916, he became Prime Minister of the wartime coalition government. He remained in this position until 1922, when his Conservative coalition partners brought him down.*

**Poor Law Report**

*A majority report simply recommended abolishing the Poor Law Guardians and instead giving responsibility to county councils. This meant keeping the workhouses which had been built as a result of the Poor Law Reform Act (1834), into which the poor had to go if they wished to receive assistance. A minority report, written by Sidney Webb and supported by a young Liberal called William Beveridge, recommended abolishing poor relief altogether. Instead, it suggested setting up a welfare state system, based on minimum standards below which the State would not allow anyone to fall, with separate government agencies dealing with issues such as unemployment.*

## Industrial relations reforms

Following the cooperation between the Liberals, the LRC (which after 1906 became the Labour Party) and the trade unions in the years after the Taff Vale Judgement, the new Liberal government introduced several reforms to deal with various trade union grievances. The Trade Disputes Act (1906) reversed the Taff Vale decision, and gave unions the right to strike without being sued for breach of contract, or loss of profits arising from a strike. The Workmen's Compensation Act (1906) provided compensation for workers who suffered accidents at work which were due to the negligence of employers, and for incapacity due to industrial diseases. However, those earning more than £250 a year were excluded. The Merchant Shipping Act (1906) improved working conditions on ships for British crews, as well as forcing all foreign ships using British ports to comply with the same standards.

The Coal Mines Act (1908) introduced the eight-hour day for miners (the first time any British government had intervened to regulate the hours of adult workers); while the Trade Boards Act (1909) set up boards to regulate the pay of workers in industries which were not covered by existing laws. The Labour Exchanges Act (1909) set up Labour Exchanges in all local authorities to help the unemployed find work. Britain was divided into 10 districts, in which public money was used to fund the keeping of a register of job vacancies, and to help employers looking for workers get in touch with those seeking work.

## Political reforms

The new Liberal government also began to carry out some important political reforms. In 1907, the Plural Voting Bill tried to establish the principle of 'one man, one vote' by stopping the practice of property owners being able to vote in all constituencies in which they owned land or buildings. However, this bill, along with several others, was blocked by the House of Lords. The Liberals succeeded in getting the Qualifications of Women Act (1907) passed.

**Source A**

A cartoon from 1908, showing William Abraham, a trade union leader, attaching a handicap weight (the Eight Hours Act) to the foot of a figure representing Britain.

### Trades Board Act

*This applied mainly to workers in what were known as the 'sweated industries', such as net mending and box making, which were mostly done in appalling conditions by women who often worked extremely long hours in their own homes.*

### Qualifications of Women Act

*This allowed women to become magistrates, and to be councillors, aldermen, mayors or chairmen of county and county borough councils, in addition to district and parish councils where this was already permitted. However, there remained many in the Liberal Party, and the Liberal government, who were still opposed to the idea of allowing women to vote in general elections.*

### Questions

1 What is the cartoon in **Source A** trying to say about the Coal Mines Act (1908)?

2 Which groups of people benefited most from the Liberal reforms?

# Opposition to the Liberal reforms, 1909-11

### The cost of the reforms

Some of the reforms pushed through were controversial, and most of them involved a large increase in government expenditure. One of the reforms which was clearly going to be expensive was the Old Age Pensions Act (1908). It gave 5 shillings (25p) a week to those aged over 70, provided they had never been in receipt of poor relief, had no criminal record and their savings did not result in more than £30 a year in interest.

### The People's Budget, 1909

To pay for the old age pensions, and the other recent reforms (as well as the increased defence expenditure felt necessary because of Germany's expanding navy) the Chancellor of the Exchequer, David Lloyd George, introduced a Budget designed to raise an extra £16 million. This included a Road Fund to modernise the roads, with the money to come from motor car licences and a tax on petrol. An increase in standard income tax was also proposed, from 1s (5p) to 1s 2d (6p) in the pound (with a reduction for those earning less than £500 a year); and a super tax of an extra 6d (2.5p) in the pound for those with an income of more than £5000 a year (on any income above £3000). Lloyd George also proposed to levy a Land Values Tax on undeveloped land and minerals, plus a 20% levy (the unearned increment) on the increase of land value when it was sold. Finally, there was also an increase in alcohol and tobacco duties, and an increase in stamp duties on the sale of houses, and in death duties on estates worth more than £5000, with a charge of 25% on estates worth more than £1 million.

**Source A**

The first payment of the Old Age Pension in a London Post Office, 1 January 1909.

### Conflict between the Commons and the Lords

Even before 1909, there had been political tensions between the two Houses of Parliament. Though this had become more serious during the last Liberal government in 1892-95, it had worsened since 1906. This was because the House of Lords (in which the Conservatives had an in-built majority) had either significantly altered or even blocked several Liberal plans for reform. When Lloyd George became Chancellor of the Exchequer in 1909, he began to attack the hereditary principle (by which members of the Lords inherited their titles and seats in the Lords), and what he called the 'idle rich' being able to prevent what the people had voted for in an election.

When the Budget was sent to the Lords, they rejected it, although one of the conventions (unwritten rules or customs) of the British constitution was that the Lords did not interfere with taxation. The Lords, most of whom were wealthy landowners, claimed they were entitled to reject this Budget as most of the increases would fall on wealthy people. Not surprisingly, the Lords supported the Conservative Budget Protest League. The Liberals were equally determined that the time had come to reform the unelected House

**Houses of Parliament**

*The Houses of Parliament (the Commons and the Lords), together with the reigning monarch, are the supreme law-making body in Britain. Before 1911, the House of Lords had the power to block (prevent) any proposals for laws coming from the House of Commons, in which the MPs elected in a general election sit. The House of Lords, then, was made up entirely of unelected hereditary lords (peers of the realm). These lords were men who inherited a title (such as duke or earl). Such lords owned large landed estates and were usually supporters of the Conservative Party. This is what gave the Conservatives their 'in-built majority'.*

of Lords. The Prime Minister, Asquith, informed the King he could not continue to govern without the extra money to be raised by the Budget, and so asked him to create enough Liberal peers to cancel out the Tory majority so that the Budget could be pushed through. Edward VII, however, only agreed to do so if the Liberals called and won another election. So Asquith called a general election for January 1910, though without publicly saying what the Liberals planned to do with the Lords if they won.

## The Parliament Act (1911)

The election result was much closer than in 1906. The Liberals won 275 seats, but the Conservatives were close behind with 273. However, the Liberals also had the support of the 40 Labour and 82 Irish Nationalist MPs, giving them a majority over the Conservatives of 124. The Liberals then re-presented the People's Budget to the Lords, but this time along with a Parliament Bill which was intended to reduce the powers of the Lords. The Lords quickly passed the Budget, but opposed the suggested reforms to the Lords. The new King, George V, said he would create enough Liberal peers to cancel the Tory majority in the Lords if the Liberals won a second election. This election took place in December 1910. It was also close, but the Liberals still had a majority and pushed on with their Parliament Bill.

The Bill said that all money bills (including Budgets) would automatically become law one month after the Commons had approved them, regardless of what the House of Lords voted. It also said that any other bill would become law after two years, even if the Lords rejected it, provided the Commons passed it three times in succession. Because this Act would reduce the power of the Lords while increasing that of the Commons, the maximum life of a parliament was reduced from seven years to five.

The Lords were divided into 'Hedgers' and 'Ditchers'. Hedgers argued the Bill should be accepted to avoid losing the Conservative majority in the Lords. 'Ditchers' wanted to reject the Bill and fight a 'last ditch' resistance. The 'Hedgers' finally won the argument, and the Lords passed the Parliament Bill by 131 to 114 votes.

*A cartoon published in Punch magazine, 28 April 1909. Lloyd George is shown as a giant threatening the rich.*

*A poster produced by the Budget League in 1909 in support of the People's Budget.*

## Questions

1 Why was the Old Age Pension Act (1908), referred to in **Source A**, such an important reform?

2 How accurate a view of the 1909 Budget is presented by **Source B**?

3 What is meant by the term 'peer' in **Source C** and what is the message of this cartoon?

4 Why was the Parliament Act (1911) passed?

# Women and the right to vote

## Women's suffrage

Since the seventeenth century, a few individuals (men as well as women) had called for equal rights for women, including the right to vote (sometimes referred to as the 'suffrage' or the 'franchise'). Support for this, though, had been slow to develop. However, in the nineteenth century, as working class men were gradually successful in gaining the right to vote for themselves, more women began to demand the same. In 1867, the Society for the Promotion of Women's Suffrage was set up. Then, in 1897, came the National Union of Women's Suffrage Societies (NUWSS). The NUWSS, led by Millicent Fawcett, believed in peaceful protest, and was prepared to work with sympathetic men in the Liberal Party. The NUWSS were sometimes known as the 'suffragists'.

They were encouraged by several reforms in the late nineteenth and early twentieth centuries which began to establish equality for women in education, legal rights and local government. These included the Married Women's Property Act (1870), which allowed women to retain possession of their personal property and wages, instead of these automatically going to their husbands. Some university colleges also finally agreed to admit female students in the 1870s. Political reforms included Forster's Education Act (1870), which allowed women who paid school rates to vote and stand in School Board elections. The County Councils Act (1880) allowed unmarried female ratepayers to vote in county and county borough council elections; and the Parish Councils Act (1894) gave them the same voting rights in parish elections, plus the right to stand for election.

## The suffragettes

Despite these reforms, women still remained without the vote in general elections. In 1903, Emmeline Pankhurst, and her daughters Christobel and Sylvia, set up the Women's Social and Political Union (WSPU). Its members soon became known as the 'suffragettes'. The Pankhursts argued that in order to get the vote, women would need to adopt the same militant, and sometimes violent, methods which men had used in their campaigns for an extension of the franchise in the nineteenth century.

When the Liberals won the 1906 election, the NUWSS's hopes for quick reform were soon dashed, despite the Qualification of Women Act (1906) which allowed women to stand as candidates in county council elections, and to become mayors and magistrates. Many women were especially disappointed when the Prime Minister, Campbell-Bannerman, and Asquith, the Home Secretary, said the need to get other reforms through Parliament meant there would not be time to consider votes for women. As a result, more women began to favour the WSPU approach. Their motto became 'Deeds not Words'. The women's movement was soon split between

### Source A

It is only simple justice that women demand. For fifty years they have been striving and have met nothing but trickery and betrayal at the hands of politicians. Cabinet ministers have taunted them with their reluctance to use the violent methods that were used by men before they won the vote in 1829, 1832 and 1867. The message of the broken pane is that women are determined that the lives of their sisters shall no longer be broken, and that in future those who have to obey the law shall have a voice in saying what the law shall be.

*An adapted extract from 'Broken Windows', a pamphlet written by Christabel Pankhurst in 1912.*

### Source B

*Emmeline Pankhurst being arrested at Buckingham Palace in 1914.*

those who favoured the peaceful protest of the NUWSS, and those who supported WSPU militancy.

## The militant campaign, 1906-13

At first, the WSPU concentrated on heckling members of the government at public meetings, and chaining themselves to the railings outside Downing Street and government buildings, as well as organising large demonstrations. The campaign was then stepped up to include smashing the windows of large department stores and waiting to be arrested. However, attempts by sympathetic MPs (especially Keir Hardie of the Independent Labour Party) to get Parliament to pass bills in 1907, 1908 and 1910, which would extend the right to vote to women, all failed. In part, this was because the main two parties, the Liberals and the Conservatives, feared such an extension would benefit their political rivals more than themselves.

Arrested suffragettes now began to refuse to pay fines and, from 1909, some went on hunger strike in prison. When prison authorities force-fed hunger-striking suffragettes, to prevent prisoners dying and so becoming martyrs for the cause, there was a public outcry. A political truce was called during the elections of 1910, but soon the window breaking resumed, along with the destruction of golfing greens. In 1912, Christabel Pankhurst went to Paris, from where she organised an even more violent campaign, which included arson attacks on post boxes, attacks on famous paintings and even bombs placed in empty buildings. At the 1913 Derby, Emily Davison tried to stop the King's horse as a protest, but was knocked down and later died.

As the number of suffragettes in prison grew, the government decided to end force-feeding, and instead passed the Cat and Mouse Act (1913). Asquith then announced that he would accept any clause that the Commons could agree on concerning women's suffrage, in a new Reform Bill he was proposing. One clause seemed likely to succeed, but it was blocked by the Speaker of the Commons and was dropped from the Plural Voting Bill.

## The coming of war

When the plan was dropped, suffragette activities were stepped up once again. As had previously happened, the huge meetings and more militant actions, which were widely reported in the newspapers, led to a big increase in membership and donations. This increased level of suffragette protests coincided with a rising number of large strikes by workers over pay and unemployment, and with growing tension in Ireland. This led some people to think that Britain was rapidly approaching a revolutionary situation. However, when Britain declared war on Germany in 1914, the WSPU suspended its actions and most members supported the war effort.

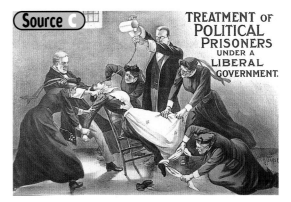

**Source C**

TREATMENT OF POLITICAL PRISONERS UNDER A LIBERAL GOVERNMENT.

*A poster against force-feeding of suffragettes, produced by the WSPU in 1910.*

**Force-feeding**

*This involved putting a rubber tube into their stomach (via the mouth or, if they refused to open their mouths, via their nose) and then pouring down a thin porridge. The women had to be forcibly restrained and were often sick several times. On a few occasions, the tube missed its target, and some of the liquid entered the lungs. Because it was an unpleasant, painful and sometimes dangerous process, some saw this as a form of political torture, designed to make women end their struggle for the vote.*

**Cat and Mouse Act (1913)**

*This allowed the authorities to release hunger-strikers temporarily to build up their strength and then re-arrest them, as many times as necessary, until they had served their sentence.*

**Questions**

1 How useful is **Source A** for finding out about the reasons why the WSPU adopted more militant methods in 1912?

2 What does **Source B** tell us about the suffragette campaign in 1914?

3 What problems of reliability might there be concerning the view presented by **Source C**?

# CHAPTER 1

# Ireland and Home Rule

## Source A

We declare our [belief] that... the right of domestic legislation on all Irish affairs should be restored to our country. We claim the privilege of managing our own affairs by a parliament assembled in Ireland. There should be in Ireland a government in Ireland for Irish affairs, controlled by the Irish parliament.

*An extract from the aims of the Home Rule League, 1873.*

## The situation in Ireland

As well as the problems associated with the campaign for women's suffrage, the Liberal government was also faced with a growing crisis in Ireland. This was Britain's oldest colony. The Liberals had supported the idea of some measure of self-government for Ireland for some time. In 1886, and again in 1893 when they were in power, Prime Minister Gladstone had tried to pass Home Rule Bills. These were demanded by the Home Rule League, formed in Ireland in 1873. Although the Conservatives were opposed, Gladstone tried to persuade the Liberals to support Home Rule. The Conservatives, in fact, were closely aligned with the 'Unionists' in Ireland, who wanted to remain directly ruled by Britain. Gladstone's first attempt in 1886 would have given Ireland its own parliament, able to decide most internal issues, though Britain would have kept control of foreign policy, the army and taxation. But this First Home Rule Bill failed as it split the Liberals. The Liberal Unionists, as well as the Conservatives, were against the idea. The second attempt, in 1893, was thrown out by the Lords.

## The Third Home Rule Bill

When the Liberals won the 1906 election with such a large majority, the Home Rule MPs (known as 'Nationalists') hoped a new Third Home Rule Bill would become law. The Nationalist MPs in Parliament (now led by John Redmond, who had replaced Charles Parnell), supported the Liberals in their struggle against the House of Lords in 1910. Their votes were crucial, as, after the second election in 1910, the Liberals had lost their overall majority in the House of Commons. As a result, the Nationalists were promised a Home Rule Bill. This was introduced in 1912 and passed the Commons but was rejected by the Lords. Since the Parliament Act (1911), however, the Bill would automatically become law in two years, provided the Commons passed it twice more.

The Unionists, though, feared Home Rule would soon lead to an entirely independent Ireland with an Irish parliament with an in-built Catholic majority. They were determined to resist. They were led by the Ulster Protestant Sir Edward Carson, and supported by several leading Conservatives, such as Lord Randolph Churchill (Winston Churchill's father). They organised huge demonstrations in protest against the Bill. In September 1912, over 500 000 signed the Solemn League and Covenant swearing to resist Home Rule. They set up the Ulster Volunteer Force and began open military training. They soon had over 100 000 members, and with more than £1 000 000 in donations, began to buy large supplies of guns and ammunition, mainly from Germany.

**Source B**

Armed Unionists marching through Portadown in protest against Home Rule, September 1912.

## The tension increases

These developments alarmed the Nationalists, and those who wanted a totally independent republic began to make their own preparations. The Irish Republican Brotherhood was revived, and set up the Irish Volunteers to oppose the Ulster Volunteers. By May 1914, they had about 80 000 members and were undertaking military training. Another more left-wing group, the Irish Citizen Army, which was led by James Connolly, also armed itself and was prepared to fight. The Republican cause was further strengthened by the new Sinn Fein Party which had been set up in 1905 and was led by Arthur Griffith.

The Nationalists and the more militant Republicans were especially angered in March 1914 by what became known as the Curragh Mutiny, in which Protestant officers at the British army's headquarters in Dublin were allowed to temporarily 'resign' their commissions rather than enforce the Home Rule Act. Ireland seemed on the point of civil war; but in August 1914, Britain declared war on Germany and the Act was suspended until the end of the war.

Many men, both Unionists and Nationalists, volunteered to join the British army. By 1916, over 150 000 had volunteered. However, the Nationalists were angered when Carson became a member of the wartime coalition government, and the army recruits from Ulster were allowed to form a special Ulster Division.

**Irish Republican Brotherhood**

*The IRB (often known also as the Fenians) had been set up in the 1860s as part of the struggle for Irish independence. They were the more militant and radical section of the Nationalist movement, but had gone into decline after the 1870s.*

**James Connolly**

*James Connolly was a leader of the Irish Transport and General Workers' Union and a revolutionary socialist. He wanted Ireland to become a socialist republic and supported Irish independence as part of that struggle. He set up the Irish Citizen Army in 1913, to provide protection for union pickets from police and troops which were attempting to break up a strike by transport workers in Dublin. Its flag was the 'Plough and Stars'.*

**Source C**

We have no foreign enemy except the treacherous government of England - a government which even whilst it is calling us to die for it, refuses to give a straight answer to our demand for Home Rule.

*The view of James Connolly, leader of the Irish Citizen Army, at the start of the First World War in 1914.*

**Questions**

1 What do you understand by the term 'Home Rule', as mentioned in **Source C**?

2 Use **Source B** and your own knowledge to explain why some people opposed Home Rule.

3 Why did the writer of **Source C** describe the English government as 'treacherous'?

4 How useful is **Source C** as evidence of the views of Irish Nationalists in 1914?

# The continuation of Liberal reform, 1911-14

## THE DAWN OF HOPE.

Mr. LLOYD GEORGE'S National Health Insurance Bill provides for the insurance of the Worker in case of Sickness.

## Support the Liberal Government
### in their policy of
## SOCIAL REFORM.

*A poster about the National Insurance Act, issued by the Liberal government in 1911.*

### New Liberalism

*This was a movement associated with Lloyd George and Winston Churchill (who was a Liberal before he joined the Conservatives). New Liberalism was influenced by the writings and welfare suggestions of such people as Charles Booth and William Beveridge. Lloyd George had also been extremely impressed by the social welfare system which already existed in Germany. It was believed that New Liberalism would revive the Liberal Party and help it stave off the political challenge presented by the new Labour Party.*

### Welfare state

*This means a country where the government helps provide health schemes and social benefits for all its citizens. It is particularly aimed at those whose incomes are too low to enable them to save money to provide decent health care or funds to see them through periods when they are unable to work, such as illness, unemployment or old age. These welfare services are paid for out of taxation as well as contributions - in this way, the wealthy contribute to the welfare of the less well-off.*

## Labour and the trade unions

The 1910 elections had reduced the Liberal majority and made them dependent on the Irish Nationalist and Labour MPs in Parliament. As well as having to deal with the women's suffrage and Irish issues, there were also problems for the Liberal government involving the trade unions. One issue had arisen in 1909, when the Osborne Judgement had ruled that trade unions could not have a political levy or subscription to raise extra money from members in order to donate money to a political party, unless members specifically asked to 'contract in'. It also said that the new Labour Party could not pay salaries to its candidates who were elected as MPs. This was a particular problem for the Labour Party, as its MPs were mainly working class and so had no private income. The Liberals helped the Labour Party in 1911 when they pushed through a Standing Order (over which the Lords had no say) which brought in the payment of MPs for the first time: MPs would get £400 a year, which was about twice the average working class wage. Then, with the Trade Union Act, the Osborne Judgement of 1909 was overturned. Trade Unions were allowed to set up political funds and to charge a political levy. Members who did not wish to contribute could sign a form to 'contract out'. The lack of trade union funds had been one of the reasons why the Labour Party had done badly in the 1910 elections. Ironically, these two Liberal reforms did much to help the growth of the political party which would soon replace them as the other major party in Britain.

## Industrial relations reforms

The Liberals passed several more reforms in the period 1911-14 which were designed to improve working conditions in a range of industries. The Mines Act (1911) improved conditions in mines, while the Shops Act gave shopworkers a half-day holiday, although it failed to deal with working hours which were often extremely long. The Minimum Wage Act (1912) set up joint boards of employers and workers in every district in an attempt to arbitrate and regulate wages.

## Social reforms

The Liberal government continued with several more 'New Liberalism' measures which many see as doing much to establish a welfare state in Britain. The most important was the National Insurance Act (1911), which had two elements. The first part dealt with sickness benefit and was supposed to cover all workers, although the better off could 'opt out' if they wished. Everyone between 16 and 70 who earned less than £160 a year paid 4d (2p) a week into a fund, while the employer paid 3d (1p) and the State 2d (1p). Medical benefits were then paid out to those suffering from illness, disablement and spells in hospital. Women were also paid a maternity grant. The scheme was operated mainly through the Friendly Societies, and a panel of doctors provided medical treatment for all workers in the scheme. However, there was opposition from various quarters. The unions thought that workers should not have to contribute, while many employers, the British Medical Association and the Press attacked it too. In the end, however, the unions were given some control over the operation of the scheme, while doctors and chemists were won over when they realised they stood to make, rather than lose, money.

The second part of the Act set up a system of unemployment benefits, based on compulsory insurance contributions. This was mainly for the low-paid, and did not cover those who worked in the seven industries most liable to periodic unemployment, such as building and engineering. Those who were covered paid 2.5d (1p) into a fund, as did the employer and the State. When unemployed, a benefit of 7s (35p) a week was paid for 13 weeks. No further payments were made until the worker had been in work and had paid another 13 weeks' contributions. Thus the cover was for short-term and transitional, not long-term, unemployment.

## Political reforms

The only significant reform here was the Plural Voting Act (1913) which finally achieved what the Lords had blocked in 1907. Apart from university seats, in which graduates could vote as well as voting where they lived, everyone else in general elections was only allowed to vote in one constituency, thus almost establishing the principle of 'one man, one vote'. As we have seen, though, an attempt to give votes to women was again defeated. This Act also reduced the length of residence needed to qualify for the vote, which made it easier for people who moved house to get on to a new electoral register.

## Strikes and syndicalism

In the years just before the First World War, the Liberals had to face another problem. While the Labour Party and the trade unions were fairly moderate, a new revolutionary movement began to attract growing support amongst many union members. This was 'syndicalism'. A series of large strikes in the period 1910-12, many of which involved violent confrontations with the police and even the army, led to the three biggest unions (the miners, the railwaymen and the transport workers) forming what was known as the 'Triple Industrial Alliance' in order to take on what they saw as a joint campaign by employers and the State to defeat legitimate strikes. However, as with women's suffrage and Ireland, the outbreak of war in 1914 brought a temporary truce.

# SUMMARY

## 1905–1909

- The Conservative Party became seriously divided. In December 1905, Balfour was forced to resign, and Campbell-Bannerman for the Liberals took over. In the January 1906 elections, the Liberals won a massive victory.
- The new Liberal government immediately began a massive programme of reform, especially on social and industrial relations issues. These reforms included: the Workmen's Compensation Act (1906), the School Meals Act and the Medical Inspection Act (1907), the 'Children's Charter' and the Coal Mines Act (1908).
- The Poor Law Report in 1909 produced differing recommendations but, in the same year, Lloyd George (the Chancellor of the Exchequer) introduced the Old Age Pension Act (1909), which gave pensions to some people over 70.

## 1909–1911

- The various Liberal reforms, and especially old age pensions, needed extra taxation to pay for them. Lloyd George introduced the 'People's Budget' in 1909, which proposed to raise most of the extra taxes from the most wealthy.
- These proposals were blocked by the House of Lords, in which the Conservatives had an in-built majority. The Lords had already altered or blocked several earlier Liberal reforms.
- After threats to increase the number of Liberal Lords, and two elections in 1910 which were narrowly won by the Liberals, the Parliament Act (1911) reduced the powers of the Lords so that they could only delay bills, not completely prevent them.
- While the Liberals were dealing with these issues, they also faced other problems. The campaign for equal voting rights for women became increasingly violent under the direction of the suffragettes (WSPU); while in Ireland, the question of Home Rule was leading to increased tension, especially as, after 1910, the Liberals depended on the support of the Irish Nationalist MPs.

## 1911–1914

- While the problems of women's suffrage and Home Rule for Ireland continued to worsen after 1911, the Liberals pressed on with their social welfare and trade union reforms.
- The most important acts were the National Insurance Act (1911), the Minimum Wage Act (1912) and the Trade Union Act (1913).
- However, after 1911, the Labour Party began to emerge as a serious political rival to the Liberals. There was also a marked increase in trade union militancy and serious strikes. But these problems, along with those of votes for women and Ireland, were put on hold when the First World War began in 1914.

# Exam Question Practice

## Cross-referencing of sources

Study Sources A and B, which are about poverty in Britain.

How far do Sources A and B agree about poverty in Britain at the beginning of the twentieth century?

### Source A

We have been used to looking upon the poverty in London as unusual [a survey by Booth in London in 1892 had shown that 30% of the population lived below the poverty line]. However, the result of careful investigation shows that the proportion of poverty in London is practically equalled in what is a typical provincial town. We are faced with the startling probability that from 25-30% of the urban population in the United Kingdom is living in poverty.

*Rowntree's main conclusions, based on his survey of poverty in York, and adapted from Rowntree, Poverty: A Study of Town Life, 1901.*

### Source B

At the beginning of the twentieth century 30% of the nation lived at or below a meanly drawn poverty line. Sixteen per cent were in such great poverty that they were actually starving.

*From a school history textbook, published in 1980.*

### Examiner's Tips

**When answering questions like this:**

◎ Remember that comparing sources does not mean just describing, copying out or re-phrasing, what the sources say or show - you must compare and contrast the sources.

◎ Remember that 'how far' means you must look for both agreements and disagreements, or similarities and differences, between the sources mentioned. For example, does one source contain extra information compared to the other?

◎ Make sure that you make detailed, precise and clear references to all the sources mentioned; however, the references do not have to be long - a brief quotation or example (or even a reference to specific lines in written sources) will be enough.

◎ It is a good idea to get into the habit of writing answers to such questions which contain sentences like these: 'Sources A and B are similar/ agree/ support each other because Source A says....and Source B says ... However, though Source A says... this is not supported by Source B which says .../ gives a different figure.'

# CHAPTER 2

## THE FIRST WORLD WAR

*A French recruitment poster appealing for volunteers.*

Source A

*An illustration from a French magazine, showing the assassination of Archduke Franz Ferdinand and his wife in Sarajevo, June 1914.*

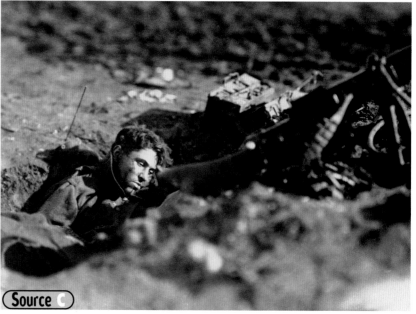

Source C

*A young German machine-gunner lies dead in a trench.*

British conscientious objectors held in a camp in Scotland.

Source E

The execution of a French mutineer, 1917.

## Key Questions

**How** could the assassination of one man and his wife in the Balkans (**Source A**) lead to a world war?

**Why** were so many men so keen to volunteer for the army at the start of the war, in response to posters like **Source B**?

**Why** were so many soldiers, like the one in **Source C**, killed in the First World War?

**Why** did some men react to the conditions of the First World War by becoming 'conchies' (as in **Source D**) or mutineers (as in **Source E**)?

These are some of the issues that we will cover in this chapter. The main focus of this chapter on the First World War will be:

* The causes which led to the outbreak of war in August 1914

* The nature of the fighting and the conditions on the Western Front

* The use of new technology and how it contributed to a situation of stalemate

* The impact of the war on life in Britain and its affect on the role of women

* The fighting and developments on the other fronts

* How the stalemate, and the war itself, were ended in 1918

# CHAPTER 2

# The long-term causes of the First World War

## Colonial and economic rivalry

The First World War began after more than 40 years of tensions in Europe. One of the long-term causes of the war was the growing rivalry between Britain, France and the relatively new state of Germany, which had not existed until 1871. The main rivalry, at first, was between Britain and France, especially in what became known as the 'Scramble for Africa' at the end of the nineteenth century. In fact, by 1900, some people began to think these two countries might even go to war against each other.

Then, in 1871, Germany came into existence. Its ruler was Kaiser (emperor) Wilhelm I and the first Chancellor was Otto von Bismarck. At first, Germany did not compete for overseas colonies, as Bismarck wanted to remain on friendly terms with Britain. In 1888, Wilhelm II became the new Kaiser. Unlike his father, he wanted Germany to establish its own empire, in order to match those already possessed by Britain and France. In 1890, he forced the more cautious Bismarck to resign. As well as competition for colonies, there was the added issue of economic growth and competition. Germany soon developed a modern industrial system which began to out-produce Britain - by 1914, the German economy was second only to the USA.

## The arms race

In order to get and protect an empire, the Kaiser knew Germany would need a navy. In 1897, Wilhelm II ordered the building of a huge navy. This angered the British government as British security in Europe had been seen for centuries as relying on having the biggest navy in the world. In 1900, the German government passed the Naval Law which ordered the building of 41 battleships and 60 cruisers. Britain responded by announcing a big increase in its navy and, in 1906, launched the first of a new and more powerful type of battleship, known as the 'Dreadnought'. The Germans decided to do the same, so the British government placed orders for yet more powerful ships called the 'Super Dreadnoughts'. In 1913, Germany widened the Kiel Canal, so that its navy could have quick access to the North Sea.

At the same time as this naval race was taking place, there was also a race between Germany on the one hand, and France and Russia on the other, to build up their armies. The French government, still wanting to regain possession of the provinces of Alsace-Lorraine, which they had lost to Germany in 1871, made a huge effort to increase the size of their army. By 1914, it numbered almost 4 million. The Russian government, which was involved in a rivalry with Austria-Hungary over influence in the Balkans, also spent vast sums on enlarging its army and on building military railways capable of rushing troops to the west. These developments caused the German government to fear it would be crushed between the French and Russian armies.

### Scramble for Africa

This refers to the race between the countries of Europe to establish new colonies in the continent of Africa. Between 1870 and 1900, virtually the whole of Africa was taken over by European countries, with Britain and France taking the biggest share. Little had been taken before 1870, as there were few reliable maps of the interior.

### Colonies

Colonies were a source of cheap raw materials and provided extra markets for the goods produced in the country which 'owned' these colonies. Yet, by 1870, most of the world - apart from Africa and parts of Asia - had already been colonised by various European countries. The only way the new Germany, and its industrialists, could carve out an empire for itself was by competing with Britain and France.

### Source A

There is no comparison between the importance of the German navy to Germany, and the importance of our navy to us. Our navy is to us what their army is to them. To have a strong navy would increase Germany's prestige and influence, but it is not a matter of life and death to them as it is to us.

Extract from a speech by Sir Edward Grey, British Foreign Secretary, to the House of Commons in 1909.

## The alliance system

In 1871, Prussia took the lead in uniting the different German states to form the new country of Germany. In the Franco-Prussian War of 1870-71, France was defeated and lost the provinces of Alsace and Lorraine. Because the German Chancellor, Bismarck, realised the French would want revenge, he tried to keep France isolated. At the time of the war, Britain and France were bitter rivals over colonies, so France's best bet was Russia. Bismarck, therefore, quickly formed the Three Emperors' League with Russia and Austria-Hungary. Although this later broke up, he signed a 'Reinsurance' Treaty with the Tsar of Russia in 1887, in which the two countries promised not to go to war. Before then, in 1879, Germany had signed the Dual Alliance with Austria-Hungary. In 1882, Italy joined this alliance, which now became the Triple Alliance.

This isolation of France continued during the 1880s, but Wilhelm II allowed the treaty with Russia to lapse. In 1892, France broke out of its isolation and signed a treaty with Russia. What Bismarck had always feared was now a possibility: that in a future war, Germany could face an attack on two fronts.

The growing arms race led Britain and France to settle their differences and, in 1904, they signed the 'Entente Cordiale'. The Kaiser tried to weaken this new agreement by interfering with French plans for Morocco. However, Britain and France stuck together at the Algeciras Conference in 1906, which was called to settle the problem. Despite the failure of his plans during the first Moroccan crisis, the Kaiser tried again in 1911 but this too failed, and only resulted in closer military ties between Britain and France. In 1907, Britain and Russia settled their differences. Therefore Britain, France and Russia were bound together in a loose 'Triple Entente'. The prospect of a war involving Britain had never occurred to Bismarck.

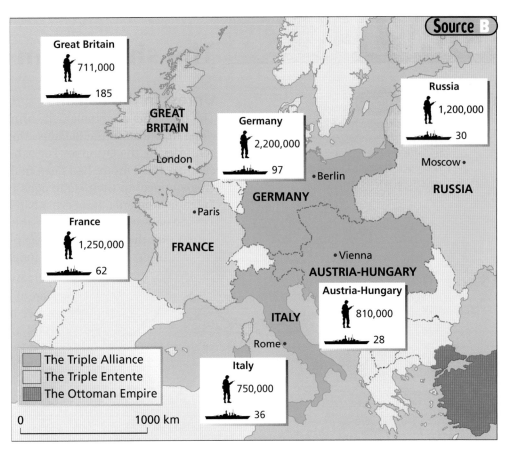

**Source B**

The two alliances in 1914, showing their military and naval strengths.

### Entente Cordiale

This means 'friendly understanding' and was the first sign of Britain and France moving closer together. Initially, it was an attempt to settle colonial rivalry in Africa, and was not a formal treaty or firm military alliance. As Germany adopted an increasingly strong foreign policy, Britain moved away from its traditional policy of not getting too involved in continental European affairs.

### Questions

1 Why did the British government place such importance on having the biggest navy in Europe?

2 How useful is **Source A** for understanding the motives behind the naval race between Britain and Germany?

3 To what extent does **Source B** support the evidence of **Source A**?

4 Use your own knowledge and **Source B** to explain how the alliance system led to increased tension before 1914.

# The short-term causes

*This refers to the struggle to win greater political independence for the various national groups, such as the Serbs, in the Balkans and eastern Europe who spoke Slavonic languages. The Russians are also Slavs.*

## Unrest in the Balkans

The problems of colonies, the arms race and the system of alliances came to a head in the Balkans. Much of this area had been ruled for centuries by the Ottoman Turkish Empire. However, since the 19th century, this Empire had been in decline as nationalist groups in the area stepped up their campaigns for independence. By 1900, Greece, Bulgaria, Romania and Serbia had already won their independence. This issue was complicated by the fact that the Austrian Empire feared that the success of Slavic nationalism might encourage some of its subjects to struggle for independence.

**Source A**

The Balkans, and the different nationalities in the Austrian Empire.

While Austria-Hungary tried to stop the spread of this nationalism by taking over the province of Bosnia-Herzegovina from Turkey in 1908, the Russians were also trying to expand in the area, as they wanted an ice-free port which would give them access to the Mediterranean Sea. Their best bet was to support Serbia, which claimed that, because Bosnia was populated by Serbs, it should be joined to them. This was also what the Serbs in Bosnia itself wanted.

In Serbia and Bosnia, secret societies were formed to force Austria out of Bosnia. Some were prepared to use terrorism to do this. In addition, some of the Balkan states joined forces to end the remaining Turkish control. In 1912, the First Balkan War broke out, in which Bulgaria, Serbia, Montenegro and Greece fought the Turkish Empire. Turkey was defeated, and one result was that Serbia gained extra territory, but this only increased Austrian fears for the survival of their Empire. Then, in 1913, the Second Balkan War broke out, this time with Greece and Serbia against their former ally, Bulgaria.

## The assassination at Sarajevo

This nationalist unrest in the Balkans reached a crisis in June 1914, when it was announced that the Archduke Franz Ferdinand of Austria would visit Sarajevo, the capital of Bosnia. One of the secret societies of Serbian nationalists decided they would assassinate him. This society was known as the Black Hand. On 28 June 1914, Franz Ferdinand and his wife, Sophia, arrived in Sarajevo. Gavrilo Princip was able to shoot dead both the Archduke and his wife in their car. Austria-Hungary, which had wanted to destroy Serbia for some time, blamed Serbia for the killings and issued a ten-point ultimatum. Although Serbia agreed to all the points but one, Austria began to prepare for war.

*This was one of several nationalist pro-Serb groups struggling to drive Austria-Hungary out of Bosnia. Princip, aged 19, was a member of 'Young Bosnia' and was given the gun by a member of the Black Hand. Princip was one of six teenagers who had decided to assassinate the Archduke while he was in Sarajevo, and they were positioned in several places along the route. An earlier attempt with a bomb failed, while the others lost their nerve and did nothing. Princip died in an Austrian prison in 1918.*

## Germany's change of policy

Previously, Germany had made it clear that it would not support Austria in any war against Serbia. This had last been shown in 1913 during the Second Balkan War, when Austria-Hungary had been involved in disagreements with Serbia and Russia over the Balkans. However, on 5 July, the Kaiser changed his mind and informed the Austrians that Germany would back it in a war against Serbia. This was despite the fact that Serbia was backed by Russia, which was unlikely to leave its main ally in the Balkans unprotected. The Kaiser's decision was partly due to growing German concerns about the growth of Russian power. When Britain and Russia tried to negotiate an agreement with Austria, the Kaiser told Austria to ignore the requests.

## The Schlieffen Plan

Ever since Russia had signed its treaty with France in 1892, German military planners had tried to work out how to deal with the possibility of an attack on two fronts at once. The plan drawn up by General von Schlieffen in 1905 was based on the assumption that Russia, which was relatively backward, would take a long time to get mobilised. So the plan relied on defeating France quickly, and then turning all Germany's armed forces to deal with the Russian army. As France had built a line of fortifications along its border with Germany, the Plan involved rushing German troops through Belgium and capturing Paris. At the time, even though Britain was committed by treaty to protect Belgium's independence, this was not seen as a problem, as Germany would make it clear that it would not occupy Belgium itself.

## The final steps

Once Austria declared war on Serbia on 28 July, the ties of the alliance system soon dragged all the major Europeans into what was to be the First World War. Russia issued orders for mobilisation on 30 July. This alarmed Germany, as the whole basis of the Schlieffen Plan was that Russia would not be ready to fight until after the defeat of France. But Russia refused a German demand to stop its mobilisation so, on 1 August, Germany declared war on Russia. When France refused to give an undertaking to stay out of the war and instead began mobilisation, Germany declared war on France too, on 3 August. The German army then tried to get Belgium to agree to German troops passing through its territory on their way to France. Belgium refused, so, on 4 August, Germany declared war on Belgium. That same day, after giving no clear indication of its intentions, Britain finally declared war on Germany. In theory, at least, this was to come to the aid of Belgium rather than France or Russia. The First World War had begun.

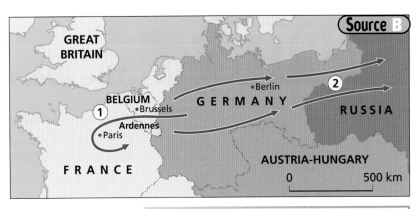

**Source B**

① German army invades through Belgium and defeats France in 6 weeks

② The whole German army then switches to fight the Russians

*The aims of the Schlieffen Plan before the start of the First World War.*

### Mobilised

*This term refers to the early stages before a war when the armed forces get their troops and equipment together, and moved to their positions in readiness for combat. Such an action means that a possible enemy needs to begin their mobilisation too, or they might be invaded before they are fully ready to defend.*

### Questions

1 How did the Austrian take-over of Bosnia in 1908 increase tensions in the Balkans?

2 By 4 August, Austria, Serbia, Germany, Russia, France and Britain were at war. For each country, outline the steps they had taken to war and explain why.

3 In what ways had the Schlieffen Plan, shown in **Source B**, been undermined by August 1914?

# The Western Front

### The failure of the Schlieffen Plan

The Plan had not anticipated that Britain would get involved. However, after declaring war on Germany, Britain sent the British Expeditionary Force (BEF) to France. These 120 000 troops delayed the German advance at Mons. Along with the unexpected resistance put up by the Belgian army, this soon meant that the German campaign was not going according to the planned timetable. To make things worse, Germany had to divert troops to the Eastern Front, where the Russians were already mobilised. On 17 August, they crossed the border into Germany, again, not in accordance with the Plan. As a result, the Germans altered the Plan and aimed their advance east of Paris instead of west. This advance was held up by the British and French armies on the River Marne. At the same time, the French war plan (known as Plan XVII), which was based on a massive French attack to recapture the provinces of Alsace-Lorraine, also failed to bring about a decisive result.

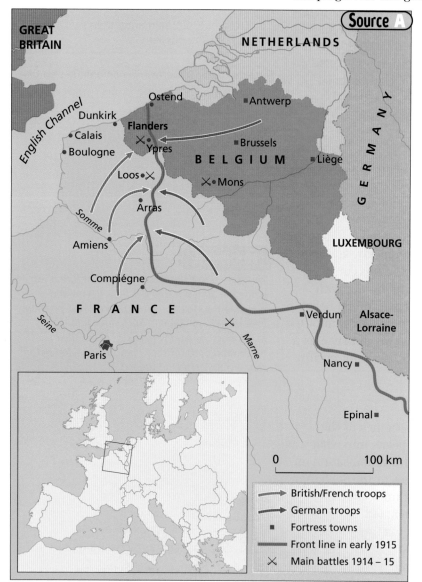

Source A

*The front line on the Western Front in 1915, following the 'race for the sea' and several major battles.*

### The race for the sea

After the Battle of the Marne, the exhausted German troops (who had been marching up to 40 kms a day) were forced to retreat over 60 kms. They then began to dig a line of defensive trenches, and there began what became known as the 'race for the sea', as each side tried to outflank the other by moving to the Channel coast. Neither side succeeded and by November 1914, a line of defensive trenches stretched from the Belgian port of Ostend to the Swiss border.

### Stalemate

Each side had expected the war would be short, and probably over by Christmas. However, as a result of the German failure to knock France out in the first few days, a situation of stalemate was reached on the Western Front, with both sides being fairly evenly matched as regards numbers and armaments. The front line established as a result of the race to the sea changed little until 1917, despite the efforts of each side to break the deadlock.

Battles to end the stalemate resulted in heavy casualties with very little gain of territory. For example, the German attempt to break through in 1916 led to the Battle of Verdun. This lasted from February to July and resulted in over 1 million casualties. In the same year, on 1 July, Britain launched an offensive on the River Somme to help relieve the pressure on the French. On the first day of the battle, over 60 000 British troops were killed. Although, by October, British forces had advanced about 10 kilometres along a 48-kilometre section of the front, the Battle of the Somme did not result in any significant breakthrough. The generals on both sides adopted a strategy known as a 'war of attrition', with the sole aim of inflicting more casualties on the enemy than they suffered themselves.

## Trench warfare

The trenches, which soon stretched across France, were dug in zigzags to limit the effects of shelling, and were protected by barbed-wire fences and reinforced with sandbags and sometimes even concrete. As the war continued into the autumn and winter of 1914, the trenches became extremely wet and muddy, and many men suffered from 'trench foot', which often led to gangrene. Soldiers were soon infested with lice and, in winter, they suffered bitterly from the cold, with frostbite common.

For over three years, the two sides faced each other across the stretch of land which soon became known as 'no man's land'. Across this space, soldiers were ordered out of their own trenches ('going over the top') to attack the enemy trenches. Attacks were usually preceded by a barrage of heavy shelling which was supposed to destroy the enemy trench defences and knock out machine gun posts. Sometimes, as in the Battle of the Somme, the shelling lasted for over a week.

In practice, however, the shelling was often inaccurate and failed to achieve its objectives. Nonetheless, the soldiers were ordered to attack across no man's land which, because of the heavy shelling, soon became a quagmire of sticky mud. Soldiers had to carry heavy packs, and many of the wounded drowned in the mud before they could be rescued. Once over the top, they were ordered to walk in lines towards the enemy who, as soon as the bombardment stopped, would come out of their dugouts and start to fire machine guns at them. If they reached the enemies' trenches, they were involved in vicious hand-to-hand fighting, using not only bayonets and pistols, but also a whole range of improvised weapons.

After all this, they were often forced to retreat to their own trenches. In theory, troops were only supposed to be in the front line trenches for eight days, but heavy shelling and the high casualties often meant men had to spend as much as three weeks at the front before being relieved.

### War of attrition

*Attrition means gradually wearing out. It was thought that the winning side in the war would be the one which inflicted greater losses on the other, even though their own losses might be extremely high too. One advantage in numbers which Britain had, was its vast Empire. Large numbers of troops came from India and Africa, as well as Canada, Australia and New Zealand.*

### Source B

We saw it, we saw men hanging on the wire, some screaming 'shoot me, do me in'. The longer they hung on the wire, the more they attracted the bullets. It was terrible.

*An account by a soldier of his experiences going 'over the top', taken from a textbook about the Somme, published in 1986.*

### Source C

*A British 18 pounder field gun, stuck in the mud in Flanders.*

### Questions

1 Why did the front line on the Western Front, as shown in **Source A**, change so little in the years from 1914-17?

2 To what does the term 'wire', mentioned in **Source B**, refer?

3 Given the terrible experiences of men who went over the top, why do you think the strategy was continued?

# New technology

## Heavy artillery

Heavy artillery barrages played a big part in the fighting on the Western Front. However, they failed to achieve any breakthrough in the stalemate. They pitted the landscape with vast shell craters, and contributed to the wet and mud at the Front by destroying the natural drainage system. They caused many deaths, inflicted dreadful injuries and reduced morale, while soldiers exposed to prolonged shelling often suffered from 'shell-shock'.

## Machine guns

These weapons played a big part in turning the First World War into a defensive rather than attacking one. They could fire up to 600 rounds per minute and had a range of over two kilometres. As a result, just one machine gun could cause massive casualties amongst the slowly advancing lines of attacking soldiers. This meant the chances of a successful attack on enemy trenches were much reduced.

## Gas

One attempt to break the stalemate, used first by the Germans at the Second Battle of Ypres in April 1915, was the deployment of poison gas. There were three main types used in the war: chlorine, phosgene and mustard. Their effects were awful - chlorine caused victims to drown in the water produced by their lungs; phosgene was much more deadly and was difficult to detect before its first effects were felt; while mustard gas burned the skin away to the bone and could also burn up the lungs. Both sides used gas attacks after 1915, even though there was the danger of killing their own troops if the wind changed direction. This, and the fact that gasmasks were developed which gave some effective protection, meant this new development did not end the stalemate.

## Tanks

As the use of cavalry, which traditionally had brought about quick victories in previous wars, was not possible in the conditions of trench warfare, governments on both sides looked for other ways to break the deadlock. Britain was the first to invent an armoured machine which could run on caterpillar tracks. To confuse German spies, they were said to be 'water tanks' and the name 'tank' stuck. They were first used by Britain during the Battle of the Somme in September 1916 and had initial successes, even though there were not enough tanks or back-up troops to achieve a decisive breakthrough. However, there were several problems. The fumes inside the tanks quickly made the soldiers ill; they were slow-moving and were thus easy targets for the enemy artillery; and they frequently got bogged down in the deep mud.

### Shell-shock

*Refers to one of the effects of the heavy shelling which troops experienced in the trenches. This, together with the dreadful injuries and dead bodies seen, and the awful trench conditions, caused some soldiers to suffer nervous breakdowns. At first, the military authorities refused to recognise this as a genuine illness, and some sufferers were shot for cowardice.*

### Source A

*An illustration from a French magazine showing Germans becoming victims of their own poison gas, following a change of wind direction, June 1915.*

### Source B

*A tank and an aeroplane during a battle on the Western Front, 1917.*

The Germans began to produce their own tanks but did not use them much. However, Britain continued to improve the design, and they were more effective in the Battle of Cambrai in November 1917. But it was not until August 1918 that they were used effectively in a way to end the stalemate. By then, the German commander, Ludendorff, considered them to be the most serious threat faced by the German army.

## Aircraft

The First World War also saw the use of aeroplanes and airships. On the Western Front, the first use made of aircraft was to act as 'spotter' or 'scouting' planes. They flew over the battlefield to observe enemy troop movements and to check on the accuracy of their own side's shelling. In 1915, they were modified by the Germans so that machine guns could be fired through the propellers to attack enemy aircraft. Britain and France then copied this technique. In 1916, the Germans were the first to use aircraft for machine-gunning ('strafing') the enemy's trenches. Bombers were also developed. Fighters and bombers were then used by both sides to attack enemy trenches. However, they did not play a major role in the war, and, as both sides had them, they did not help to end the stalemate.

## Submarines

These were known as U-boats (Unterseeboten) and were used by the Germans to counter British control of the surface of the sea. They were first used in 1915 to sink any ships trading with Britain which were thought to be carrying war-related materials. As the shipping of neutral countries was attacked without the traditional warning, this was known as 'unrestricted submarine warfare'. In 1915, the British passenger liner *Lusitania* was hit: 1198 passengers were drowned, including 128 Americans. This act played a part in the USA eventually entering the war against Germany in 1917. For a time, Germany halted the unrestricted U-boat campaign.

At first, the Germans were only using 21 submarines and, by the end of 1915, had only sunk about 5% of British and neutral shipping bringing supplies of food and materials to Britain. However, by 1917, the Germans had over 300 U-boats and unrestricted submarine warfare was resumed. This time, it was much more successful and the Germans believed it would soon lead to Britain's surrender. By April 1917, 25% of British shipping was being lost and the British authorities calculated there was only six weeks' food supply left. However, the British developed new ways of limiting submarine damage by using the convoy system and hydrophones. By November 1918, British merchant shipping losses were down to 4% again. So, once again, new technology failed to end the stalemate.

Source C

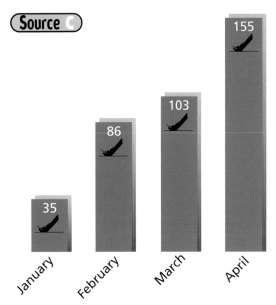

The number of British ships sunk by U-boats, January–April 1917.

### Convoy system

This was an effective way of countering the losses inflicted by submarine warfare. British merchant ships sailed together in convoys in zig-zag patterns to make it harder for the submarines to work out their movements. They were also protected by escort warships.

### Hydrophones

These were special microphones used to detect submarines in the water. Depth charges were then dropped to destroy the U-boats.

### Questions

1 Why did the use of gas, shown in **Source A**, fail to produce any decisive results during the First World War?

2 What early problems were associated with the use of tanks, shown operating on the Western Front in **Source B**?

3 How did Britain overcome the U-boat damage shown in **Source C**?

# CHAPTER 2

# The Home Front

**Conscientious objectors**

*These were people opposed to the war, and were often referred to as 'conchies'. They included religious people and pacifists who believed all killing was wrong, and revolutionary socialists who believed worker should not kill worker in a war which they felt was in the interests of the rich. Tribunals were set up to decide who were genuine conscientious objectors. In 1916, when conscription was first introduced, there were over 15 000. About half agreed to do non-combatant work at the Front, but the rest refused to do any war work and were eventually sent to prison. Conchies were very unpopular and were given a hard time. After the war, they were not allowed to vote for five years.*

**Zeppelin**

*Zeppelins were filled with hydrogen and powered by an engine. The crew were in a cabin below the airship's body, and could observe the ground below and drop bombs. In 1915, there were 20 Zeppelin raids on London which killed 188 civilians. Other towns, such as Southend, were also bombed. However, Britain developed searchlights, barrage or barrier balloons, incendiary bullets and night fighter planes to counter this new weapon. The Zeppelins were also vulnerable to bad weather and had poor navigational instruments.*

## Recruitment

At first, thousands of young men rushed to volunteer for the war, which most people thought would be short, as most recent wars in Europe had been. The common belief was that it would be 'over by Christmas'. A series of campaigns was launched in an attempt to recruit 2.25 million men by October 1915. One way of doing this was to create 'pals battalions', promising all those who volunteered from the same town, street or factory that they would stay together. However, as the war dragged on, the number of recruits began to fall, while the high casualties at the front threatened to seriously weaken the army.

As a result, the Military Service Act in January 1916 introduced conscription (compulsory military service) for all single men aged between 18 and 41. In March, this was extended to married men. There were some categories of men who were exempt from having to fight. These included the medically-unfit and those in essential jobs (such as miners and farmers), as well as conscientious objectors. As the war continued and the casualties mounted, the upper age limit was changed to 51 in 1918.

## Propaganda and censorship

To encourage men to join up, untrue or exaggerated stories about the Germans were spread by the Press, such as German soldiers eating Belgian babies or using the bodies of dead British soldiers to make fats and oils. In Germany, similar lies were spread about the British and the French.

The government was given extra powers by the Defence of the Realm Act (DORA) which was passed on 8 August 1914. As well as banning people from discussing military affairs in public or spreading rumours, it also allowed the government and military authorities to censor newspapers and the letters sent home by troops. As a result, bad news was suppressed, the true number of casualties was often hidden, and any successes were exaggerated. Poster campaigns were also used to encourage people to eat less and do voluntary work.

## Bombing raids

New war technology also affected civilians at home. In 1914, the Germans decided to use a new weapon to bomb British cities and so break civilian morale. This was the airship, or Zeppelin. In 1917, the Germans switched to the more efficient Gotha IV bomber planes which killed over 3000 civilians in air raids on Britain. Britain also developed its own bombers.

## Rationing

In 1916, there were serious food shortages as a result of the increasing German U-boat (submarine) attacks on merchant shipping. In 1917, the government introduced voluntary rationing in order to reduce food consumption and distribute more equally what food there was. However, the voluntary system failed, as poor people could not buy even the reduced amounts of sugar and meat allowed, while the rich could afford to buy more illegally on the 'black market'.

The government also used DORA to take over public parks and other unused land to turn into fields and allotments for growing extra food. Between 1914 and 1918, more than 1.2 million hectares of land were ploughed up. But even these measures were not enough, so, in 1918, full-scale compulsory rationing was introduced which actually improved on the diets poor people had had before 1914.

## The role of women

The Defence of the Realm Act also gave the government power to control mines, the railways and any factory connected to war production. This was particularly important in view of the number of men who were sent to the Front. Soon, labour shortages created new opportunities for women which allowed them to play an important role in the war effort. Many worked in munitions factories producing weapons, bullets and shells. Such women were known as munitionettes. Others worked in engineering factories, or acted as conductors on trams and buses, while over 400 000 replaced men as clerks and secretaries. Many joined the Women's Land Army to do farm work, or volunteered for the Voluntary Aid Detachments (VADs) which undertook a variety of jobs. Some were used in traditional women's work (as laundresses, maids, cooks and nurses) but others acted as ambulance drivers or motorbike messengers at the Front.

During the war, most of the suffragettes joined campaigns to encourage men to volunteer for the army. Some gave out white feathers (a symbol of cowardice) to young men in civilian clothes, although sometimes these were soldiers home on leave. They also supported the war effort in other ways, in part because they believed it would persuade people that women did deserve the vote. In 1915, Mrs Pankhurst organised a march to encourage employers to employ more women. The costs of the march were paid for by Lloyd George who, as Minister of Munitions, was worried by the 'shell shortage'.

**Source B**

A British poster to recruit more women to build aeroplanes. Issued by the Ministry of Munitions.

### Munitionettes

*This was the name given to the women who worked in the munitions factories. The work was dirty and dangerous, as there were fires and explosions, while the chemicals were highly poisonous. The women's skin often turned yellow because of the chemicals, so they were sometimes known as 'canaries'. After the war, as with other women who had helped the war effort, they lost their jobs and were expected to return to their traditional roles.*

**Source C**

Members of the Women's Land Army at work, March 1918.

### Questions

1 How useful is **Source A** for finding out about opposition to the war?

2 What roles were played by British women during the First World War?

# CHAPTER 2

# The other fronts

### The Eastern Front

As well as having to fight Britain and France on the Western Front, Germany, along with its ally Austria-Hungary, was also involved in fighting against Russia in the east. At first, in August 1914, the Russian army did not perform as effectively as German military planners had feared. Russia invaded eastern Germany to take the pressure off its allies in the west, but the Russian troops were poorly armed and badly led. This allowed the Germans to inflict two heavy defeats on the Russians at Tannenberg and the Massurian Lakes, capturing over 130 000 Russian prisoners and thus removing the immediate threat in the east.

Although the Russians did better against the Austro-Hungarian armies, German troops were able to invade Russia itself in 1915 and by 1916 were continuing to advance. In June 1916, the Russian General Brusilov launched a counter-offensive which resulted in over 250 000 Germans being taken prisoner. In March 1917, the first of two revolutions (the other was in November) broke out in Russia. After this second revolution, Russia was effectively out of the war. This was later formalised by Russia signing the Treaty of Brest-Litovsk with Germany in March 1918.

### The Italian Front

Although Italy was a member of the Triple Alliance, it at first stayed neutral, but was persuaded by the Allies to sign the secret Treaty of London in which it was promised much Austrian territory if it joined the Allies against Germany. The Italian army was not really combat ready in 1915 and suffered many casualties fighting the Austrians. Later, the Allies sent troops to assist and, in 1918, the Italians won a decisive victory at Vittorio Veneto.

### Gallipoli

By February 1915, some members of the British government came to believe that the way to end the stalemate on the Western Front was to attack Germany's weakest ally, Turkey. This would allow the Allies to invade the Balkans, draw German troops from Russia, re-open the supply route to the Russian army through the Black Sea and invade Germany's other ally Austria-Hungary. Those in favour of this decided on the capture of Gallipoli which would give the Allies control of the Dardanelles. They said the navy would do the bulk of the work. A rapid invasion by Allied troops would then occupy the area without the need to fight trench warfare.

The British and French naval bombardment of Turkish defences began in March 1915, and was at first successful. But, after several Allied ships were sunk or damaged by shells and mines, the naval force withdrew. Instead, it was decided to launch a land invasion in April, using British, French and ANZAC troops, most of whom were inexperienced. German advisers had improved the Turkish defences

## Brusilov's counter-offensive

*After initial success, Brusilov's offensive began to slow down as he lacked sufficient reserve troops, and the Germans were able to advance again. Over the following months, the Russians suffered over 1 million casualties and, by December 1916, low morale and revolutionary unrest led to over 1 million desertions from the Russian army.*

**Source A**

*The location and strategic importance of Gallipoli and the Dardanelles.*

## The Dardanelles

*This is the narrow stretch of water which allowed access between the Aegean Sea and the Black Sea, and also protected the Turkish capital, Constantinople (now Istanbul). Turkey signed an alliance with Germany in August 1914 and went on to fortify the Straits, preventing Allied supplies reaching Russia via the Black Sea. Because Turkish power had been declining for some time, the Allies thought it would be easy to defeat Turkey and then move up the 'soft underbelly of Europe' to attack Austria-Hungary.*

and had taught them modern fighting tactics. After some initial success, the Allied troops failed to make significant advances and were ordered to dig in. An attempt to end the deadlock was made in August by landing fresh troops in Suvla Bay, but again the attack failed. The combination of determined Turkish resistance, hot weather and disease led to high casualties on both sides; and in December, the Allies decided to withdraw.

## The Middle East

Over 1 million British, ANZAC and Indian troops were also involved in campaigns to capture the Turkish territories of Palestine (now Israel) and Mesopotamia (now Iraq). As in Gallipoli, the Germans had trained the Turkish forces and there was stiff resistance which at first resulted in two unsuccessful Allied offensives. But the Turks were outnumbered, and T.E. Lawrence (Lawrence of Arabia) successfully encouraged many Arab groups to revolt against Turkish rule (in large part because the British government promised them independence after the war). Eventually, after its defeat at Megiddo in September 1918, Turkey finally surrendered on 3 November 1918.

## The war at sea

Despite the fact that the naval race had been an important factor leading to the start of the war, there were few important sea battles, as both sides knew that to lose control of the seas would mean defeat. This was because the victorious side could impose a naval blockade and so prevent vital supplies of food and war materials being delivered. Apart from the small battle at Heligoland in August 1914, the only major battle was at Jutland in 1916. Although the British lost 14 ships to the Germans' 11, the larger British fleet was able to keep the German navy cooped up in its ports. This enabled the Allies to maintain a strict blockade which played an extremely important part in their eventual victory. It was this failure to break British control on the surface of the sea which led the Germans to turn to unrestricted submarine warfare.

> ### Questions
>
> 1 What was the aim of the Gallipoli campaign, and why did it fail?
> 2 The war began as a conflict between two European Alliances. Explain how it became a 'world war'.

**ANZAC**
*This stands for the Australian and New Zealand Army Corps.*

**Source B**

*The capture of Jerusalem by British forces in 1917.*

**Source C**

*A French postcard, 'Our Allies', from July 1916, showing the various nationalities from the British and French Empires which fought in the First World War.*

# The end of the stalemate

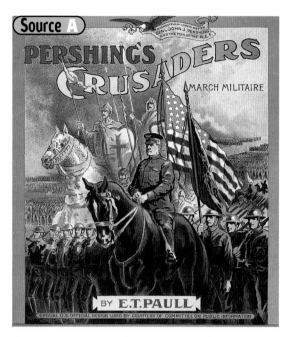

*The cover page of an American music sheet, showing General Pershing and American troops. Pershing was the commander of US forces in Europe during the First World War.*

## The continuing stalemate

During 1917, the stalemate on the Western Front continued and attempts on other fronts also failed to achieve a breakthrough. In April 1917, the French General Nivelle launched an attack on the German lines. Although this was more successful than previous offensives, the casualties were high and resulted in a serious mutiny in the French army. This was eventually crushed by a new French commander, Petain, who executed the leaders and improved conditions for the rest. A British attack at Passchendaele, near Ypres, from July to November 1917 also failed to achieve the desired breakthrough, while casualties numbered over 500 000. In November 1917, the battle of Cambrai saw a successful use of tanks by the British, but they were eventually forced back.

## The USA joins the Allies

However, in April 1917, the USA decided to enter the war on the side of the Allies. Although officially neutral since 1914, the USA had been giving loans and selling equipment to the Allies. This had angered the Germans who, from 1916, relaunched unrestricted submarine warfare against American shipping, including some passenger ships. When Britain revealed the contents of the Zimmermann Telegram, which showed that Germany was trying to encourage Mexico to join them against the USA, this finally led the USA to declare war.

It was not until November 1917, however, that large numbers of fresh American troops began arriving in Europe. By then, the Allies had effectively lost Russia, their ally in the east, as mutinies and revolution destroyed the ability of the Russian army to keep fighting. The new Bolshevik government then began negotiations for a general end to the war. When the rest of the Allies and Germany refused, they began talks with the Germans for a separate peace. This meant the Germans could consider transferring their eastern army to the Western Front.

## The German spring offensive

In March 1918, after the Treaty of Brest-Litovsk had ended the fighting in the east, several hundred thousand German troops were switched to the west. By then, Germany's situation was becoming desperate, as the Allied naval blockade had resulted in serious food shortages for German troops and civilians alike. At the same time, over 50 000 American troops were arriving in France each month. So the German commander, Ludendorff, planned a massive spring offensive to achieve a decisive victory before more American troops arrived.

However, the French called up their reserve forces and were also reinforced by American soldiers. German casualties had been high (about 400 000) and their rapid advance had left them exhausted,

### Spring offensive

*This offensive began on 21 March 1918 and attacked the Allies' weakest points on the Somme front. There had been no major German offensive since 1916, and thick fog gave the Germans an added element of surprise. After five hours of heavy shelling, the Germans attacked with specially-trained and highly mobile 'storm troops' armed with light machine guns, grenades and flame throwers. Over the next few weeks, the Allies retreated to within 35 miles of Paris, which was soon being shelled by heavy German artillery.*

## Source B

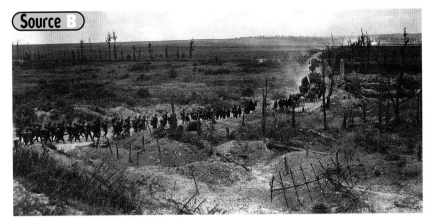

German troops advancing across Champagne, 1918.

## Source C

The sudden and dramatic entrance of the 2nd and 3rd Divisions into the shattered and broken fighting lines and their dash and courage in battle produced a favorable effect on the French soldiers... The Germans, who had been filled with propaganda about the poor quality of our training and war effort, must have been surprised at the strong resistance offered by the Americans.

*An extract from the war memoirs of General J. J. Pershing. He is describing the role of the US army in stopping the German 'spring offensive' in 1918.*

with low morale and with little food or extra ammunition. They were also suffering from what soon became a major flu epidemic, so the offensive began to slow down from May. By August, it was clear even to the German commanders that they could not win the war. By October, Germany's allies were close to collapse.

## The collapse of Germany

By the end of September, the German commanders Hindenburg and Ludendorff told the Kaiser they could no longer hold the Allies, and advised him to appoint a civilian government which should begin negotiations for a ceasefire (armistice). During October, food and fuel shortages led to strikes and revolutionary unrest in Germany itself, which became much more serious after 29 October when a mutiny by sailors at Kiel soon spread to other parts of Germany. By early November, revolutionaries had taken control of Berlin, Munich and some other cities, and the Kaiser abdicated and fled to Holland. A new democratic provisional government then signed an armistice with the Allies on 11 November. Germany had clearly lost the 'Great War'.

## Why did Germany lose?

Apart from the factors already examined, some historians now believe another important factor in the final defeat of Germany was the strategy adopted by Allied commanders, such as Field Marshal Haig. At the time, and subsequently, many people felt that the tactics followed by generals like Haig in battles such as Verdun and the Somme were simply horrifically wasteful failures. Some historians now think, however, that the heavy losses the Germans also suffered during these offensives eventually weakened their morale and, in particular, resulted in huge casualties amongst experienced non-commissioned officers. Thus, these dreadful battles in 1916-17 can be seen as just as important as the arrival at the end of 1917 of American soldiers.

## Field Marshal Haig

*He was the Commander-in Chief of the British armies in France from 1916-18, and was promoted to Field Marshal after the Battle of the Somme in 1916. After the war, he was made an earl and given £100 000 by Parliament. However, historians are divided on the question of his leadership. Some see him as the 'butcher of the Somme', while others point out that British losses were no worse than those of France and Germany. It is also true that he did not have overall control over the troops in France. The final decisions were always taken by the French.*

## Questions

1 What can you learn from **Source B** about the German offensive launched in the spring of 1918?

2 How reliable is **Source C** about the impact of US troops on the Western Front in 1918?

3 What were the main factors involved in the collapse of the German war effort in 1918?

4 Why do you think historians have held different views about Field Marshal Haig?

# SUMMARY

## 1870–1911

- After the creation of the new state of Germany in 1871, tensions increased between the major European nations, especially as France had been defeated by Prussia in 1871, and German industry began to overtake that of Britain.

- The main problems were to do with nationalism and colonial rivalry. As problems continued to arise, the major countries started to form alliances in order to provide extra protection. Soon, Germany had created the Triple Alliance with the central powers, while Britain was part of the Triple Entente.

- The growing tensions also led to an arms race - a naval one between Britain and Germany, and a military one between France and Germany. There were also serious differences between Russia and Austria-Hungary over the Balkans.

## 1912–1914

- Tensions in Europe were increased by nationalist unrest in the Balkans. Russia sided with the Serbs against Austria-Hungary, which had seized Bosnia in 1908.

- Two Balkan Wars added to the tensions and, in June 1914, Serbian nationalists assassinated the heir to the Austrian throne in Sarajevo.

- The assassination set off a chain reaction which, because of the alliance system, soon resulted in an all-out European war.

## 1914–1916

- At first, both sides expected a short war but, by the end of 1914, it had settled into the stalemate of trench warfare.

- Numerous battles resulted in high casualties for both sides, and the war became a war of attrition.

- Despite launching campaigns elsewhere, such as Gallipoli and the Middle East, there was no breakthrough for either side.

- New weapons, such as gas, tanks, aircraft and submarines also failed to end the deadlock, as both sides copied each others' technology. However, the German U-boat campaign caused serious food shortages in Britain, while the Allied naval blockade of German ports caused more serious shortages in Germany.

## 1917–1918

- In April 1917, the USA joined the Allies, although Russia dropped out after the November Revolution. A separate peace between Russia and Germany in March 1918 allowed Germany to switch large numbers of troops from the Eastern to the Western Front.

- Alarmed at the prospect of large numbers of fresh American troops, the Germans launched a massive spring offensive on 21 March 1918. However, although the Germans made rapid and significant advances, the attack was stopped by the exhaustion of their troops and the lack of food and supplies.

- After August 1918, the Allies counter-attacked and the German commanders informed the Kaiser that the German army could no longer carry on. Mutinies and revolutionary unrest in Germany resulted in the abdication of the Kaiser.

- A new provisional government in Germany signed an armistice on 11 November, and the fighting came to a halt.

# Exam Question Practice

## Reliability of sources

Study Sources A and B, which are about the final steps to war.

Which is the more reliable statement about Germany's attitude to the Balkan crisis after the assassination at Sarajevo in June 1914? Use the two sources and your own knowledge to explain your answer.

**Source A**

The Kaiser told me that Austria-Hungary might rely upon Germany's full support. It was Kaiser Wilhelm's opinion that action must not be delayed. Should war break out between Austria-Hungary and Russia, Germany would stand at our side. Kaiser Wilhelm would regret it if we do not make use of the present situation, which is all in our favour.

*The Austro-Hungarian Ambassador's report of a discussion with the German Kaiser on 5 July 1914.*

**Source B**

In Moltke's opinion there was no alternative to making preventive war in order to defeat the enemy while we still had a chance of victory...I pointed out that the Kaiser... would only agree to fight if our enemies forced war upon us....

*Written comments by the German Foreign Secretary, von Jagow, made from memory soon after the war. Von Moltke was the German Chief-of-Staff.*

## Examiner's Tips

**When answering questions like this:**

◎ Make sure you comment on ALL the sources mentioned in the question AND that you use your own knowledge to assess the sources/put them in their historical context.

◎ When considering reliability, don't forget to comment on more than the content/information given by the sources - you must also use the provenance details provided by the Principal Examiner (in this case, who wrote them, and when).

◎ You will also need to comment on the nature of each source, i.e. was it a private document (like a personal diary), or was it meant to be read by other people?

◎ Make sure you also comment on the possible purpose(s) of the sources, i.e. in this case, is someone trying to justify their country's actions?

◎ Finally, don't forget to make a final choice as to which source you think is more reliable. You will lose marks if you only comment on the reliability of the sources concerning Germany's attitude, without indicating which one you think is probably the most reliable one.

◎ If you think both are equally reliable, then attempt to show why you cannot choose between them.

## THE PEACE TREATIES

> **Source A**
>
> 1 There should be no secret deals or treaties between states.
>
> 4 The level of armaments should be reduced in each country.
>
> 5 The future of colonies should be reviewed and the wishes of local people taken into consideration.
>
> 6 Other countries should leave Russian territory.
>
> 10 The different peoples of Austria-Hungary should be given their freedom.
>
> 12 Non-Turkish people in the Turkish Empire should be free to have their own governments.
>
> 14 A League of Nations should be set up to preserve the future peace of the world.

*A summary of some of the Fourteen Points issued by US President Woodrow Wilson in January 1918. He thought this was the way to secure peace in the future.*

PEACE AND FUTURE CANNON FODDER

The Tiger: "Curious! I seem to hear a child weeping!"

> **Source B**

*A cartoon of 1919 by the British artist Will Dyson. It shows the 'Big Four' leaving the Paris Peace Conference, and implies that the settlement is bound to lead to war – the suggested date is 1940.*

*Allied officers in the Hall of Mirrors watching the handing over of the Treaty of Versailles, 7 May 1919.*

### Key Questions

**What** did President Wilson of the USA hope to achieve with his 'Fourteen Points' (**Source A**)?

**Why** could he not get Britain and France to accept many of these Points during the peace conferences, like the one shown in **Source C**?

**Is** it fair to suggest, like **Source B** does, that the peace treaties of 1919-23 made another war inevitable?

These are some of the issues we will cover in this chapter. The main focus of this chapter on the peace treaties will be:

- The leading personalities of the 'Big Four' countries which determined the outcomes of the peace negotiations

- How their aims differed over what to do, and why these aims differed

- The main terms of the Treaty of Versailles with Germany

- What was decided in the other peace treaties signed between the 'Big Four' and Germany's former allies

- Whether these treaties were unfair to Germany and its allies

- How far these treaties contributed to the outbreak of a future war

# The main personalities and their aims

*Lloyd George, Clemenceau and Wilson, after the signing of the Treaty of Versailles in June 1919.*

### Self-determination

*This refers to the right of national or ethnic groups which have a language, history or culture in common to be allowed to decide (determine) whether they want to have their own independent country or be joined with similar people in another country. President Wilson was a great believer in this, and plebiscites (referendums) were held after the peace treaties so that some national groups could indeed decide for themselves.*

### Source B

England and France have not the same views with respect to peace that we have by any means. When the war is over we can force them to our way of thinking because by that time they will, among other things, be financially in our hands.

*The views of Woodrow Wilson, written by him in a private note, 1917.*

## The 'Big Three'

Britain, France, Italy and the USA (the Allies) won the First World War. They were known as the 'Big Four'. In January 1918, their leaders met in Paris to decide on the peace terms to present to the defeated Central Powers. They were officially known as the Council of Four.

Although Italy and Japan (plus 22 smaller states, such as Serbia) had fought on the Allied side, the main decisions were made by the 'Big Three': Britain, France and the USA. The leaders of the 'Big Three' were: David Lloyd George (Prime Minister of Britain), Georges Clemenceau (Prime Minister of France) and Woodrow Wilson (President of the USA).

## The leaders' different aims

### The USA

In January 1918, Woodrow Wilson issued his Fourteen Points. These set out what Wilson thought should be the basis for peace in Europe once Germany had been defeated. In particular, he wanted an end to secret diplomacy and treaties, a general disarmament, national self-determination for people living under the rule of other countries, and the setting up of a new international organisation to maintain peace and independence for all countries. Both the British and French leaders disagreed with several of his Points. Once the fighting was over, these disagreements began to emerge during the peace negotiations in Paris.

The USA had not suffered any destruction of industries or land during the war. In fact, the American economy had benefited from the war and the USA had, therefore, been able to lend money to Britain and France. Also, as it had not entered the war until 1917, it had not suffered heavy casualties. Wilson, therefore, pushed for what he called a just peace for Germany that would not be too harsh.

However, Wilson's position at the peace conferences was weakened by the fact that his party, the Democrats, had lost control of the Senate to the Republicans in the elections of November 1918. The Republicans were not keen to maintain American involvement in European affairs, and Britain and France used this to make Wilson give way on several of his Points. In the end, Wilson was prepared to make compromises, provided Britain and France backed his idea for a League of Nations.

### Britain

Lloyd George did not want to be too hard on Germany, despite strong anti-German public opinion in Britain. The main reasons for this were that he wanted the German economy to recover quickly so Britain could sell it industrial goods, and he did not want the Germans to feel bitter and so seek revenge in another war. He also believed that if Germany was made poor, it might lead to a communist revolution. Instead, he saw a prosperous Germany being able to act as a 'buffer' between western Europe and Bolshevik Russia. As a result, Lloyd George wanted a 'compromise' peace, which would weaken Germany enough militarily so that it would no longer pose a threat to the British navy and the British Empire (and also take away all its colonies), but otherwise would not seek to punish Germany. His aims were midway between those of France on one side and the USA on the other.

## France

While the war had been economically damaging for Britain, it had been an economic disaster for France. Most of the fighting had been on French soil, so there had been massive destruction of farmland, factories, railway lines, roads, bridges and homes. There had also been 3.5 million French casualties, compared to 2.25 million suffered by Britain. Because of this, and the massive war debts the French government had run up with the USA, the French wanted Germany to pay heavy reparations. Also, as France had earlier been defeated by the Germans in the Franco-Prussian War, 1870-71, Clemenceau wanted Germany to be virtually disarmed so it would never again be a threat to French security. For the same reason, France wanted Germany to lose a significant amount of European territory. Because Clemenceau wanted such a harsh peace, he was nicknamed 'The Tiger'. Yet, in fact, he at first asked the USA to cancel French war debts so that there would be no need to make Germany pay massive compensation. When the USA refused, he then adopted a harder line with Germany.

## The negotiations

When the Allies met in Paris, these different aims threatened to slow up the peace treaties. Despite this, the terms were rather hastily worked out for a number of reasons. These included the fact that the Austro-Hungarian Empire was already breaking up; communism seemed to be sweeping across many parts of Europe; and, as the armistice was only a temporary truce, the Allied naval blockade on Germany was now causing German civilians to die of starvation. One way of speeding up the decision-making process was to exclude the defeated countries from the discussions; they were then presented with the agreed terms on a 'take it or leave it' basis. In the end, there were five separate treaties in the years 1919-20.

**Source C**

*The ruins of the French town of Cambrai in 1914, resulting from heavy shelling.*

### Reparations

*This term means 'compensation'; sometimes the word 'indemnity' is also used. The reparations were the compensation Germany was forced to pay for having 'caused' the First World War. Because the Allies could not agree on how much Germany should pay, a special Reparations Committee was set up to avoid delaying the signing of the peace treaty. In 1920, the figure agreed on was £6000 million but this was increased on the insistence of France and Britain in 1921 to £6600 million. The first payments had already been taken by then in the form of coal, iron, railway engines, machinery and other materials. The rest was to be paid in instalments over the next 42 years.*

### Questions

1 Why did the writer of **Source B** think the USA would have financial power over Britain and France by the end of the First World War?

2 How useful is **Source B** as historical evidence about American aims in 1918?

3 What impact did scenes such as that shown in **Source C** have on French aims in 1918?

# The Treaty of Versailles

## The problem of Germany

The biggest problem facing the peace negotiators was what to do with Germany, which before the war had been the most powerful nation on the European continent. The German delegates were not allowed to take part in the discussions which began in January 1919. However, they did believe the terms would be based on Wilson's Fourteen Points. The issue was further complicated because Britain and France did not agree on how far Germany should be weakened militarily and economically, and the final terms of the Treaty were not finally agreed by the Allies until June 1919. The first 26 Articles of this treaty (and of all the others) dealt with the setting up of the League of Nations. There were four other main issues dealt with in the Treaty of Versailles which Germany was given to sign:

### Land losses in Europe

In all, the Treaty of Versailles took away about 13% of Germany's territory and 10% of its population in Europe. The Big Three agreed that the provinces of Alsace and Lorraine should be returned to France, without there being a plebiscite (referendum) to find out the wishes of their inhabitants. Germany also lost considerable territory to the newly-recreated country of Poland (West Prussia, Posen and part of Upper Silesia). This gave Poland a 'corridor' to the sea, and also split East Prussia from the rest of Germany. Poland benefited mainly because France wanted a strong ally on Germany's eastern border in order to weaken Germany's position. However, although Clemenceau also wanted Poland to get the port of Danzig, Lloyd George and Wilson insisted that it became an international 'Free City' controlled by the League of Nations. The three Baltic Sea states of Estonia, Latvia and Lithuania, which Germany had taken from Russia by the Treaty of Brest-Litovsk, also became independent states.

Smaller amounts of land were also lost to Belgium and Denmark: Eupen-Malmedy went to Belgium and North Schleswig to Denmark. France had also wanted to weaken Germany by taking over the important coal-producing region of the Saar, and by making the whole of the Rhineland area into a new separate country. The Saar was put under the control of the League of Nations for 15 years while the Rhineland was demilitarised. Any union (Anschluss) with Austria was also forbidden.

**Source A**

- Germany 1914
- Land taken from Germany
- Land under League of Nations control
- Demilitarised zone

*The territorial losses imposed on Germany by the Treaty of Versailles.*

### Rhineland

*This was the land which lay between the River Rhine and the French border. As France had twice been invaded by Germany (in 1870 and again in 1914), Clemenceau wanted this to become an independent country, but Britain and the USA refused. Instead, the Germans were banned from having any troops in this area, along with a 50 km strip of land along the eastern side of the river. The Rhineland became a de-militarised zone with Allied troops in occupation for 15 years.*

### Loss of colonies

The Allies were only agreed on the fact that Germany should lose all its colonies in Africa and Asia. While Britain and France wanted to add them to their own empires, the USA argued they should be run by the League of Nations before becoming independent. In the end, it was agreed that the colonies would be shared out between the Allies, who were given 'mandates' by the League to run them and prepare them for independence.

### Military restrictions

The German army was reduced to only 100 000, and conscription was forbidden. Germany was also banned from having tanks or heavy artillery, and could not station any troops or military equipment in the Rhineland. Germany was also restricted to a few small military aircraft; while its navy was reduced to six battleships and 30 smaller ships, with submarines completely outlawed. The rest of its navy was to be handed over to Britain and France, but the German commanders eventually scuttled their ships in Scapa Flow rather than hand them over.

### The 'war-guilt' clause

In addition, Germany was forced to accept Article 231, which stated that Germany alone was totally responsible for causing the First World War. This 'war-guilt' clause committed Germany to paying compensation. Because of Allied disagreements about the amount, the final figure of £6,600 million, payable over the next 42 years, was only agreed by the special Reparations Committee in 1921. Before then, in 1919, all of Germany's foreign currency and assets abroad were seized by the Allies.

## A 'Diktat'?

The German delegation were angry that the terms were much harsher than Wilson's Fourteen Points, but they were only given 22 days in which to accept or reject the draft treaty which had over 400 clauses. Although they made many criticisms, very little was altered. In view of the serious food shortages and revolutionary unrest in Germany, the German representatives reluctantly accepted the Treaty, rather than face renewed fighting. But, because they had in practice been forced to sign, this was seen as a dictated peace - or 'diktat'. Most Germans were angered by the terms of the Treaty, and blamed the new Weimar government for accepting it. At times in the 1920s and the 1930s, resentment at the Treaty of Versailles was a major factor in the rise of extreme nationalism and the far Right in Germany. At the same time, British governments came increasingly to see the Treaty as harsh, and were prepared to 'revise' parts of it. This, in part, explains the policy of appeasement followed in the 1930s.

**Mandates**

*These were permissions or licences to take over and rule Germany's former colonies in Africa and Asia, authorised by the League of Nations. They were given to various countries which had fought on the Allied side. Apart from Britain and France, Japan took over Germany's possessions in China and the Pacific Ocean. Different mandated areas were run on behalf of the League by Britain, France, the British dominions of Australia, New Zealand and South Africa, and Japan which had helped the Allies in Asia.*

**Source B**

*Some of the German delegation going over the terms of the Treaty of Versailles.*

**Questions**

1  How serious an impact did the land losses in Europe, imposed by the Treaty of Versailles and shown in **Source A**, have on Germany's strength?

2  Why did France want newly-created Poland to be given as much German and Austrian land as possible?

3  Why did some of the German delegation, shown in **Source B**, see the Treaty of Versailles as a 'diktat'?

4  Look back at the aims of each of the Big Three. How satisfied would each one have been with the final Treaty?

# The other treaties

*How the Treaties of 1919 and 1920 dealt with the territories of Austria-Hungary.*

**Successor states**

*This was the term used to describe the new nations which appeared in central and eastern Europe after the First World War and the various peace treaties. In the main, they arose out of what had been the Austro-Hungarian Empire - thus they were the 'successors' to this collapsed empire. Two states were completely new (Czechoslovakia and Yugoslavia) while Poland (which had been carved up between Austria, Prussia and Russia at the end of the eighteenth century) was recreated. They all had various weaknesses and problems, including Czechoslovakia which was the only one to remain a democracy during the inter-war period.*

**Source B**

Our firmest guarantee against German aggression is that behind Germany, in an excellent strategic position, stand Czechoslovakia and Poland.

*An extract from a speech by Clemenceau, the Prime Minister of France, made in 1919.*

## Germany's allies

The Paris peace conferences also had to deal with the other Central Powers which, like Germany, had been defeated in 1918. These were Austria-Hungary, Turkey and Bulgaria. Treaties between these countries and the Allies were worked out in the years 1919-20. Because the Austro-Hungarian Empire was already beginning to break up, with Austria and Hungary becoming two separate countries, two different treaties were needed. As with the Treaty of Versailles with Germany, all these treaties began with the 26 Articles on the setting up of the League of Nations.

### Austria

The treaty with Austria was the Treaty of Saint-Germain, signed in September 1919. Under it, Austria lost some land to Italy (Istria and the South Tyrol), and a lot more of its wealthiest areas to the new states which largely came out of the old Austro-Hungarian Empire. In particular, large areas (containing over 3 million German-speakers) went to Czechoslovakia and Poland, while the new state of Yugoslavia took over the Austrian possessions in the Balkans. These countries became known as the 'Successor' states. In all, Austria was reduced to a small country of just over 6 million people. This treaty, like the Treaty of Versailles, permanently forbade any unification (Anschluss) with Germany. Finally, the Austrian army was limited to only 30 000.

### Hungary

During the peace negotiations, a revolution had broken out in Hungary. This was led by the communist Bela Kun, who proclaimed Hungary to be an independent soviet republic. The Allies delayed signing any treaty with Hungary until after the communist revolution had been crushed. Eventually, a new right-wing dictatorship was set up under Admiral Horthy who, in March 1920, was forced to sign the Treaty of Trianon. This gave about 60% of Hungarian territory and 11 million of its citizens to the new 'Successor' states of Czechoslovakia and Yugoslavia, with some also going to Romania. As a result, Hungary was reduced to a population of only 7 million. The size of its army was reduced to 35 000.

### Turkey

The Turkish (or Ottoman) Empire had been in decline since the eighteenth century, long before the First World War. In 1920, the Turkish Sultan (emperor) was forced to sign the Treaty of Sevres with the Allies. This gave most of its European lands to Greece; while its provinces in the Middle East were shared out between Britain and France as mandates, despite earlier promises to Arab leaders that they would gain independence if they fought on the Allies' side. In the end, France was given Syria, while Britain got Palestine, Jordan and Iraq. Turkey was also made to pay compensation. Many Turkish people were angry at the Treaty, and a nationalist general, Mustafa Kemal (known as Ataturk) led a successful rebellion against the Sultan in 1921. Kemal then occupied the territories given to Greece. In 1923, the Allies agreed to sign a new treaty with Turkey. This Treaty of Lausanne returned most of the land previously given to Greece, and cancelled the payment of reparations.

### Bulgaria

In November 1919, the Treaty of Neuilly was signed between Bulgaria and the Allies. Some land was lost to Greece, Yugoslavia and Romania, while its army was reduced to 20 000.

## Assessing the treaties

In view of the territorial and military changes imposed by the Treaty of Versailles and the other treaties, historians have argued about whether they were unfair, and about the new problems they might have caused. There is particular discussion about the Treaty of Versailles.

In practice, the Treaty of Versailles was less harsh than the Treaty of Brest-Litovsk imposed on Russia by Imperial Germany in March 1918. It was also quite leniently applied. Disarmament, for instance, was carried out by the Germans, under Allied supervision, by commissions of control. These frequently pointed out that throughout the 1920s, Germany was not complying, and restrictions were later evaded by military agreements with Soviet Russia.

Furthermore, Germany was left largely intact, with a population still almost double that of France, despite the losses imposed by the Treaty. Also significant was that Germany had not been invaded, while France's ten richest departments (provinces) had been devastated by the fighting. As far as reparations were concerned, during the 1920s, the 'final' figure was progressively reduced.

When compared to the other peace treaties of 1919-1920, especially the Treaties of St. Germain and Trianon (with Austria and Hungary respectively), the Treaty of Versailles also seems quite lenient. These other treaties broke up the economic stability of the old Austro-Hungarian Empire, and led to the creation of many smaller states, several of which (especially Czechoslovakia and Poland) had large numbers of different nationalities within their borders which resulted in ethnic tensions. For instance, in Czechoslovakia only 65% of its population were Czechs or Slovaks, while most of the west border areas were inhabited by German-speakers known as the Sudeten Germans. The Slovaks in the poorer east also complained of unfair treatment by the Czechs. Poland was not satisfied with its borders and in the years 1919–21, it fought wars against Czechoslovakia, Lithuania and the Soviet Union in order to gain more territory.

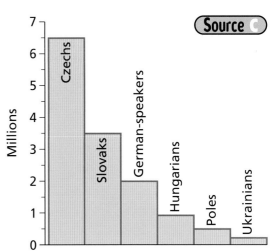

**Source C**

The different national groups in Czechoslovakia in 1920.

### Reparations

The payments were rescheduled over a longer period by the Dawes Plan, 1924 and the Young Plan, 1929. While in the 1930s, Germany was able to finance large-scale rearmament. Overall, the basic strength of the German economy was not seriously weakened by the Treaty, and Germany was soon restored to being the most successful European economy. By 1925, Germany's steel production was already twice the size of Britain's.

### Sudeten Germans

These were German-speakers who had been part of the Austro-Hungarian Empire. There were over 3 million of them, and they mostly lived in the border area known as the Sudetenland, next to the Czech frontier with Austria and Germany. Although, like all Austrians, they spoke German, they had not been part of Germany. There was no plebiscite to allow them to decide which country they wanted to be transferred to.

### Questions

1 What can you learn from **Source B** about the importance of the 'successor states'?

2 In practice, what effect did the imposition of reparations have on the German economy?

# SUMMARY

## 1918–1919

- The main Allied countries of Britain, France and the USA (known as the 'Big Three') began to work out the kind of peace they wanted to end the fighting. In January 1918, Wilson of the USA issued his Fourteen Points without consulting the other two countries.

- In January 1919, the various Allied countries met in Paris to begin peace negotiations, but the defeated countries were not allowed to take part.

## 1919–1920

- The Big Three leaders (Lloyd George, Clemenceau and Wilson) presented the Treaty of Versailles to the German delegation, who were not allowed to make any significant changes. They were told that if they refused to sign, the Allies would re-start the war. As sections of the German armed forces were involved in mutiny or revolution, the Germans signed under duress.

- The Treaty imposed many territorial and military restrictions on Germany, including the loss of all its colonies. Unification (Anschluss) with Austria was forbidden.

- The 'war-guilt' clause, forced Germany to accept full responsibility for starting the war, and thus the obligation to pay huge reparations (compensation) to the Allies. Many Germans saw the new government as 'November Criminals' who had 'stabbed Germany in the back' by signing the armistice and accepting the Treaty.

- Other treaties were signed in the coming months with the other defeated Central Powers. These, too, involved the transfer of land and people to new or existing countries in central and eastern Europe, along with military restrictions and, for some, the payment of compensation.

- As a result, there was economic dislocation and much national and ethnic unrest in the 'Successor states', especially as the German-speaking inhabitants of the former Austro-Hungarian Empire were in the main denied any rights of self-determination.

- Further instability in the region was caused by Poland, which fought several short wars to extend its borders.

## 1921–1923

- In 1921, the Reparations Committee decided that Germany should pay a total of £6600 million in compensation over the next 42 years.

- After the Treaty of Sevres had been signed with Turkey, the Sultan was overthrown by a nationalist revolt, and fighting broke out between the new rulers and Greece, which had gained most of Turkey's European territories. Eventually, in 1923, the Allies signed a new treaty (Lausanne) with Turkey, which restored most of its European lands.

- There was also ethnic tension in Czechoslovakia as only 65% of its population were Czechs or Slovaks. The main problems were between the Czech government and the large German-speaking population, which had been transferred from Austria. The Slovaks also complained of unfair treatment.

# Exam Question Practice

## Recall of knowledge and description

Study the information below and answer the questions which follow.

## Information

The Treaty of Versailles was signed between the Allies and Germany in June 1919. It imposed several territorial and military changes which were unpopular with many Germans, who saw the Treaty as a 'diktat'. The German cartoon in Source A gives a view of the Treaty which was widespread in Germany.

**1** Explain what was meant by the term 'diktat'? **(2)**

**2** Describe the main points of the Treaty of Versailles. **(6)**

**Source A**

'Greed, revenge and other devils gloat over the Treaty of Versailles.' The view of the German cartoonist, Lindlott, published in the magazine 'Simplicissimus' in 1919.

### Examiner's Tips

**When answering questions like this:**

◎ Look to see how many marks are available If it's 5 or 6, try not to write more than about two or three paragraphs (save your essays for those giving 8, 9 or 10 marks!).

◎ Don't spend too long on answering questions which only carry 1 or 2 marks, like question (1) above. In such cases, just write one or two sentences at the most - but make sure you give precise/detailed facts, even on such low-scoring questions.

◎ Make sure you avoid making vague statements (e.g. 'Germany lost a lot of land') you will not score very high marks.

◎ Remember that for questions worth about 5 marks, you will need to give a few specific supporting facts about several different aspects. For this question, you would need to deal with land losses in Europe, Germany's colonies, the various military restrictions, the question of union with Austria, and the issue of 'war-guilt' and reparations.

# CHAPTER 4

## THE LEAGUE OF NATIONS, 1919-29

Citizen.]       [Brooklyn, U.S.A.

### An Expected Arrival.
Will the stork make good as to this infant ?

*'The Birth of Hope', an American cartoon from 1919 about the formation of the League of Nations.*

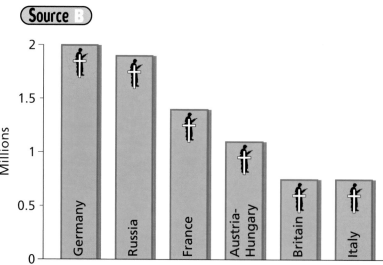

*The number of soldiers killed in the First World War.*

**Source C**

*An illustration of the first meeting of the League of Nations, from an Italian journal in 1922.*

## Key Questions

**Why** did many people in 1919 place great hopes in the League of Nations, as suggested by **Source A**?

**What** effect did the terrible losses suffered during the 'Great War' (shown in **Source B**) have on the foreign policies of the main countries involved?

**Why** did the League of Nations shown in **Source C**, fail to stop future wars?

These are some of the issues which we will cover in this chapter. The main focus of this chapter on the League of Nations will be:

• The role and organisation of the League of Nations

• The problems of its membership and powers

• How the League was able to solve several disputes in the period 1920-29

• What failures the League experienced during the 1920s

• Why the League found it difficult to deal with all the conflicts during this period

# CHAPTER 4

# The role and organisation of the League

## The Covenant

The first 26 Articles of all five of the peace treaties of 1919-20 were about setting up a new international organisation meant to keep the peace. This body was called the League of Nations, and was mainly the idea of Woodrow Wilson, President of the USA. He believed that the traditional secrecy of European diplomacy had been a major factor in causing the First World War. His Fourteen Points included a call to set up a 'general association of nations' to guarantee the 'political independence and territorial integrity' (borders) of all nations. He believed the USA should use its new global economic and military power to create a 'new international order' which would 'make the world safe for democracy'. His plans were also partly a result of fears triggered by the 1917 Bolshevik Revolution in Russia.

In January 1919, a commission had been set up to work out a Constitution for the League. Fourteen states were involved: the Big Five (the USA, Britain, France, Italy and Japan) with two delegates each, and nine other (minor) states with one delegate each. Though all agreed that the main aim should be to prevent future wars, they disagreed as to how this should be achieved. However, by February 1919, it was agreed that a new international body should be established, and its rules, or Covenant, would be set out in the first Articles of the Treaties.

## The role of the League

The League was to be a permanent international body, with four main roles. These were to guarantee the territory of states via collective security, prevent conflicts, settle disputes peacefully and bring about disarmament. The League also had an administrative job to supervise the former colonies or provinces of Germany and Turkey, and an economic and social role - helping to stabilise currencies and assisting with world health issues, the problem of illegal drugs, etc. A permanent Court of International Justice was also set up, based in the Netherlands, at The Hague, which was to settle legal disputes between countries.

## Membership

From its beginning, although it started off with 45 members, three of the great powers of the world were absent from the League. Even though it was an American President who had pushed hardest for the League to be set up, the US Congress, dominated by the Republicans, refused to sign the Treaties or to join the League. From 1920-26, Germany and its former allies were not allowed to join the League. Despite Germany being allowed to join in 1926, as one of the permanent Council members, the League was still seen as a 'victors club'. These were serious early weaknesses, which were made worse by the fact that the fear of communism meant Soviet

Russia was also not allowed to join. In fact, the Russian government condemned the League as a capitalist club dominated by imperialist powers. Though the number of Council members elected by the Assembly increased to six in 1926 and nine in 1929, it was essentially seen as a European club.

## Organisation

The League's administrative system was based at Geneva in Switzerland. The Assembly met once a year, with all member countries having one vote each. Any member with a dispute was to bring the matter to the Assembly, instead of resorting to violence. The original founder members were made up of 32 Allied states, and 13 neutral powers. If the Assembly was unable to prevent conflict, then the smaller Council would take action to implement collective security. This Council consisted of the Big Four (Britain, France, Italy and Japan) as permanent members, plus 4 smaller countries elected at intervals by the Assembly. Its main powers were the pressure of world opinion and, if necessary, the imposition of economic sanctions. If these failed, then force could be used, but the League was never given its own army, so this sanction depended on the more powerful nations agreeing to use their own troops.

The routine administration and secretarial work was to be carried out by the Secretariat, which acted as the League's civil service. Its first Chairman and Secretary-General was Sir Eric Drummond. To administer the former territories of the defeated powers, a system of mandates was set up, to be operated by League members (mostly Britain, the British Dominions, France and Japan) on agreed conditions, and with annual reports to the League. The League also set up Special Commissions to administer areas such as Danzig and the Saar. Finally, in order to carry out its economic and social roles, the League established various bodies, such as the International Labour Organisation (to establish fair and humane conditions of labour) plus other Commissions to end slavery, illegal drugs, and the arms trade, to prevent and control the spread of disease, and to maintain the freedom of trade and communications.

**Source C**

The defeat suffered by Wilsonism in the United States strikes at the very existence of the League of Nations. America's place will remain empty at Geneva, and the two countries that dominate, France and Great Britain, are divided on almost every one of the topics to be discussed.

*A French politician, in 1920, commenting on the implications for the League of the non-membership of the USA.*

**Economic sanctions**

*These are actions taken or applied to put pressure on a country to force it to do, or to stop doing something; economic sanctions might include a trade ban or boycott, especially of vital products such as armaments or coal. These could only work if all the powerful countries involved in such trade stuck to the sanctions.*

**Questions**

1 Draw up a list of all the tasks that the League of Nations was supposed to carry out. For each task note which parts of the League were responsible for the job.

2 What does **Source C** see as the likely consequences of the American decision not to join the League?

3 Explain in your own words how the idea of collective security was supposed to work. What problems might there be getting it to work in practice?

# The League in action

## Successful actions by the League

The League, with its headquarters at Geneva, formally began its work in January 1920, and was able to achieve several successes during the period 1919-1929. These included:

- Yugoslavia v. Albania, 1920 – In this dispute, the League was able to persuade Yugoslavia to withdraw its troops from Albania.

- Aaland Islands, 1920 - This was a dispute between Finland and Sweden, over these islands (which were owned by Finland, although the majority of the population was Swedish). Britain brought it to the attention of the League, which settled it peacefully, in Finland's favour.

- Upper Silesia, 1921 – The League successfully resolved a dispute between Poland and Germany over this territory. The Treaty of Versailles had decided that the people of Upper Silesia should vote in a plebiscite to decide whether they wished to be part of Poland or Germany. The result was close and resulted in rioting, so the League was asked to resolve it. The League finally decided to divide it between Poland and Germany, though the drawing of the borders was extremely complicated. Germany got most land.

- Mosul, 1924 – Here the League resolved a dispute between Iraq and Turkey over this important oil-rich area in Iraq's favour. (Iraq was a British mandate area.)

- Greece v. Bulgaria, 1925 – Greece was ordered by the League to withdraw its troops, and to pay compensation to Bulgaria for damage caused. They had argued over neighbouring Macedonia.

## General work

The League was successful in running the Saar and Danzig, and stabilised the currencies of Austria and Hungary in the 1920s. The League Secretariat also helped revive the world economy, by arranging world conferences on tariffs and trade agreements. Its humanitarian work with refugees and prisoners of war (especially after the Russo-Polish war, 1920-1921, and the Greco-Turkish War, 1920-1922) was also a significant achievement. In addition, it did much to deal with tropical diseases, such as yellow fever and malaria. The International Labour Organisation was set up to improve workers' rights and working conditions across the world. Its main achievement was to limit child labour in some countries.

## Failures

However, even during the period 1920-1929, before the Depression, the League of Nations' success as a peace-keeping organisation was limited. Its failures included:

- Vilna, 1920 – In 1919, Lithuania was re-created as one of the independent Baltic States (it was formally part of Tsarist Russia).

**Source A**

*Refugees arriving in France.*

**Source B**

*The League of Nations Malaria Committee, meeting in Singapore in 1924.*

### Depression

*Sometimes called the Great Depression, this refers to the global economic distress (high unemployment, inflation, industrial decline in production and trade, poverty), which hit most capitalist countries in the 1930s, following the Wall Street Crash of 1929. Communist Russia was unaffected, and actually experienced tremendous economic growth.*

It wanted Vilna to be its new capital (as it had been in the past). But Vilna had a large Polish population and, in 1920 was seized by Poland. Although Lithuania asked the League to intervene, Poland ignored it.

- Russo-Polish War, 1920-1921 – Poland was not content with its eastern border (the Curzon Line) as decided by the peace treaties of 1919-1920. In 1920, Poland crossed the Curzon Line to seize White Russia and the Ukraine. The League was unable to prevent this war. In fact, Poland was backed by Britain and France, the two most important members of the League. (These two countries, along with the USA, Italy, Japan and several other countries had also intervened in the Civil War in Russia, against the communist government).

- Greece v. Turkey, 1920-1922 – The Treaty of Sevres, 1920, had given most of Turkey's European lands to Greece. Turkish nationalists, led by Mustafa Kemal, overthrew their Sultan for signing the Treaty. Greece decided to invade Turkey in order to overthrow this new government, which was determined to overturn the Treaty of Sevres. The Turkish army defeated the Greeks and then threatened the British forces occupying parts of Turkey. Further warfare was avoided by Britain agreeing that a new treaty should be signed (Lausanne, 1923). The League had been unable to either prevent or halt this war, in large part because Britain supported Greece, while France supported Turkey. However, its Refugee Committee and Health Organisation did much useful work over the next 3 years in assisting with the 1.4 million Greek civilians driven from their homes.

- Memel, 1923 – The port of Memel and the land around it was mainly inhabited by Lithuanians, but had been put under League administration by the Treaty of Versailles. However, the League was unable to prevent Lithuania seizing it in 1923. The League did finally persuade Lithuania to accept the port becoming an 'international zone', with Lithuania retaining the surrounding area.

- Invasion of the Ruhr, 1923 – The League was unable to prevent France and Belgium from invading the Ruhr after Germany failed to pay its second reparations instalment. In fact, France did not even consult the League before it took action.

- The Corfu Incident, 1923 – The League also failed to stop another of its leading members, this time Italy, from invading the Greek island of Corfu. This occurred after 5 Italians (sent by the Conference of Ambassadors to help survey a disputed border between Greece and Albania) were killed in an ambush. Greece asked the League for help, but Mussolini ignored the League as he argued it was a Conference of Ambassadors' matter.

## Conference of Ambassadors

*This was set up by, and was made up of, Britain, France, Italy and Japan. It was meant to ensure that the terms of the peace treaties were kept to. It met regularly, and was often used by the more powerful countries as a way to settle disputes without having to go through the League of Nations.*

*This body met at regular intervals, and often resulted in confusions of responsibility with the League of Nations. Several disputes in the period were, in fact, settled by the Conference of Ambassadors, not by the League. A conflict between Poland and Czechoslovakia in 1919, over the border town of Teschen (which had important coalmines) was settled by the Conference, as was the 1920 dispute between Lithuania and Poland over Vilna. The Conference of Ambassadors finally decided in Poland's favour.*

## Questions

1 Why was the League relatively successful in the kind of work shown in **Sources A** and **B**?

2 How did the League solve the dispute over Upper Silesia in 1921?

3 How did the Conference of Ambassadors undermine the international role of the League during the 1920s?

4 What other reasons can you suggest for the failures of the League in the 1920s?

# Weaknesses of the League

### Decision-making in the League

The absence of three important nations from the League, meant the two most important members were Britain and France. Unfortunately, these two countries often disagreed over what to do. In addition, the League's procedures to prevent aggression also had several practical problems. Firstly, while members of the Assembly could bring any issue to the League which threatened a military conflict, the Assembly could only 'advise' (recommend). Only the Council could make decisions. If a dispute arose, member states had to submit the dispute to the Council, and avoid all use of force until 3 months after the League had reported. The League had 6 months to investigate and report to the Council. However, Council decisions had to be unanimous and if no agreement had been reached after another 3 months, the members in dispute could resort to force.

### Powers of the League

Attempts to strengthen the League's ability to guarantee the terms of the 1919-1920 peace treaties also failed. In 1923, a draft Treaty of Mutual Assistance, suggested by France to give the League powers to take rapid military action in the event of unprovoked aggression, was blocked by Britain. This was because the new Conservative government feared a powerful League would be used by France to push its own interests in Europe. France tried again in 1924 with the Geneva Protocol, which aimed to commit all members to undertake collective military action. This was supported by the new Labour Prime Minister of Britain, Ramsay MacDonald, but he fell from power later on in 1924. In March 1925, Austen Chamberlain, on behalf of the new Conservative government, blocked this scheme as well.

**Unanimous**

*This means everybody had to agree. This method of making decisions proved to be one of the League's weaknesses. If just one of the countries which was represented in the Council refused to agree to an action, then the League could not do anything.*

### Dealing with powerful countries

Countries trying to by-pass the League of Nations by using the Conference of Ambassadors undermined the League. A more serious weakness was shown when a more powerful nation was involved in conflict, especially if that country was also an important member of the League. This was shown by the Corfu Incident of 1923, which was finally settled by the Conference of Ambassadors in Italy's favour. France, which saw Italy as an important potential ally against Germany, did not want to upset Mussolini (the Italian leader), and so blocked any action against Italy by the League. Italy had earlier cooperated with France over its invasion of the Ruhr. Also, the British government had been advised by experts that applying economic or

**Source A**

*Italian troops in Corfu, September 1923.*

naval sanctions against Italy would damage British interests. So both the unanimous-decision process and the use of sanctions were shown to be ineffective in practice, when effective collective action was required.

## Disarmament

Article 8 dealt with disarmament, but the League was unable to bring this about. This was despite the fact that many countries believed that the build up of armaments before 1914 (the arms race) had created insecurity in Europe and had thus been a major factor in the outbreak of the First World War. In part, this was because the 1920s were very unstable. The existence of communist Russia and the power vacuum in central and eastern Europe meant many states, such as Poland and Czechoslovakia, were reluctant to disarm. More importantly, France was extremely concerned about disarming, given Britain's refusal to give the League real military powers, and the refusal by both Britain and the USA to give any military guarantees. Although Britain was willing to reduce its own level of weapons, the non-membership of the USA meant disarmament talks often bypassed the League.

## Non-League agreements

The steps which were taken to reduce tensions and maintain the Treaties during the 1920s were all the result of direct diplomacy, not because of the League. In 1921-22, the Washington Conferences resulted in the Washington Naval Treaty (1922), by which the USA, Britain, Italy and Japan agreed to limit their navies. In 1925, the Locarno Treaty saw Germany agree to accept the demilitarisation of the Rhineland and its new borders with France and Belgium. Although Germany did not promise to accept its eastern borders, it did agree that changes would be made by negotiation not war. This Treaty led to Germany being allowed to join the League in 1926, and to an optimistic feeling about peace, known as the 'spirit of Locarno'. In 1928, 45 countries (including Germany) signed the Kellogg-Briand Pact. This said that all countries would never resort to war again. Later, the number of countries signing it went up to 65. Finally, the problem of Germany's reparations payments was solved by two agreements which reduced their level, increased the time-period, and provided American loans: the Dawes Plan of 1924 and the Young Plan of 1929.

Despite talk of self-determination, the League often failed to carry this out. For example, it was able to do very little to protect the rights of ethnic minorities in the new central and eastern European states. However, despite these problems and failures, by 1929 the League had grown to 54 members, and had helped to promote a greater level of international cooperation than had existed before 1914.

### Military guarantees

*Because Britain refused to allow the League to have any of its own military forces, the French government wanted Britain and the USA to give it definite promises of military assistance if Germany should ever try to undo any part of the Treaty of Versailles. When such promises were not made, France felt insecure.*

*France's fears were also linked to the fact that Germany possessed greater industrial resources and had a population of 66 million compared to France's 39 million.*

### Source B

The French position remained as brittle as ever. There was no firm entente with Britain. In 1928 the RAF drew up plans for a 'Locarno' war against France should she ever violate German territory. The Eastern alliances were a poor substitute. Germany, revived economically and secretly re-arming, had said nothing about her eastern frontier at Locarno. The French knew that when Germany was strong enough, French security would once again be in the melting-pot.

*Extract from a history textbook, published in Britain in 1989, outlining French concerns about the Locarno Treaty of 1925.*

### Questions

1 Why was the League unable to deal with the Corfu Crisis of 1923, shown in **Source A**?

2 What do you understand by the terms 'no firm entente' and the 'Eastern alliances' mentioned in **Source B**?

3 Britain and France both made things difficult for the League. Why did they do this?

4 You have now looked at lots of reasons for the League's failures. Which of these reasons do you think was the most serious. Explain why.

# SUMMARY

## 1919–1920

- Wilson of the USA persuaded the Allies to work out a Covenant (set of rules) for the new international peace-keeping organisation he wanted. It was decided to call it the League of Nations.
- The rules became the first 26 Articles of the five peace treaties signed with the defeated Central Powers. The League's main aims were to protect the independence of all countries, and to bring about disarmament.
- Decisions had to be unanimous before action could be taken. The strongest action was to enforce economic sanctions against any country which resorted to war, as the League did not have its own military force.
- Although 45 countries joined as founder-members, the USA decided not to join, while Germany and its former allies were temporarily excluded. Communist Russia was also not invited to join. At the same time, the Conference of Ambassadors was set up by Britain, France, Italy and Japan.
- The headquarters of the League was in Geneva in Switzerland. There was an Assembly where all the members met once a year, but the power to take action lay with the permanent Council. The routine administration was done by the Secretariat; and there were also several Special Commissions. The League's first meeting was in 1920.

## 1920–1923

- The League had a number of successes in ending or preventing conflicts. It also began to do good work through its various Commissions, such as dealing with refugees, trying to wipe out diseases and attempting to improve working conditions across the world.
- Its successes in dealing with conflicts included: Yugoslavia v. Albania, 1920; the Aaland Islands, 1920; and Upper Silesia, 1921. In the main, however, these were all disputes involving smaller countries.
- However, it also failed to bring about disarmament and to solve several problems which, in the end, were dealt with by the Conference of Ambassadors. These failures included: Vilna, 1920; the Russo-Polish War, 1920-21; Greece v. Turkey, 1920-21; Memel, 1923; the occupation of the Ruhr, 1923; and the Corfu Incident, 1923. Several of these involved the more powerful members of the League. The League was also not involved in the Washington Naval Treaty of 1922.

## 1924–1929

- The League continued to have some success when dealing with disputes involving smaller states. These included: Mosul, 1924; and the war between Greece and Bulgaria, 1925.
- In 1926, Germany was allowed to become a member of the League.
- Several agreements to reduce tensions and improve relations during this period were made outside of the League. These included: the Dawes Plan, 1924; the Locarno Treaty, 1925; the Kellogg-Briand Pact, 1928; and the Young Plan, 1929.
- Nonetheless, by 1929, the League had 54 members, and had played an important part in helping to reduce the risk of war by promoting cooperation and the peaceful settlement of disputes.

# Exam Question Practice

## Explanation/Analysis questions

Study Source A below, which is about the Kellogg-Briand Pact of 1928, and then answer the following question.

Why, despite the improvement of international relations which led to the signing of the Kellogg-Briand Pact, did the League of Nations often have problems in preventing conflicts in the 1920s? **(10)**

**Source A**

1  The parties... condemn war as a means of solving international disputes and reject it as an instrument of policy.
2  The settlement or solution of all disputes...shall only be sought by peaceful means.

*An extract from the terms of the Kellogg-Briand Pact, 1928.*

## Examiner's Tips

**When answering questions like this:**

◎ Remember you are being asked to explain something, so don't just describe the successes and failures of the League in the 1920s, as this will not answer the question, even if many of the facts you give are accurate and relevant. You must show the examiner that you are aware of reasons/factors, as well as knowing the facts.

◎ Make sure you try to give a number of different reasons to show the problems of the League, and make sure you can give one or two precise examples to illustrate each of the factors you have identified. If you just list several different factors without giving supporting facts, you will not score the higher marks.

◎ Check the number of marks available. Such questions often carry high marks, so you will find it helpful to do a rough plan first - that way, you can check to see you are giving several different reasons.

◎ Try to see if you can sort the reasons out into more/less important ones where this is possible/relevant.

# CHAPTER 5

## BRITAIN BETWEEN THE WARS

The Jarrow Crusade marchers on their way to London in 1936.

An illustration published in an Italian magazine, of a battle between the British Army and Sinn Fein forces in Dublin during the 'War of Independence'.

*An armoured car accompanying a food convoy in Aldgate, London, during the General Strike, May 1926.*

## Key Questions

**What** happened to Britain after it won the First World War?

**Why**, less than 20 years after its victory, was Britain experiencing 'hunger marches' like the one shown in **Source A**?

**Why** did violence, such as that shown in **Source B**, break out in Ireland?

**Why** was it decided that armed food convoys like the one in **Source C** were necessary in Britain in 1926?

These are some of the issues that we will cover in this chapter. The main focus of this chapter on Britain between the two world wars will be:

• The economic and social problems resulting from Britain's involvement in the First World War

• The growing tensions in industrial relations, and the General Strike

• The outbreak of conflict in Ireland and attempts to end it

• The economic and political impact of the Great Depression on Britain

• How British governments tried to deal with the problems caused by the Depression

# The impact of the First World War

## Cost of the war

The cost of the war had meant that the government had had to find additional finance. Income tax was doubled and several new indirect taxes were introduced, such as a luxuries tax and amusement taxes. In addition, loans were raised. Even then, 75% of public spending went on the war, and the government ended up with a £10 billion debt, and, more importantly, a large balance of trade deficit (when the country spends more money buying goods from elsewhere than it makes by selling its own goods to other countries). In part, this was because over 25% of British assets overseas had been sold off to help finance the war. In the past, these 'invisible' earnings had helped close the gap between imports and exports. This trading deficit was made worse by the fact that British industry had concentrated on war production instead of exports. As a result, Britain lost its customers to other industrial nations, especially to the USA and Japan.

## Industrial decline

An additional problem was that much of British industry was using old-fashioned and inefficient machinery, compared to some other nations which had industrialised later. Even before 1914, Britain had been overtaken by Germany and the USA. Although banking, insurance and shipping continued to prosper, Britain's 'staple' industries, such as coal, iron and steel, were in decline. The textile industries were also old-fashioned and suffered from increased competition from abroad.

## Slump and unemployment

After the war these problems were not obvious at first. But, by the end of 1920, the loss of wartime government contracts and the demobilisation of the large army combined to produce a post-war depression. By mid-1921, there were over 2 million unemployed. At first, there was no immediate panic, as it was assumed that this 'slump' in exports and industrial production would be short-lived. However, although the situation did slowly improve, there was no return to pre-war conditions. The state of British industry compared with its competitors meant unemployment never fell below 1 million in the period before the start of the Second World War.

Originally, unemployment benefit had only been seen as temporary assistance for people between jobs. However, the slumps of the 1920s and 1930s led to many long-term unemployed. The Unemployment Insurance Act (1921) allowed for the payment of 'uncovenanted' (uninsured) benefit once the period of insured benefit had passed. This was known as the 'dole'. The Unemployment Fund was allowed to borrow up to £30 million from the Treasury to cover this. Further Unemployment Insurance Acts

**Staple industries**

*This refers to the main established 'old' industries. The coal industry was finding it hard to operate on a profitable basis, while the iron and steel industries faced growing competition from the more advanced foreign producers. An added problem for them was that their biggest customers in Britain, the engineering and ship-building industries, were also in decline and thus placing smaller orders.*

**Source A**

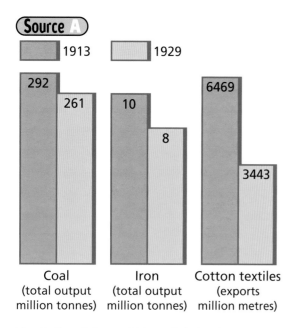

| | 1913 | | 1929 |

| Coal (total output million tonnes) | Iron (total output million tonnes) | Cotton textiles (exports million metres) |
| --- | --- | --- |
| 292 / 261 | 10 / 8 | 6469 / 3443 |

*The decline of three British staple industries, 1913-29.*

(1927 and 1929) lowered some benefits and abolished extended benefits.

## Social reform

The horrors and sufferings of the war led to a strong desire to build a better peace. As Lloyd George had promised before the war ended, Britain was to become a 'fit country for heroes to live in'. In part, this was because the mass conscription had revealed the poor physical condition and the lack of education of many of the working-class soldiers. The Education Act (1918) raised the school-leaving age to 14; introduced medical inspections for secondary school children; and allowed councils to set up 'Day Continuation Schools' for 14 to 18 year-olds, and nurseries for children aged between two and five. The employment of children under 12 was made illegal.

The poor housing conditions were tackled by the Addison Housing Act (1919), which set out to build 200 000 new 'council' houses for ordinary people. Although these were often cramped, they were an improvement on the slums which they replaced. Rate-payers, however, disliked the extra costs involved and, under the Conservatives in this period, the emphasis was shifted to private housing. In 1923 the Minister of Health, Neville Chamberlain, passed an act which allowed subsidies to be given to builders of new houses. From then until 1929, about 500 000 new houses were built, although only about 150 000 of these were built by councils. The Wheatly Housing Act (1924) raised State subsidies for rent-controlled houses and was widely used by many councils, resulting in the building of over 500 000 new council houses until the subsidy was withdrawn in 1933.

## Political reform

Before the war, the government had been facing growing protest and disruption as a result of the suffragette campaign to get votes for women. During the war, women had played an extremely important and active part in the war effort. In addition, women had been able to experience a more liberated social life, such as smoking in public and going into pubs. Their range of clothing had also become less restrictive and more practical, with many wearing trousers. The Representation of the People Act (1918) gave votes to women over the age of 30 who were householders or married to householders. At the same time, the voting age for men was set at 21, although some ex-servicemen were able to vote at 19. Most of those still entitled to plural voting (voting in more than one place) had this right removed.

However, it was not until the Representation of the People Act (1928) that women gained equal voting rights, when all women over the age of 21 were given the vote.

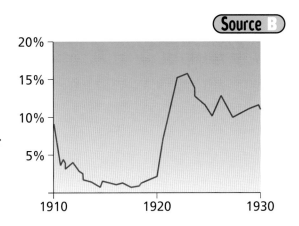

*The percentage of workers unemployed in Britain in the years 1910-30.*

## Questions

1 According to **Source A**, by how much did coal production in Britain decline in the years 1913-29?

2 How useful are **Sources A** and **B** for finding out about the state of the British economy in the 1920s?

3 Look at the economic problems and the social and political reforms described here. Do you think people felt that their lives were better or worse than they had been *before* the First World War?

# Industrial conflict

## Trade union militancy

Before 1914, industrial tensions between employers and trade unions had been building up, with many workers being influenced by syndicalist ideas (the use of militant industrial action to force political change). On several occasions the government had used the police, and even the army, to deal with mass strikes in transport and the coal mines. The unions had responded by setting up a 'Triple Industrial Alliance' and drawing up plans for a general strike. The outbreak of war had put these plans on hold, and, during the war, trade union members had benefited from government control of wages and prices, and of industries such as the railways and the mines.

## The impact of the post-war slump

After the war, employers were keen to regain control of their companies. However, between 1913 and 1919, trade union membership had almost doubled, and workers wanted to maintain the improved living standards they had enjoyed during the war. During 1919 and 1920, there was a marked increase in the number of strikes, many of which led to wage increases which took account of rising prices. Even the police went on strike!

However, after a depression began in 1921, employers tried to improve their profits by cutting wages and increasing the hours of work. The high unemployment meant unions found it much harder to use strikes to improve wages. These problems were particularly bad in the older industries such as coal mining.

## 'Black Friday'

In 1919, the Miners' Federation of Great Britain (MFGB) had persuaded the government to appoint a Commission of Inquiry into whether the coal mines should be nationalised (taken over permanently by the government). Although the majority had argued that nationalisation should take place, the government decided to do nothing, and announced that government control would end in March 1921. In 1921, the owners announced drastic wage cuts and a return to different wages for different areas. The MFGB opposed this and called on the transport and the railway unions to strike in their support. But, at the last moment, on Friday 15 April, the railway workers' union withdrew its support and the Triple Industrial Alliance began to collapse. This day became known by trade unionists as 'Black Friday'. The miners fought on alone until July, but failed to gain any significant improvements.

## The continuing problems of the coal industry

Although there was a slight improvement after 1921, there was another serious crisis in the coal mines in 1925. As prices fell sharply once again, the owners responded with further wage cuts

**Government control**

*This had meant that, in practice, they only had one employer to negotiate with. Miners, in particular, benefited from the fact that wages no longer varied from area to area. Thus, from 1914-18, with one or two exceptions, an 'industrial truce' existed, and most unions wanted to see government control continue after the war.*

**Source A**

*A strikers' demonstration during the General Strike of 1926.*

and an increase in the working day of one hour. By then, other unions were facing similar problems, so the Triple Industrial Alliance was revived. The Conservative government, led by Stanley Baldwin, decided to postpone a conflict by giving a £24 million subsidy to the mine owners, so that wages would not yet have to be cut. This was announced on Friday 31 July, and the trade unions, who believed they had won an important victory, called it 'Red Friday'. Baldwin also set up a Royal Commission of Inquiry, under the chairmanship of the Liberal Sir Herbert Samuel, to suggest possible remedies.

However, the subsidy would run out at the end of April 1926, and the government began to make preparations to deal with a massive strike. These plans included the use of troops and the setting up of a semi-official Organisation for the Maintenance of Supplies.

## The General Strike

The Samuel Commission rejected the miners' call for the coal industry to be nationalised, but also declared that the massive wage cuts demanded by the employers should not go ahead. When the employers made it clear that the wage cuts would go ahead anyway, when the subsidy ended, the MFGB persuaded the Trades Union Congress (TUC) to agree to a general strike in their support.

The miners went on strike on 1 May against the wage cuts, and the General Strike began on 4 May 1926. The first wave of strikers called out were the railwaymen, transport workers and printers, and the response was solid. On subsequent days, second and third groups of workers joined the strike, with many coming out before the time planned by the TUC. In many parts of the country, despite the involvement of police and troops to try to ensure the delivery of food, the strike was remarkably peaceful. However, in more than 70 towns, the local strikers went way beyond the TUC's instructions.

The government got round the printers' strike by appointing Winston Churchill to oversee the production of a daily newspaper called *The British Gazette*, which accused the unions of unconstitutional action intended to intimidate Parliament. The TUC responded with *The British Worker*, which denied these charges and said the strike was simply in solidarity with the miners. Baldwin also used the BBC to keep the public informed, and to put the government's case. The TUC and the Labour Party leader, however, were denied access to the BBC.

Yet, despite its apparent success, the TUC called off the strike on 12 May, after only nine days, saying that they had been told by the government that a solution could be found. The miners, and many of the strikers, were furious when they learned that no definite promises had been received.

### Organisation for the Maintenance of Supplies

*The OMS spent months recruiting and training volunteers to drive buses and trains in the event of a general strike, and to act as special constables.*

*The members of the OMS were mainly drawn from university students and the middle classes; several members of the British Fascist movement also joined. Special constables recruited by the government also tended to come mainly from the middle classes.*

### TUC's instructions

*Despite TUC instructions, some local strikers set up councils of action or strike committees to control all transport in the town. In some places, workers' defence groups were set up to combat attempts by OMS volunteers to perform the work of those on strike.*

### no definite promises

*The MFGB struggled on alone for six more months before admitting defeat and accepting the owners' original terms. In fact, many of the smaller pits closed down and, by mid-1927, over 250 000 miners were unemployed. The Conservative government pushed through the Trades Disputes Act (1927), which made general and 'sympathetic' strikes illegal. Despite Baldwin's promises that those who had supported the General Strike would not be victimised, many strikers were sacked, and many employers would only let them return if they signed a pledge to leave their union. As a result, unemployment increased, and trade unions lost members and money.*

### Questions

1 Why did many workers want the government controls to continue after 1918?

2 What can you learn about the conduct of the General Strike from **Source A**?

3 Why do you think the TUC called off the Strike, even though they had not been given any definite promises?

# Ireland and the 'War of Independence'

## The Easter Rising

The outbreak of war in 1914 led the Liberal government to postpone putting the Home Rule Act into operation (see page 16). Most Irishmen, Catholic and Protestant, supported the British government in the war, and many volunteered for the army. However, a minority of Republicans saw Britain's involvement in a major war as an opportunity to grab full independence for Ireland. A shipment of arms for the Republicans, carried by a German ship, was intercepted by the British, and Sir Roger Casement, an important Irish Nationalist, was arrested. Despite this setback, on Easter Monday, 24 April 1916, a small group of about 2000 from the Irish Volunteers and the Irish Citizen Army, led by Padraig Pearse and James Connolly, took over important buildings in Dublin, including the General Post Office, which became their headquarters. Although they had no chance of success, they proclaimed the independence of Ireland and raised the green, white and orange tricolour flag over the Post Office.

For the next six days, fighting between the rebels and British troops took place across Dublin. It ended when the British shelled the occupied buildings from a warship on the River Liffey. The surviving rebels were taken prisoner and marched to prison. At that point, most Dubliners were angry with the rebels for the damage they caused and for betraying their countrymen, who were fighting in Europe on Britain's side. But the British authorities then made a big mistake. They put the prisoners on trial for treason, and, when they were found guilty, executed 15 of them by firing squad, in batches, from 3-12 May. In August, Roger Casement was hanged.

## The growth of Sinn Fein

These executions turned the rebels into national heroes, and resulted in a massive increase in support for Sinn Fein. This rose further when Britain put Ireland under martial law and imprisoned people like the Sinn Fein leader, Arthur Griffith. By 1917, Sinn Fein was committed to the creation of a totally independent Ireland. Later that year, it won two by-elections in what had been safe seats for the more moderate Nationalist Party. Eamon de Valera (one of its leaders) then won the East Clare seat. By the end of 1917, Sinn Fein had over 250 000 members. An attempt to introduce conscription into Ireland in May 1918 led the Irish Nationalists to walk out of Westminster and join Sinn Fein in an anti-conscription campaign. After a series of strikes and the signing of a National Pledge, Lloyd George decided to drop the plan. In the December 1918 general election, Sinn Fein won 73 out of Ireland's 105 seats, and the Irish Nationalists won 7 seats. There were 23 Ulster MPs. Led by Eamon de Valera, the Sinn Fein MPs refused to go to

### Source A

*The destruction suffered by Dublin during The Easter Rising, 1916.*

### Source B

English rule in this country is and has always been based on force...

We confirm the establishment of the Irish Republic and pledge ourselves and our people to make this Declaration effective by every means at our command.

We solemnly declare foreign government in Ireland to be an invasion of our national right which we will never tolerate, and we demand the evacuation of our country by the English garrison.

*Extract from the Irish Declaration of Independence, 21 January 1919.*

Westminster and, in 1919, set up their own Irish Parliament in Dublin, called the Dail Eireann (Parliament of Ireland). One of the Sinn Fein MPs elected was Countess Markievicz, who had commanded a section of Volunteers during the Easter Rising. She had been imprisoned by the British for her involvement in the rebellion and in the 1918 elections became the first woman to be elected to the British House of Commons - though, like all the Sinn Fein MPs, she refused to go to London. At its first meeting on 21 January 1919, the MPs passed the Irish Declaration of Independence. Later in the year, de Valera was made President, while Griffith became Vice-President and Michael Collins became Minister of Finance. This 'government' then began to collect taxes.

## The 'War of Independence'

This rebellion soon led to a guerrilla war between the British army and the Irish Republican Army (IRA), which was led by Michael Collins. Although Collins was on the run, he managed to fulfill his role as Finance Minister, as well as master-minding the activities of the IRA. Their first attack was on two members of the Royal Irish Constabulary (RIC) in January 1919. Sinn Fein saw this as the first shots in their 'war of independence'. Britain responded by banning the Dail and Sinn Fein. During 1920, the IRA killed 176 policemen and 54 soldiers. One result was that members of the RIC resigned rather than risk being shot.

As the fighting continued, the police increasingly lost control of the country. To strengthen the police, almost 10 000 special troops were recruited by Britain from unemployed ex-soldiers. The officers were known as the Auxiliaries, while the ordinary soldiers were called the 'Black and Tans' (so-called because of their mixed use of police and army uniforms). During 1920, both sides were responsible for several atrocities but the British atrocities tended to push more and more Irish into supporting Sinn Fein. Collins had several spies in Dublin Castle, which was the British HQ. This enabled him to avoid capture and, on Sunday 21 November 1920, he was able to order the killing of 12 British Army undercover agents who had just arrived in Dublin with orders to eliminate Collins and his spies. Two Auxiliaries were also killed, and this led to the Black and Tans killing 12 spectators at a Gaelic football match - this day became known as 'Bloody Sunday'.

The British government began to believe it would be unable to defeat the IRA so it passed the Government of Ireland Act. This set up two separate parliaments for the north and south of Ireland, with proportional voting to protect the rights of minorities. Under the Act, Ulster would become Northern Ireland. This was supported by the Ulster Unionists but not Sinn Fein, who were not prepared to accept a divided Ireland, so the fighting continued.

**Source C**

*Black and Tan troops search a suspected Sinn Fein supporter. Another lies dead in the background.*

## Questions

1 How reliable is **Source B** for finding out about the reasons behind Sinn Fein's 'War of Independence'?

2 In 1914 most Irish people were prepared to support Britain in the war. Why had so many turned against Britain by the end of the war?

3 How was the Government of Ireland Act different from the Home Rule Act that was postponed in 1914? Why did the British government pass it?

# The division of Ireland

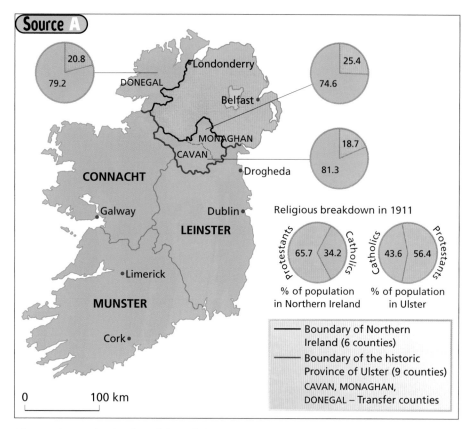

**Source A**

Religious breakdown in 1911

% of population in Northern Ireland

% of population in Ulster

— Boundary of Northern Ireland (6 counties)
— Boundary of the historic Province of Ulster (9 counties)
CAVAN, MONAGHAN, DONEGAL – Transfer counties

0    100 km

*The provinces of Ireland, and the religious breakdown in the north in 1911.*

**Dominion status**

*This offered slightly more independence than Home Rule. The south would be a self-governing territory within the British Empire (like Canada was, for example). But this meant that Irish MPs would still have to swear an oath of loyalty to the British Crown and that the south would have to help Britain in any war.*

**Source B**

Although at the beginning there are to be two parliaments and two governments in Ireland, the Act contemplates and affords every facility for union between north and south, and empowers the two parliaments by mutual agreement and joint action to terminate partition and set up one parliament and one government for the whole of Ireland.

*An extract from the Government of Ireland Act, 1920.*

## Partition and the Irish Free State

By June 1921, both sides had had enough of the bitter fighting, and Lloyd George, the British Prime Minister, suggested to de Valera that a conference be held in London to discuss a settlement. A truce was called in July, and talks began between the British government and Sinn Fein leaders in October. Lloyd George offered dominion status to the 26 southern counties, provided that six counties of the  province of Ulster in the north remained part of the UK, as Northern Ireland, until such time as the majority of its people voted to join the rest of Ireland. At this stage, the permanent partition of Ireland seemed unlikely. De Valera and several other Sinn Feiners, though,  were opposed to splitting Ireland and accepting anything less than full independence.

De Valera refused to attend the talks, and instead sent Griffith and Collins. The majority of Sinn Fein, however, were prepared to accept these terms as they believed that full independence for the whole of Ireland could now be achieved peacefully. This was because the Government of Ireland Act had promised to set up a Boundary Commission to decide the exact boundaries between the two parts of Ireland, and a Council of Ireland to work for reunification. Collins and his supporters believed it would be possible to persuade some Catholic-dominated areas of the six counties in the north to join the south. This would then make Northern Ireland unviable in the long term. Lloyd George, himself, did not think Northern Ireland would be able to exist for very long. There was bitter argument in the Dail, about accepting dominion status. However, in the end, the Dail voted 64 to 57 to accept. So, on 6 December 1921, an Anglo-Irish Partition Treaty was signed.

## The Republicans split

In 1922, the south of Ireland became the Irish Free State (Saorstat Eireann), with its own parliament, but still having to swear an oath of loyalty to the British crown. The nine counties of Ulster were reduced to the six most Protestant ones, with the three overwhelmingly Catholic ones being transferred to the south.

However, the new administration of Northern Ireland then refused to participate in the promised Boundary Commission. This disappointed those who had signed the Treaty, as the prospects of a peaceful reunification now seemed very unlikely.

De Valera resigned as President, and Griffith took his place, while Collins became Prime Minister. The pro-Treaty group then won a general election in the south in June 1922.

De Valera's anti-Treaty IRA supporters – known as the 'Irregulars' or Republicans – refused to accept the Treaty, the partition terms and especially the oath to the British Crown. In June, anti-Treaty forces took over the Four Courts in Dublin. The Irish Free State then came under intense pressure from Britain to deal with the anti-Treaty faction. Eventually, using guns borrowed from Britain, Collins ordered the bombardment of the Four Courts.

## Civil war, 1922-23

This action by the Free State government triggered a bitter civil war, as the anti-Treaty forces took up arms against the new Irish Free State government. Although they managed to assassinate Michael Collins in an ambush in August 1922, the anti-Treaty forces were outnumbered and the fighting came to an end in April 1923. This was partly because the British government helped the Irish Free State and partly because the Irish people had had enough of a bitter conflict which had been going on for most of the time since 1918. During the conflict, the Free State government executed 77 Republicans, and imprisoned almost 12 000.

With the war over, the Free State government asked Britain to implement the promise concerning the Boundary Commission. Although this finally met, the only change which took place was to transfer a large part of Donegal to Northern Ireland. Many Free Staters felt they had been tricked, and by 1925 the partition of Ireland was firmly established.

## After partition

In 1926, de Valera split from Sinn Fein and set up his own party called Fianna Fail (Warriors of Ireland). This gradually increased its support during the rest of the 1920s, including from IRA members. This was despite the fact that de Valera then stated he was prepared to take the oath of loyalty to the British Crown. In 1932, Fianna Fail defeated Finne Gael (the United Irish Party - which had remained loyal to Collins and Griffiths) and formed its first government, with de Valera as Prime Minister. De Valera immediately began to try to re-negotiate the terms of the Anglo-Irish Treaty. The oath of loyalty was abolished and the British Governor-General was stripped of his powers. Finally, in 1937, the Irish Free State was renamed Eire and became a republic in all but name, to be confirmed in 1949 when Eire left the Commonwealth.

**Source C**

*Pro-Treaty forces shell anti-Treaty forces in the Four Courts building in Dublin in June 1922.*

### Questions

1 Why did the removal of the counties of Donegal, Cavan and Monaghan from Ulster, as shown in **Source A**, make it more unlikely that Northern Ireland would vote for reunification?

2 Why did some members of Sinn Fein, as shown in **Source C**, refuse to accept the Partition Treaty of 1922?

# The Great Depression

### Economic recovery

After the General Strike, there was some improvement in the British economy. Unemployment fell to about 1 million, profits improved and trade recovered. However, many workers still experienced problems, and there was an expectation that a Labour government would help solve some of their grievances. In the 1929 elections, Labour won 287 seats and, for the first time, was the largest party in the House of Commons. However, although Labour's Ramsay MacDonald became Prime Minister for the second time, it was a minority government, as the Conservatives had 261 seats and the Liberals 59.

### The start of the Great Depression

In October 1929, the US stock market on Wall Street 'crashed'. This soon brought an end to economic recovery world-wide, as trade declined by over 60% and production fell. In Britain, exports fell from £850 million to £460 million between 1929 and 1931, and unemployment soon rose to over 3 million. In order to pay the increased demand for unemployment benefit, the government had to use ordinary income from taxes, as the insurance fund could not cope. Unfortunately, with so many out of work, the income from taxation also fell. By 1931, Britain was facing a serious economic crisis.

### Economic policies

To deal with these problems, MacDonald set up an Economic Advisory Council to suggest radical changes, but these were blocked by conservative Treasury officials. An attempt to reform unemployment benefits with an Unemployment Insurance Bill in 1929 was attacked by the Conservatives as being too generous. In 1931, an Anomalies Bill proposed taking benefit away from those who 'abused' the system. These attempts did little to help solve the problems, which became worse as the USA called in its loans to European countries such as Germany. To help stave off the total economic collapse of Germany and Austria, Britain loaned them over £200 million. This, too, was attacked by the Conservatives as being too extravagant. To help fund the payment of unemployment benefit, the government increased the amount the insurance fund could borrow to £30 million a year.

### The May Committee

To counter the growing criticism, MacDonald then appointed a special Committee of Inquiry under Sir George May to report on the financial situation. The Report of the May Committee was not published until August 1931, after Parliament had broken up for the summer.

Source A

I KNOW 3 TRADES
I SPEAK 3 LANGUAGES
FOUGHT FOR 3 YEARS
HAVE 3 CHILDREN
AND NO WORK FOR
3 MONTHS
BUT I ONLY WANT
ONE JOB

*An unemployed man during the Great Depression.*

May reported that the government was running into debt, and said the deficit for 1932 would be £120 million. To prevent this, he recommended large cuts in government spending; a large reduction in the insurance fund's ability to borrow money; cuts in unemployment benefits; and big reductions in the salaries of public officials, such as civil servants and teachers.

## The formation of a National Government

Britain had already borrowed over £100 million to deal with the crisis, and the USA would only lend more if the Budget was 'balanced' by sweeping cuts in government spending on the social services. At the same time, the May Committee's Report led to investments being withdrawn from Britain and a drain on the Bank of England's gold reserves.

MacDonald and Philip Snowden (the Chancellor of the Exchequer) were influenced by the Treasury's senior civil servants and reluctantly agreed to make the cuts, including a 10% cut in unemployment benefit. Most of the other Labour ministers, and the Labour Party, were opposed and MacDonald resigned.

Instead of calling another general election or inviting the Conservatives to form a government, the King instead asked MacDonald to form a coalition 'national' government made up of the leading members of the other parties. MacDonald agreed, and the new National Government met the House of Commons in early September 1931.

## Early policies

Under MacDonald, Snowden (who remained as Chancellor) introduced a supplementary Budget in September. This raised income tax from 22.5p to 25p in the pound; reduced allowances and exemptions; and greatly increased indirect taxes on beer, tobacco and petrol. The National Government also introduced a bill to make drastic cuts in government spending. Salaries of public officials and employees were cut by 15%; benefits were cut by 10%, while the length of benefit was reduced; at the same time, national insurance contributions were raised. Finally, Britain 'came off the Gold Standard' and bank rates were raised from 4.5% to 6%.

### Questions

1 How did the Great Depression affect British politics?

2 What was the May Committee?

3 Why did most of the Labour Party see MacDonald as a traitor for joining the National Government

**Source B**

It is clear that MacDonald never really accepted the socialist faith of a classless world, built on unselfish service... Without consulting his Cabinet colleagues, without even informing them of his plans to set up a National Government with himself as Prime Minister, he proceeded to carry out his long thought out plan.

*The views of MacDonald's secretary writing in 1938.*

**National Government**

*It was supported by the entire Conservative Party, most of the Liberals (although Lloyd George, who was ill, was opposed), but only a small number of Labour MPs. The bulk of the Labour Party was now the Opposition, and saw MacDonald as a traitor.*

**Gold Standard**

*This was the system by which the British government linked the value of the pound to a fixed amount of gold, which was itself linked to the US dollar. Being 'on the gold standard' was seen as a sign of Britain's financial strength. However, being on the 'gold standard' tended to make British exports more expensive and, therefore, resulted in unemployment. Coming off the 'gold standard' made it easier to export but sometimes led to inflation (as it did during the First World War).*

# CHAPTER 5

# The National Government in action

### The 1931 and 1935 elections

In October 1931, MacDonald called a general election. The leaders of the National Government drew up a vague election manifesto known as the 'Doctor's Mandate', so that each Party's candidates could campaign for slightly different policies. The National candidates won 556 seats, of which only 13 were National Labour; the rest were mostly National Conservative. The official Labour Party won 46 seats and, along with the Independent Labour Party's 5 and Lloyd George's Liberals, who won 4 seats, these formed the Opposition in the Commons. Shortly afterwards, MacDonald and the other National Labour MPs were expelled from the Labour Party. In practice, the National Government was now a Conservative government. This was confirmed by the 1935 election result, in which 387 'National' MPs were elected, as opposed to 154 Labour MPs. MacDonald retired and was replaced by the Conservative Stanley Baldwin who, in 1937, was replaced by Neville Chamberlain. He remained as Prime Minister until a wartime coalition was formed in 1940.

### Protectionism and the National Government

In 1930, the Economic Advisory Committee recommended protectionism, and the Abnormal Importations Act (1931) gave the government power to impose up to 100% import duties on selected foreign products. In the end, about 100 products were made liable. However, Snowden was against protectionism and resigned. He was replaced as Chancellor by the Conservative Neville Chamberlain, the son of Joseph Chamberlain. He brought in the Import Duties Act (1932), which marked the complete end of free trade. This imposed a 10% import duty on all foreign goods, although the Ottawa Imperial Economic Conference in August 1932 agreed preferential rates should be applied to goods coming from the Empire. Although there was a 'free list' of exempt goods, the Import Duties Advisory Committee was set up to recommend further duties. As a result, most manufactured goods had 20% duties, while luxury goods had 30%.

### Financial and industrial policies

In 1931, Chamberlain reduced the bank rate to 2%, to make it easier to borrow money. At first, in the 1932 and 1933 Budgets, Chamberlain continued with Snowden's taxation policies. But, in 1934, several of the cuts were reversed and income tax was reduced to 22.5p in the pound again.

From 1932, the government also turned to planning and State subsidies as ways of ending the slump. For instance, they invested in the improvement of railways and roads, and public works schemes in the most distressed areas, such as the north east,

---

**Protectionism**

*This is the use of 'tariffs' or 'duties' on foreign imports to make them more expensive and protect British industry from competition. Until the 1920s, the Conservatives had been associated with the maintenance of free trade. Attempts by Joseph Chamberlain to introduce protectionism had split the Party in the first years of the twentieth century. However, in the early 1920s, Stanley Baldwin had come to support a protectionist policy. Although this policy was defeated at the 1923 election, in 1925 the new Conservative government returned to the 33% 'safeguarding duties' which had first been imposed on over 6000 goods in 1921. The Safeguarding of Industries Act (1926), allowed more firms to apply to the Board of Trade for protection.*

**Source A**

Everybody knows that there at present in England prosperous districts and 'depressed areas'... The Rhondda [south Wales] is part of a depressed area, and 35% of the industrial population were out of work...63% were [long term unemployed] in the Rhondda... the difference between a prosperous and a depressed area is thus not in the neighbourhood of 1:7, but of 1:70.

*Extract from a study of the effects of the Depression in Britain, published in 1938.*

Lancashire and West Cumberland (Cumbria) and south Wales. The Depressed Areas Act (1934) renamed them 'Special Areas' and spent some £2 million a year to help economic recovery.

Apart from protection against foreign goods, the government also tried to help the older industries by promoting reorganisation in the coal, steel and ship-building industries, though with limited success. New industries, such as electrical goods, cars and man-made fabrics, however, did well and increased their volume of exports.

## Unemployment

By 1934, the cost of unemployment benefits had risen to £400 million a year, although much of this was covered by the rates and indirect taxes paid by ordinary people. The *Unemployment Insurance Act* (1934) set up the Unemployment Assistance Board to take over the job of dealing with extra temporary payments from the Public Assistance Committees. These were now mainly covered by the Treasury. Also in that year, most of the benefit cuts made in 1931 were reversed, with the benefit rising from £1.50 to £1.80 a week. But a 'means test' (to check a family's finances) was also introduced, and local officials were ordered to save as much as possible by asking questions about savings, and whether any children in the family were earning. These incomes were to be deducted from any benefits to be paid. The means test was much resented. Mostly, the unemployed suffered in silence, but there were 'hunger marches' in the worst hit areas. The most famous was the Jarrow Crusade of 1936.

## Social policies

Housing Acts (1933 and 1935) continued with the earlier policy of slum clearance and new council house building, until this spending was limited in 1938. However, there was a boom in private house building, reaching some 350 000 a year until 1939. Many new private 'estates' were built and the suburbs were expanded. Most working-class people could still not afford to buy their own homes, although building societies were developed to lend money at interest.

Despite many protests about taxation levels, the number of rich people increased during this period. The vast majority of the population, however, remained poor, with many earning £2 a week if they were lucky. Despite this, living conditions were improving for many. About four million were now covered by national insurance, while 20 million had health cover through their trade union or friendly society. The percentage of children not receiving education was very low, and some 20% of children won scholarships at 11 to grammar schools.

**Source B**

Ellen Wilkinson MP accompanying the Jarrow Marchers.

### Jarrow Crusade

*About 200 unemployed men marched from Jarrow, near Durham, to take a petition to the government in London. They walked over 450 kms. Although this may have made some people in London much more aware of their suffering, it had no real effect on government policy.*

### Questions

1 What was the 'means test', and why did so many people resent it?

2 What were the 'depressed areas' referred to in **Source A**?

3 What was the Jarrow Crusade, shown in **Source B**?

# SUMMARY

## 1918–1922

- Lloyd George continued as Prime Minister of a coalition government after the war. One of its first acts was to give votes to women over 30.
- The impact of the war on the British economy led to a short post-war depression. 'Old' industries, in particular, lost markets during the war and faced increased foreign competition.
- One result of these economic problems was a rise in industrial disputes. Many unions wanted wartime government controls to continue, but employers wanted to cut wages. Problems were worst in the mining industry.
- There was also trouble in Ireland after 1918. When Sinn Fein won the majority of Irish parliamentary seats, a 'War of Independence' broke out between the IRA and the British army. Eventually, in 1922, a ceasefire resulted in the partition of Ireland.
- Tensions between the Liberals and the Conservatives eventually led to Lloyd George's fall in 1922.

## 1923–1929

- Under the Conservatives, problems in the mining industry continued. At the same time, the Labour Party began to replace the Liberals as the main opposition party. In 1924, Ramsay MacDonald became the first Labour Prime Minister, but his minority government fell later in the year.
- In 1925, the government gave a subsidy to mine owners to prevent wage cuts, and set up the Samuel Commission. In 1926, the miners succeeded in getting the TUC to call a General Strike. This was called off after nine days, leaving the miners on their own.

## 1929–1931

- In 1929, Labour won the election. Although Labour was the largest party in the Commons, MacDonald's second government was still a minority.
- After the Wall Street Crash in the USA in 1929, the Depression soon caused high unemployment in Britain. The Labour ministers disagreed over what action to take, and the May Committee was set up. When it recommended sweeping cuts in government expenditure, MacDonald resigned.

## 1931–1939

- MacDonald then formed a coalition National Government with the Conservatives. As unemployment rose, a 'means test' was introduced for those claiming the 'dole'.
- In the worst hit areas, there were 'hunger marches'. The most famous was the Jarrow March in 1936.
- By 1937, the National Government was really a Conservative government in all but name.

# Exam Question Practice

## Source sufficiency

Study Sources A and B below, and then answer the question which follows.

Do Sources A and B provide enough information to explain why a War of Independence broke out in Ireland in 1918?

**Source A**

KILMAINHAM MAY 1916

*A drawing of the execution of one of the rebel leaders of the Easter Rising of 1916.*

**Source B**

Sinn Fein aims at securing the establishment of the Irish Republic by:

(a) withdrawing the Irish MPs from Westminster ... and opposing the will of the British Government or any other foreign government to make laws for Ireland....

(b) making use of any means available to render useless the power of England to hold Ireland in subjection by military force.

(c) establishing a parliament as the supreme national authority to speak and act in the name of the Irish people.

*An extract from the Sinn Fein election manifesto of 1918.*

## Examiner's Tips

**When answering questions like this:**

◎ Make sure that you use both the sources given.

◎ Try to comment on the content of the sources AND any possible problems of reliability.

◎ Don't forget to also use your own knowledge of the topic, otherwise, you will not be able to comment fully on the amount of information provided by the sources. You will be expected to use your knowledge to give facts which explain other events/factors which are not contained in the sources. If you don't, you will not score high marks.

# CHAPTER 6

## RUSSIA AND THE USSR, 1900-1941

Source A

*The Tsar and Tsarina dressed in their robes of state.*

Source B

*A painting showing Lenin addressing Red Guards during the November Revolution, 1917.*

Source C

*Women in Tashkent in the Soviet Union, being taught to read and write, 1928.*

*Gulag prisoners working in a labour camp, 1934.*

## Key Questions

**How** did the people shown in **Source A** come to lose power in 1917?

**Why** did some of those involved in the November Revolution (**Source B**) feel it necessary to kill the Tsar and his family just one year later?

**Why** was it necessary in the 1930s to teach so many adults, like those in **Source C**, basic reading and writing skills?

**How** could the party responsible for the idealism shown in **Source C** also be responsible for scenes like **Source D**?

**Were** people's lives better or worse than they had been under the Tsar?

These are some of the issues which we will cover in this chapter. The main focus of this chapter on Russia will be:

- The problems existing in Russia before 1914

- The role of the First World War in sparking off revolution in 1917

- How the Bolsheviks came to power and were able to win the Civil War

- The main policies and changes during Lenin's rule

- Why there was a power struggle after 1924, and why Stalin won

- The economic changes brought about by Stalin in the 1930s, and their impact

- Why Stalin plunged the Soviet Union into the horrors of the Great Terror

- How the USSR's foreign policy during the 1920s and 1930s failed to prevent its involvement in another major war

# CHAPTER 6

# Tsarist Russia, 1900-14

*An extract from a speech made by Tsar Nicholas II in 1895.*

## The Tsarist regime

In 1900, Russia was ruled by Tsar Nicholas II, who had succeeded his father in 1894. His powers were absolute and he ruled a large Empire of 125 million people, containing over 20 different nationalities. Russia was a vast Empire which stretched from Europe into Asia. Despite development of the railway system and the telegraph from the 1860s, communication across the Empire was still poor, and this limited the powers of central government. In most local areas, it was the landed gentry, the Church and provincial officials who ran things. Order was maintained by the Ministry of the Interior, the Okhrana (secret police) and especially the 2.6 million-strong army. The Orthodox Church taught obedience to a 'divinely-appointed' Tsar, who was the 'father' of the people.

There was no national parliament or consultative body, and only the Tsar could appoint and dismiss ministers. Although there were two advisory bodies, the State Council and the Senate, the people had no say in government, no political parties and no opportunities even to debate political issues freely.

## Russian society

Tsarist Russia in 1900 was still in many ways a semi-feudal society, very different from countries such as Britain, Germany and France. The vast majority of its population, over 85%, were peasants. These were mostly illiterate, religious, superstitious and very conservative. Until 1861, they had still been serfs (a form of slavery). After emancipation (freedom), most were heavily in debt. Until 1911, they had to pay yearly instalments to their former masters for the land they had been given. A population increase, and their tradition of sub-dividing their land between all their sons, led to very small farms and a land shortage. Most used very old-fashioned farming methods, and food production was limited. There was an increase in the numbers of poor peasants and landless labourers.

Over 25% of the land was owned by the Tsar and the important nobles, who made up about 1% of the population. Below them, the upper classes (lesser nobles, the Church leaders and the top government officials) owned much of the remainder. There was also a growing middle class. Most were in the legal or other professions, but there was also a growing number of bankers, merchants and factory owners. All these were very wealthy.

There was also a small industrial working class concentrated in the major cities. Most worked in large factories, where conditions were extremely poor. Hours were long and pay was low; their housing, too, was overcrowded and substandard. They were not allowed to join unions, and frequently had insufficient food and fuel.

## Serfs

*Serfdom was a form of slavery. The serfs owed labour services in return for their use of the land. They were effectively tied to the land, unable to move freely.*

## Source B

*Women barge-haulers on the River Volga, in about 1910.*

## Russian economy

Under Sergei Witte (Minister of Finance, 1893-1903, and then Prime Minister from 1903-06) some industrialisation took place, helped by capital and technical assistance from western European countries such as Britain, France and Germany. This economic growth, known as the 'Great Spurt', led to a significant increase in Russia's national wealth. In the periods 1890-99 and 1907-13, industrial production increased considerably. This industrial expansion was assisted by a world-wide boom in the 1890s. However, by 1900, this boom had ended and, overall, the Russian economy was still relatively backward. The recession which followed, led to high unemployment. Although the situation began to improve after 1908, high inflation and lagging wages in Russia meant unrest continued to simmer.

## Political opposition

There were many who opposed the Tsarist regime. Many middle-class people resented the fact that they had no political power. They wanted a democratic system with an elected parliament. These liberals wanted reforms but were against revolution. Another group, the Social Revolutionaries (SRs), had been in existence since the mid-nineteenth century. They believed the peasants could be roused to carry out a revolution to overthrow the Tsar and share out the land. They used terrorism against government and police officials in their struggle, and in 1881 even assassinated Tsar Alexander II.

The other main opponents of Tsarism were the Russian Social Democratic Labour Party (RSDLP). This was a Marxist party (following the views of Karl Marx) which was formed in 1898. They were in favour of a revolution led by the industrial workers, allied with the peasants. At their 1903 conference, they split into two groups: the Bolsheviks, led by Lenin, who believed conditions in Russia meant the Party should be made up of a small number of committed revolutionaries; and the Mensheviks who wanted a mass party like those in western Europe.

### Marxist

*Karl Marx was a German philosopher in the nineteenth century. He had predicted that private ownership of land and factories (the means of production) would eventually be replaced by shared ownership. In a communist state (which would be brought about by revolution) all the means of production would be owned by the community as a whole.*

### Bolsheviks

*The Bolsheviks also came to believe that the middle class in Russia was too weak to modernise a semi-feudal society. They argued that the workers would have to take power in a revolution. Then they could modernise society and begin to move towards Socialism at the same time. The Mensheviks did not believe a workers' revolution would be possible for a long time. In 1918, the Bolsheviks changed their name to 'Communists'.*

### Questions

1 What can you learn from **Source B** about the life of ordinary people in Tsarist Russia in the early years of the twentieth century?

2 What do you understand by the term 'autocracy' in **Source A**?

3 Why might some people in Russia have been disappointed by the contents of the Tsar's 1895 speech?

# CHAPTER 6

# Wars and revolutions

## The 1905 Revolution

By 1904, political and social unrest was growing. In that year, partly to take people's minds off politics, the Tsar got involved in a war with Japan over control of Korea and Manchuria. He expected an easy victory and, at first, most of the people rallied behind him. But defeats on land and sea, and price rises and food shortages, led to a mass protest on Sunday 22 January 1905. The crowd was fired on by soldiers and the incident became known as 'Bloody Sunday'.

This sparked off a Revolution in which the middle classes, as well as the RSDLP and the SRs, demanded changes. During the summer, there were a few mutinies, and many strikes and peasant uprisings. In October, the workers organised a general strike. Although the Russo-Japanese War had been ended by the Treaty of Portsmouth in September, most of the soldiers were not yet back from the war. So Count Witte advised Nicholas II to meet some of the demands of the liberals. In the October Manifesto, the Tsar promised elections to a Duma (national parliament) and the right to form political parties.

This satisfied the liberal middle classes, who formed the Constitutional Democrats (Kadets) but the workers also wanted increased wages and shorter working hours. They continued their campaign and formed revolutionary soviets (workers' councils) in the major cities. With the opposition now divided, in December the Tsar ordered the newly arrived soldiers to close down the soviets and arrest the leaders. By January 1906, the Revolution had been crushed.

## Suppression and reform

Nicholas dismissed Witte and replaced him with Peter Stolypin, who supervised a bloody suppression in the countryside. The Tsar also rigged the voting system for the Duma to ensure greater representation for the wealthier landowners. Although the Fundamental Law declared that the Duma could have no say on most government matters, the first two Dumas, in 1906 and 1907, still contained many critics. So the Tsar simply dismissed them and changed the law to exclude socialists. Once he had got a Duma made up of loyal supporters, the Tsar ignored it and, by 1912, he was ruling without it.

From 1906-11, Stolypin tried to win over the peasants by introducing reforms. He abolished the yearly land payments, and helped peasants buy their own land. The richer peasants began to produce more food for the cities, and Stolypin also set up a health insurance scheme to improve things for the workers. However, he was assassinated in 1911, and from 1912 strikes and unrest began to increase once again.

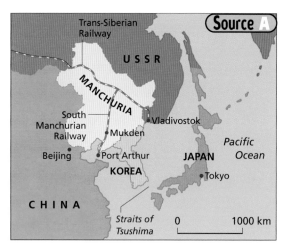

Source A

The Russo-Japanese War, 1904-5.

| Source B | | |
| --- | --- | --- |
| Year | Strikes | Strikers |
| 1905 | 13 995 | 2 863 173 |
| 1906 | 6 114 | 1 108 406 |
| 1907 | 3 573 | 740 074 |
| 1908 | 892 | 176 101 |
| 1909 | 340 | 64 166 |
| 1910 | 222 | 46 623 |
| 1911 | 466 | 105 110 |
| 1912 | 2 032 | 725 491 |
| 1913 | 2 404 | 887 096 |
| 1914 | 3 534 | 1 337 458 |

Industrial unrest in Russia, 1905-14. These statistics were published by the Tsar's Ministry of Trade and Industry.

## The impact of the First World War

By 1914, many sections of Russian society had serious social and economic grievances. But it did not seem that Russia was on the verge of revolution. It was the effects of Russia's participation in the First World War which pushed Tsarist Russia from crisis to revolution. The economy was broken by the strains of three years of total war. All sections of society were badly affected, especially the peasants and the industrial workers.

The backward agricultural system was highly dependent on manpower and horses. By 1916, over 15 million men and over 60% of the horses had been sent to the Front, and the system began to crumble. There was also high inflation, resulting in peasants hoarding rather than selling their grain.

The peasants' actions, and the need to supply the vast Russian army, led to serious food shortages in the cities. The war also disrupted the transport system so that, by 1916, the railway network was on the point of collapse. This made it difficult to send what food and fuel there was to major cities such as Moscow and Petrograd. The winter of 1916-17 was particularly cold, while inflation led many firms to go bankrupt, leading to more unemployment. Those still in work saw their real wages drop by as much as 30% in 1917 alone. The number of strikes and food riots increased, causing many factory owners to shut down their firms and flee, adding to the problems of unemployment and hunger in most major cities.

## The March Revolution, 1917

After Russian troops had suffered several major defeats, Nicholas II assumed personal command of the army and left for the Front. On 8 March 1917, women in Petrograd organised a demonstration to mark International Women's Day. This soon spread and developed into a general strike. The soldiers of the Petrograd garrison became unreliable and many units began to join the demonstrators. There was serious fighting, in which over 1500 were killed. The police and Cossacks were unable to disperse the crowds, and many of the Tsar's ministers fled from the capital. When the Duma set up a Provisional Government, the Tsar was persuaded to abdicate by his generals.

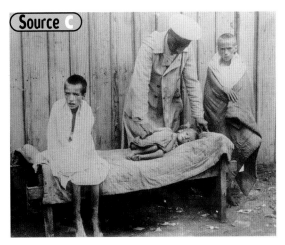

**Source C**

Russian patients suffering from scurvy (a disease caused by a lack of fresh fruit and vegetables) during the First World War.

**Source D**

Military defeats brought the masses to a clearer understanding of the war - unfair distribution of foodstuffs, an immense and rapid increase in the cost of living, an inadequacy in sources of supply. Everywhere there are exceptional feelings of hostility and opposition to the government because of the unbearable burden of the war and the impossible conditions of everyday life.

An extract from a secret Petrograd police report, written in October 1916.

**8 March 1917**

At this time, the Russian calendar was 13 days behind the one used in western Europe. So the March and November Revolutions are often referred to as the February and October Revolutions. In 1918, Russia adopted the modern calendar.

**Questions**

1 How useful is **Source B** as evidence of the degree of unrest amongst Russian factory workers in the period 1905-14?

2 How do **Source C** and **Source D** support the view that Russia's involvement in the First World War caused serious problems for the Tsarist system?

# The Bolshevik Revolution

### Dual Power, March to November 1917

The Provisional Government was made up of liberal Kadets, with Prince Lvov as Prime Minister. It only really represented the wealthier sections of society. On the same day, the Petrograd Soviet was revived by the workers. At first, the Soviet was dominated by the Mensheviks and SRs, who were prepared to support the Provisional Government. The Soviet's Order Number 1 told workers and soldiers to obey the Provisional Government, but only if the Soviet agreed with their decisions. This potentially undermined the Provisional Government's control of the armed forces, and led to a situation of dual (or shared) power. This was not a problem, though, while the Bolsheviks were only a minority in the Soviet.

### Policies of the Provisional Government

The Provisional Government immediately allowed free speech and released political prisoners. However, it decided to continue Russia's involvement in the war, although the army was already beginning to disintegrate. It also said that land reform would have to wait until the war was over.

At first, the Bolsheviks in Russia (including Stalin) gave limited support to the Provisional Government, even though it was continuing to fight in the war. However, in April Lenin returned from exile and immediately published his 'April Theses'. These urged the Bolsheviks to take a more revolutionary position, and contained two important slogans: 'All power to the soviets!' and 'Peace, Bread and Land'. At the same time, many factory workers and ordinary soldiers became more revolutionary. As a result, the Mensheviks and SRs began to lose their seats to the Bolsheviks and the even more militant anarcho-syndicalists. These political groups were not prepared to keep in power an unelected government which refused to end Russia's involvement in the First World War.

The provisional government moved further to the right, and experienced one political crisis after another. After the failure of the army's June offensive, Lvov resigned and his liberal Kadet government fell in early July.

### The rise of the Bolsheviks

Lvov was replaced by Alexander Kerensky, who headed a coalition government of Kadets and SRs. But he too insisted on keeping Russia in the war. In July, about 20 000 soldiers and anarcho-syndicalists tried to overthrow him in what became known as the 'July Days'. But he was able to defeat this with the support of loyal troops. Kerensky then banned the Bolsheviks who, although they had not planned the attempt, had eventually been involved in the demonstrations. Many of their leaders were imprisoned and Lenin escaped to Finland.

---

**Source A**

The Bolshevik speaker would ask the crowd: 'Do you need more land?' 'Do you have as much land as the landlords do?' 'But will the Kerensky government give you land? No, never. It protects the interests of the landlords. Only our party, the Bolsheviks, will immediately give you land...'

Several times I tried to take the floor and explain that the Bolsheviks make promises which they can never fulfil... but I saw that the crowded square was unsuitable for this kind of discussion.

*Comments made by a member of the Mensheviks about events during the summer of 1917.*

In August the Provisional Government faced a new threat. General Kornilov, who had only recently been appointed as commander-in-chief of the army by Kerensky, tried to overthrow it. Kerensky panicked and was forced to release the Bolsheviks and seek support from them. Their Red Guards organised defences, and were able to persuade Kornilov's troops to desert. This further weakened the authority of the Provisional Government, while increasing support for the Bolsheviks. In September, they won many new seats in town and city council elections, and especially in the soviets (winning majorities in both Petrograd and Moscow).

This encouraged Lenin to urge the Bolshevik central committee to plan the overthrow of Kerensky and his government. Although two prominent Bolsheviks, Zinoviev and Kamenev, were opposed to this, the majority supported Lenin and, under the day-to-day organisation of Trotsky, the Bolsheviks began their preparations. Even though his authority was clearly breaking down, Kerensky still refused to hold the long-promised elections to a Constituent Assembly. Elections to the soviets, on the other hand, were frequent, and the All-Russian Congress of Soviets was the only nationally elected body in Russia.

## The November Revolution, 1917

Because Kerensky refused to deal with the land question until after the war, rural soviets and individual peasants began to take over large estates and to divide the land amongst themselves. In the towns, workers began to occupy factories and establish factory committees. By the autumn of 1917, Kerensky's government was almost totally isolated. When Kerensky finally decided to take action against the Bolshevik-dominated Soviet, on 6 November, it was too late. Trotsky had become Chair of the Petrograd Soviet's Military Revolutionary Committee, and had already got the Petrograd garrison to promise to support the Soviet should there be any moves against it. During 6 and 7 November, the Bolsheviks' Red Guards, and about 20 000 workers and soldiers, took control of the main buildings in Petrograd, and Kerensky fled. The November Revolution, the second revolution in 1917, was carried out without conflict in Petrograd. Only later in propaganda films was the 'storming' of the Winter Palace portrayed as involving fighting. There was, however, more serious conflict in Moscow. On 8 November, the power to rule Russia was handed over to the Second All-Russian Congress of Soviets, which had just begun its first meeting.

**Source B**

People of Russia! Our great motherland is dying. I, General Kornilov, declare that under pressure of the Bolshevik majority in the soviets, the Provisional Government is acting in complete accord with the plans of the German General Staff. It is destroying the army and is undermining the very foundations of the country.

*Extract from an open telegram sent by General Kornilov, in August 1917.*

**Source C**

*Red Guards outside the Petrograd Soviet's headquarters in the Smolny Institute, at the start of the November Revolution.*

## Questions

1 To what extent do **Source A** and **Source B** agree about the significance of the Bolsheviks in the summer of 1917?

2 How did Kornilov's actions help to increase support for the Bolsheviks?

3 Why was the Provisional Government so unpopular by the autumn of 1917?

# The problems of peace

## The coalition

The Bolsheviks had 300 out of the 670 seats in the Congress, which, in November 1917, was declared to be the ruling body of Russia. Several of the other parties in the Soviet, including the Mensheviks and the SRs, opposed Kerensky's overthrow and some walked out of the Congress in protest. So the Congress elected a purely Bolshevik government. This was called the Council of People's Commissars (Sovnarkom). Lenin, its first Chairman (Prime Minister) was happy with this, but several leading Bolsheviks wanted to have a coalition with other parties represented in the Soviet. Eventually, in December, the SRs split into Left and Right and the Left SRs joined the Bolsheviks in a coalition government.

## The Constituent Assembly

Just before he fell from power, Kerensky finally arranged the elections for a Constituent Assembly but, by the time they were held, he had already been overthrown. Many of the voters in the rural areas of Russia were unaware of the split in the SRs, or even that Kerensky had been overthrown.

The results were a disappointment for the Bolsheviks as they only won 175 out of 717 seats. The Right SRs won 370 and the Left SRs 40. The Constituent Assembly met in January 1918 and immediately refused to accept the new Soviet government or the decisions already made by the Congress of Soviets. As some Right SRs and Kadets had begun taking military action against Sovnarkom, Lenin ordered the Red Guards to close the Assembly.

## The Treaty of Brest-Litovsk

One of the biggest problems facing Lenin's government was the question of Russia's involvement in the First World War. The Provisional Government's continuation of the war had been a major reason for its fall. By November 1917, because of defeats and poor conditions, combined with Bolshevik propaganda, the Russian army was breaking up. Many soldiers were deserting and, in several mutinies, the soldiers killed their officers.

On the first day after the Revolution, a Bolshevik decree calling for an immediate and just peace had been accepted by the Congress. However, it proved impossible to get a peace that was both just and immediate, as the Allies refused to discuss peace and the Germans simply demanded huge areas of Russia in return for an end to the fighting.

So Lenin argued that peace should be made whatever the terms. He believed that a revolution would soon break out in Germany; and that the new government would then return Russia's land. This split the Bolsheviks for a time, as Bukharin and the Left argued for a revolutionary war against Germany. Trotsky, who was Commissar

### Constituent Assembly

This was to be Russia's first democratic parliament, and elections had been promised since March 1917. The Bolsheviks at times tried to embarrass the Provisional Government by demanding the elections, even though they believed Russia should be ruled by the soviets.

### Source A

To hand over power to the Constituent Assembly would again be compromising with the malignant bourgeoisie [evil middle classes]. The Russian Soviets place the interests of the toiling masses far above the interests of treacherous compromise....as long as behind the slogan 'All power to the Constituent Assembly' is concealed the slogan 'Down with the Soviets', civil war is inevitable.... And when the Constituent Assembly again revealed its readiness to postpone all the ...urgent problems and tasks that were placed before it by the soviets, we told [them] that they must not be postponed for a single moment. And by the will of the Soviet power, the Constituent Assembly, which has refused to recognise the power of the people, is dissolved.

*Lenin's explanation of the decision to dissolve the Constituent Assembly, in January 1918.*

for Foreign Affairs, argued instead for 'neither peace nor war': the fighting would stop but Russia would not sign a treaty. Lenin felt so strongly that signing a treaty was the only option that he offered to resign from the government in order to campaign for peace amongst ordinary party members. At first, some of those in favour of waging a revolutionary war were prepared to consider arresting Lenin. But when the Germans advanced even further into Russia, the Russian army disintegrated and Trotsky sided with Lenin.

The harsh Treaty of Brest-Litovsk was signed in March 1918. This forced Russia to pay 300 million gold roubles to Germany, and to give up its richest areas containing 30% of its farmland and population and over 75% of its coal and iron mines. All the territory lost then came under direct or indirect German control. When the government and then the Congress accepted this Treaty, the Left SRs left the coalition and in July 1918 began terrorist attacks on government officials.

**Source** B

Our impulse tells us to rebel, to refuse to sign this robber peace...[but] Russia can offer no physical resistance because she is materially exhausted by three years of war. It is true that there may be people who are willing to fight and die in a great cause. But they are romanticists, who would sacrifice themselves without prospects of real advantage....The Russian Revolution must sign the peace to obtain a breathing space to recuperate for the struggle.

*Extract from a speech by Lenin in March 1918, arguing in favour of signing the treaty demanded by Germany.*

**Source** C

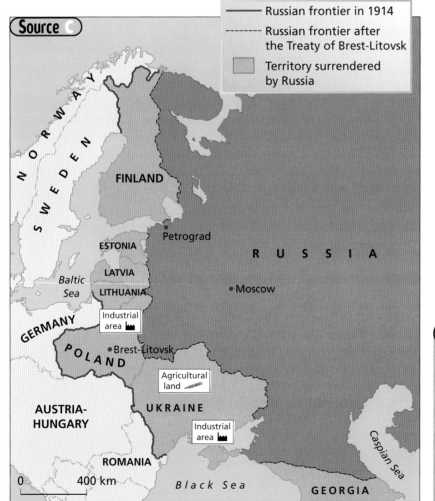

- —— Russian frontier in 1914
- ------ Russian frontier after the Treaty of Brest-Litovsk
- ☐ Territory surrendered by Russia

*The land lost by the Treaty of Brest-Litovsk, March 1918.*

**Questions**

1 How useful is **Source A** as historical evidence of the reasons behind the dissolution of the Constituent Assembly?

2 What can we learn from **Source B** about the decision to sign the Treaty of Brest-Litovsk?

3 What effect did the signing of this treaty have on the coalition between the Bolsheviks and the Left SRs?

# The Civil War 1918–1921

## Civil War and foreign intervention

By the time the Treaty of Brest-Litovsk had been signed, civil war had already begun. The Communists (the Bolsheviks had changed their party's name in March 1918) were known as the Reds. All those against them were known as the Whites. At first, it seemed that the Reds were bound to lose as they faced many different enemies. The Whites included supporters of the Tsar, Kerensky's supporters, several army leaders, various national separatist and anarchist movements, the Kadets and the SRs. Once the Civil War had begun, 14 different nations - including Britain, France, Poland, Japan and the USA - sent in troops. At first, they tried to prevent military supplies they had given to the Provisional Government falling into the hands of the Germans. But they soon began to help the Whites. At the start, the Whites also had more weapons and trained soldiers. To begin with, the Communists were restricted to the central areas of Russia and it looked as if they were bound to lose. Because of this crisis, the Mensheviks and Left SRs returned to take their seats in the soviets.

However, the Whites had many different leaders and were slow to form armies. This gave Trotsky time to create a Red Army from Red Guards, workers and ex-soldiers who volunteered. But conscription was soon introduced and the Red Army eventually grew to 5 million. Trotsky began by using officers of the Tsar's army. He argued that these were the only ones with the necessary experience, and he ordered their families be held hostage to reduce the risks of desertion and betrayal. Although Lenin agreed it was necessary to use these officers, many Communists and Left SRs were angry and some became Trotsky's bitter enemies.

In May, the Civil War finally became serious for the Reds when the Czech Legion took control of the Trans-Siberian Railway and then joined up with Kolchak's White Guards in the east. One result was that, to stop the Tsar and his family (who had been imprisoned and were awaiting trial) being rescued by the Whites, the Reds decided to execute them.

The critical year was 1919, when the Bolsheviks faced attacks on all three fronts. However, these attacks were not co-ordinated and the Red Army was able to defeat each one in turn. At the end of 1919, most of the foreign forces were withdrawn from Russia.

## The Russo-Polish War

By early 1920, it was clear that the Reds would win, although fighting continued. Then, in March 1920, Poland (with weapons and troops supplied by France and Britain) invaded Russia again in order to gain more land. Although the Red Army was able to push them back, Lenin then made the mistake of ordering the Red Army into Poland to help Polish Communists overthrow the military

### Whites

*There were four main leaders - General Yudenich in the west, General Denikin and Baron Wrangel in the south and Admiral Kolchak in the east. Although at first some of them wanted to put the Tsar back in power, each one soon tried to make himself the ruler of Russia once the Tsar and his family had been executed.*

### Source A

*A Communist poster showing a Red Army soldier removing Baron Wrangel's cloak to reveal foreign capitalist powers behind him.*

### Czech Legion

*A group of about 40 000 Austro-Hungarian prisoners of war who had formed an army to fight against the Central Powers (Germany and Austria-Hungary). They feared, wrongly, that the Communists were about to hand them over to the Germans, so they revolted and took over a large part of Asian Russia.*

dictator of Poland. The Red Army was defeated and a ceasefire was agreed in October 1920. Soviet Russia was eventually forced to accept the Treaty of Riga in March 1921, which gave Poland a large area of Russian land.

## Why the Communists won

The various White leaders were divided and their armies were geographically separated. The Communists, however, controlled the central part of Russia. This meant it was easier for the Reds to use the railways to supply their different armies and defend their supply lines. They also held the main industrial centres, and so could keep their armies supplied with ammunition and weapons. Many nationalist Russians resented the fact that the Whites relied on foreign interference. The Communists also had a united leadership, and Trotsky was able to develop the Red Army into a disciplined force which he directed from his special armoured train. Finally, although the majority of peasants tended to support the SRs, they saw the Communists as the only force that could prevent the return of the rich landlords.

*Japanese troops posing with the bodies of Reds recently killed by them.*

*The Civil War and foreign intervention.*

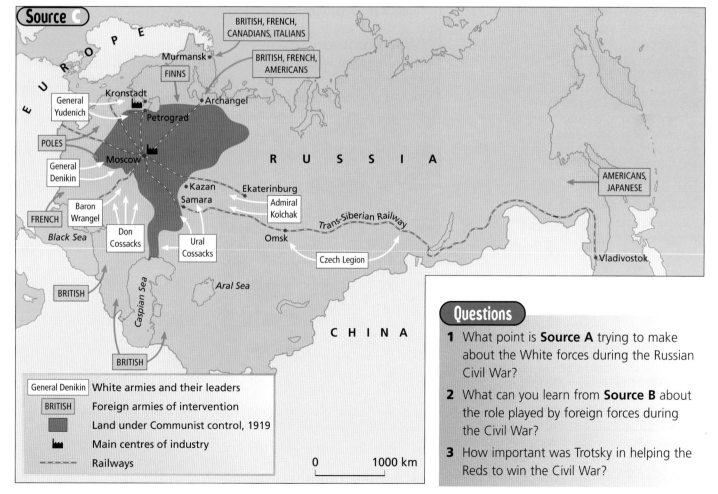

**Source C**

BRITISH, FRENCH, CANADIANS, ITALIANS

BRITISH, FRENCH, AMERICANS

Murmansk

FINNS

General Yudenich

Kronstadt

Archangel

Petrograd

POLES

Moscow

General Denikin

• Kazan

Samara

Ekaterinburg

Admiral Kolchak

AMERICANS, JAPANESE

Baron Wrangel

FRENCH

Black Sea

Don Cossacks

Ural Cossacks

Omsk

Trans-Siberian Railway

Czech Legion

Vladivostok

Caspian Sea

Aral Sea

BRITISH

C H I N A

BRITISH

R U S S I A

E U R O P E

| General Denikin | White armies and their leaders |
| BRITISH | Foreign armies of intervention |
| ■ | Land under Communist control, 1919 |
| ☗ | Main centres of industry |
| - - - - | Railways |

0        1000 km

## Questions

1 What point is **Source A** trying to make about the White forces during the Russian Civil War?

2 What can you learn from **Source B** about the role played by foreign forces during the Civil War?

3 How important was Trotsky in helping the Reds to win the Civil War?

# Lenin's Russia

## Early actions

The first meeting of the All-Russian Congress of Soviets, which voted for the Decree on Peace, also decided two other important issues. These were the land question and what to do about factories and mines. The Communists wanted the large estates of the wealthy to become State collective farms, which would be able to use modern machinery. They also wanted to let capitalists remain as the owners of their factories, as they hoped this would speed up industrial recovery and encourage foreign investment. This policy was known as 'State capitalism', and Lenin's government set up Vesenka (the Supreme Council of the National Economy) to work with the private owners. At first, only the banks and the railways were nationalised (taken over by the State).

However, the peasants wanted all the land broken up into small farms to be shared out amongst themselves, and many workers wanted to control their factories. In fact, many peasants and workers had already begun to take over land and factories, causing many factory owners to leave the cities. So Sovnarkom had to accept Decrees on the Land and Workers' Control which they didn't think were sensible.

## 'War Communism'

When the Civil War broke out in 1918, the Communists introduced emergency economic measures known as 'War Communism'. All factories were nationalised and the workers' committees which ran them were put under central control. This was done to make sure the Red Army was kept supplied with weapons and ammunition. However, many workers resented this increase in government power. To prevent starvation in the towns and cities, peasants were forced to hand over surplus food. However, most peasants hated this and began to grow less food. This, combined with the loss of important farmland to Germany and the disruption of Civil War, eventually led to starvation in parts of Russia by 1921.

## The Kronstadt Rebellion

By the end of the Civil War, the Russian economy was beginning to collapse. This was not just the result of the Civil War but of the First World War, Revolution, and foreign intervention as well. Although many Communists wanted to continue with War Communism, Lenin came to believe a change in economic policy was necessary. At first, the Party rejected his plans. Then, in March 1921, sailors and workers in the important naval base at Kronstadt rose up in protest. The rebels in this Kronstadt Rebellion demanded an end to War Communism and the restoration of full soviet democracy. In the end, Trotsky was ordered to crush the rising, and thousands of Red Army soldiers and rebels were killed before it was ended.

### Source A

Every food requisition detachment is to consist of not less than 75 men and two or three machine guns.

A commander is to head each detachment. He is to be appointed by the chief commissar responsible for the organisation of food armies. A political commissar is to be appointed by the Commissariat of Food.

...The political commissar's duties are (a) to organise local committees of the rural poor and (b) to ensure that the detachment carries out its duties and is full of revolutionary enthusiasm and discipline.

*An extract from 'Instructions for Requisitioning Grain', which was part of a 'War Communism' decree issued in August 1918.*

### Soviet democracy

*During the Civil War, political parties such as the Mensheviks and SRs were allowed to operate, although at times their newspapers were banned and their leaders imprisoned. This happened when the SRs, for instance, assassinated Bolshevik officials. Elections to soviets also took place at times. However, during the Civil War, the Bolshevik government often by-passed the soviets.*

## The New Economic Policy

The Kronstadt Rebellion took place during the 10th Congress of the Communist Party. It shocked the majority of the Party into accepting Lenin's earlier suggestions for a change in economic policy. This was known as the 'New Economic Policy' (NEP). It involved a partial return to capitalism in some aspects of the economy. Although the 'commanding heights' of the economy remained nationalised (such as the railways), smaller factories and shops were either returned to their former owners or bought by those who believed they could make a profit. The forcible seizure of surplus grain was stopped. Instead, peasants were able to sell a part of their extra grain privately, once a certain amount had been sold to the State at a fixed price.

Many Communists were against this, as it would revive capitalism at a time when the Kronstadt Rebellion had shown how isolated the Communists now were. To deal with this threat, the Congress also decided to ban other parties, and the operation of factions (rival groups) in their own party. This was supposed to be a temporary ban which would be lifted as soon as the NEP had improved the economy.

By 1924, the NEP had achieved several successes. Agricultural and industrial production was increasing, and in many cases had returned to the levels which had existed in 1913, before Russia had got involved in the First World War. Despite this, many Communists were worried by the growing number of wealthy peasants (kulaks) and businessmen (nepmen).

*A typical NEP market in the 1920s.*

| Source C | 1921 | 1922 | 1923 | 1924 |
|---|---|---|---|---|
| Grain (million tons) | 37.6 | 50.3 | 56.6 | 51.4 |
| Coal (million tons) | 8.9 | 9.5 | 13.7 | 16.1 |
| Steel (million tons) | 183 | 39 | 709 | 1140 |
| Electricity (million Kwhs) | 520 | 775 | 1146 | 1562 |
| Av. monthly wage of factory worker (roubles) | 10.2 | 12.2 | 15.9 | 20.8 |

*Statistics calculated by a Western historian, showing production during the first four years of the NEP.*

## Lenin's death

Also in 1924, while the NEP was beginning to improve the economy, Russia adopted a new constitution. This set up a federal system which established greater central control over the different republics which made up the country. Russia now became known as the Union of Soviet Socialist Republics (USSR). Much of the work for this new constitution had been done by Josef Stalin who was Commissar for Nationalities. Lenin had become increasingly worried about Stalin's work on the constitution but, in 1922, Lenin had suffered the first of a series of strokes. These kept him out of active politics and, in January 1924, he died.

### Questions

1 Why did grain requisition detachments, as shown by **Source A**, need to have military protection?

2 Using **Source C** and your own knowledge, explain how successful the NEP had been by 1924.

3 Why were some Communists opposed to the NEP?

# The struggle for power

### The rivals

Even before Lenin's death in 1924, there had been divisions between the leading Communists. Apart from Lenin, the most important Communists were Trotsky, Zinoviev, Kamenev, Bukharin and Stalin. Of these, the closest to Lenin in his ideas was Trotsky. He had only joined the Bolsheviks in August 1917, but as Commissar for War and head of the Red Army, he had become popular with the ordinary members of the Party.

However, his popularity was resented by those 'Old Guard' Bolsheviks who had sided with Lenin when the RSDLP split in 1903. Zinoviev, in particular, thought he should be the next leader. But both he and Kamenev had weakened their position by the fact that they had opposed Lenin's plans to overthrow Kerensky in October 1917, and had even revealed the decision to opposition parties.

These two thought they could use Stalin to help them in their plan to prevent Trotsky from taking over. Stalin had become General Secretary of the Communist Party in 1922. This was a routine job but it gave him the power to control Party membership and appointments.

### Lenin's 'Testament'

Lenin became increasingly aware of these tensions and decided to outline the strengths and weaknesses of the main leaders. This was his Testament, written in December 1922. Shortly afterwards, he had serious disagreements with Stalin over policy towards the different national groups. So, in January 1923, he wrote a Postscript recommending that Stalin be removed from all positions of power. However, when he died, Zinoviev and Kamenev persuaded the Party leadership not to act on Lenin's advice, and Stalin kept his jobs. The leaders also decided not to publish the Testament.

### Policy differences

However, there were also serious political differences between these Communist leaders. By 1924, Trotsky had decided that the NEP had been successful and should be ended. He believed it was now necessary to begin an industrialisation programme and to start creating large collective farms. In addition, Lenin and the Bolsheviks had always believed that only revolutions in economically advanced countries could achieve Communism. Thus, Russia would never be able to become Socialist without outside help. After Lenin's death, Trotsky continued to believe in the importance of world revolution. However, Stalin countered Trotsky's theory of Permanent Revolution with his own view of Socialism in One Country. This said Russia could become Socialist on its own, provided Lenin's NEP was followed.

---

> ### Trotsky
>
> *From 1903-04, he sided with the Mensheviks when the RSDLP split into two factions. From 1904 until 1917, he led his own faction; but, when he returned to Russia in May 1917, he worked closely with the Bolsheviks. Because Lenin was in hiding following the July Days, Trotsky soon became their main speaker, although he did not formerly join them until August 1917. Many founder-members of the Bolsheviks resented his rapid rise. Trotsky was also arrogant at times, and did not bother to maintain close relations with other Communist leaders.*

---

> ### Source A
>
> Comrade Stalin, having become General Secretary, has concentrated an enormous power in his hands; and I am not sure that he always knows how to use that power with sufficient caution...
> Stalin is too rude and, although we Communists might put up with this, it is hardly a quality that we would expect in a General Secretary of the Party. That is why I suggest he be removed from his post.

*Adapted extracts from Lenin's* Testament *and* Postscript*, written at the end of 1922 and the beginning of 1923.*

---

> ### Source B

*Trotsky's last official public appearance, at Dzerzhinsky's funeral, Moscow, 1926. Trotsky is shown on the left, with Stalin on the right – the man between them is Kamenev.*

## Defeat of Trotsky and the Left

Even before Lenin died, Zinoviev, Kamenev and Stalin had joined together, in what became known as the 'Triumvirate', to prevent Trotsky becoming the next leader of the Party. They began their campaign against him by publishing the disagreements which had arisen between Trotsky and Lenin during the years 1903-17. Trotsky and his supporters were known as the Left Opposition. Using Stalin's control of the Party organisation and the 1921 ban against factions, the Triumvirs began to remove Trotsky's supporters from influential positions. Trotsky was increasingly outvoted and isolated. In 1925, he was forced to resign from his powerful position as Commissar for War.

## The defeat of the United Opposition

By then, however, Zinoviev and Kamenev were becoming suspicious of Stalin's motives and policies. In particular, they now realised that Stalin was using his position to appoint and promote his own supporters. So, in April 1926, they joined forces with Trotsky in what was known as the United Opposition. Their plan was to restore Party and Soviet democracy, and to end the NEP. However, Stalin joined forces with Bukharin and the Right to maintain the decisions taken in 1921. By using his control of Party Congresses and elections, Stalin was able to outvote his ex-partners. By December 1927, Trotsky, Zinoviev, Kamenev and other left-wing Communists had lost important positions and had been expelled from the Party.

## The defeat of Bukharin and the Right

Stalin then began to turn against Bukharin and the Right. Towards the end of 1927, Stalin began to indicate that he favoured a change in economic policy. He decided to adopt Trotsky's earlier suggestions for a programme of industrialisation and the ending of NEP. Bukharin continued to defend the existing policies, so Stalin began to use his position to remove Bukharin's supporters. In desperation, Bukharin turned to Trotsky, who had been exiled to Siberia earlier in 1928. Bukharin was particularly worried that Stalin intended to execute his opponents, and suggested to Trotsky that they join forces to restore Party and Soviet democracy before it was too late.

However, their supporters would not cooperate, and Bukharin was defeated. In 1929, Trotsky was expelled from the Soviet Union. Stalin was left as the most important leader of the Communist Party.

**Source C**

An official cartoon of 1927, attacking the United Opposition. Trotsky is shown as the head of the house, in charge of Zinoviev and Kamenev.

### Questions

1 How did Stalin use his position as General Secretary of the Party?

2 Why was Stalin able to keep his post as General Secretary, despite the advice given by Lenin in **Source A**?

3 What message was Stalin trying to give about his opponents in **Source C**?

# CHAPTER 6

# Stalin's revolution: Agriculture

## Stalin's 'turn to the left' and abandoning of NEP

Despite the successes of NEP, only about 20% of the population was employed in industry. In addition, from 1926, the amount of grain sold by the peasants to the State began to decline. In that year, State purchases were 50% less than expected. This was because peasants reduced their surplus by growing less and consuming more, in part because Soviet industry was only able to produce a limited amount of consumer goods for them to buy. Similar results were experienced after the 1927 harvest, leading to shortages in what became known as the 'grain crisis'.

As early as 1925, Stalin seems to have started to favour an industrialisation programme. However, because of his power struggle with first the Left Opposition and then the United Opposition, he said little about his changing views. By the end of 1927, however, the United Opposition had been defeated, and Stalin announced that Soviet agriculture and industry needed to be modernised.

## Crisis in agriculture

Before industry could be expanded, agriculture had to be modernised. This would enable fewer peasants to produce more food. The surplus workers could then move to work in factories. An agricultural surplus would also allow the USSR to export food and so earn foreign currency, which could be used to buy modern machinery from abroad.

The grain crisis of 1927-28 led Stalin to order the seizure of grain from the kulaks. This was unpopular and led to protests and serious riots, and Bukharin was able to get Stalin to stop the seizures and instead to increase the price the government paid for grain. Although the problems continued, by 1929 Bukharin and the Right had been defeated, so Stalin was able to press ahead. At first, he called for voluntary collectivisation - the merger of small peasant farms into large collective farms (kolkhozes). But as grain shortages persisted, in 1930 Stalin ordered more seizures of grain and forced collectivisation of kulak farms. As before, there was armed resistance and government officials were even murdered in some areas. This led other Communist leaders to persuade Stalin to call a halt, and a number of collectives were returned to private ownership.

## Forced collectivisation

However, once the 1930 harvest was in, Stalin renewed the forced collectivisation programme. By 1931, over 50% of farms had been collectivised; and by 1937, the official figure was given as 90%. Although Stalin had carried out a 'revolution from above', which effectively ended private ownership of the land, his methods did

*A Soviet government poster, contrasting the modern methods used on collective farms with the old-fashioned methods of the past.*

much damage to Russian agriculture. This was because many kulaks slaughtered their animals, and destroyed equipment and food rather than hand them over to the collective farms. Stalin punished those who resisted by executing the main leaders of resistance, while forcibly moving others to poor farming areas or sending them to gulags. As a result, many were killed or died, and food production was seriously disrupted. To avoid starvation in the towns, grain was seized from rural areas, causing a serious famine in parts of rural Russia in which millions died. Production figures did not return to 1928 levels until 1941, and Soviet agriculture remained weak for decades after.

### Gulags

*These were forced labour camps, to which workers who broke the labour code were sent. Most inmates (called 'zeks') were peasants who had resisted collectivisation. Later, there were also the victims of Stalin's purges. By 1939, there were about 3 million prisoners.*

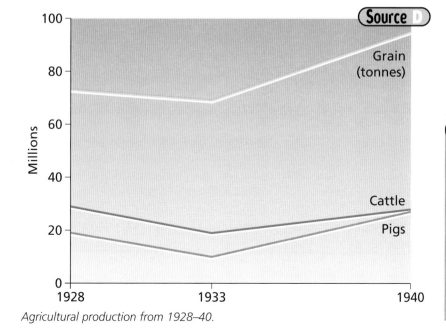

*Agricultural production from 1928–40.*

### Questions

1 Why, by 1928, was Stalin worried about the level of grain purchases by the State?

2 How useful is **Source B** for finding out about how peasants reacted to forced collectivisation?

3 Study **Source C** and **Source D**. Which source is more reliable for finding out about the impact of forced collectivisation in the period before 1941?

# CHAPTER 6

# Stalin's revolution: Industry

Source A

Throughout history Russia has been beaten again and again because she was backward...It is sometimes asked whether it is not possible to slow down industrialisation a bit... To slow down the pace [of the Five-Year Plan] would mean falling behind. And those who fall behind get beaten. No, we refuse to be beaten! In the past, Russia was beaten for her backwardness by British and French capitalists and by Japanese barons. That is why Lenin said: 'Either die, or overtake and outstrip the advanced capitalist countries'. We are 50 to 100 years behind the advanced countries. Either we make good the difference in 10 years or they crush us.

*Extracts from a speech made by Stalin in February 1931.*

*A Soviet poster of 1928, claiming 'Industrialisation is the path to Socialism'.*

## Speeding up industrialisation

As early as 1925, Stalin had mentioned the need to modernise and develop Soviet industry; and in 1926, he had said it was necessary to 'catch up' with western industry. This drive increased after 1927, when he became worried that the USSR might be invaded once again. The economic planning bodies, Gosplan and Vesenka, were told to draw up plans for increasing production. The result was a series of targets which were set for each industry, and then broken down for each individual factory.

## The Five-Year Plans

The First Five-Year Plan ran from 1928-32 and concentrated on heavy industry, especially coal, iron, steel, electricity and oil. This was because increased industrialisation would need plentiful supplies of these products, and lots of energy, in order to build and run new factories.

The government claimed the Plan had been so successful that the targets set had been met or exceeded by the end of 1931, so Gosplan began drawing up a Second Five-Year Plan in 1932. This was to run from 1932-37, and concentrated more on transport and mining, although heavy industry in general was still emphasised. A Third Plan, to run from 1938-42, put more emphasis on light industry and consumer goods. But this Plan was disrupted when the threat posed by Nazi Germany led to a switch to military production. In 1941, it was completely ended by the Nazi invasion.

## The success of the Plans

Overall, these Plans were extremely successful. Despite exaggerated claims by Stalin's government, western historians believe industrial production in the USSR increased by over 260% between 1928 and 1940. Many new factories were built, and new industrial centres were established, such as Magnitogorsk. This was achieved in a number of ways. Skilled foreign workers were employed to teach Russians new work methods. Large numbers of women and peasants were encouraged to work in factories - creches and canteens were provided to make work easier. 'Super' workers were encouraged to follow the example of Stakhanov, a miner who had greatly increased his daily production of coal. Soon, Stakhanovism had spread to all industries. Government propaganda gave publicity to 'Heroes of Socialist Production', and showed how they were making the USSR and Communism stronger. Medals and better housing were also given to workers who exceeded their work targets.

## The Soviet experience of industrialisation

Not everything about these plans was positive. Targets were often unrealistically high, and many managers falsified their production figures to avoid punishment. Other ways of increasing production included increasing the hours of work, linking pay to production, and imposing a strict work discipline which fined workers for being late. Many workers were sent to the gulags for repeated offences. Along with many other prisoners, they were made to build canals and dams, or work in mines. At first, 'real' wages fell, and there were shortages of housing and consumer goods during the first two Plans. However, the Plans ended unemployment, and workers received free health care and education. This was in contrast to the capitalist countries which suffered high unemployment and poverty during the Depression in the 1930s. Despite these problems, by 1941, the Soviet Union was sufficiently industrialised to withstand and eventually defeat Nazi Germany.

**Source C**

Nothing strikes the visitor to the Soviet Union more forcibly than the lack of fear. No fear of not having enough money at the birth of a child. No fear for doctor's fees, school fees or university fees. No fear of underwork, no fear of overwork. No fear of wage reduction in a land where none are unemployed.

*The views of Dr. H. Johnson, the Dean of Canterbury Cathedral, during his visit to the USSR in 1939. He was sometimes known as the 'Red Dean'.*

| Source D | Production in 1928 | First Five-Year Plan | | Second Five-Year Plan | |
|---|---|---|---|---|---|
| | | **Real** | **Planned** | **Real** | **Planned** |
| Electricity (million Kwhs) | 5.05 | 13.4 | 17.0 | 36.2 | 38.0 |
| Coal (million tonnes) | 35.4 | 64.3 | 75.0 | 128.0 | 152.5 |
| Oil (million tonnes) | 11.7 | 21.4 | 22.0 | 28.5 | 46.8 |
| Pig iron (million tonnes) | 3.3 | 6.2 | 8.0 | 14.5 | 16.0 |
| Steel (million tonnes) | 4.0 | 5.9 | 10.4 | 17.7 | 17.0 |

## Questions

**1** Why did Stalin fear the USSR might be attacked in the future?

**2** Apart from propaganda posters like **Source B**, what other methods did Stalin use to get industrial workers to increase production?

**3** In view of what you know, how accurate a picture of the results of the Five-Year Plans is provided by **Source D**?

# Show trials and purges

## Stalin's insecurity

By 1929, Stalin had defeated his main opponents within the Communist Party. Yet several of his supporters had been against expelling leading Oppositionists, and after 1930 his policy of forced collectivisation led to criticism from within the Party. In 1932 and 1933, other Communists criticised Stalin's policies and methods, and were eventually expelled. However, Stalin's demands that they be executed had been resisted by the other Party leaders. Stalin also remained aware that expelled leaders, such as Trotsky and Zinoviev, had always been closer to Lenin than he had.

## The Kirov Affair, 1934

Because of the disruption caused by collectivisation and the early Five-Year Plans, there was no Party Congress from 1930 to 1933. At the 17th Congress, held in 1934, Kirov (who was head of the Party in Leningrad) seemed as popular as Stalin. What is more, there is evidence that some Party officials saw him as a likely replacement for Stalin. Shortly afterwards, Kirov was murdered in suspicious circumstances. Whatever Stalin's involvement was, he used it as an opportunity to launch another purge of the Communist Party.

## The Great Purge and the Show Trials

Although there had been purges before, this was much larger than previous ones. Thousands of Party leaders and officials were arrested. They were then interrogated by the NKVD, in an attempt to get them to 'confess' their involvement in attempts to assassinate Party leaders and to overthrow the Revolution. They were even accused of being agents of Nazi Germany!

Although a few refused to admit their 'guilt', most did. About 100 Party members were executed, and many were imprisoned, including Zinoviev and Kamenev. Stalin then organised a series of 'show trials' in which those arrested were forced to openly admit their 'crimes'. In 1936, at the 'trial of the sixteen', Yagoda, the head of the secret police, succeeded in getting death sentences passed on Zinoviev, Kamenev and 14 others. Yagoda was then replaced by Yezhov, who was even more extreme. In 1937, as a result of the 'trial of the seventeen', another 13 Communist leaders were executed. In 1938, came the 'trial of the twenty-one'. In this, Bukharin was the main 'culprit', but he refused to 'confess'. He, along with 17 others, was executed. This turned out to be the last of the show trials.

## The Great Terror

By then, however, the purge had turned into terror. As early as 1937, Stalin had turned his attentions to the armed forces. Red Army commanders were arrested and executed. They were accused of spying for Nazi Germany and Japan. By 1939, five Red Army

### NKVD

These were the initials of the People's Commissariat for Internal Affairs, set up in 1917. In July 1934, it took over the secret police (OGPU) and kept this responsibility until 1943. OGPU (United State Political Administration) was the name of the secret police from 1923-34; from 1917-22, the Cheka had been the secret police and, from 1922-23, the GPU.

### Source A

The predominant view in Party circles was that Stalin had led the country into a dead-end by his policy, that he had roused the peasants against the Party, and that the situation could be saved only by his removal. Many influential members of the Central Committee were of this opinion.

*The private views of Bukharin, made a few months before his execution in 1938.*

### Source B

The teacher showed us her school textbooks where the portraits of Party leaders had thick pieces of paper pasted over them as one by one they fell in to disgrace - this  the children had to do on instructions from their teacher... with every new arrest, people went through their books and burned the works of disgraced leaders in their stoves.

*A Soviet writer describing how school history books were constantly revised during the 1930s.*

marshals and all the admirals of the navy had been shot. In all, about 20% of all army officers were executed.

This Great Terror now spread beyond the Party and military leaders. Increasingly, ordinary people were denounced by neighbours or workmates, and about 3 million in all were arrested or sent to the gulags. As the Great Terror started to affect industrial production, some of Stalin's supporters began to raise concerns. In 1938, Yezhov was replaced as head of the secret police by Beria. In 1939, after admitting that 'mistakes' had been made, Stalin called off the Great Terror. By then, all the 'Old Guard' Bolshevik leaders except Trotsky had been executed or had committed suicide. Trotsky, who had been expelled from the USSR in 1929, was assassinated by one of Stalin's agents in Mexico in 1940.

## The cult of personality

Stalin also used censorship and propaganda to build up his dictatorship. Only the successes of his policies were broadcast. If there were mistakes, these were either blamed on 'enemies' or not reported at all. The Press, radio, the Arts and cinema were all heavily censored.

At the same time, Stalin set out to show he was Lenin's true successor. Statues, paintings and posters of Stalin appeared everywhere, while many towns and streets were named after him.

Young people, in particular, were targeted, as they would not have experienced the early history of the Party. Stalin made sure that all leaders of the Young Communist League (Komsomol) were carefully vetted before being appointed. Any unreliable ones were removed.

## Stalin's achievements

Despite the many harsh features of Stalin's rule, there was also some genuine support. Medical care had been improved and all health services were free. By 1939, the Soviet Union had more doctors per head of the population than Britain. Education was also expanded so that more could enjoy secondary education, while drives to improve literacy were successful. In some respects, women continued to benefit from greater equality at work. Although towards the end of the 1930s, some rights they had gained after the November 1917 Revolution were increasingly restricted (such as divorce and abortions). After the early problems of the Five-Year Plans, living standards for most workers did improve. There were also benefits such as cheap public transport and recreational facilities such as swimming pools and cinemas.

**Source C**

*A show trial against 8 engineers accused of sabotage.*

### Lenin's true successor

*All history books were re-written to show that Stalin, and not Trotsky or the other Communist leaders, had been Lenin's second-in-command. All other leaders' names were either erased, or they were described as 'enemies of the revolution'. Even photographs were altered to remove evidence that other leaders might have been associated with Lenin.*

### Questions

1 What evidence do you know of to support the claim made in **Source A** that there was serious opposition to Stalin from within the Communist Party during the 1930s?

2 How reliable is **Source A** as evidence of this opposition?

3 Why did Stalin finally end the Great Terror?

# The approach of war

## Early isolation of Soviet Russia

After the November Revolution in 1917, the Bolsheviks withdrew Russia from the First World War in March 1918. This led to the intervention of 14 different countries in the Civil War on the side of the Whites. Although the Communists won the Civil War, the new workers' state remained isolated. It was not invited to help draw up the peace treaties which ended the First World War, or to join the new League of Nations.

As the Communists were committed to helping revolutions break out across Europe, this did not worry them too much. Instead, in 1919, they set up the Communist (or Third) International, soon known as the Comintern.

## Relations with other countries in the 1920s

By 1922, the other revolutions had all been crushed. So Soviet Russia turned to the other 'outcast' in Europe - Germany. In 1922, the Treaty of Rapallo gave Russia modern German technology and technical assistance. In return, Germany was allowed to buy weapons forbidden by the Treaty of Versailles and to carry out military training in Russia. These arrangements were extended by the Treaty of Berlin in 1930. In 1927 Britain broke off diplomatic relations with the USSR following Soviet connections with the Trades Union Congress. This resulted in a war scare in the USSR.

## Collective security

After the Wall Street Crash and the Great Depression, German politics began to move to the right. This caused concern to both the USSR and France. In 1932, these two countries promised not to attack each other. Soviet fears increased after 1933, when the Nazis came to power in Germany, especially when one of Hitler's first acts was to take Germany out of the League of Nations. Stalin was particularly worried as Hitler made it clear he wanted to destroy Communism, and to get 'Living Space' for Germany in the east of Europe. The USSR was also alarmed by Japanese military aggression against China from 1931, which seemed to threaten its own Asian republics.

The Commissar for Foreign Affairs, Litvinov, was told to try to get an anti-Fascist alliance with Britain and France. At the same time, Stalin tried to improve relations with Capitalist countries. In 1933, the USA at last officially recognised the USSR and, in 1934, the Soviet Union was allowed to join the League of Nations. Stalin now urged the League to combine to oppose Fascist aggression, and to take collective action to ensure the security of all threatened countries. At the same time, the Comintern now ordered Communist Parties in Europe to form Popular Fronts with all those who opposed Fascism.

### Comintern

*Its job was to help workers' revolutions wherever they broke out. Zinoviev was its first President, and from its base in Moscow, it gave literature, funds and advice to the Communist revolutions which had begun in several countries in the years 1919-21. After the November 1917 Revolution, those who sympathised with the Bolsheviks set up Communist Parties in their own countries. These Communist Parties then joined Comintern. At first, the Russian Communists did not try to force other Communist Parties to agree with them. However, this changed under Stalin.*

### Source A

We turn our eyes to the east. This huge empire in the east is ripe for ending. The future aim of our foreign policy ought to be to acquire such eastern territory as is needed by our German people. Only a large space on this earth assures a nation of freedom... If we speak of soil in Europe today we can have in mind only Russia and her border states.

*An extract from Hitler's book Mein Kampf, written in 1924.*

### Fascist

*Fascism was the name given to the extreme right-wing, nationalist principles first adopted in Italy under Mussolini. Similar principles, stressing the absolute authority of the nation's leader, were adopted by the Nazis in Germany under Adolf Hitler.*

## Appeasement and the League

Hitler openly broke the terms of the Treaty of Versailles several times in the years after 1935. Despite this, the British government followed a policy of appeasement towards Germany, while France felt unable to take any action without British support. As a result, Hitler was able to re-occupy the Rhineland, and then intervene in the Spanish Civil War, in 1936. In 1938, Hitler was able to bring about Anschluss (union) with Austria, again without the League taking any action. When Hitler began to make demands on Czechoslovakia, Stalin began to think that Britain and France were encouraging Hitler to expand in the east so that he would attack the USSR.

When a crisis arose over the Sudetenland area of Czechoslovakia in September 1938, Stalin's fears seemed confirmed. Britain persuaded France to agree to Hitler's demands, and the Czech government was forced to give up this important border area. Stalin was particularly suspicious as France and the USSR had signed a treaty promising to protect Czechoslovakia.

## The Nazi-Soviet Non-Aggression Pact

In March 1939, the rest of Czechoslovakia was taken over and, again, Britain and France took no action. Although the USSR continued to press Britain and France to sign an anti-Nazi treaty, Stalin decided to buy time. Stalin was particularly worried as he realised his purges of the armed forces had left them demoralised and weakened. In May, Litvinov was replaced by Molotov, who was prepared to negotiate with Germany, which had recently opened new contacts with the USSR. The result was a Non-Aggression Pact between these two countries.

## Preparing for the Great Patriotic War

This Pact gave Stalin time to rebuild the Red Army, and was meant to ensure that any future war would be fought on non-Russian soil. Stalin was convinced Hitler would eventually attack the USSR. After Hitler invaded Poland in September 1939, Britain and France declared war on Germany. Stalin stayed out of the Second World War at first, and instead moved the Red Army into the Polish areas agreed with Hitler. Attempts to persuade Finland to exchange territory to strengthen the defences of Leningrad failed and, in November 1939, war broke out between Finland and the Soviet Union. The Red Army, still recovering from the effects of the purges, did not do well at first in this 'Winter War'. Eventually though, the Finns were forced to make peace. In June and July 1940, Stalin occupied the other areas agreed in 1939.

**Source B**

France and Britain don't want to get involved in a war with Hitler. They are still hoping to push Hitler into a war with the Soviet Union. By refusing to make an agreement with us, they tried to allow Hitler to attack the Soviet Union. They will have to pay the price for their short-sighted policy.

*Stalin's view of the British and French policy of appeasement in 1939.*

**Source C**

It will be asked how it was possible that the Soviet government signed a non-aggression pact with so deceitful a nation, with such criminals as Hitler and Ribbentrop [the German foreign minister] ... We secured peace for our country for eighteen months, which enabled us to make military preparations.

*An extract from a speech made by Stalin in 1941.*

**Non-Aggression Pact**

*This was signed in August by Ribbentrop for Germany and Molotov for the USSR. By it, the two countries promised not to attack each other – it was not a treaty of friendship between allies.*

*This pact, however, also contained a secret clause. Germany and the USSR agreed to re-draw the map of eastern Europe. Western Poland would go to Germany. In return, Hitler agreed that the Soviet Union could have land it had lost at the end of the First World War and after the Russo-Polish Wars. This included eastern Poland, parts of Romania, and the three Baltic republics of Estonia, Latvia and Lithuania.*

**Questions**

1 Do **Sources A** and **B** fully explain why, by 1938, Stalin feared an invasion by Nazi Germany?

2 Why did Stalin replace Litvinov with Molotov as the USSR's Commissar for Foreign Affairs?

3 What were the main terms of the Non-Aggression Pact of August 1939?

# SUMMARY

## 1900–1917

- In 1900, Russia was ruled by an all-powerful Tsar. An attempt at revolution in 1905 failed, and Nicholas II's rule seemed secure after reforms helped some peasants and set up a Duma (parliament).
- Russia's involvement in the First World War resulted in the March Revolution of 1917. The Tsar abdicated and a Provisional Government took over. In April, Lenin returned and, in November, the Bolsheviks overthrew the Provisional Government.
- Immediately, the All-Russian Congress of Soviets approved decrees on ending the war, and reforming land and factory ownership.

## 1918–1921

- The newly-elected Constituent Assembly was dismissed in January 1918, and in March the Treaty of Brest-Litovsk ended Russia's part in the First World War.
- This peace ended the Bolshevik coalition with the Left SRs. At the same time, a Civil War broke out. Despite foreign intervention, the Red Army created by Trotsky eventually won the war.
- To fight the war, Lenin's government was forced to take emergency economic measures known as 'War Communism'. This was unpopular and provoked the serious Kronstadt Rebellion in 1921. Lenin then persuaded the Communists to introduce a New Economic Policy.

## 1922–1929

- Lenin's Testament outlined the strengths and weaknesses of the other Communist leaders; his 1923 Postscript recommended Stalin be removed from power.
- Lenin's death in 1924 resulted in a struggle for power. Zinoviev and Kamenev joined with Stalin to oppose Trotsky. Stalin then allied with Bukharin against Zinoviev and Kamenev. Finally, Stalin turned on Bukharin. By 1929, Stalin had defeated all his main rivals.

## 1929–1941

- Stalin then introduced fundamental changes to the Soviet economy, to rapidly expand and modernise Soviet industry.
- In agriculture, he introduced forced collectivisation. Opposition from kulaks meant that production declined at first and there was famine in parts of the USSR.
- Soviet industry was more successfully transformed, by the adoption of Five-Year Plans. These mostly concentrated on heavy industry.
- Stalin also began a Great Purge of the Communist Party and the armed forces. A series of show trials resulted in the execution of all his main opponents. Several million victims ended up in the gulags.
- After 1933, Stalin began to fear attack from Nazi Germany. The USSR joined the League of Nations in 1934, but failed to get an alliance with Britain and France. In 1939, Stalin signed a Non-Aggression Pact with Hitler.

# Exam Question Practice

## Judgement or interpretation questions

Study Sources A and B below, and then answer the question which follows.

'Stalin's attempts to modernise Soviet agriculture in the 1930s were a great success'. Do you agree with this statement? Use the sources and your own knowledge to explain your answer.

**Source A**

*Peasants working under the Tsarist regime.*

**Source B**

*Soviet tractor drivers on a collective farm.*

## Examiner's Tips

**When answering questions like this:**

◎ Make sure you do the two things the question asks you - use your own knowledge AND the sources.

◎ Don't just say 'Yes' or 'No' - the Principal Examiner will be expecting a balanced answer which tries to look at both sides of the question ('Yes' and 'No'). You should try to spend roughly the same amount of time on putting both sides, even if you have a strong view one way or the other.

◎ Make sure you give reasons for your conclusions. Don't just give different arguments and then simply identify the one you prefer.

◎ Make sure you deal with a range of issues/factors. You will not score high marks if you only comment on one aspect.

◎ When you are using your own knowledge, try to give detailed and precise bits of information, e.g. don't just say the peasants objected to collectivisation - mention that they destroyed crops, animals and equipment rather than hand them over to the collective farms.

◎ If you can't make a decision one way or the other, say so and show why, e.g. Stalin's methods led to a decline in production and to famine in some areas, but Soviet agriculture was able to function despite the great destruction following the Nazi invasion of 1941.

## GERMANY, 1918-1945

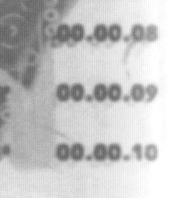

*An illustration from a German children's book, published in 1935. The title of the book was 'Trust No Fox on the Heath and No Jew on his Word'.*

*A Jewish child being taken from his home in the Warsaw ghetto in 1943.*

Source C

*A mass grave discovered by Allied troops when they liberated Belsen Concentration Camp in April 1945.*

## Key Questions

**How** was it possible for a drawing such as **Source A** to lead to scenes like those shown by **Sources B** and **C**?

**How** was it possible that a twentieth-century government could order and arrange the mass murder of millions of people?

**Why** did so many (including fathers and mothers) help carry it out?

**Why** did so many people do so little to stop it?

This is just one of the issues that we will cover in this chapter. The main focus of this chapter on Germany will be:

- The problems of Germany following the First World War

- The impact of the Great Depression

- Nazi beliefs and the importance of Hitler

- How Hitler and the Nazis got to power in the 1930s

- How the Nazis controlled Germany and tried to prevent opposition

- What life was like for different groups in Nazi Germany, including young people, women and Jewish people

- How some Germans did try to oppose the Nazis

# Germany, the First World War and the Weimar Republic

**Source A**

Children at a street soup kitchen in Berlin, 1918.

## Impact of the First World War

Germany's defeat in 1918 had a great effect on its people and on the political system. Most Germans were convinced that they had been fighting a defensive war and, right up to 1918, the Kaiser's government had led the people to think that they were winning the war. However, the Allied naval blockade of German ports had caused serious shortages of food and medicines in Germany. These had been made worse by the winter of 1916-17 and the loss of the potato crop. Many German civilians had to live on turnips in what came to be known as the 'turnip winter'.

## Mutiny and revolution

In 1917, these food shortages began to affect Germany's armed forces, and when rations for the navy were cut, there was a mutiny. In addition, coal shortages led to electricity cuts and the closure of cinemas and theatres. So, by 1918, many Germans were fed up with the war.

To make matters worse, Germany was then hit by an influenza epidemic which killed many civilians and soldiers. In October 1918, the German High Command admitted to the Kaiser that Germany could not win the war. At the same time, the USA told the Kaiser that there could be no peace negotiations until Germany became more democratic, but the Kaiser refused to share power with the Reichstag (the German parliament).

Anger amongst the sailors in the naval base at Kiel led to another mutiny on 28 October, which, unlike the one in 1917, quickly spread to other ports. In Kiel and elsewhere, the sailors were joined by soldiers and workers. Imitating the Bolsheviks in Russia in November 1917, the mutineers and the striking workers quickly set up workers and soldiers' councils which took over several towns; while socialists in Bavaria and Saxony declared their provinces to be independent republics. By 9 November, Berlin was in the hands of the revolutionaries. With the army refusing to back him, the Kaiser abdicated and fled to the Netherlands on 10 November 1918.

**Source B**

German painting of the Kiel Mutiny, November 1918.

**Armistice**

*This is a ceasefire, or a pause, in the fighting to see if peace terms can be agreed. If not, the fighting resumes; so do not confuse an armistice with peace.*

## Defeat and the Weimar Republic

With the Kaiser gone, Germany became a democratic republic and a new provisional government took over. It was a centre-left coalition (made up of several parties), and was headed by Friedrich Ebert, the leader of the Social Democratic Party (SPD). As the generals told the new government that the German army could no longer fight, Ebert felt there was no choice but to sign an armistice with the Allies. As a result, the fighting of the First World War ended on 11 November. However, many Germans were deeply shocked to learn that Germany had been defeated, especially as no Allied troops had been able to cross into German territory. Germans, particularly the conservatives and nationalists, began to think of the politicians who had signed the armistice as the 'November Criminals'. Many only accepted the establishment of a republic because they thought that this would lead the Allies to give Germany a better deal.

## The Treaty of Versailles

The new provisional government thought that the final peace treaty would be based on Woodrow Wilson's Fourteen Points, issued in January 1918. But these had been rejected by the Kaiser and the previous government earlier in 1918, and Britain and France now insisted on harsher terms.

The representatives of the German government were not even allowed to take part in the peace negotiations in Paris, which began in January 1919. Instead, in June 1919, they were simply presented with the terms as agreed by the Allies and informed they could only accept them or reject them. Several members of the government, including the Chancellor, Scheidemann, who had taken the place of Ebert when the latter had become the first President of Weimar Germany, resigned in protest. As rejection would have meant continuing the war, a new German government was quickly formed which reluctantly accepted the Treaty which they, and most Germans, felt was a diktat (literally a dictated peace).

Many Germans thought the terms of the Treaty of Versailles were harsh, as Germany lost all its overseas colonies and several important parts of its European land. Germans were also angry that German speakers in the lands given to the 'successor states' in central and eastern Europe (such as Czechoslovakia) were denied the right to self-determination. Many also resented the military restrictions, and the 'war-guilt' clause, in which Germany was forced to accept sole responsibility for starting the First World War, and to pay compensation. In 1921, a figure was finally set for German reparations (compensation) of £6600 million. This also caused great anger in Germany.

| Source C |
| --- |
| We are told that we should acknowledge that we alone are guilty of having caused the war. I would be a liar if I agreed to this. We are not trying to avoid all responsibility for this world war. However, we emphatically deny that the German people should be seen as the only guilty party. Over fifty years the imperialism of all European states has poisoned the international situation. |

*The view of Count Brockdorff, the leader of the German delegation, about the Treaty of Versailles, May 1919.*

| Self-determination |
| --- |
| *This was the belief, held by President Wilson of the USA, that significant national groups which had a language, history or culture in common, should be allowed to decide (determine) whether they wanted to live in their own country or be joined with similar people in another country.* |

| Questions |
| --- |
| **1** How useful is **Source A** for finding out about the situation in Germany at the end of the First World War? |
| **2** Why did many Germans see the Treaty of Versailles as a 'diktat'? |
| **3** How reliable is **Source C** for finding out about German reactions to the 'war-guilt' clause of the Treaty of Versailles? |
| **4** Why did some Germans see those who signed the armistice and the Treaty of Versailles as the 'November criminals'? |

# The Weimar Republic, 1919-23

## The Weimar Constitution

Before June 1919 (when the terms of the Treaty were known), some important political developments had already taken place in Germany. The provisional government, headed by Ebert, called elections for January 1919. But unrest in Berlin forced the newly elected government to meet in the small town of Weimar. Here, it drew up a new democratic Constitution - the first Germany had ever had. This gave the vote to everyone over 20. Because it used a system of proportional representation for elections to the Reichstag (parliament), a large number of small parties tended to win seats. As a result, German governments were always coalitions, made up of several parties. Because they found it difficult to agree on policies, the coalitions were often short-lived.

The Constitution also provided for the election of a President, who had the power to appoint Prime Ministers, provided they could command a majority in the Reichstag. Under Article 48, the President could declare a state of emergency and rule by issuing decrees which did not have to be approved by the Reichstag.

## Opposition to the Weimar Republic

Right from the start, the provisional government had faced opposition from more radical left-wing parties. During December 1918 and January 1919, revolutionary socialists, known as the Spartacists, tried to organise a Bolshevik-type revolution in Berlin. This alarmed the German army and Ebert was forced to do a deal allowing the army, and a para-military group known as the Freikorps, to crush the rising. This was done with considerable bloodshed, including the brutal murder of the leaders of the Spartacists. The survivors later formed the German Communist Party (KPD) which remained extremely hostile to the SPD. The elections which Ebert had arranged eventually took place on 19 January, six days after the defeat of the Spartacists. In March 1919, the KPD tried again to organise a revolution in Berlin but, once again, the government allowed the Freikorps to suppress it. At the same time, the far left in Bavaria set up an independent soviet republic; but this too was crushed by the army and Freikorps units in May.

As well as opposition/uprisings from the far left, the Weimar Republic also faced much opposition from the conservative and nationalist right. Most civil servants, judges, and police and army commanders, who had been appointed by the Kaiser, stayed in their posts. They were used to the more authoritarian system of the Kaiser, and tended to see democracy as a foreign idea, which had been forced on the German people by the victorious Allies. These right-wing political attitudes resulted in much violence, including the political murders of leading 'November criminals', e.g. Rathenau, the Foreign Minister, in 1922. Then, in March 1920,

### Proportional representation

*This means that seats in the parliament are allocated according to the number of votes for each party across the country as a whole. If 10% of the voters vote for a particular party, then that party gets 10% of the seats in parliament.*

### Spartacists

*This was a revolutionary Marxist group similar to the Bolsheviks in Russia, and was led by Karl Liebnecht and Rosa Luxemburg. They wanted Germany to have a government based on workers and soldiers' councils or soviets. Liebnecht and Luxemburg advised against a rising in 1918-19, but were outvoted.*

### Freikorps

*These were groups of right-wing nationalist, anti-socialist and anti-communist soldiers. At the end of the war, they acted as armed vigilante squads against left-wingers. They hated the democracy of the Weimar Republic. Noske, the SPD Defence Minister, appeared only too happy to use them to crush the Spartacists.*

Captain Wolfgang Kapp led several units of the Freikorps in an attempt to overthrow the government in Berlin. The police and some of the army were sympathetic to his aims and so did little to protect the government (in fact, the army refused a government request to intervene), but Kapp's Putsch (coup) was defeated by the workers who paralysed Berlin by organising a general strike.

Later that month, the communists organised a 'Red Rising' in the Ruhr valley and in several other areas. Once again, these were defeated by the army and Freikorps units: in all, about 2000 workers were killed before the army gained control.

**Source A**

A Freikorps unit in Berlin in 1920. Note the skull and cross-bones emblem on the front of the armoured car.

## The occupation of the Ruhr, 1923

The Weimar Republic also faced serious economic problems which, in part, stemmed from the high level of reparations which Germany had to pay to the Allies. When the German government announced they could not afford to pay the second instalment, French and Belgian troops invaded the Ruhr, Germany's richest industrial area, in order to take food, coal, iron ore and steel as payment. The German government tried to organise 'passive resistance' and strikes, but many Germans were angry at what they felt was a weak response. Anger increased when German workers were shot in clashes with French troops. The German government then tried to cope with this crisis by printing more money to make up for the loss of income. However, this led to a rapid and serious hyperinflation. Having more paper money but no more goods being produced meant that the German currency soon came to be seen as worthless. While this affected all Germans, some of the worst hit were those on pensions and with savings. This only increased the hatred which many middle-class Germans had for the Weimar Republic.

### Hyperinflation

*This is when prices rise so quickly (inflation) that paper currency rapidly becomes worthless. For instance, German workers soon had to be paid daily instead of weekly because prices were going up so quickly. Soon, they were being paid twice a day, and had to use handcarts or wheelbarrows to take their wages home. Banknotes were so worthless that they were even used to light fires. In 1921, £1 was worth 500 marks, by November 1923, it was worth 14 billion marks!*

### Source B

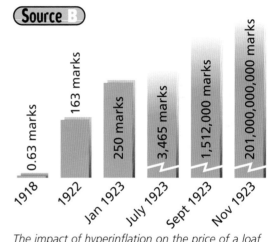

The impact of hyperinflation on the price of a loaf of bread.

### Source C

May I give you some recollections of my own situation at that time? As soon as I received my salary I rushed out to buy the daily necessities. My daily salary... was just enough to buy one loaf of bread and a small piece of cheese or oatmeal...

An acquaintance of mine, a clergyman, came to Berlin from a suburb with his monthly salary to buy a pair of shoes for his baby; he could only buy a cup of coffee.

*Memoirs of a German woman who lived through the hyperinflation of 1923.*

### Questions

1 Explain the rapid price rises in 1923 shown in **Source B**.

2 How far does **Source C** support **Source B** about the effects of the hyperinflation?

# The Nazi Party and the crisis of 1923

**Gustav Stresemann**

*He was the leader of the conservative/liberal DVP Party who, as first Chancellor and then Foreign Minister, played an important part in German politics in the years 1923-29. Although he wanted to undo ('revise') many parts of the Treaty of Versailles, he believed the best way to do this was by peaceful cooperation with the Allies. Under him, Germany later experienced a 'Golden Age' in the 1920s as Europe came out of the depression which had followed the First World War.*

**Source A**

Gustav Stresemann.

**Anti-Semitism**

*This means hatred of Jewish people, and had existed in many European countries for hundreds of years. Mostly, Jews had suffered from discrimination in employment and housing over the years, and at times had been forced to live in Jewish-only 'ghettos'. However, in some countries, such as Tsarist Russia and pre-1900 Poland, violent attacks and riots (pogroms) occasionally took place in which thousands of Jews were injured and killed.*

## Hitler and the crisis

As the crisis continued, a new government was formed in September 1923. This was headed by Gustav Stresemann, who had been appointed by the President. He immediately called off passive resistance and replaced the old mark with a new currency known as the Rentenmark. However, this was extremely unpopular with German nationalists. One of the more extreme groups decided to use the crisis as an opportunity to overthrow Stresemann's government. This group was the Nazi Party, led by Adolf Hitler.

## Hitler and the foundation of the Nazi Party

Hitler was born in Austria in 1889. In 1913, he moved to Munich in Germany and joined the German army when war broke out in 1914. Like many Germans, Hitler was shocked when news of Germany's surrender reached him. After the war and the suppression of the attempt at socialist revolution in Bavaria, Hitler worked for the army in Munich as a political instructor. His main task was to indoctrinate new recruits against the ideas of socialism and democracy, but he was also asked to spy on any new left-wing group that might be set up.

In 1919, he attended a meeting of the small German Workers' Party (DAP) which was led by Anton Drexler. Although it sounded left-wing, the DAP was a right-wing group, with strong nationalist, anti-communist and anti-Jewish ideas. The army soon saw this group as being useful in spreading nationalist ideas. Hitler decided to join it and soon began moves to take control of the DAP. In 1920, he got the party to change its name to the National Socialist German Workers' Party (NSDAP). It soon became known as the Nazi Party and, later that year, Hitler helped design a new Party emblem - based on the swastika.

## Nazi Party beliefs

The NSDAP then adopted a new Twenty-five Point Programme, which was partly written by Hitler and which contained a mixture of nationalism, anti-Semitism and some socialist-sounding policies. In 1921, he became leader of the Nazis and set up the Stormtroopers (SA). Its members were recruited from ex-soldiers and the unemployed, and wore a uniform based on brown shirts. Their main tasks were to protect Nazi meetings, and to break up the political meetings and demonstrations of left-wing groups. Hitler was an effective speaker, and blamed the Treaty of Versailles and all Germany's economic problems on the Weimar government, communists and Jews. The NSDAP grew quickly in southern Germany as a result of Hitler's speeches, SA violence, and donations from various sources including the army. In particular, Ernst Rohm, a local army captain, was able to get funds from the army to enable the Nazis to buy up the *Volkischer Beobachter*, a weekly newspaper. By 1923, the Nazi Party had over 50 000 members.

## The Beer Hall Putsch, 1923

When Stresemann ended passive resistance to the French occupation of the Ruhr in 1923, German nationalists and conservatives were extremely angry. Hitler decided to organise a 'national revolution' against the Weimar government in Berlin. It was to start in Munich and the rest of Bavaria, where the Nazis were strongest and where they received backing from some of the senior army officers and police chiefs. The idea was to take control of Munich and then begin a march on Berlin. In November, Hitler and the SA took over a meeting in a beer hall which was being addressed by von Kahr, the Bavarian leader, and the army and police chiefs, von Lossow and von Seisser. At first, these officials were persuaded to join the plan, but they later changed their minds. The following day, this 'Beer Hall' Putsch failed when the Nazi march of 3000 SA members (led by Hitler, Goering and General Ludendorff) was blocked by the police. In the fighting which followed, one policeman and 16 Nazis were killed. Hitler fled but was later captured while hiding in an attic.

**Source B**

The Beer Hall Putsch. Nazis arrest the mayor and councillors of Munich, 9 November 1923.

Though charged with treason, Hitler was able to use his trial to attack the whole Weimar system, and his supporters gave his speeches wide national exposure for the first time. He was given the lightest possible sentence (5 years instead of life) and sent to Landsberg prison. While he was there, he wrote *Mein Kampf* in which he set down his beliefs and plans. In December 1924, he was released early from prison by the sympathetic authorities in Bavaria, after only serving nine months of his sentence.

**Source C**

If our putsch was high treason, then Lossow, Kahr and Seisser must have been committing high treason along with us, for during all these weeks we talked of nothing but the aims of which we now stand accused.

I alone bear the responsibility for the putsch but I am not a criminal because of that. There is no such thing as treason against the traitors of 1918. I only wanted what is best for the German people.

*An extract from a speech by Hitler during his trial.*

**Mein Kampf**

*This book (the title means 'My Struggle'), written by Hitler while in prison, was a confused ramble which nonetheless contained most of his ideas. In particular, it contained his belief that democracy was bad and that Germany should be ruled by an all-powerful 'Fuhrer' (leader) - the 'Fuhrerprinzip' or 'Fuhrer principle'. He also wrote down his racist beliefs about Jewish people being inferior and the 'Aryans' being the 'Master Race'; and his desire to conquer 'Living Space' ('Lebensraum') for Germany in the east. Because it was so poorly written, not many people read it at the time.*

**Questions**

1 What do you understand by the term *anti-Semitism*?

2 Why did Hitler stage his Beer Hall Putsch in November 1923?

3 What can you learn from **Source B** about the nature of the attempted Nazi putsch in Munich?

4 How reliable is **Source C** as evidence about the involvement of Bavarian officials in Hitler's attempted putsch?

# From recovery to Depression

## Stresemann and recovery

By 1924, Germany was beginning to return to more stable economic and political circumstances. This owed much to the work of Stresemann who, from 1924-29, was extremely influential in government as Foreign Minister. He was able to renegotiate reparation repayments with the Allies on easier terms.

Under the Dawes Plan in 1924, the payments were to be limited to what Germany could afford each year, while the USA agreed to provide loans to help restart German industry. In 1929, the Young Plan extended the repayments timetable, reduced the reparations bill to less than £2000 million and brought further American loans for German industry. Unemployment began to fall, and wages rose every year until 1930.

Stresemann also improved Germany's diplomatic position in Europe. In 1925, he signed the Locarno Pact which promised to accept Germany's western borders as established by the Treaty of Versailles and to keep the Rhineland de-militarised. In return, Allied troops began to withdraw. In 1926, he persuaded the Allies to let Germany join the League of Nations and, in 1928, signed the Kellogg-Briand Pact by which all countries promised to settle disputes peacefully. As a result of these agreements, foreign investment in Germany increased and, by 1929, Germany was the world's second most advanced industrial nation.

## The Nazis' 'Lean Years', 1924-30

On his release from prison, Hitler found that Stresemann's policies were already beginning to improve Germany's economic situation. As a result, support for extreme political parties began to decline. In addition, the Nazi Party had begun to break up into various factions. Thus, from 1924-30, the Nazis experienced their 'Lean Years', in which they received little electoral support. After winning 32 seats in the first elections in 1924, they won only 14 in the second election in that year and only 12 in 1928.

However, Hitler quickly set about reasserting his control over the Party. Regional Party leaders (Gauleiters) were appointed who were answerable only to Hitler. He also set up a series of different sections for the Party in order to recruit more members, for instance, the Hitler Youth, and sections for students and teachers. In 1925, he set up the Schutz Staffel (SS). Hitler also decided that the Nazis would have to use elections in order to gain power, but the Nazis continued to use violence in the streets against left-wing parties. Hitler also began to establish links with wealthy industrialists. An added boost came in 1928, when the newspaper owner Alfred Hugenberg, became leader of the conservative DNVP and joined in a national campaign with the Nazis against Stresemann's policies.

### Schutz Staffel (SS)

*This protection squad was set up in 1925, as part of the SA. In 1929, Himmler became its leader, and it rapidly grew in size (from 200 to 50 000). The recruits for the SS and the SD, its security branch (Sicherheitsdienst) which was set up in 1932, tended to come mostly from the educated middle classes. Later, after Hitler had become Chancellor of Germany, it was used by him to murder the SA leaders in 1934 and it became a separate organisation. In 1936, all police organisations, including the Gestapo, were placed under Himmler's control. Heydrich, Himmler's deputy, was put in charge of the SD. Its Death's Head Units ran the concentration and extermination camps, and the Waffen SS were special military units which fought alongside the regular army.*

**Source A**

*Himmler and Heydrich, leaders of the SS. This photograph was taken after the Nazis were established in power.*

## The Depression

By 1929, the German economy seemed to be booming. However, it was not as strong as it seemed. Although new industries had been created, much of this was based on foreign loans and investments, and Germany always had a balance of trade deficit (imports were greater than exports) which it tried to ignore by increased borrowing. As a result of these factors, and an increase in population, unemployment never dropped much below 1.3 million. Then, in October 1929, Stresemann died and a few weeks later, the USA's stock market on Wall Street crashed. The USA stopped further loans to Germany, which now had to repay earlier ones. Industry soon went into depression as world trade declined, and unemployment grew rapidly - by 1932, it had risen to six million.

### Source B

However, the rapidity of the German recovery [after 1923] was deceptive. There was economic growth but the balance of trade was consistently in the red. Unemployment never fell below 1.3 million in this period and it was averaging 1.9 million during 1929. The population increased during the 1920s pushing up the jobless total... The German economy depended on foreign money... The Government balanced the budget in 1924 but from then on had a deficit. Rather than cut back they spent more and borrowed from abroad to pay for it... All this suggests the German economy was in a precarious state long before the Depression.

*Extract from a history textbook, published in 1997.*

*"Millions stand behind me" A photomontage by the anti-Nazi John Heartfield, 1933.*

### Questions

1 What, according to **Source B**, was the main weakness of the German economic revival in the years after 1924?

2 What is the poster in **Source C** trying to suggest about the connection between the Nazi Party and big business in Germany?

3 What problems of reliability are there with this source?

4 Why were the years 1924-30 known as the Nazis' 'Lean Years'?

# Hitler's rise to power

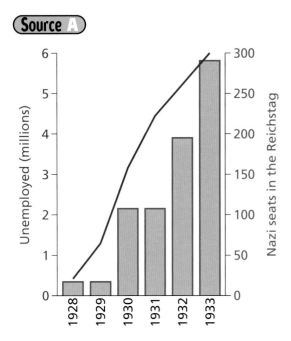

*The rise of Nazi seats in the Reichstag and the growth of unemployment in Germany, 1928-1933.*

## Elections, 1930-32

It was the Wall Street Crash and the subsequent Depression which gave Hitler the chance to achieve power. The growing unemployment and poverty made it difficult for the coalition governments of the Weimar Republic to agree on what policies should be adopted. As a result, there were frequent changes of government, and President Hindenburg (who had become President in 1925 but, unlike Ebert, had never liked the Weimar system) increasingly used his powers under Article 48 to rule by decree.

The Nazis stepped up their violence against the communists and, at the same time, blamed all Germany's problems on the Weimar governments, the Treaty of Versailles and the Jews. The violence seemed to prove to many that the government was weak and that only the Nazis were strong enough to take action against the communists. As more and more conservatives and nationalists turned to the Nazis, the number of Reichstag seats for the NSDAP began to increase. In September 1930, they went up to 107 after Chancellor Bruning had failed to get acceptance of his new government's policies and had called for fresh elections. Bruning failed to get enough votes for his centre-right coalition, so Hindenburg used his power to issue decrees to push through Bruning's plans for cuts in government spending and increased taxes in 1931. By 1932, over 15 million Germans were dependent on State benefits or charity, and Bruning became known as the 'Hunger Chancellor'. He was then brought down by his right-wing opponents in May 1932, and was replaced as Chancellor by von Papen who was on the right of the Centre Party and whose new government was known as the 'cabinet of barons' as almost all were members of the German aristocracy.

## Political rivalries

Under the control of Goebbels, the Nazi propaganda machine, helped by increased donations from large industrialists and land owners, gave wide coverage of Nazi promises to overturn the Treaty of Versailles, and to make Germany great again, as it had been under the Kaiser. This, combined with Hitler's speaking powers and the worsening economic situation, led to even more election successes. In the March 1932 Presidential election, Hitler polled 13 million votes to Hindenburg's 19 million; and in the July 1932 elections, the Nazis won 230 seats and became the largest single party in the Reichstag. However, in the November 1932 elections, their number of seats dropped to 196, while the communists' share increased again, to 100 seats. In December, Hindenburg sacked von Papen and appointed von Schleicher (head of the German army) as Chancellor. However, political rivalries led to von Papen persuading Hindenburg to sack von Schleicher and instead appoint Hitler as Chancellor of a conservative-dominated

### Goebbels

*He joined the Nazi Party in 1922 and, at first, had joined with Strasser and other more militant members to oppose Hitler. However, in 1926, he was persuaded to change sides. In 1929, Hitler put him in charge of Nazi propaganda. He excelled in this, and after the Nazis took power in Germany, he was made Reichsminister of Popular Enlightenment and Propaganda.*

### 1932 Presidential election

*Goebbels made good use of the increase in Nazi funds for this election. Hitler was flown to meetings by plane as part of a 'Hitler over Germany' campaign.*

coalition government in which von Papen felt he would be the real power. So, on 30 January 1933, Hitler became Chancellor of Germany.

*Hitler speaking in Berlin during the presidential election campaign, March 1932. Goebbels is directly behind him.*

## The March 1933 election

Although there were only three Nazis in the Cabinet, one of them, Wilhelm Frick, was Minister of the Interior and so in charge of the police. Hitler decided to move quickly to increase Nazi power and control. He called an election for March 1933, and stepped up SA and SS violence against anti-Nazis, especially the communists. Just before voting was to take place, the Reichstag building caught fire on 27 February and a young Dutch ex-communist, Marinus van der Lubbe, was arrested at the scene and later executed for the crime. Hitler used this Reichstag Fire to accuse the KPD (Communist Party) of trying to start a revolution, and got Hindenburg to agree to an emergency law (the Decree for the Protection of the People and the State) on 28 February.

In Prussia, a state that covered two-thirds of Germany, the Nazi official in charge of police was Hermann Goering. He simply enrolled 50 000 SA men as police 'auxiliaries' to round up the Communists. The KPD's newspapers were banned and many Communists were arrested and some murdered, while other parties (especially the SPD) were intimidated by arrests and the breaking-up of their meetings. However, the Nazis still failed to win an overall majority. This was also despite the fact that the Nazi Party election fund had been boosted by 3 million Reichsmarks which had been promised after a meeting with wealthy industrialists on 20 February.

**Reichstag Fire**

*Van der Lubbe was eventually given a pardon by the West German government almost 50 years after the events. Historians are not certain whether the Nazis started the fire themselves. However, the fire seems to have started in several places at once, which makes it unlikely that it was the work of one man. Even if van der Lubbe was involved, there is no evidence to suggest that van der Lubbe was acting on the instructions of the KPD.*

**Questions**

1 How does **Source A** suggest a link between the Depression and the Nazis' rise to power?

2 Draw up a list of all the factors that helped the Nazis' rise to power. For each one explain briefly how it helped.

3 How important was Hitler himself in the Nazis' rise to power?

# CHAPTER 7

# The Nazi dictatorship

## Source A

The other parties have had 14 years to prove their abilities. The result is a heap of ruins. Now, German people, give us four years and then judge us.

*Extract from Hitler's 'Appeal to the German People', 31 January 1933.*

## Source B

The Communists reacted to the news of Hitler's appointment by arranging a protest demonstration in the city centre at which a general strike was to be announced. ...When Communist supporters began to assemble, about 500 Stormtroopers decided to march through the square. The police kept about 500-600 Communist supporters out of the square while the SA paraded around; when the planned demonstration did start, the police quickly intervened to stop it.... The SPD in Breslau had adopted a 'wait and see' attitude; they saw the results of the Communist demonstrations as justifying their own decision to do nothing.

*An eye-witness account of events in Breslau on 31 January 1933, published in 1987.*

## 'Second Revolution'

*This was the call made by the more militant members of the Nazis who wanted the anti-capitalist points of the 1920 Party Programme carried out, now that the Nazis were in power and had defeated the Communists (the 'First Revolution'). These promises had included making large firms share profits with workers and the confiscation of some firms, along with vague policies to limit 'international high finance', as well as improvements in pensions and other State benefits. However, these views had been extremely unpopular with the upper classes and the military elites and, since 1925, most of the Nazi leadership had been quietly moving away from these promises.*

## The Enabling Act and dictatorship

Although the Nazis had failed to win an outright majority in the March 1933 elections, von Papen's small nationalist party (the DNVP) had won 52 seats. Even though they supported the Nazis, Hitler only got a majority in the Reichstag after the KPD deputies (MPs) had been excluded. But Hitler wanted a two-thirds majority so he could destroy the Weimar Constitution altogether. To achieve this support, he made promises to the Centre Party to respect the Catholic Church in Germany, and they agreed to his plans. With SA and SS members crowded round them, all but the SPD deputies voted for an Enabling Act which gave Hitler the power to declare a state of emergency and rule by decree for four years, without having to get the approval of the Reichstag.

The Nazis then moved quickly to establish their dictatorship by a process of 'coordination' (Gleichschaltung). To begin with, Communists and other 'politicals' were put into concentration camps run by the SA. By the end of July, there were already over 25 000 prisoners in these camps. In April, Nazi officials known as Gauleiters took control of all of Germany's 18 Lander (provinces). The Nazis began to abolish all state governments and then to appoint Nazi governors. In May, all trade unions (which had mostly supported the SPD or the KPD) were banned, their leaders arrested and their assets seized. In June, the SPD were banned, and three other parties disbanded themselves. In July, the Centre Party also disbanded and, on 14 July, after continued attacks and arrests, all opposition parties were banned by the Law against the Formation of Parties. Germany thus became a one-party state.

## The Night of the Long Knives

Although Hitler had secured control of Germany, he still faced some opposition from within his own party. It came from the more militant sections of the NSDAP who now wanted a 'Second Revolution' to carry out the 'socialist' promises made in the Party Programme. An important leader of this opposition was Ernst Rohm, head of the SA since 1930, who wanted the German army to be merged with the SA under his control. By 1934, there were over 1 million men in the SA. But some Nazi leaders, such as Himmler and Goering, despised the SA men and their more militant political demands.

Rohm's plans also worried the Nazis' industrialist backers and alarmed the army - both important groups in Hitler's rise to power. In addition, he would need a loyal army to conquer the 'Living Space' he wanted for Germany. After discussions with some of the army leaders, Hitler ordered the SS to murder Rohm and other SA leaders. This took place in June 1934 and became known as the Night of the Long Knives. In all, about 400 people were murdered.

THEY SALUTE WITH BOTH HANDS NOW.

*A cartoon by David Low, published in Britain in 1934.*

## Hitler becomes Fuhrer

Shortly after this event, in August 1934, Hindenburg died and the army (which had provided weapons and transport for the Night of the Long Knives) then supported Hitler combining the jobs of President and Chancellor, and so becoming Fuhrer (Leader) of Germany. The army also agreed to swear an oath of loyalty to Hitler since 1930 as Commander-in-Chief of the armed forces. The Nazis now moved to create a totalitarian dictatorship in order to prevent any possible opposition in the future.

### Questions

1  How does **Source B** help to explain the rapid Nazi takeover in 1933?
2  What event of June 1934 does **Source C** refer to?
3  What can you learn about this event from **Source C**?
4  Construct a timeline of the main events in the creation of the Nazi dictatorship during the years 1933-34.

# Maintaining power

## Propaganda and censorship

Once in power, the Nazis wasted no time in ensuring the maintenance of their role. Goebbels, who was placed in charge of propaganda and culture, established control over newspapers, the radio and the cinema, and over the arts in general. Newspapers were either closed down, or taken over by the Nazis' own publishing company; while the Editors' Law in October 1933, reduced the powers of the owners who remained, and instead simply told editors what they could and could not publish. All Communist, Socialist and Jewish journalists were sacked. This control was extended in November 1933, when the Nazis set up the Press Chamber and, by 1939, the Nazis owned almost 70% of the Press. At the same time, all newspapers had to use the state press agency (the DNB) as the only source for news stories.

Goebbels also ensured that cheap radios (volksempfanger - the 'people's receivers') were made available to make sure Nazi views were heard regularly by as many people as possible - by 1939, 70% of German households had a radio. Loudspeakers were also placed in factories, the streets and public places, while the mass Party Nuremberg rallies were filmed and shown at the cinemas.

## Terror and the police state

As well as censorship and propaganda, the Nazis also relied on terror. In April 1933, Himmler was given control of all the political police in Bavaria, but soon extended his power at the expense of Frick, the Interior Minister. By 1934, helped by his deputy, Heydrich (who ran the SD), he had control of all states except Goering's Prussia. Here, a secret police force known as the Gestapo was given the power to arrest and murder, while they and the NSDAP used informers everywhere to discover any potential opponents. In 1936, Himmler took control of all police forces when he became head of the new Reich Central Security Office (RSHA). In 1939, Heydrich became its head.

## The Nazi state

In theory, Hitler was supposed to be in complete control of the Party and the State, and Goebbels deliberately created a 'cult of personality' around Hitler - the 'Hitler Myth'. However, instead of the disciplined and ordered structure which was presented to Germans and the rest of the world, the reality was often quite different. Hitler in fact was lazy and often did not even begin to work until the afternoon. Also, in order to make sure he stayed in control, he deliberately set up conflicting government and Party organisations, and encouraged rivalries between the different Nazi leaders - such as Goering and Himmler. The SS, for instance, was eventually able to establish a massive economic empire of its own, via the occupied territories and the extermination camps, and often

**Gestapo**

*This was the Secret State Police (the Geheime Staatspolitzei), which had been set up by Goering in Prussia in 1933. Its job was to find all opponents of the Nazi regime, and it was allowed to use any means necessary. Thus it was able to break the law by torturing and even murdering arrested suspects. Its method of arresting suspects in the early hours of the morning was known as the 'Night and Fog' tactic. It also encouraged all 'loyal' Germans to spy on their neighbours and family and denounce all critics of Hitler and the Nazi state. In 1936, it was placed under Himmler's control, when he became Reichsfuhrer SS in charge of all police forces in Germany.*

acted as a powerful 'state within the state'. Nonetheless, Hitler made all the important decisions, and his personal reputation remained unaffected, even when some Nazi leaders or policies were unpopular.

## The economy

However, as well as using coercion and propaganda, the Nazis also tried to maintain power by adopting popular economic policies. Hitler's economic plans were not precise, but he wanted to make Germany self-sufficient and to re-arm the country in defiance of the Treaty of Versailles. Despite the promises made previously to limit the wealth and power of big firms, there was no attempt to achieve State ownership of the economy. In order to reassure the business world, Hitler appointed Schacht (a non-Nazi and head of the Reichsbank) as Minister of the Economy, a post he held until he resigned in 1937. Schacht's job was to develop a 'New Plan' to provide Germany with the raw materials needed for rearmament, and to finance public works to reduce unemployment, without increasing Germany's foreign debts.

## Unemployment

First of all, Hitler concentrated on reducing unemployment. He was helped in this by the fact that the earlier policies of previous governments were beginning to have an effect, while international trade was starting to pick up. He expanded the National Labour Service (Arbeitdienst), which had been set up before he became Chancellor. This service used government money to fund public works' schemes, which included the building of autobahns (motorways) and houses. In 1935, the Reich Labour Law made working for the NLS compulsory for all 18-25 year olds for six months. Unemployment was also reduced by forcing women and Jews out of work, while the Communists, Socialists, trade unionists and Jews put into concentration camps were not counted as unemployed. When trade unions were abolished in 1933, workers were forced to join the Nazi Labour Front (DAF), which was led by Robert Ley. Strikes were made illegal, and the hours of work were increased. Though there were price controls, real wages remained below the levels workers had enjoyed before 1929. To distract the workers' attention from this, the DAF began two schemes. The 'Beauty of Labour' (Schonheit der Arbeit) tried to improve working conditions, but achieved little. More was done via the 'Strength through Joy' (Kraft durch Freude) scheme, which provided free or subsidised holidays, cultural and sporting events and facilities. However, its Volkswagen (people's car) scheme tricked workers into putting 5 marks a week into a fund to buy a car. The few cars which were built went to Nazi officials, and most of the money was spent on rearmament.

*An Extract from a speech by Robert Ley, May 1933.*

**Source C**

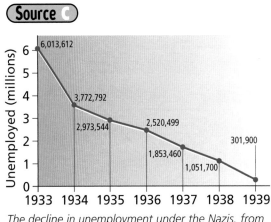

*The decline in unemployment under the Nazis, from 1933-39.*

# Nazi policies and their impact

## Agriculture

In order to achieve self-sufficiency, agriculture was encouraged to increase production, while imports were reduced and firms were encouraged to develop substitutes for foreign imports wherever possible. Attempts were made to keep food prices down below the 1928-29 levels, and the Reich Entailed Farm Law in 1933 stopped peasant farmers from splitting up their farms between their sons. Although the law also gave farmers protection from being evicted for debts, many farmers who had been strong supporters of the Nazis were disappointed. Smaller businesses, which had also been promised help by the Nazis against big businesses before 1933, found that although restrictions were placed on interest charges, the Nazis now encouraged bigger firms to take over smaller ones.

## Rearmament

Rearmament, which began secretly after 1933 and then openly after 1935, resulted in the building of thousands of tanks, aircraft and warships and helped further reduce unemployment. Conscription was also introduced, which increased the army from the 100 000 allowed by the Treaty of Versailles to over 1.4 million. This, too, reduced unemployment levels. Rearmament was stepped up in 1936, when Goering was put in charge of a Four Year Plan to prepare Germany for war. Goering's growing demands for resources worried Schacht, who realised that Germany was already spending more money than it was earning. When Hitler refused his request that the rearmament programme be slowed down, Schacht resigned in 1937.

## Women

The Nazis had strong ideas on the role of women and how they could contribute to making the Third Reich a powerful country. These ideas and policies were based on the traditional 'Three Ks': Kinder, Kucher, Kirche (Children, Kitchen, Church). Laws were passed to remove women from civil service and other government and professional jobs so these could be given to unemployed men. Interest-free loans were given to young women who gave up work to marry, and labour exchanges and employers were told to give preference to men. Women were also encouraged to marry and have large families, by a system of marriage loans, improved maternity benefits, grants for each fourth child and above, and bronze, silver or gold medals ('The Mother Cross') for having six, eight or ten children. Abortion was made illegal, and contraceptive advice and family planning clinics were reduced.

The Nazis made sure no woman held any important leadership post in the Party, and opposed the idea of equality for women. They even tried to control women's appearance so that they conformed to traditional images: make-up and hair-dyeing were

**Source A**

'Family' - a 1930s painting by W. Willrich, depicting the stereotypical Nazi ideal of an Aryan family.

**Three Ks**

The Nazis believed there was a 'natural' division between the genders. While men were 'born' to work, engage in politics and fight in wars, women were 'intended by nature' to reproduce and be passive, so they should remain housewives and mothers. If they did work outside the home, they should stick to jobs related to their 'natural' function, e.g. nursing or social work. This attitude meant that, during the war, Germany had far fewer women working in war industries than the Allies.

discouraged, and women seen smoking in public were criticised. The Nazi organisations for women - the NSF (National Sozialistische Frauenschaft - National Socialist Womanhood) and the DFW (Deutsches Frauenwerk - German Women's Enterprise) - constantly promoted the Nazi views about a woman's role.

To 'improve' the Aryan stock, infertile women could be divorced, and forced sterilisation was carried out to prevent the birth of any children who might not be 'fit' Aryans. By 1939, over 375 000 Germans had been sterilised.

## Young people

The Nazis tried to ensure that the younger and future generations would be loyal supporters of Hitler and the NSDAP. Schools were placed under central government control, and a new national curriculum was imposed which emphasised the greatness of Hitler and Germany. All teachers had to join the Nazi Teachers' League (by 1937, 97% of teachers were members), and all Jewish or politically 'unreliable' teachers were sacked. In 1934, Bernhard Rust became Minister for Science and Education, and under him a much greater emphasis was placed on nationalist history, and all textbooks were replaced by a new official one which attacked the 'enemies' of Germany and showed how the Nazis were saving the country. Biology lessons were centred on the Nazis' 'race science', which tried to indoctrinate pupils into thinking that the 'Aryans' were a 'superior' race (Herren Volk), while Jewish, Slavic and black people were inferior. The amount of time devoted to PE was tripled, and a great emphasis was placed on getting boys fit for war and girls fit for producing large families. One result was a decline in educational standards. Those with any physical handicap were not allowed to receive any secondary education.

Outside of school, the Nazis also made great efforts to control and indoctrinate young people with Nazi ideas and values. All young people were encouraged to join one of the various Hitler Youth (Hitler Jugend - HJ) movements for boys and girls of all ages.

### Questions

1 What did the Nazis do to try to achieve the 'ideal' woman shown in **Source A**?

2 How useful is **Source B** as evidence of the reactions of young Germans to the Hitler Youth?

3 Were the Nazis' attempts to indoctrinate young people always successful? Use **Source B** and your own knowledge to explain your answer.

### Source B

When I became a leader in the Jungvolk the negative aspects became very obvious. I found the compulsion and the requirement of absolute obedience unpleasant. I appreciated that there must be order and discipline in such a large number of boys, but it was exaggerated. It was preferred that people should not have a will of their own and should totally subordinate themselves... when I moved to Bann headquarters and acquired rather more insight I had the first serious doubts. The Hitler Youth was interfering everywhere in people's private lives. If one had private interests apart from the Hitler Youth people looked askance.

*Extract from A. Klonne's memoirs 'Youth in the Third Reich', published in 1982, describing his experiences in the Hitler Youth.*

### Aryans

*According to Hitler, the 'Aryans' were the north European (Nordic) 'races' who, with their blue eyes and blond hair, were superior to the dark-haired and dark-eyed Mediterranean 'races', and especially to 'inferior races' such as Jewish and Slavic peoples. He wanted to create a 'pure' Aryan race of Germans (hence no 'inter-breeding') who would be allowed to belong to the 'folk community' (Volksgemeinschaft) and go on to dominate Europe and the world as the 'Master Race'.*

### Hitler Youth

*In July 1933, von Schirach, the leader of the HJ, was made Youth Leader of the Reich, and rival youth organisations were shut down. At times, there was rivalry betwen Rust and von Schirach over the conflicting demands made on children's time. In December 1936, the Hitler Youth Law made the HJ officially as important as school and family, and it increased pressure on parents to ensure their children joined the HJ. In 1939, membership was made compulsory.*

# Anti-Semitism and the Final Solution

## Nazi racism

The Nazis were strongly racist and believed that the Germans, and other 'Aryans', were the 'Master Race' which alone created 'culture'. They saw other groups as racially inferior, especially Jews, but also Slavs, the Roma and Sinti (gypsies) and blacks. Their obsession with 'racial purity' also led them to order the compulsory sterilisation of disabled people and criminals and, later, the murder of mentally and physically handicapped people.

## Anti-Semitism, 1933-38

However, it was the Jews who were the main victims of Nazi racism. Hitler and the Nazis justified their treatment of the Jewish population by blaming them for communism and Germany's defeat in the First World War. They also used the pseudo-scientific ideas of what was known as 'Social Darwinism' to push their idea that 'inferior' races were a threat that had to be dealt with in order to 'save' the German nation. Although there were only about 600 000 German Jews (one per cent of the population), the Nazi regime persecuted them in a number of ways which became increasingly violent. Apart from general anti-Jewish propaganda both within and outside schools, the new Nazi government wasted no time in putting pressure on the Jewish community in Germany. The SA and SS almost immediately launched a boycott of all Jewish-owned shops and businesses in April 1933. However, this did not receive widespread support, and so was called off after only one day.

Hitler then decided to use the law against Jews. The first law (the Law for the Restoration of the Professional Civil Service), in 1933, banned all Jews from holding State jobs. This was followed, once the Nazis were securely in power, by the Nuremberg Laws in 1935. These were a number of laws, such as the Reich Citizenship Law which removed all citizenship rights from Jews, and the Law for the Protection of German Blood and Honour which banned any marriage or relationship between Aryans and Jews. From 1936, after the Olympic Games had been held in Berlin, there were further laws which restricted Jewish ownership of property, banned Jews from all professional jobs and removed all Jewish children from State schools. Many Jewish business owners had no choice but to sell up at low prices, and many decided to emigrate to other countries. In 1938, all Jewish men and women had their passports stamped with a large letter J.

## Increased violence, 1938-41

After 1938, Nazi policy towards Jews became more violent. When a Jewish student shot dead a German diplomat in Paris, as a protest against the discrimination against Jews (including his own parents) in Germany, the Nazis responded with what became known as Kristallnacht (Night of Broken Glass) in November 1938. The SA

**Source A**

A humiliated Jewish man with a shaved head is forced to walk the streets wearing this sign declaring that he is a Jew.

**Source B**

In the summer of 1941... I was suddenly summoned to the Reichsfuhrer SS [Heinrich Himmler]... he said to me in effect "The Fuhrer [Hitler] has ordered that the Jewish Question be solved once and for all and we, the SS, are to implement that order..."

The final solution of the Jewish Question meant the complete extermination of all Jews in Europe. I was ordered to establish extermination facilities at Auschwitz in June 1941....

I visited Treblinka to find out how they carried out their extermination. The camp commandant at Treblinka told me he had liquidated 80 000 in the course of half a year...

He used monoxide gas and I did not think his methods were very efficient. So when I set up the extermination building at Auschwitz, I used Zyklon B.... It took from three to fifteen minutes to kill all the people in the death chamber... We knew when the people were dead because the screaming stopped.

Extracts from the evidence given by R. Hoess, commandant of Auschwitz, at the Nuremberg Trials, 1946.

and SS, encouraged by Goebbels, organised attacks on Jewish homes, shops and synagogues in a week-long campaign of terror. Over 100 Jews were killed, 20 000 were put in concentration camps, and thousands of homes and shops were destroyed. The Nazi government then fined the Jewish community one billion marks for the damage done. By 1939, nearly all Jewish businesses had been closed down or forced to sell.

Jews in Germany were then forced to live in ghettoes and the violence increased. Once the war began, these policies were applied to all the Jews living in the newly-conquered states of western and eastern Europe. In Poland, Jewish people were deliberately deprived of food, which forced them to work in labour camps where many died from starvation and disease.

## The Final Solution

By June 1941, the Nazi invasion of Poland and then the USSR had brought even more Jews under Nazi control. From July 1941, it was decided to eliminate all Jews in what became known as the 'Final Solution' (Endlosung) of the 'Jewish Question'. At first, this was carried out by Himmler's SS, which formed special action groups (Einsatzgruppen) to organise mass shootings of Jews. In all, these units had murdered about 2 million Communist officials and Jews by 1943. It was decided to coordinate plans and to exterminate the Jewish population of Europe more methodically. On 20 January 1942, the Wannsee Conference took place in Berlin, at which leading Nazis agreed on a programme of mass extermination, with Adolf Eichmann given overall planning responsibility. Special extermination camps were constructed in parts of Poland, which would be able to kill large numbers in gas chambers. Once these were built, special trains transported millions of Jews across Europe for mass extermination in camps such as Auschwitz. In all, about six million Jews were murdered. In addition to Jewish people, other groups deemed by the Nazis as 'inferior' - such as Slavs, Sinti and Roma, and homosexuals - were also murdered. Their numbers came to about five million.

### Questions

1 Look at **Source A**. How else did the Nazis persecute Jews in the years 1933-35?

2 What were the main steps towards the 'Final Solution' referred to in **Source B**?

3 What, according to the evidence of **Source B**, was the role played by Hitler in this 'Final Solution'?

4 How useful is **Source B** as historical evidence concerning the planning of the 'Final Solution'?

### Final Solution

*From 1939-41, Nazi leaders considered various policies for dealing with the Jewish population of Europe, including the 'Madagascar Plan' to forcibly deport them to the island of Madagascar. At one time, Hitler seems to have preferred this option but, although he did not finally abandon it until February 1942, from the end of 1940 he had begun to consider mass extermination as an alternative. Another plan was simply to work them to death as slave labour. By May 1941, Hitler had come to favour a combination of these second and third options, and appears to have given orders for this, but no written evidence survives. However, in July 1941, Goering sent a written order to Heydrich to prepare the 'final solution'. Hitler stayed away from the Wannsee Conference, but it is extremely unlikely that such actions would have been taken without his order to do so. Hoess, the commandant of Auschwitz, claimed Himmler had told him that Hitler had ordered the SS to solve the 'Jewish Question' 'once and for all'. This mass murder is often known as the 'Holocaust'.*

### Extermination camps

*These should not be confused with the concentration camps which had been set up in Germany from 1933 to imprison and punish political opponents, and later Jews as well. While many people were killed or died in these concentration camps, there was no deliberate policy of extermination. In all, six mass extermination (or death) camps were built in Nazi-occupied Poland - Auschwitz-Birkenau, Belzec, Treblinka, Sobibor, Chelmno and Majdanek. Although the SS and SD were in overall charge, very large numbers of ordinary German and local officials and personnel were also involved. These included the Ordnungspolizei (Order Police) which consisted of the uniformed German police and locally-recruited auxiliaries, the army which at times provided transport and guards for the Einsatzgruppen, and large numbers of civil servants, industrial firms (such as I.G. Farben, which made the gas) and medical staff.*

# Popularity, opposition and the war

## Support for Hitler and the Nazis

In the last free elections in Germany in November 1932, the Nazis had only received 34% of the vote. In March 1933, despite much intimidation and violence, they had only been able to push this up to 43%. From then on, it is difficult to assess just how many Germans supported Hitler and his Nazi dictatorship. However, many Germans (who were not Jewish, Socialist or Communist) were content with early Nazi policies on unemployment and German rearmament. Until 1942, when the war began to go badly for Germany, many approved of his destruction of the Treaty of Versailles and the early German conquests which brought increased food supplies and raw materials to Germany.

## Opposition

However, despite Gestapo and SS terror and Nazi propaganda, there were Germans who were prepared to risk punishment in order to resist the Nazi regime. Although the KPD and the SPD still refused to cooperate with each other, both political parties set up underground organisations which published newsletters, put up posters and even carried out industrial sabotage in order to weaken the Nazi war machine. The Communist Red Orchestra (Rote Kapelle) group also passed on military secrets to the Soviet Union until they were betrayed and arrested by the Gestapo.

Young people also resisted. Many hated the Hitler Youth groups and refused to join, even after it became compulsory in 1936. Some formed rebel music and fashion groups, such as the Meuten, the Edelweiss Pirates or the Swing Movement. These listened to music which the Nazis said was 'degenerate' (such as jazz and swing) and danced forbidden dances. At times, the working-class groups (the Meuten and the Pirates) even beat up members of the Hitler Youth. Other youth opposition groups were more political. The White Rose Group at Munich University was made up of students who issued anti-Nazi leaflets and called on people to resist the Nazis. Their leaders, Hans and Sophie Scholl, Christoph Probst, Alex Schmorell and Willi Graf (along with their professor, Kurt Huber) were eventually arrested and beheaded in February 1943.

Some members of the Churches also offered some resistance: some individuals opposed the growing persecution of Jews, while the Catholic Church in particular forced Hitler to end the policy of euthanasia of the 'mentally-ill'. The most outspoken critic was von Galen, the Archbishop of Munster. When Hitler tried to control the Protestant Churches by setting up a Reich Church, Pastor Niemoller formed the Confessing Church in opposition, and was later sent to a concentration camp.

Some upper-class Germans had initially supported the Nazis because of their strong actions against the Communists. Later

**Source A**

*The execution of twelve Edelweiss Pirates in Cologne, 10 November 1944. They were hanged for anti-Nazi activities.*

**Source B**

The day of reckoning has come, the day when German youth will settle accounts with the vilest tyranny ever endured by our nation. In the name of German youth, we demand from Adolf Hitler's state the restoration of personal freedom...

We grew up in a state where every free expression of opinion has been ruthlessly suppressed. Hitler Youth, storm troops, and SS have tried...to regiment... and to narcotise [drug] us....

There can be but one word of action for us: Fight the Party! Quit the Party organisations... Students! The eyes of the German nation are upon us. Germany expects from us, from the might of the spirit, the destruction of the National Socialist terror in 1943....

*An extract from a pamphlet distributed by the White Rose Group in Munich, February 1943.*

many (especially those who were part of what was known as the Kreisau Circle, which met at the home of the aristocrat von Moltke) became alienated by the corruption which was widespread amongst the Nazi Party's leaders and government officials. The Kreisau Circle were eventually executed in the years 1944-45.

In some ways, the most serious opposition to Hitler came from within the High Command of the German army. There had been some officers (the Beck-Goerdeler Group) who had feared Hitler's policy over Czechoslovakia in 1938 might lead to war; but the most serious threat to Hitler came in July 1944. Many officers feared Hitler was leading Germany to destruction, and some had tried to contact the Allies to see if peace could be made with the USA and Britain, so allowing Germany to concentrate on defeating Russia. In July 1944, von Stauffenberg and others decided to blow Hitler up. Although the bomb went off, Hitler survived. The plotters either committed suicide or were tortured and then executed.

## The impact of the war

Whatever support the Nazis had before 1939, it is clear that they lost support as the war went on. Despite Goering's Four Year Plan, Germany was not ready for a long war in 1939. To begin with, the period 1939-40 saw an uninterrupted series of successes for German Blitzkrieg methods. Within a year, Germany had conquered or defeated the western half of Poland, the Netherlands, Belgium, France and Norway. At first, the invasion of the Soviet Union which began in June 1941 was also extremely successful. However, from the winter of 1941-42, Germany began to suffer reversals in the USSR and in North Africa. Rationing had to be introduced because of food shortages, and, after 1942, Germany experienced increasingly heavy Allied bombing. The longer the war continued, the more the hardships and suffering increased. By 1945, Germany was in ruins. With the Soviet Red Army entering the suburbs of Berlin in May 1945, Hitler committed suicide. Yet many Germans still believed in the 'Hitler Myth' - that Hitler knew everything and that all his actions were for the good of Germany.

### Questions

1 Who were the Edelweiss Pirates (shown in **Source A**), and what were their main activities?

2 How useful are **Sources A** and **B** for finding out about opposition to the Nazis amongst young people?

3 Why was most opposition to the Nazis not very effective?

4 What does the July bomb plot, shown in **Source C**, tell us about the nature and extent of opposition to Hitler?

### The Beck-Goerdeler Group

*This was the main conservative resistance to the Nazis amongst the army and civil service leadership. Colonel Beck was Chief of the Army General Staff from 1935-38, and Goerdeler was Mayor of Leipzig until he was replaced in 1936. In 1938, Beck feared Hitler's policy over Czechoslovakia would provoke a war which Germany would lose, but his attempts to get backing from Britain for a coup failed, and so he resigned his post. Beck continued to work closely with Goerdeler to build up a network of opponents to the Nazis in the army, foreign office and various police and intelligence organisations, including the Abwehr (military intelligence).*

### Von Stauffenberg

*Colonel von Stauffenberg came from an aristocratic Catholic family and, along with Major-General von Tresckow and Field Marshal von Witzleben, was one of the leading army resisters after 1938. He was the main organiser of the attempted assassination of Hitler in July 1944, which he began plotting in 1943. Unlike the Beck-Goerdeler group which also became involved, he wanted Germany to return to democracy after Hitler's assassination. Although von Stauffenberg successfully left the bomb (hidden inside his briefcase) next to Hitler who was chairing a meeting, someone moved it after von Stauffenberg had left, and Hitler suffered only slight injuries. Many of the leading conspirators were hanged with piano wire, suspended from meathooks. Their execution was filmed so Hitler could watch it later.*

**Source C**

Goering and Bormann examining the damage caused by the bomb planted by von Stauffenberg in July 1944.

# SUMMARY

## 1918–1923

- The Kiel Mutiny sparked off a revolution. A new provisional government signed the armistice in November 1918.
- The Weimar Republic was established. The Nazi Party was formed.
- The Treaty of Versailles led to Kapp's Putsch in 1920. Opposition to Weimar democracy from the right increased.
- The French occupied the Ruhr in 1923. Hyperinflation was ended by Stresemann. The Nazis' Beer Hall Putsch fails.

## 1924–1929

- Reparation payments were reduced by the Dawes and Young Plans. Germany was allowed to join the League of Nations in 1926.
- Hitler was released from prison, and began to reorganise the Nazi Party.
- In October 1929 the US Wall Street Crash began the Great Depression. Loans from the USA ceased, and unemployment in Germany rose rapidly.

## 1930–1933

- By 1932, 6 million Germans were unemployed and Nazi support grew.
- President Hindenburg increasingly ruled by using Article 48.
- Wealthy industrialists increased donations to the Nazi Party. In July 1932, the Nazis became the largest party in the Reichstag.
- The Nazis lost seats in the November 1932 election, while the Communists increased their seats again. Some of the German elites persuaded Hindenburg to appoint Hitler as Chancellor on 30 January 1933.

## 1933–1939

- After the Reichstag Fire in February 1933, the Communists were banned and the Enabling Act was passed. By July 1933, Germany was a one-party state.
- Political opponents were silenced by the use of terror. After The Night of the Long Knives the army supported Hitler becoming Fuhrer in August 1934.
- The Nazis dealt with unemployment by public works schemes. Women were pushed out of some jobs and were encouraged to marry and have large families. The Nazis also tried to control young people.
- The Nazis began their anti-Semitic policies with a boycott of Jewish shops, and the expulsion of Jews from the civil service. Then the Nuremberg Laws were passed in 1935. Violence increased after the Night of Broken Glass in 1938.
- Hitler increased Nazi support by overturning parts of the Treaty of Versailles.

## 1939–1945

- From 1939-41, Nazi Germany was successful in the Second World War. The 'Final Solution' began.
- In 1941-42, the German army suffered setbacks. From 1943, Germany suffered heavy Allied bombing.
- The Red Army reached the suburbs of Berlin and Hitler committed suicide. The Third Reich ended.

# Exam Question Practice

## Descriptive essay

Study Sources A and B, which are about the Nazi takeover in Germany in 1933.

Using these sources, and your own knowledge, show how the Nazis established their dictatorship in the years 1933-34.

**Source A**

*Communists rounded up by the Nazis in Berlin, shortly after Hitler became Chancellor in January 1933.*

**Source B**

The following offenders will be hanged. Anyone who does the following in the camp, at work, in the sleeping quarters, in the kitchens and workshops, toilets and places of rest: discusses politics, carries on controversial talks and meetings, forms cliques, loiters around with others; who for the purpose of supplying the propaganda of the opposition with atrocity stories, collects true or false information about the concentration camp... All punishments will be recorded on files.

*Part of the regulations of Dachau concentration camp, near Munich, set up in March 1933.*

## Examiner's Tips

**When answering questions like this:**

◎ Make sure you stick to the period specified by the question, i.e. do not write about actions after 1934.

◎ Make sure you only write about what the question has asked, i.e. how the Nazi dictatorship was established – so do not write about social or economic policies.

◎ Remember to use both of the sources AND your own knowledge - if you only use the sources OR your own knowledge, you will only get half marks at most.

◎ Do not make the mistake of only describing one method – such as the arrest and imprisonment of political opponents as shown by the two sources. For essays, you will need to give a range of different methods, such as the use of the legal powers of the Weimar Constitution, the use of informers, censorship, etc, as well as the use of terror and intimidation (Gestapo and the SS).

◎ Because you will be expected to write about several different aspects or factors in an essay, it is always a good idea to do a rough plan first, to make sure you are covering a range of points.

◎ Finally, make sure you give precise information wherever possible, e.g. dates, names of acts, parties etc. Vague or generalised knowledge will not get you the highest marks.

# THE USA, 1918-1941

An American business poster praising American prosperity and values.

Unemployed workers in a New York Mission Sleeping Hall.

**Source C**

The St Valentine's Day Massacre in 1929 in Chicago, involving rival gangs of mobsters.

**Source D**

The lynching of two African-Americans, in Marion, Indiana, in 1930.

## Key Questions

**How** could the 'Land of liberty and opportunity' contain such contrasting images of wealth and poverty as **Sources A** and **B**?

**How** was it possible for the country which boasted about the 'American Dream' to also be home to the shocking violence shown in **Sources C** and **D**?

These are some of the questions that we will be examining in this chapter. The main focus of this chapter on the USA will be:

- The prosperity of the 1920s 'Boom'
- The divisions and problems existing in the USA before 1929
- The Wall Street Crash and the impact of the Great Depression
- Roosevelt and his New Deal
- The relative success of the New Deal in coping with the Great Depression
- Why the USA went to war in 1941

# The Republican boom

*An American cartoon attacking the way big business trusts dominated American politics. This was published before the First World War.*

## Laissez-faire

*This is an economic policy based on the belief that governments should not interfere in the economy, but should leave businesses to make their own decisions (the words are French for 'leave alone'). The Republicans, in particular, believed in this, so, in the 1920s, they reduced taxes on the wealthy, and removed all restrictions on companies and trusts (big companies that took over smaller ones to create a monopoly). This gave them the sole right to trade in particular goods, without any competition.*

## Tariffs

*These are charges or import duties placed by a government on foreign goods coming into the country. These charges are intended to make foreign goods more expensive, thus helping to increase the sales of the cheaper home-produced goods and protect domestic industry.*

### The impact of the First World War

The USA had stayed out of the First World War until 1917. The Democratic President, Woodrow Wilson, described it as a European 'civil war' and both political parties were united in the belief that America should stay neutral. Wilson was re-elected in 1916 and the following year he changed his mind about America's involvement. But even then there was no fighting or destruction in the USA itself. In fact, the USA had done well out of the war. Since 1914, it had been supplying weapons and food to many European countries, and was able to sell its own industrial products to colonial markets previously supplied by Britain, France and Germany. In particular, the disruption caused by the war enabled the American chemical industry to overtake Germany's, which, before 1914, had been the biggest in the world. The profits made by American industries, banks and investors during the war were then invested in new industries and technologies in the USA, such as electricity and the telephone.

### Republican Presidents

Woodrow Wilson lost the 1920 Presidential elections, and for the next 12 years the USA was ruled by a succession of Republican presidents – Warren Harding (1921-23), Calvin Coolidge (1923-29) and Herbert Hoover (1929-33). These Presidents not only returned the USA to a policy of isolationism towards Europe, they also ended the restrictions on industry and commerce which had been introduced by the Democrat Wilson in order to protect the less well-off members of the public. Warren Harding referred to this as a 'return to normalcy', while Calvin Coolidge said the 'business of America is business'. The Republicans believed in the economic policy of 'laissez-faire'. Republicans also put tariffs on foreign goods. This was known as 'protectionism'.

### The Boom

Other factors also enabled the American economy to expand rapidly after 1918. In particular, the USA had massive supplies of raw materials such as oil, coal and iron. These enabled American companies to undertake the rapid development of new industries, such as the car industry. This then led to an expansion of other industries connected to car production, such as rubber, steel and leather. New methods of mass production provided more jobs and made more and more consumer goods, such as radios and refrigerators, available for people to buy.

Industrial expansion was also aided by new techniques of advertising, especially on commercial radio, and new methods of buying consumer goods, such as hire purchase. As a result of all these factors, the American economy boomed in the 1920s, with a tremendous increase in industrial production, especially of consumer goods such as radios and cars.

*A photograph taken in July 1925 of cars parked at Nantasket Beach, Massachusetts. This was a popular seaside resort near Boston.*

## The 'Roaring Twenties'

As a result of this economic boom, the Republican era in the USA became known as the 'Roaring Twenties'. As well as many clubs and bars springing up and contributing to what many called the Jazz Age, there was a significant migration of people into the towns and cities of America. By the end of the 1920s, the majority of Americans were living in urban not rural areas. Cities expanded and huge skyscrapers were built which dominated the skylines of American cities and seemed to be a symbol of the new wealth and prosperity in the USA. Department stores, chain stores and cinemas also spread, and the number of cars and lorries built and sold greatly increased.

In 1913, Henry Ford set up the world's first moving production line in Detroit. By 1925, over 15 million cars had been produced, and by 1927 one car was being produced every 10 seconds. The car industry became the USA's largest employer and by 1929 there was one car to every five people. The ratio in Britain was 1:43. During the same period, the cinema industry took off, especially after the first 'talkie' was made in 1927. It was estimated that over 100 million cinema tickets were sold each week throughout the 1920s.

**Source C**

...work is planned on the drawing board and the operations sub-divided so that each man and each machine do only one thing...the thing is to keep everything in motion and take the work to the man, not the man to the work.

*Henry Ford explaining the system of mass production used in his car factory.*

**Questions**

1 How did the economic trusts referred to in **Source A** benefit during the Republican era from 1920-33?

2 What can you learn about the American economy in the 1920s from **Source B**?

3 Why was Ford's new system of production so successful?

# A divided nation

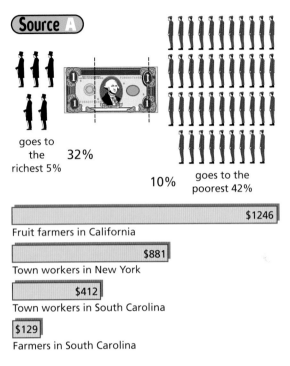

goes to the richest 5% — **32%**

**10%** goes to the poorest 42%

$1246
Fruit farmers in California

$881
Town workers in New York

$412
Town workers in South Carolina

$129
Farmers in South Carolina

*The distribution of income in 1925, and monthly wages in 1929. Note the variations between rural and urban areas, and between the relatively poorer South compared to the more prosperous areas.*

### Flappers

*These were young women (mostly from the urban middle and upper classes) who, having got the vote in 1920, were determined to throw off many of the traditional restrictions placed on women. They wore more daring clothes, smoked and kissed in public, went out with men without chaperones, drove cars and took on paid employment.*

**Source B**

By sheer force of violence, the flapper has established the feminine right to equal representation in such hitherto masculine fields of endeavor as smoking and drinking, swearing, petting and upsetting the community peace.

*An extract from an article, critical of the rising social freedoms of women, which appeared in the New York Times in 1929.*

## Inequality and poverty

Despite the economic boom, there were many divisions in American society, and not all Americans were able to share in the prosperity of the 1920s – they experienced 'poverty in the midst of plenty'.

## Workers

During the whole of the 'Roaring Twenties', almost 50% of the American people lived below the poverty line. Six million families had an income of less than $1000 a year, when, in 1929, it was estimated that a family needed $2000 just to provide the bare essentials. Particularly affected were those who worked in the older industries, many of which were in decline during this period. Unskilled workers and casual labourers had very low wages in comparison to those with skills who worked in the newer industries. With no welfare system, the unemployed suffered great hardship, which was made worse by being surrounded by the many signs of the affluence being enjoyed by others. In comparison with the towns and cities, the rural areas had very little share in the new wealth of the 1920s.

## Women

After the First World War, women experienced several social and political reforms. In particular, divorce was made easier and, in 1920, all women were given the vote. Some middle-class young women, such as the flappers, also enjoyed more social freedoms like smoking in public places. However, although the war had led to a big increase in the number of women working in factories, women's pay remained significantly lower than that for men. Politics and many other professions were not equally open to women.

## Farmers

Many farmers also experienced problems and growing poverty during the 1920s. In the main, this was the result of increased competition from European farmers, who were able to resume normal production after 1918. At the same time, the newer industries and technologies made some farm products unnecessary. The spread of cars replaced horses, so less fodder was needed, and cotton lost out to man-made fabrics such as rayon and nylon. These problems were made worse by the introduction of tariffs which made it harder to sell abroad and so led to many goods being unsold. This overproduction led to a fall in prices.

## Black or African-Americans

One group which suffered from poverty in this period was black Americans, who numbered about 12 million in 1920 (about 10% of the total American population). Although they had been freed from slavery at the end of the American Civil War in 1865, they remained victims of poverty and discrimination, especially in the southern states of the USA, where most of them still lived. For instance, there was segregation between black and white people. Black Americans in the South were prevented from voting in elections by what were known as the 'Jim Crow' laws.

In addition to the poverty and discrimination, Black Americans in the southern states also suffered from the violence carried out by the Ku Klux Klan. Many law officials in the rural South were sympathisers and even members of the KKK.

As a result, between 1920 and 1930, over 1.5 million black Americans migrated from the South to the cities in the North, where, because of the economic boom, there were better chances for employment and education. However, although there was no official segregation in the North, there was still discrimination in jobs, wages and housing and, at times, outbreaks of racist hatred and even violence.

## Segregation

*This was the separation of whites and blacks in the southern states of the USA, in all public places such as schools, and on all forms of public transport. Even prisons were segregated. It was like the apartheid system in South Africa. Segregation had been upheld by the Supreme Court in 1896. It ensured that blacks were discriminated against, and received the worst education, housing and jobs. Washington DC, the capital of the USA, which was just in the South, was also strictly segregated.*

## Jim Crow laws

*These were various laws used by the white authorities in the southern states to uphold segregation, and to stop black people from registering to vote (for instance, by imposing literacy tests on blacks, even though illiterate whites were still allowed to vote). Jim Crow had been a white racist comedian who had been popular in the nineteenth century.*

## Ku Klux Klan

*This organisation had been formed in the southern states during the American Civil War to maintain white supremacy. It had later gone into decline but there was a resurgence in white racism after 1915 and the KKK was refounded by William Simmons. In 1923, Hiram Wesley Evans became its 'Imperial Wizard', and by 1925 claimed it had 5 million members. Although blacks were its main victims, the KKK also had a fanatical hatred of Catholics, Jews, Socialists and Communists. In fact, of anyone who was not a WASP (White Anglo-Saxon Protestant). Its main methods were beatings, burnings and lynchings (hangings).*

### Source C

A Ku Klux Klan initiation ceremony.

## Questions

1 How can you explain the big variation in average wages, and the distribution of incomes, shown in **Source B**?

2 What were the main activities of the KKK, shown in **Source C**?

3 Why do you think there was still so much discrimination in the USA, even 60 years after slavery was abolished?

4 What other tensions were there in American society?

# Violence and intolerance

## Prohibition and gangsters

As well as poverty, the USA in the 1920s also experienced other social problems. One of these was the rise of powerful gangster bosses who became so wealthy that they were able to bribe judges, police chiefs and elected officials in many towns. The most notorious examples were Al Capone and 'Bugs' Moran. They had been able to grow so powerful partly because of the policy of prohibition. This was introduced in 1919, as a result of pressure from women in the Anti-Saloon League and the Women's Christian Temperance Union. The Eighteenth Amendment to the American Constitution made the sale, manufacture or transport of alcohol illegal, and then the Volstead Act also made buying it illegal.

However, many people were prepared to break the law in order to drink alcohol, and, as a result, many 'speakeasies' (drinking clubs) were opened selling 'moonshine' (illegal alcohol) which had been 'bootlegged' (smuggled in) by the gangsters. Consequently, many ordinary citizens who simply wanted a drink became 'criminals' while real gangsters were able to make an awful lot of money. Violence increased, both between the gangsters and the police, and between rival gangs, but prohibition was not finally ended until the Twenty-First Amendment in 1933.

## The 'Red Scare'

As well as racism, American society in the 1920s was also scarred by political intolerance which was aimed mainly at recent Catholic immigrants from southern and eastern Europe. Many powerful and wealthy people in the USA (such as Henry Ford) were opposed to left-wing ideas and had been worried by the Russian Revolution in 1917. Many saw Europe after 1917 as a place full of dangerous revolutionary ideas and parties, and viewed with horror the many attempts at revolution which had exploded in several parts of Europe in the period 1918-23.

A 'Red Scare' developed in which Socialists, Communists and Anarchists were harassed by the police and even the Federal Justice Department, while some were even deported from the USA. Henry Ford was only one of many industrialists who refused to allow people to join trade unions and often used violence against those attempting to recruit members. Not surprisingly, trade union membership in the 1920s dropped from 5 million to 3 million.

---

### Al Capone

Capone was the most notorious of the gang leaders. He used intimidation, extortion and murder to gain control of many illegal activities, such as gambling, prostitution and brothels, as well as supplying alcohol and running 'speakeasies'. He used his money and power to control Chicago by bribing policemen and politicians, including the Mayor of Chicago. By 1927, Capone's income was probably more than $27 million a year. Among the many murders he ordered was the killing of members of a rival gang led by Bugs Moran in 1929. This became known as the St. Valentine's Day Massacre. He was eventually imprisoned for tax evasion.

---

### Source A

The steamship companies haul them over to America and as soon as they step off the ships the problem of the steamship companies is settled. But our problem has only begun – Bolshevism, red anarchy, kidnappers challenging the authority of our flag... Thousands come here who will never take the oath to support our Constitution and become citizens of the USA. They pay allegiance to some other country while they live off our own.

*An extract from a speech made by a Republican senator in 1921. It shows that one of the main fears about immigration were the political beliefs of some of these immigrants.*

# Immigration

As part of this campaign against the left, American governments in the 1920s passed various laws to restrict the number of immigrants coming into the country. Before 1900, most immigrants had come from northern and western Europe, and had been White Anglo-Saxon Protestants (WASPs). Since 1900, a growing number had come from elsewhere in Europe. Many of these were non-Protestants, and some were Socialists or Anarchists (who believe all governments should be abolished). Consequently, attempts were made to limit their number. A literacy test was imposed on immigrants in 1917, and a quota system was introduced by an Immigration Act in 1921. The case of the Italian Anarchists Sacco and Vanzetti, who were executed for robbery and murder in 1927 on very little real evidence, was a clear example of the political hysteria which affected the USA at times in this period.

## Sacco & Vanzetti

*Because they admitted to being Anarchists, their trial in 1920 was more about their revolutionary political views than the extremely weak evidence presented by the police in an attempt to link them to a serious crime. Although 107 people swore that the two men were elsewhere, the judge turned down every appeal against their conviction and sentence of death.*

## Source C

I have known Judge Thayer all my life...I say that he is a narrow-minded man; he is a half-educated man; he is an unintelligent man; he is full of prejudice; he is carried away by fear of Reds, which [has] captured about ninety per cent of the American people.

*The views of a leading US lawyer about the judge in the Sacco and Vanzetti Case.*

## Source B

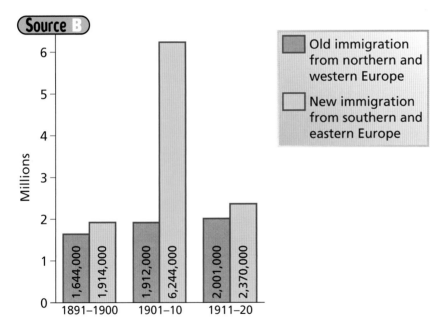

The numbers of immigrants to the USA, coming from different parts of Europe, in the period 1891-1920.

## Questions

1  Why were gangsters able to become so powerful in the USA during the 1920s?

2  How do you explain the kind of fears shown in **Source A**?

3  What does **Source B** tell us about the origins of immigrants to the USA in the period 1891-1920?

# The Wall Street Crash and the Great Depression

## Share speculation

During the boom of the 1920s, there was a tremendous increase in share trading. The number of people owning shares rise from 4 million in 1920 to 20 million by 1929. Many of these owners were speculators who bought their shares 'on the margin'. This meant they only made a down payment (deposit) on the shares, hoping to pay the rest when they had sold them for a profit.

## Over-production

By 1929, there were signs of several other weaknesses in the American economy. In particular, by the end of the 1920s, the USA was approaching a crisis of over-production as the result of a number of factors. Firstly, because almost a half of the American population still lived in poverty, those who could actually afford to buy the new consumer goods had eventually bought most of what they wanted. The companies were producing goods they could not now sell in America. Secondly, because the Republican governments had imposed tariffs on foreign goods (such as the Fordney-McCumber Act (1922), other countries had retaliated by placing them on American goods.

## The Wall Street Crash

In the autumn of 1929, some investors and speculators lost confidence that the boom could continue. Afraid of overproduction, they began to sell shares. This set off panic selling by thousands of investors. Soon millions of shares had been sold and prices fell rapidly. On 24 October, over 13 million shares were sold off. This became known as 'Black Thursday'. The collapse of share prices led to many firms closing down, so large numbers of people became unemployed. This situation soon became worse as investors lost confidence and workers lost jobs. With fewer people with money to buy goods, sales of most products fell, leading to even more people becoming unemployed in what developed into a downward economic spiral.

## The Great Depression

The Wall Street Crash and its consequences led to what became known as the Great Depression, which eventually reached its peak in 1933. By then, industrial production had dropped by 40% and share prices had fallen by 80%. Unemployment had risen to 14 million. Farmers too were badly hit. Because food prices fell, many farmers were unable to keep up their mortgage repayments to the banks and so were forced to sell their farms. Thousands who lost their farms in Oklahoma and Arkansas decided to cross the country to find work in the more prosperous state of California. However, these 'Okies' and 'Arkies' were often given a hard time by locals and forced to move on. This situation was made worse in the

---

### Fordney–McCumber Act (1922)

*As a result of foreign retaliation at American tariffs like this, American firms and farmers found it increasingly difficult to export their goods, and even began to lay off workers. As early as 1927, unemployment began to increase and by the middle of 1929 there were clear signs of an economic downturn.*

### Black Thursday

*This was surpassed on 29 October, when 16 million shares were sold. Share prices continued to fall until June 1932. The problem was made worse by the banks which had given large loans to speculators so they could buy 'on the margin'. In order to cover these loans, the banks joined the rush to sell shares.*

*Those who had invested in shares were ruined and many were bankrupted. In addition, many of the smaller banks collapsed and thousands of people lost their savings. By 1932, more than 20% of such banks had folded.*

### Great Depression

*This refers to the serious downward economic spiral which hit the USA (and then most of the rest of the world) after the Wall Street Crash in 1929. Depressions are situations in which there are many bankruptcies and consequent unemployment, as sales continue to fall, unemployment rises, and another round of bankruptcies and unemployment is set off. Soon, millions of people are living in great poverty.*

Midwest, where soil erosion led to what became known as the Dust Bowl, in which thousands of farmers were unable to farm when the wind blew away millions of tons of top-soil. These dust storms were sometimes so large that homes and people were buried.

## Hoover and the Depression

The Republican President at this time was Herbert Hoover. Like other Republicans, he believed in laissez-faire and 'rugged individualism'. Because of this, the USA had no system of unemployment benefit, so hard-hit people in the cities were utterly dependent on charity soup kitchens and hand-outs. At first, Hoover did little to help, as he believed that if the government left businesses alone, they would soon start to overcome the problems. His beliefs were summed up in his statement that 'prosperity is just around the corner'.

However, the situation continued to worsen and, in many areas, the unemployed and homeless were forced to live in cardboard shacks. These collections of shacks were then called 'Hoovervilles'. Former soldiers grouped together in what became known as the 'Bonus Army' and asked for their pensions to be paid early. They camped outside the White House in an attempt to publicise their cause, but their protest was broken up by police and soldiers. In 1932, Hoover finally decided that the government would have to do something, and so he introduced an Emergency Relief and Reconstruction Act. In the main, however, it was too little, too late.

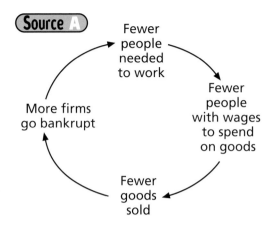

**Source A**

Fewer people needed to work → Fewer people with wages to spend on goods → Fewer goods sold → More firms go bankrupt →

*The downward economic spiral.*

**Herbert Hoover**

*Born in 1874, he had started as a mining engineer and had become a multi-millionaire by the time he was 40. He believed in 'rugged individualism', the idea that people should look after themselves and should not rely on government help. He entered politics as a Republican. He won the 1928 Presidential elections and became President in 1929, just before the Wall Street Crash.*

**Source B**

*A Hooverville, built on wasteland.*

**Questions**

1 What were the main causes of the Wall Street Crash?

2 Why were the shacks and shanty towns like those in **Source A** called 'Hoovervilles'?

3 Why did Hoover take so long before trying to end the Depression?

# Roosevelt and the New Deal

## Franklin Delano Roosevelt

*He was born in 1882 into a wealthy family. In 1910, he became a Democratic Senator for New York. In 1921, he was partially paralysed by polio. However, he fought hard to overcome much of his disability and, though he still often needed to make use of a wheelchair, he remained in politics, having gained some idea of the problems facing the less fortunate. Although he remained a strong believer in the 'American Dream' (that anyone could become rich if they worked hard enough), he also came to think that the power of government should be used to build a fairer society with a more equal distribution of wealth. After winning the 1932 election, he promised the American people a 'New Deal' which seemed partly influenced by socialist ideas. He used the radio to deliver 'fireside chats' to try to restore confidence in American banks and companies, and was nicknamed 'the Champ'. He won four Presidential elections in a row. The American Constitution was then changed to limit a President to a maximum of two terms of office.*

## Source A

*Roosevelt about to deliver the first of his 'fireside chats'.*

## Federal

*The American Constitution is a federal one. This means that there is a central federal (national) government and a Congress (parliament) which deal with issues (such as foreign affairs) of concern to all of the 50 states which make up the USA. Each of the states also has its own local government which deals with issues such as education and law and order. There is a strong tradition that central government should not interfere too much in local state affairs.*

## The 1932 Presidential elections

When the Presidential elections took place in November 1932, Hoover was opposed by the Democratic candidate, Franklin Delano Roosevelt. Unlike Hoover, Roosevelt believed that the government would have to intervene and spend money in order to help the American economy. Though he had no firm policies, he did promise the American people a 'New Deal' in which the American government would use all its powers to get the country out of the Depression. He and the Democrats won the November elections with a large 'landslide' majority in all but six of the states. However, because the American Constitution at that time did not allow a newly elected President to take over until the following March, Roosevelt had to wait four months before he could begin to take action. This period was known as the 'lame duck months', during which Hoover began to take some action to deal with the effects of the Depression.

## The First Hundred Days

Roosevelt wasted no time in beginning to tackle the problems caused by the Depression, and asked for emergency powers for 100 days. His first act was to restore confidence in the American banking system. By the Emergency Banking Act, all banks were ordered to close until government inspectors had examined their accounts. The weaker ones were shut down, and about 5000 were allowed to reopen, with government financial backing if necessary, to prevent further collapses. At the same time, the Economy Act imposed cuts in the salaries of government employees, and set up the Securities Exchange Commission to prevent any future reckless speculation of the kind that had helped to start the Wall Street Crash. For the first time, the USA had a government that was prepared to intervene directly in the economy and to limit the activities of large companies.

## The 'Alphabet Agencies'

Also during the First Hundred Days, Roosevelt got Congress to approve the setting up of 16 new government agencies to tackle the many different problems resulting from the Depression. These became known as the 'Alphabet Agencies' (from the abbreviations of their names). These were mainly approved and set up by Congress between April and June 1933. Roosevelt's main aim was to offer help to the poor, the homeless and the unemployed. This was done via a series of acts.

In May, the Federal Emergency Relief Administration (FERA) gave $500 million of food and aid to the hungry and the homeless. At the same time, various schemes were set up to provide the unemployed with jobs and an income. In April, the Civilian Conservation Corps (CCC) provided work for 2 million unemployed single people (mostly male) by directing them to undertake conservation work, such as creating forests, nature reserves and footpaths. In June, the Public Works Administration (PWA) was set up by the National Industrial Recovery Act (NIRA) to provide work for those with skills, by financing the construction of schools, hospitals, railways, bridges, airports and dams. In the same month, the Home Owners Loan Scheme (HOLS) was also set up to provide low interest mortgages. Later, in November 1933, the Civil Works Administration (CWA) helped find work for about 4 million unemployed people, but the wages were low and this scheme was later abandoned in 1934.

The New Deal also tried to help farmers by various schemes. In May, the Agricultural Adjustment Act (AAA) paid farmers subsidies and set quotas to produce less food, and even to destroy surplus crops and livestock, in order to increase food prices. Help was also given to farmers to modernise and to use methods which would prevent soil erosion. The Farm Credit Association (FCA) provided help for needy farmers to pay their mortgages and to prevent evictions. The main help for industry came via the National Industrial Recovery Act (NIRA) in June 1933 which, as well as setting up the PWA, also established the National Recovery Administration (NRA). This was an attempt to get employers to set fair wages and prices voluntarily, and to get them to improve working conditions and to recognise trade unions. The NRA made child labour illegal. Firms that agreed, were able to display the 'Blue Eagle' sign to show they had the approval of the federal government. In all, about 2 million employers joined the scheme.

In May 1933, Roosevelt also set up the Tennessee Valley Authority (TVA) to solve the many problems which existed in this massive area which covered seven different states. The valley area suffered from both flooding and soil erosion which created a desert-like dust bowl out of the farming land alongside the river. There was also great poverty and deprivation in these areas, but the different states did not have the resources to solve them, and anyway rarely cooperated. The TVA was a federal body which cut across local state governments to build a series of dams which would solve these problems, as well as providing hydro-electric power and work for thousands of unemployed people.

**Source B**

[We discovered]... the existence of over a hundred sweatshops hiring young girls for as little as 60c to $1.10 for a 55 hour week. A family of six, including four children, were found stringing safety pins on wires late into the night for 4 to 5 dollars a week.

*An extract from an official report into working conditions in Connecticut in 1932, during the Great Depression. This was one of the things the NRA tried to stop.*

**Source C**

*The building of the Norris Dam, in the Tennessee Valley.*

**Questions**

1 Identify, and briefly describe the work of five New Deal 'Alphabet Agencies'.

2 How was Roosevelt's approach to solving the economic problems of the Depression different from the outlook of previous Republican Presidents?

3 How did the Tennessee Valley Authority (whose work is shown in **Source C**) help solve the problems of this area?

# Opposition to the New Deal

## Opposition

Although the New Deal measures introduced by Roosevelt restored confidence in the federal government, there was soon opposition to his policies. Conservatives and industrialists, who had always disliked any government interference in business, and increased taxation, saw the New Deal as a form of socialism, and accused Roosevelt of being a 'traitor to his class'. The American Liberty League received large donations from wealthy industrialists to campaign against Roosevelt's restrictions on private enterprise. Traditional Republicans took the same view, and the conservative judges in the Supreme Court ruled several of the New Deal laws to be unconstitutional, because the federal government was attempting to tell individual states what to do. For instance, the NRA was judged unconstitutional in 1935 in what became known as the 'sick chickens' case', when federal officials prosecuted a farmer for selling diseased chickens. This was seen as federal interference with the powers of individual states. In all, Roosevelt's government lost 11 out of 16 cases involving New Deal policies when the Supreme Court eventually judged them unconstitutional. Even some Democrats objected to the taxation needed to pay for all the New Deal projects, while many state governments objected to the increasing interference of the federal government in what they saw as local issues.

There was also opposition from the left, as many radicals believed that the New Deal was not doing enough for the poor. In 1933, Huey Long (a Democratic Senator and the populist but authoritarian Governor of Louisiana) began the 'Share Our Wealth' Movement. He wanted Roosevelt to tax the rich more heavily, and called for the confiscation of all fortunes of more than $5 million, which could then be shared out by giving every family $6000. As they spent this money, he argued, the USA would be pulled out of the Depression more quickly. Although he claimed over 7.5 million people joined his SOW clubs, he also faced opposition, and was assassinated in 1935. He was succeeded by Gerald Smith. Also in 1935, Father Charles Coughlin, a Catholic priest who was known as the 'radio priest', set up the National Union for Social Justice. In 1936, Frances Townsend (a retired doctor) joined forces with Coughlin and Smith to stand against Roosevelt in the Presidential elections.

## The Second New Deal

Despite this opposition, the American people had been favourably impressed by Roosevelt's first attempts to tackle the problems resulting from the Depression, and many had approved of his 'fireside chats' on the radio. As a result, he received another massive win in the Presidential elections in 1936, winning in all but two of the states. This enabled him to continue with his plans to

---

### Supreme Court

*This is a special court made up of nine senior judges appointed by the President. Their job is to make sure that the three branches of the State – the legislative (Congress), the executive (the President and his Cabinet) and the judiciary (the courts) stay separate and do not try to exceed their powers. The Supreme Court has the power to rule acts of the President or Congress unconstitutional (illegal).*

### Source A

THE ILLEGAL ACT.
PRESIDENT ROOSEVELT. "I'M SORRY, BUT THE SUPREME COURT SAYS I MUST CHUCK YOU BACK AGAIN."

*A cartoon published in the British magazine* Punch *in June 1935. It is criticising the actions of the Supreme Court, which had recently ruled several New Deal acts to be unconstitutional.*

take the New Deal further. In fact, his 'Second New Deal' had begun as early as 1935. Its main measures were the Wagner Act, the Social Security Act and the Works Progress Administration. In 1936, the Soil Conservation Act replaced the AAA, which was one of the New Deal agencies which had been declared illegal.

The Wagner Act was passed to replace the NIRA, which had been blocked by the Supreme Court. The new act now forced employers to recognise trade unions and the right of workers to have them negotiate wages and conditions on their behalf. The Wagner Act also gave workers the same benefits they had been given under the NIRA, and extended coverage to employers such as Henry Ford who had refused to join the original scheme. The Social Security Act set up for the first time a system of state pensions for the old and for widows, and also worked with state governments to provide help for the sick and the disabled. It also established a system of national insurance for unemployment benefits to which both employers and employees contributed. The Works Progress Administration coordinated all the different organisations which tried to provide work for the unemployed, and also tried to create jobs for office workers and unemployed artists, photographers and actors through the Federal Arts Project.

*WPA workers clearing away flood debris.*

## The Supreme Court

As part of the Second New Deal, Roosevelt re-introduced many of the policies which had been rejected by the Supreme Court. In fact, encouraged by his second massive election victory, Roosevelt tried in 1936 to get Congressional approval for the Judicial Reform Act, giving him the power to appoint new judges, which would thus prevent the Supreme Court from blocking any more of his policies. This caused great opposition, even from some of his supporters, and he was forced to back down. However, the Supreme Court was less hostile to Roosevelt's policies after this constitutional crisis, and as judges died or retired, he was able to appoint more sympathetic ones.

> **Source C**
>
> By bringing into the Supreme Court a steady stream of new and younger blood, I hope to make justice speedier and less costly. Also I intend to bring in younger men who have had personal experience and contact with today's circumstances and know how average men have to live and work.

*An extract from a radio speech made by Roosevelt in 1937, concerning his proposals to appoint new judges to the Supreme Court.*

### Questions

1 Explain the background which led to the publication of the cartoon shown in **Source A**.

2 Why was it felt necessary to introduce a Second New Deal?

3 What did Roosevelt mean by the reference to 'today's circumstances' in **Source C**?

# Assessing the New Deal

## Source A

Was the New Deal successful? Roosevelt failed to reduce unemployment below ten million until the outbreak of war in Europe brought extra work to American factories. But unemployment was far lower by 1939 than it had been in 1932, and America survived the Depression without the threat of dictatorship which affected millions of people in Europe.... He worked with the trade unions, and the ordinary working man gained greater protection and increased wages.

*Extract from a school history textbook, published in 1996.*

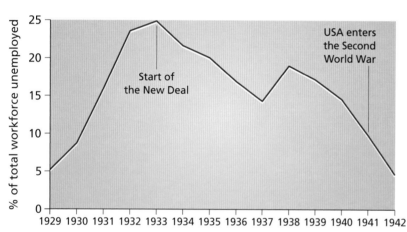

## Source B

*The level of unemployment in the USA, 1929-42.*

## Women

*The Depression had led to increased discrimination against women, as many saw female workers as filling jobs that should be given to men at a time of high unemployment. Although many of the New Deal laws continued to discriminate against women as regards pay and job security, Roosevelt helped increase opportunities for women by appointing several women to important government posts. For example, Frances Perkins was made Secretary of Labor – she was responsible for the 1935 Social Security Act, and draft parts of the NRA regulations. Roosevelt's wife, Eleanor, played a prominent political role as First Lady – in particular, she tried to persuade her husband to outlaw racial segregation and generally to adopt more liberal policies. As a result, she was very popular with working class and black Americans.*

## Unemployment

However, despite the Second New Deal, the Depression still continued to cause problems. In particular, the New Deal failed to fully solve the unemployment problem. Although the number had dropped from the high of nearly 13 million in 1933, it did not drop below 10 million until 1936, and was still almost 6 million in 1941 when the USA joined in the Second World War. In fact, there was a mini-Depression in the period 1937-38, when Roosevelt felt prosperity was returning and so decided to cut government spending on the New Deal. Many workers on New Deal projects were laid off, and the budget cuts made affected many other firms. As a result, unemployment actually rose again to over 10 million. This setback allowed the Republicans to do better in the 1938 elections to Congress, and so made it more difficult for Roosevelt to get his later policies accepted. It was really war production which solved the unemployment problem.

## Problems with New Deal policies

Because unemployment continued to be a significant problem during the 1930s, consumer spending also failed to recover quickly – by 1937, it was still only 75% of what it had been just before the Wall Street Crash in 1929. An additional problem was that policies to help farmers by destroying surplus food and animals in order to keep up prices and farmers' incomes actually made food too expensive for the really poor. The quotas established by the AAA, which were designed to take land out of cultivation also led to many poor black farmers being forced off the land altogether, and the introduction of more modern machinery led to many farm labourers being put out of work. While the Blue Eagle scheme did much to improve general conditions of work, nothing was done to end the unequal pay received by women and black Americans. In fact, the wage code actually allowed employers to pay black Americans and women less than whites and men.

## Roosevelt's popularity

As well as these problems, there was also much industrial conflict in the years 1937-38. After the passing of the NIRA and the establishment of the National Recovery Board, there had been a big increase in union membership. In 1937, the Congress of Industrial Organisations (to which many different unions belonged) organised a series of sit-in strikes to obtain improved wages. The larger companies, such as Ford, General Motors and General Electric, employed strike-breakers and this led to many cases of violence. The worst violence took place at the Republic Steel Works in Chicago on 31 May 1937, when the police killed nine strikers and wounded over 100 others in a crowd who were marching on this public holiday. This became known as the 'Memorial Day Massacre'. Roosevelt, however, refused to get involved; in the end, many strikes were successful, and most trade unionists became Democratic rather than Republican supporters.

In 1938, Roosevelt pushed through the Fair Labour Standards Act in an attempt to improve child labour laws. This also tried to set a national minimum wage for all those working in businesses which operated across state borders. However, it was the last important piece of New Deal legislation; after 1938, Roosevelt was more concerned with foreign affairs.

Despite all these problems, Roosevelt continued to remain popular with the voters, although his majorities in the 1940 and 1944 elections were reduced, as the Republicans began to recover from their poor performances in 1932 and 1936.

**Source C**

This is our weakness. The New Deal has done a great deal during the last seven years. But we have not been able to force from those who own and control the main part of our wealth the security that people have a right to.

*Extract from the diary of Harold Ickes, a former Secretary of the Interior under Roosevelt, written in May 1940. Ickes was a strong supporter of Roosevelt, and had organised the PWA.*

**Source D**

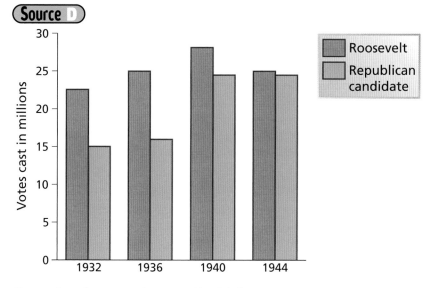

*The number of votes cast in US presidential elections, 1932-44*

**Questions**

1 Why does **Source B** show an increase in unemployment in the years 1937-38?

2 How were black Americans and women discriminated against as regards New Deal legislation?

3 What can you learn from **Source D** about Roosevelt's popularity in the years 1932-44?

# American foreign policy, 1918-1929

**Source A**

..this League is primarily a political organisation, and I object strongly to having the politics of the United States turn upon disputes where deep feeling is aroused but in which we have no direct interest.... I wish to limit strictly our interference in the affairs of Europe and of Africa...

*An extract from a speech made in August 1919 in the USA by Senator Henry Cabot Lodge. Lodge was leader of the Republican opposition to Woodrow Wilson – earlier, he had drawn up his 'Fourteen Reservations' to counter Wilson's Fourteen Points.*

## Isolationism

It was a Democratic President, Woodrow Wilson, who took the USA into the First World War. This was not only a reversal of the usual American foreign policy of 'isolationism' as regards European diplomacy, it was also a complete U-turn for Wilson who had been re-elected as President in 1916 after campaigning in favour of the argument that the USA should stay neutral in the First World War.

Wilson had more sympathy with Britain than Germany, but many Americans were recent immigrants from Germany, who tended to want the Germans to win. However, the USA had more trade with Britain, and Germany was the USA's main industrial competitor, so a German victory would have been financially damaging for the USA. Early German U-boat (submarine) attacks aroused public anger when American passengers were among those killed. By January 1917 the USA had already loaned the Allies $2 billion. In that month, the Germans attacked an American liner. In March came news of the Zimmermann Telegram, in which the Germans promised to return to Mexico land taken by the USA in the nineteenth century, if Mexico would support Germany in the war. This finally led Congress to declare war on Germany in April 1917.

In January 1918, Wilson drew up his 'Fourteen Points' as proposals for peace and, during the peace negotiations in 1919, he pushed hard for the establishment of the League of Nations. Although he wanted to continue the USA's involvement in Europe, this was not something which was supported by the Republicans or even by several in his own Democratic Party. In the mid-term elections in 1918, the Republicans won control of the Senate. In March 1920 they blocked Wilson's attempts to get the USA to sign the peace treaties and join the new League of Nations. Instead, the USA finally signed a separate peace with Germany in 1921.

In particular, many Americans saw Europe and its 'Old World' quarrels as the cause of the deaths of 100 000 American soldiers killed in the war. Many were especially concerned that if the USA joined the League of Nations, the US Congress would lose its sole power to decide whether to get involved in a war. Instead, the Republicans promised to return the USA to its traditional policy of isolationism as regards European diplomacy and the joining of alliances with other countries.

## Europe

Despite refusing to join the League of Nations, however, the Republicans did not totally stay out of European affairs. For instance, although they refused requests to cancel British and French war debts, they did bring about the Dawes Plan in 1924 and the Young Plan in 1929, which were designed to help the German economy to recover, and so help increase American trade with

Germany and Europe. The USA was also involved in the Kellogg-Briand Pact of 1928, which tried to prevent the use of force in international disputes.

## Latin America

America's policy of isolationism certainly did not apply to other areas of the world. In particular, the Republican Presidents of the 1920s continued the policy of extending American interests and influence in Latin America. This policy had been established since the Monroe Doctrine of 1823, when the USA had declared its 'special interest' in the area it saw as its own 'backyard'. In 1898, the USA had gone to war against Spain and had ended up controlling the Caribbean islands of Cuba and Puerto Rico, and the Philippines in the Pacific, all of which had been Spanish colonies. Later, the USA had gone on to 'take' Panama, and set up a protectorate over the Dominican Republic.

President Theodore Roosevelt's view of relations with Latin America was that the USA should 'speak softly and carry a big stick'. In 1904 he announced what became known as the 'Roosevelt Corollary' to the Monroe Doctrine. This basically justified any American intervention in Latin and Central America, to protect private property, to maintain order or to protect American lives. During the 1920s and early 1930s, the USA militarily intervened in several states, including Nicaragua and Haiti.

## The Pacific

Since the nineteenth century, American governments had also been interested in expanding their influence in Asia. This eventually brought America into conflict with Japan, which was trying to extend its influence in the area at the same time. During the First World War, the USA and Japan had been on the same side, but Japan took over several of Germany's colonies in China and the Pacific, and during the peace negotiations in 1919, Wilson was unable to persuade the Japanese government to transfer territory to China.

In 1922, the Washington Naval Treaty attempted to limit the respective sizes of the American, British and Japanese fleets in the Pacific on a 5:5:3 ratio.

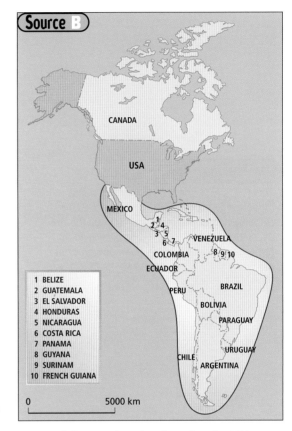

**Source B**

1 BELIZE
2 GUATEMALA
3 EL SALVADOR
4 HONDURAS
5 NICARAGUA
6 COSTA RICA
7 PANAMA
8 GUYANA
9 SURINAM
10 FRENCH GUIANA

0       5000 km

*A map of the Americas showing what the USA believed was their 'backyard'.*

### Questions

**1** To what extent were the Republicans 'isolationists' in the 1920s?

**2** Why did the USA and Japan come into increasing conflict in the Pacific?

# The road to war

## Roosevelt's foreign policy

Although Roosevelt was less committed to isolationism than the Republicans, he at first continued with it. In 1934, the Johnson Act forbade loans to countries involved in wars, and in 1935 and 1937, two Neutrality Acts placed further restrictions on American companies and individuals becoming involved in the wars of other countries.

The policy of isolationism was not applied to Latin America. In 1933, the USA adopted the 'Good Neighbour' policy, which in many ways was a continuation of a less aggressive policy begun under Hoover. Under Roosevelt, the USA had, by 1939, invested over $3 billion in Latin American countries. Some saw this as a form of 'dollar imperialism'.

## The Depression and Japan

However, it was developments in Asia which finally caused the USA to get involved in another world war. The Great Depression had a serious effect on the Japanese economy and, after 1929, governments came to power in Japan which adopted a more aggressive foreign policy as a way of solving their economic problems. Japan soon began to expand its navy beyond the 1922 agreements. The Japanese invasion of Manchuria in 1931 was followed by the full-scale invasion of China in 1937. The USA, which had its own interests in China, was concerned by this but, at first, refused to support the League of Nations' call to impose a trade boycott on Japan, as it did not want to lose valuable trade.

## The end of isolationism

However, when war broke out in Europe in 1939, the USA slowly began to change its policy. In November 1939, Congress agreed to the 'Cash and Carry' Plan, which changed the Neutrality Acts to allow the sale of goods and weapons to Britain and France, provided they paid for them in advance, and transported them themselves. When France was defeated in 1940, the USA gave Britain 50 destroyers to protect its merchant ships carrying supplies across the Atlantic. In return, the USA insisted on the right to build military bases in British territory in the Americas. In March 1941, Congress approved the Lend-Lease Act, which allowed the USA to loan Britain military equipment free of charge. This was later extended to the Soviet Union.

## Pearl Harbor

Meanwhile, in the Pacific, relations between the USA and Japan had continued to decline. In 1938, the Japanese government had announced its plans to establish a Japanese-controlled economic empire in Asia. The USA had reacted angrily to this 'New Order' and had imposed a brief trade boycott on Japan. This was renewed

---

### 'Dollar imperialism'

This refers to a policy based on extending influence over countries by using economic resources and finance, rather than by the use of military means. By investing heavily in a poorer country and being the main importer of its products, richer countries could increase their influence.

### Source A

Some of our people like to believe that wars in Europe and Asia are no concern of ours. But it is a matter of most vital concern to us that European and Asiatic war-makers should not gain control of the oceans which lead to [this continent]. If Great Britain goes down the Axis powers [Japan, Germany and Italy] will control the continents of Europe, Asia, Africa, Australasia and the high seas. All of us would be living at the point of a gun.

An extract from a radio speech made in the USA by Roosevelt in 1940.

and widened in 1939, when Japan refused to agree to a compromise. When Japan, which was already allied to Germany and Italy, invaded the French colony of Indo-China in May 1941, the USA imposed an oil and steel embargo on Japan, and 'froze' Japanese assets in the USA. This angered the Japanese as it slowed down their invasions of China and Indo-China. Roosevelt also ordered the strengthening of American military bases in Hawaii and the Philippines. As the American Pacific fleet was the only serious threat to Japanese ambitions in Asia, Japan decided to attack Pearl Harbor, the main American naval base in the Pacific. The attack, on 7 December 1941, destroyed five battleships, five other ships and 177 planes; eight other ships were seriously damaged. in addition, almost 2500 people were killed and over 1000 wounded. The day of the attack was a Sunday, and the base at Pearl Harbor was caught completely unawares. This was despite the fact that US intelligence had already broken Japan's secret code and had learned of Japanese military preparations and the movements of the Japanese navy across the Pacific. Some historians believe that the information was deliberately withheld by the US government so that it would have an excuse to enter the Second World War. Although Japan had carried out a daring raid, the three US aircraft carriers, which had been the main targets, were not hit as they were at sea on manoeuvres. This was soon to prove a costly failure for Japan. This attack on Pearl Harbor was followed by the USA declaring war on Japan on 8 December. Three days later, on 11 December, the USA also declared war on Japan's allies, Germany and Italy.

"**I am looking forward to dictating peace to the United States in the White House at Washington**"
— *ADMIRAL YAMAMOTO*

**What do YOU say, AMERICA?**

*A poster issued by the US government, shortly after the attack on Pearl Harbor.*

## Questions

1 Why did tension build up between the USA and Japan before 1941?

2 What is the purpose of the poster, **Source B**?

3 Why did the USA decide to give military equipment to Britain after 1939?

**Source C**

So we had won after all!... We should not be wiped out. Our history would not come to an end... Hitler's fate was sealed. As for the Japanese they would be ground to powder.

*The view of Winston Churchill, the British Prime Minister in 1941, on the attack at Pearl Harbor and the USA's entry into the Second World War.*

# SUMMARY

## 1918–1928

- After the First World War, the Republican candidate, Warren Harding, won the 1920 Presidential election. He promised to return the USA to 'normalcy' in foreign affairs (isolationism) and economics (laissez-faire).
- From 1920, the USA experienced an economic and industrial boom under the Republicans, who reduced restrictions and taxes on big companies. Many ordinary people began to buy shares in companies in order to make a profit. But not all sections of American society shared in this new wealth.
- During this boom, there were several problems: prohibition of alcohol and the rise of gangsters; racism and violence towards black Americans by the Ku Klux Klan; restrictions on immigration; a 'Red Scare'.

## 1929–1933

- Herbert Hoover won the 1928 Presidential election for the Republicans. But in October 1929, the collapse of the American Stock Market on Wall Street began what soon became the Great Depression.
- At first, although sales fell, firms closed and unemployment soared, Hoover refused to act. By 1932, almost 25% of American workers were unemployed. Although Hoover started to take some action, he lost the 1932 elections to the Democratic candidate, Roosevelt, who promised a 'New Deal'.

## 1933–1936

- As soon as Roosevelt took over in March 1933, he began a series of 'fireside chats' to restore confidence, and in his 'Hundred Days' set up a series of 'Alphabet Agencies' to deal with the various problems.
- However, the First New Deal encountered opposition from both left and right. In particular, the conservatives in the Supreme Court ruled most of Roosevelt's policies unconstitutional.
- Roosevelt's response was to announce a Second New Deal. Despite these problems, Roosevelt won an even bigger majority in the Presidential election in 1936. He then tried to get approval to add extra judges to the Supreme Court, but this was blocked by Congress.

## 1937–1941

- As the Second New Deal began to have an effect, Roosevelt decided to cut government spending. But this coincided with another drop in world trade and resulted in a mini-Depression in 1937-38 and a rise in unemployment.
- However, from 1938, Roosevelt became increasingly concerned about the approach of war in Europe, and especially about Japanese expansion in China and the Pacific. An American oil embargo on Japan resulted in the Japanese attack on Pearl Harbor in December 1941, which brought the USA into the Second World War.

# Exam Question Practice

## Comprehension in context

Study Source A below, which is a cartoon about opposition to the New Deal.

Explain what Source A is telling us about some criticisms of Roosevelt's New Deal policies.

*A cartoon published in the USA in 1937 and called 'Share the Burden'.*

## Examiner's Tips

**When answering questions like this:**

◎ Try to extract as much information as possible from the source itself (such as dates, figures, etc) and/or from the information about the source provided by the Principal Examiner.

◎ Try to comment on what kind of impression the cartoon seems to be giving or suggesting.

◎ Remember to use your own knowledge to explain what is in the source, and to explain what the cartoonist is referring to, by adding extra information.

## THE SECOND WORLD WAR

Source A

Chamberlain of Britain, Daladier of France, Hitler of Germany, and Mussolini of Italy meeting at Munich in September 1938.

Source B

German troops entering Prague in March 1939.

Source C

A young child injured following the Japanese bombing of Shanghai railway station in China.

*The centre of Hiroshima after the dropping of the atomic bomb on 6 August 1945.*

## Key Questions

**How** important a part did the meeting in **Source A** play in the outbreak of war in 1939?

**Why** was Nazi Germany able to invade countries such as Czechoslovakia, shown in **Source B**, without meeting opposition from Britain and France?

**Why**, as **Source C** shows, did civilians suffer so much more in the Second World War than they had in the First?

**Why** did the USA decide to drop the world's first atomic bombs, as shown in **Source D**?

These are some of the issues which we will cover in this chapter.
The main focus of this chapter on the Second World War will be:

• The effect the Great Depression had on international relations after 1929

• Why the League of Nations became increasingly ineffective in the period 1929-1939

• How Hitler was able to break the Treaty of Versailles from 1933-1936

• The policy of appeasement, and the reasons behind it

• The outbreak of the Second World War in 1939, and its early stages

• The setbacks suffered by the Axis forces after 1941, and the defeat of the Third Reich

• How the war in the Pacific was fought and won

# The impact of the Great Depression

## The weaknesses of the League of Nations

Although the League had had some successes in the 1920s, it had often been unable to deal effectively with disputes which involved the more powerful countries. This had been seen, for example, as early as 1923, when the League failed to prevent aggression in two separate instances. These were France's invasion of the Ruhr, and Italy's invasion of Corfu.

An additional weakness was the fact that, by 1929, two significant countries were still not members of the League. These were the USA and the Soviet Union. On top of this, was the fact that Britain and France, its two most important members, often had conflicting policies. Conflicts were, thus, frequently settled outside the League for instance by the Conference of Ambassadors.

Source A

*A dole queue in Hanover, in the early 1930s.*

## The Great Depression

When the Wall Street Crash happened in the USA in October 1929, it soon began what became known as the Great Depression. This was a serious economic crisis which affected almost the entire world, and led to widespread unemployment and social suffering. It also contributed to the emergence of extreme political parties in many countries.

Italy had already become a Fascist dictatorship before 1929, but both Japan and Germany came under the control of extreme nationalist and dictatorial governments during the early 1930s. Yet all three countries at first remained members of the League.

These governments increasingly turned to aggressive foreign policies in an attempt to solve their economic problems at the expense of other countries. At the same time, other countries tended to put their own economic interests first - even if they were members of the League. This meant many were reluctant to impose economic sanctions on an aggressive country in case they lost trade to their foreign competitors.

### Isolationism

*This was a belief (held mainly by Republicans, but also by many Democrats) that the USA should stay out of international politics and diplomacy, especially in relation to Europe (the 'Old World'). This was based on the belief that American interests were centred on areas closer to home – Latin America and the Caribbean, and the Pacific region. The outbreak of the First World War confirmed this view, and, after it, many Americans wanted no further involvement in European affairs.*

## The USA and isolationism

The response of the USA in this period was to become even more isolationist than it had been in the 1920s. This trend continued under Roosevelt, whose main concern was to push through his New Deal policies. Some American politicians even said that the USA should remain neutral if another war broke out in Europe. One result of this was that Britain and France, both of which also suffered from the Depression, were reluctant to risk any conflict, in case they had to fight on their own. The one other non-member country which could have strengthened the League of Nations' ability to curb aggressive actions, was the Soviet Union. But Britain and France did not trust its Communist government, even after Stalin successfully applied for membership of the League in 1934.

## The rise of Japan

The first country to take aggressive action following the Wall Street Crash was Japan. During the early nineteenth century, many Japanese people watched in alarm as the USA and west European countries carved out empires and areas of influence for themselves in Asia. In 1868, angry at growing US interference in Japan, a group of nobles seized control of the government. They were determined that Japan would not lose its independence. The Japanese economy and the armed forces were modernised, and Japan was able to inflict an unexpected defeat on Russia in 1905.

From then until 1929, Japan attempted to gain its own empire in Asia, for the same reasons (raw materials and extra markets) as European nations. This, however, was resented by countries such as Britain and France. In the First World War, Japan fought on the side of Britain and France. Although it gained the German possessions in the Pacific after the war, Japan was disappointed not to be given more territory in China by the peace treaties of 1919-20. This led to resentment against Britain, France and the USA.

## Japan and the Depression

One area of China which was of particular interest to Japan was the northern province of Manchuria. Japanese investments in the area were increased during the 1920s, and a part of the Japanese army was stationed in the province to safeguard these investments. However, Japan was badly hit by the Depression; especially as it was not self-sufficient in coal, iron, oil, tin or rubber. By 1931, 50% of its factories had closed down, while Japan's rice farmers were badly hit. Japan's main export, silk, declined sharply, and Japanese goods in general were hit by trade tariffs.

The Japanese army (already a powerful force in Japan by the late 1920s), was linked to the Zaibatsu, which also pressed for a more aggressive foreign policy. The army increasingly dominated or ignored the civilian governments of Japan. In 1930, the serious drop in exports caused by the Depression led to a political crisis. This resulted in military factions having a greater influence. Earlier attempts at parliamentary democracy collapsed, as extreme nationalists even resorted to the assassination of liberal political leaders.

### US interference in Japan

*In July 1853, a US fleet, commanded by Commodore Perry, had brought a 'request' from the US President for Japan to open up its trade to American companies - up to then, Japan had followed a policy of seclusion from the western world. Perry, as instructed, made it clear that an even larger US fleet would arrive next spring, and that Japan would be wise to accept this American 'request'.*

### Source B

.... Japan was not welcomed as one of the leading nations of the world by the peacemakers at Versailles... The limitations that the Great Powers were to place on Japanese [expansion] were revealed at the Washington Conference from November 1921 to February 1922, at which Japan was represented in company with the USA, Britain, France, and some other nations... the Japanese agreed that their navy was to be smaller in size than the navies of the USA and Britain, and that they would not undertake hostile action against China.

*An extract from a British history textbook, published in 1973.*

### Zaibatsu

*These were the large industrial companies in Japan in the inter-war period. Many had close links to those army officers who saw military conquest as a way of solving the problems caused by the Depression.*

### Questions

1  How did the effects of the Great Depression, such as those in **Source A**, lead to increased international tensions?

2  What resentments did Japan have against the USA and Britain in the 1920s?

# The decline of the League of Nations

### Mukden (Shenyang) Incident

*Japan had gained the South Manchurian Railway during the Russo-Japanese War of 1904-05 and, by 1927, had come to control most of Manchuria's mines, factories and ports. To protect these, they had a large army in the Kwantung area of southern Manchuria. At this time, Manchuria was ruled by an ineffective Chinese warlord (military-ruler), but Japan feared the new nationalist government of China might soon provide effective control over Manchuria. Officers of the Japanese Kwantung army in Manchuria claimed Chinese soldiers had tried to blow up the South Manchurian Railway near the town of Mukden (Shenyang).*

### Source A

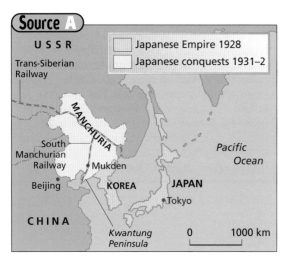

*The Japanese take-over of Manchuria, 1931-32.*

### Source B

*Chinese civilians rounded up by Japanese troops in Manchuria in 1931.*

## Crisis in Manchuria, 1931-1932

The first serious test of the League after 1929 came in 1931, when Japan invaded Manchuria on 18 September. Both Japan and China were members of the League. The Japanese army staged the Mukden (Shenyang) Incident in order to justify sending in a Japanese army of occupation. Though the civilian government of Japan tried to get the military to withdraw, the army refused to listen and instead continued their invasion. This Japanese invasion clearly broke the League's collective security system. The invasion of Manchuria was also against the Washington Naval Treaty of 1922, by which Japan had promised not to attack China.

## The League's reaction

The League did set up the Lytton Commission of Enquiry (on Japan's suggestion) in December 1931 to investigate the situation. This committee did not report until October 1932. By then, Japan had been in complete control of Manchuria for nearly a year, and had renamed it Manchukuo. The report did not recommend either economic or military sanctions. The League accepted the report, agreeing that Japanese claims were valid, but that Japan was wrong to have used force and should, therefore, withdraw its troops. Japan then simply left the League in February 1933.

## Why did the League fail to act?

The Manchurian Crisis occurred during 1931-1932, when the Depression was at its peak. European countries - and the USA - were thus more concerned with the problems created by the Depression. The USA had much trade with Japan, and was reluctant to get involved in the conflict between China and Japan. Despite growing disagreements with Japan, the USA refused to consider the idea of economic sanctions. As a result, most League members feared any trade ban imposed on Japan would merely result in losing that trade to the USA. In addition to trade concerns, Britain was worried that a conflict with Japan might endanger British colonies in Asia, such as India, Hong Kong and Singapore. Although France was concerned that its colony of Indo-China might be at risk from Japanese aggression, it was more worried about German intentions. Italy was not interested in Asia and, more importantly, because of the affects of the Depression, was already planning to increase its own empire.

The other important non-League member, the USSR, saw Japan's aggression as a threat to its Asian territories, and was willing to act. However, no west European state was prepared to co-operate with Stalin in any military action. The Soviet Union, on the other hand, was not prepared to risk any intervention on its own.

## The World Disarmament Conference, 1932-33

This Conference, organised by the League, failed to agree limits on weapons. It was attended by 61 member nations, and 5 non-members, including both the USA and the USSR. France again unsuccessfully attempted to give the League its own army. The main problem, however, was over disarmament and Germany's insistence on 'equality of treatment'. In 1932, German delegates walked out of the Conference, and said they would not return until they had been granted 'equality of treatment'. After Hitler became Chancellor of Germany in January 1933, Germany left the Conference for good. In October, Hitler took Germany out of the League and soon began to rearm. Other countries soon did the same; in part, it was seen as a way of reducing unemployment and stopping industrial decline.

## The invasion of Abyssinia, 1935

Mussolini was so encouraged by the lack of effective League action during the Manchurian Crisis that, from 1932, he began detailed planning for the conquest of Abyssinia.

In October 1935, Italy invaded Abyssinia (now known as Ethiopia). This was the first serious act of aggression by a major European power since 1920. Haile Selassie, the Emperor of Abyssinia, appealed to the League for help.

The British Foreign Secretary, Hoare, asked the League to impose economic sanctions on Italy. However, oil was not included in the list of banned goods, and was allowed to pass through the British- and French-owned Suez Canal, to the Italian invasion force. In addition, many non-League members continued to trade with Italy. One reason why Britain and France were reluctant to take strong action against Italy was that the three countries had, earlier in 1935, formed the Stresa Front. This was meant to act as a check on Hitler's foreign policy actions.

## The Hoare-Laval Pact

Instead of effective action, Britain and France drew up the secret Hoare-Laval Pact, which offered Italy the bulk of Abyssinia. However, it was leaked to the Press. Hoare was forced to resign and the plan was dropped. The League, now supported by Britain and France, began to take a tougher line. In March 1936, they decided to ban the sale of oil and petrol to Italy. However, this did not fully come into effect until May 1936. By then, the Italian conquest was complete. The British and French reaction angered Mussolini, who began to move closer to Hitler. This broke up the Stresa Front and meant that now Britain and France had to rely on each other. In addition, the League had been shown in a bad light and, once again, had failed to take strong action to stop aggression. In July 1936, all sanctions against Italy were ended.

---

### Equality of treatment

*This meant that either all nations should disarm to the German level set by the Treaty of Versailles, or Germany should be allowed to rearm up to the levels of other major powers. In fact, though, Germany had never fully complied with the Versailles restrictions.*

**Source C**

*An illustration from an Italian magazine, published in 1935, showing an Italian air-attack on an Abyssinian supply convoy.*

### Questions

1  Why did the League fail to take firm measures against the Japanese invasion of Manchuria? Try to think of at least two separate reasons.

2  What can you learn about the Italian invasion of Abyssinia from **Source C**?

3  How did the Italian invasion of Abyssinia and the League's reponse to it affect international relations?

# CHAPTER 9

# Hitler's actions 1933-1936

### Hitler and the Treaty of Versailles

When Hitler became Chancellor of Germany in 1933, the weaknesses of the League became even more obvious. His book *Mein Kampf* had set out his beliefs about the foreign policy which he thought Germany should follow. His aims were to unite all German-speakers in one Greater German Empire (Reich), and to take land from east European countries. These clearly went against the Treaty of Versailles and would involve war. So he also said Germany should rearm. In order to hide his ambitions, and to weaken France's connections to Poland, he signed a Non-Aggression Pact with Poland in January 1934.

### Failed takeover of Austria, 1934

Once he was securely in power in Germany, Hitler began to put his ideas into practice. He had noted the failure of the League to prevent Japan's conquest of Manchuria. After taking Germany out of the Disarmament Conference and the League in 1933, he turned his attention to Austria. In July 1934, he encouraged Austrian Nazis to cause trouble, and then tried to send in German troops. But this was blocked by Britain, France and Italy. Although Mussolini was a Fascist and so shared many of Hitler's political ideas, he himself wanted to take land from Austria that had not been given to Italy after the war. He did not want a strong Germany to control Austria, so he moved Italian troops up to the border. Hitler was forced to back down, as the German army was not ready for a major war. In September 1934, the Soviet Union's fears about the intentions of Germany and Japan finally led it to join the League of Nations.

### The Stresa Front

In January 1935, the Saar, which contained important coal mines and iron deposits, voted to rejoin Germany. These extra resources allowed Hitler to speed up German rearmament, and he also re-introduced conscription. In April 1935, Britain, France and Italy formed the Stresa Front to prevent future aggression by Germany.

However, in July 1935, Britain and Germany signed a secret Naval Agreement which allowed Hitler to build up the German navy beyond the restrictions set by Versailles. Britain had done this partly because it disapproved of France which had just signed an agreement with the Soviet Union. However, this Naval Agreement (signed without consulting France or Italy), weakened the Stresa Front. Although Mussolini had opposed his attempt to achieve Anschluss with Austria in 1934, Hitler was determined to get Mussolini to make an alliance with Germany. During the crisis over Abyssinia, he supported Italy. Before the crisis was over, the Stresa Front had collapsed.

**Source A**

A celebration outside the German Reichstag in January 1935. They are celebrating the return of the Saar to German control.

**Source B**

The launch of a German battleship, under the terms agreed in the Anglo-German Naval Agreement of 1935.

## Re-occupation of the Rhineland, 1936

Hitler's actions became bolder after 1935 and the end of the Stresa Front. In March 1936, he took advantage of the League's problems over Abyssinia and ordered German troops into the Rhineland. According to the Treaty of Versailles, this was to be a permanently de-militarised zone. His action was a big gamble, as the German High Command told him the German army could not deal with any military action Britain and France might take. However, Hitler believed that previous crises showed they would take no action. He was proved right. Many people in Britain, and in the British government, believed that as it was German territory, the German army had a right to be there. The French government felt unable to take action on its own. So, although the French protested, no action was taken. Hitler's gamble had paid off.

## The Spanish Civil War

After his successful re-occupation of the Rhineland, Hitler continued his efforts to get an alliance with Mussolini. In July 1936, a civil war broke out in Spain between its elected Popular Front government and Nationalists backed by the army. The following month, Hitler and Mussolini decided to help the Nationalists with troops and weapons. Hitler, in particular, saw this as a useful opportunity to test German military equipment in action. He also introduced a Four-Year Plan designed to get Germany ready for a major war by 1940. The Soviet Union then gave help to the Popular Front government. The League did nothing to stop these developments in Spain, although it did set up a Non-Intervention Committee.

## The Rome-Berlin-Tokyo Axis

This military cooperation in Spain brought Germany and Italy closer together and, in October 1936, they signed the Rome-Berlin Axis. In November, Germany signed an Anti-Comintern Pact with Japan. When Italy joined this in October 1937, these three aggressive countries were joined together in what was known as the Rome-Berlin-Tokyo Axis.

### Questions

1 What were the consequences of the Anglo-German Naval Agreement referred to in **Source B**?

2 Why was no action taken by the League of Nations to stop the German re-occupation of the Rhineland?

3 **Source D** shows the kind of devastation that German weapons caused in Spain. What do you think the effect of this war was on

a Fascist countries like Germany and Italy;

b non-Fascist countries;

c the reputation of the League of Nations?

### Source C

The 48 hours after the march into the Rhineland were the most nerve-racking in my life. If the French had then marched into the Rhineland we would have had to withdraw with our tails between our legs, for the military resources at our disposal would have been wholly inadequate for even a moderate resistance.

*Comments made by Hitler several years after the re-occupation of the Rhineland.*

### Source D

*The ruins of part of Guernica, a town in northern Spain, which was bombed by German planes during the Spanish Civil War, on 26 April 1937.*

### Anti-Comintern Pact

*'Comintern' was an abbreviation for 'Communist International', which was the body set up the Bolsheviks in 1919 to help the spread of revolution across the world. The Anti-Comintern Pact was designed to combat and destroy Communism and the Soviet Union. At the time, the Japanese were split between those who wanted to gain territory from the Asian territories of the USSR, and those who wanted to avoid war with the USSR so that Japan could safely expand in the Far East.*

# Appeasement and the approach of war

*A German soldier surrounded by cheering crowds in Vienna, after the German occupation in March 1938.*

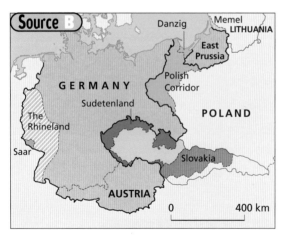

*German expansion, 1935-1939.*

## Neville Chamberlain

*Chamberlain became Prime Minister in 1937. His experience of the First World War made him determined to avoid another war. Like many in Britain, he believed it would be better to negotiate acceptable changes to Versailles with the Germans. In November 1937, he sent Lord Halifax to Germany to tell Nazi officials that Britain would support legitimate German claims in Europe, provided they were negotiated peacefully. However, Eden, the Foreign Secretary, objected to this, and later resigned.*

## Anschluss with Austria

Hitler was encouraged by these foreign policy successes, and by the fact that Italy was now firmly allied with Germany. In 1938, Hitler decided to move once again against Austria. As before, the Austrian Nazi Party had been causing trouble. In January 1938, the Austrian government discovered a plot which was intended to force German intervention. In February, Hitler ordered the Austrian Chancellor, Kurt Schuschnigg, to allow some Austrian Nazis to join his government. Although Schuschnigg at first agreed, in March 1938 he announced plans for a referendum on whether Austrians wanted to keep their independence.

Hitler did not wait for the vote to take place. Instead, on 11 March, he ordered the German army to invade Austria. Although Anschluss (union) between Germany and Austria was forbidden by the Treaty of Versailles, Britain and France again did nothing.

## The Sudetenland

The possession of Austria made it easier for Hitler to move against his next target, Czechoslovakia. Czechoslovakia was the wealthiest of the 'successor states' and had a small but modern army. The Treaties which had been signed with Austria and Hungary in 1919-20 had given the new state of Czechoslovakia an area known as the Sudetenland. This was previously part of the Austro-Hungarian Empire, and now formed the Czech border with Austria and Germany. It contained over 3 million German speakers, many of whom felt that they were discriminated against by the majority population of Czechs and Slovaks. There was a pro-Nazi Sudeten German Party led by Konrad Henlein, and financed by Germany. In March 1938, Hitler told Henlein to make impossible demands on the Czech government and to create more trouble in the area.

## The Crisis

In 1925, France had signed the Little Entente with Czechoslovakia, and the other successor states. This promised French help if they were attacked by Germany. But in 1938, Daladier became Prime Minister of France, and he was not keen to go to war over Czechoslovakia. Britain had no treaty with Czechoslovakia and Neville Chamberlain, the British Prime Minister, made it clear that they would not send troops to defend it. In April, Mussolini told Hitler he would support Germany and, on 30 May, Hitler told his generals that he intended to destroy Czechoslovakia. In public Hitler then threatened to invade Czechoslovakia to 'protect' the Sudeten Germans.

## Appeasement

Britain responded in July by sending Lord Runciman to put pressure on the Czechs to make concessions to Germany. He sympathised with the German claims and his report to the British government recommended that the Sudetenland should be given to Germany. However, Hitler wanted to go to war so, in September, Henlein was ordered to renew his violent campaign. Hitler then used this as an excuse to break off negotiations. He now increased his demands.

## The Munich Agreement

Britain and France were determined to avoid war over Czechoslovakia. Instead, they decided to continue with their policy of appeasement. In September 1938, Chamberlain flew three times to Germany in order to prevent Hitler resorting to the use of force. At the Berchtesgaden and Bad Godesberg meetings, Hitler continued to increase his demands. Finally, on 29 September, the Munich Conference began between Germany, Italy, Britain and France. Although it was to decide the fate of Czechoslovakia, the Czechs were not invited. The Soviet Union, which had said it would defend Czechoslovakia if Britain and France acted as well, was also excluded.

Britain and France quickly agreed that Germany should have the Sudetenland, and the Czech government was informed that there would be no help from Britain and France. On 1 October, German troops occupied the Sudetenland, which contained the important Czech armaments firm of Skoda, without having to fire a shot.

## Invasion of Czechoslovakia

Hitler's foreign policy now concentrated on destroying the rest of Czechoslovakia. The Slovaks were bullied into declaring their independence, while Poland and Hungary were encouraged to make their own territorial demands. On 15 March 1939, Nazi Germany finally invaded Czechoslovakia. Though Daladier did put France on a war footing, no action was taken by Britain or France. Hitler now turned his attention to the Lithuanian port of Memel which its German inhabitants were demanding be returned to Germany.

## The threat to Poland

Soon after the Munich Conference, Germany began to request the return of Danzig (run by the League of Nations as an International Free City), and the building of road and rail links across the Polish Corridor to East Prussia. Once Czechoslovakia and Memel had been taken, it became clear to most people that Poland was Hitler's next target. At the end of March 1939, Britain and France made a significant policy change, and guaranteed to protect Polish independence.

Hitler was not convinced these would be acted on. However, the USA moved a battle fleet from the Atlantic to the Pacific which allowed British and French fleets to move to the North Sea. Britain then announced conscription for all males aged 20-21.

**Source** C

The Pact of Munich is signed. Czechoslovakia as a power is out. The genius of the Fuhrer and his determination not to avoid the risk of world war have again won us victory without the use of force.

*An extract from the diary of General Jodl of the German army. It was made on 30 September 1938, the day the Munich Agreement was signed.*

**Appeasement**

*This meant trying to avoid war by making concessions to a possible aggressor. Britain and France had followed this policy since the early 1930s. At first, it was done to keep Mussolini happy. After 1933, it was done to keep Hitler happy by agreeing to 'revise' parts of the Treaty of Versailles which many in Britain now felt had been too harsh on Germany.*

*For many years, this policy was criticised for encouraging Hitler's aggressive policies and so helping cause the Second World War. Although some, such as Churchill, called for a grand anti-Fascist alliance, many saw this as impractical. The League was failing; and Germany, Italy and Japan were no longer members. The USA was still isolationist. Chamberlain (like many) was anti-Communist, while Stalin's purges of the Red Army commanders seemed to have weakened the USSR. The Stresa Front had collapsed and France was not strong.*

*Also, military advisers told Chamberlain in 1937 that British armed forces were too weak to support France, or even to defend British cities from air-raids. In addition, he was told that the British Navy could not protect British colonies in the Far East from Japan. The Dominions (such as Australia and Canada) also informed him that they would not fight a war over Czechoslovakia. Furthermore, the majority of British citizens were opposed to Britain rearming.*

**Questions**

1 How useful is **Source A** as evidence of the views of Austrian people on the Anschluss (union) carried out by Germany in March 1938?

2 Why did Hitler wish to take over the Sudetenland?

# The war in Europe 1939-1940

## The importance of the Soviet Union

Hitler had already set the date for the invasion of Poland, but wanted a pact with the powerful Soviet Union to make sure it stayed out of the fighting. He calculated that, without Soviet help, Britain and France would not honour their pledges to protect Poland. The Soviet Union had been offering Britain and France an anti-Nazi alliance for some time, but Chamberlain had rejected the offers. In part, this was because it might provoke Germany, and because Poland was opposed to Soviet troops crossing its territory. However, by mid 1939, there was strong public support in both Britain and France for such an alliance. So Chamberlain, reluctantly, agreed to open negotiations. But only at a low-level. Eden, the former Foreign Secretary, who offered to conduct them, was excluded from the initial negotiations.

## The Nazi-Soviet Non-Aggression Pact

Since the Munich Conference in September 1938, however, Stalin suspected that Britain and France were prepared to accept German conquests in the east. Britain's slow responses to these low level negotiations in the summer of 1939 seemed to confirm this fear. Stalin began to see German requests for a non-aggression pact as giving the USSR more time to prepare its defences. So, when the negotiations with Britain seemed to stall, discussions began between Molotov and Ribbentrop, the Soviet and German Foreign Ministers. As a result, the Molotov-Ribbentrop Pact of Non-Aggression was concluded on 23 August 1939. It was supposed to last for 10 years, and included secret clauses for the splitting of Poland and a Soviet takeover of the Baltic States.

## The invasion of Poland

On 29 August, Hitler 'offered' Poland the choice of peaceful dismemberment (by negotiation) or war. Poland refused, and, on 1 September, Germany invaded Poland. Two days later, on 3 September, Britain and France declared war on Germany. This surprised Hitler. Britain felt able to take this action as, since 1934, its defence expenditure had increased by over 400%. In fact, Chamberlain had used the period of appeasement to step up rearmament, in case his policy should fail. The Dominions had also decided to drop appeasement and support a tough stand against German aggression. Britain and France were also encouraged by the fact that Italy and Japan had been angered by Hitler's Pact with the Soviet Union. As a result, these two stayed neutral. This was despite the fact that Mussolini had signed the Pact of Steel with Hitler in May 1939, promising military assistance. So, although the invasion of Poland is seen as the start of the Second World War, it was really only a war between Germany and Poland. The defeat of Poland was rapid, as the Polish army was overwhelmed by the German 'Blitzkrieg' method of warfare.

### Source A

Everything that I undertake is directed against Russia; if the West is too stupid and too blind to understand this, then I will be forced to reach an understanding with the Russians, smash the West, and then turn all my concentrated strength against the Soviet Union. I need the Ukraine so that no one can starve us out again as in the last war.

*Comments made by Hitler, on 11 August 1939, to the League of Nations' High Commissioner in Danzig.*

### Source B

*German troops watching Warsaw burn, September 1939.*

### The Dominions

*These were self-governing countries like Canada and Australia, with their own elected parliments, but which acknowledged the British ruler as their Head of State.*

### Blitzkrieg

*This term is German for 'lightning war' - it was based on the use of tanks, aircraft and paratroops, in overwhelming force, in order to achieve rapid movement and the crushing of the enemy in as short a time as possible. It was used by Nazi Germany with great success in the early stages of the war.*

### The 'Phoney' War

In fact, despite British and French promises of support for Poland, there was no fighting with Germany. From October 1939 to April 1940, there existed what became known as the 'phoney war'; although during this period, German U-boats and mines sank several hundred Allied ships. In April 1940, the Allies began to mine the sea around Norway to try to prevent supplies of iron ore reaching Germany. On 11 April, Germany occupied Denmark and invaded Norway; on 1 May, Norway surrendered. One result of this was that both Chamberlain and Daladier were replaced by new Prime Ministers. In Britain, Winston Churchill took charge of a wartime coalition government in May 1940.

### The fall of France and the Low Countries

On 11 May, Hitler launched invasions of the Netherlands, Belgium and France. The Blitzkrieg tactics resulted in more German victories. The Germans rushed to the French Channel coast. From 26 May to 3 June, the British Expeditionary Force and some French soldiers were evacuated from Dunkirk to avoid encirclement and capture. This encouraged Mussolini, on 10 June, to at last declare war on Britain and France. He believed it was clear that Germany would win the war. On 22 June, France surrendered and German troops marched into Paris. Germany took direct control of most of France, while the south and south east was run by a puppet government based in the small town of Vichy.

### The Battle of Britain

Britain was now without an ally. In July, the German Luftwaffe began bombing merchant shipping in the Channel. In August, Hitler ordered the bombing of British military, industrial and shipping centres. In particular, the Luftwaffe tried to destroy radar stations and air bases. This was to prepare the way for the invasion of Britain, known as Operation Sealion. However, the British airforce, the RAF, fought back in what became known as the Battle of Britain. Hitler then ordered the Luftwaffe to begin bombing London. In the end, the Luftwaffe failed to win control of the skies and, in September 1940, Hitler was forced to postpone his plans for the invasion of Britain. However, Britain remained without an ally for over a year.

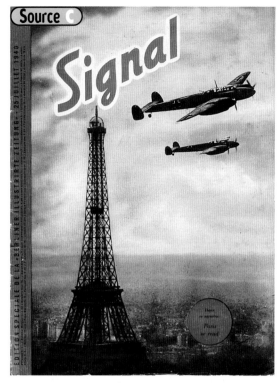

**Source C**

The front cover of the French edition of the German magazine, Signal, published on 25 July 1940. It shows German planes flying over Paris.

**Puppet government**

*This term refers to any government set up by another, stronger, power. Although such a government rules in theory, in practice it is controlled by the stronger power. This was the case with the Vichy government, set up by the Nazis after they had defeated France in 1940. The Vichy government was led by Petain - its job was to rule part of France and to cooperate with the part of France directly occupied by the German army.*

### Questions

1 What can you learn from **Source A** about Hitler's motives in signing the Non-Aggression Pact with the Soviet Union in August 1939?

2 What do you understand by the term 'Phoney War'?

# The conflict widens, 1940-41

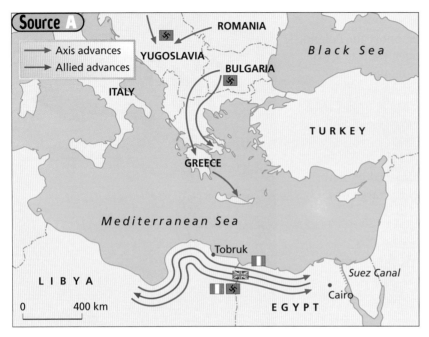

Source A

Axis advances
Allied advances

ROMANIA
YUGOSLAVIA
BULGARIA
ITALY
GREECE
Black Sea
TURKEY
Mediterranean Sea
Tobruk
Suez Canal
Cairo
LIBYA
0    400 km
EGYPT

*North Africa and the Balkans 1940-1941.*

## North Africa and the Balkans

Mussolini was desperate to win some new lands for Italy. So, in August 1940, he ordered the occupation of British Somaliland and, in September, his 240 000-strong army began an invasion of Egypt. This threatened Britain's important shipping route through the Suez Canal. In October, he also began an invasion of Greece. However, the Italian forces did badly in Greece, and part of the African army was sent there. Then, in December 1940, Britain counter-attacked in Egypt and invaded the Italian colony of Libya. Meanwhile, by March 1941, Germany had forced Romania, Hungary and Bulgaria to sign treaties of alliance. However, Hitler was unable to get Yugoslavia to do the same. So, in order to be in a better position to help Italian forces in Greece, Hitler ordered the invasion of Yugoslavia and Greece in April 1941. Within two weeks, Yugoslavia had been defeated and divided up. By the end of May 1941, Greece was also defeated. Germany and Italy now controlled most of the Balkans. A German army under the command of Rommel was also sent to North Africa, in April 1941. This Afrika Korps helped recover Libya for the Italians, and went on to invade Egypt once more.

Source B

*A line of Russian refugees trying to escape from advancing German troops in 1941.*

## The invasion of the Soviet Union

Hitler had been angered by Italy's poor performances, as he had had to divert troops to assist them. This forced him to delay his planned invasion of the Soviet Union, which was further delayed by the failure to build extra airfields and by bad weather. This attack on the USSR had always been his intention, and in December 1940 had originally been planned to start in the spring of 1941. The attack, code-named 'Operation Barbarossa', finally began on 22 June 1941. Stalin had believed that Germany would not attack the Soviet Union until Britain had been defeated. When Hitler failed to secure victory in the Battle of Britain in 1940, Stalin began to slow down Russia's military preparations. Stalin ignored warnings from his intelligence services and from Britain that Hitler was about to attack and, as a result, most Soviet defence forces were taken completely by surprise. This allowed the German forces to make a rapid and massive advance deep into the USSR. Most of the Soviet airforce was destroyed on the ground, and over 700 000 Soviet troops were captured. By October 1941, the total collapse of the USSR seemed imminent, as it suffered these tremendous defeats in the early stages of what became known as the 'Great Patriotic War'.

## The Eastern Front

Determined to crush the Soviet Union, Hitler had diverted most of Germany's military resources to Operation Barbarossa. Over 3 million German, plus another 2 million Axis, troops were involved in the initial invasion. However, as the Russians retreated, they moved 4000 factories and 10 million workers to safety behind the Ural Mountains. They immediately began to replace the military equipment that had been destroyed or captured by the Germans. Anything they could not move which might be useful to the enemy was destroyed in their 'Scorched Earth' policy. The rapid German advance stretched their supply lines which were then attacked by partisan (resistance) groups set up behind enemy lines. The brutal Nazi treatment of Communists, Jews and Slavs in general, allowed Stalin to unite most Russians behind him.

> **Source C**
>
> I... affirm that in March 1941... Hitler called the chiefs of command of the three parts of the armed forces... to a conference... In that conference Hitler said as follows: 'The war against Russia will be such that it cannot be conducted in a knightly fashion. This struggle is a struggle of ideologies and racial differences and will have to be conducted with unprecedented, unmerciful and unrelenting harshness.'

*Part of the statement made by Franz Halder, chief of staff of the German army from 1938-42, at the Nuremberg tribunal, on 22 November 1945.*

*The Eastern Front, 1941-1942.*

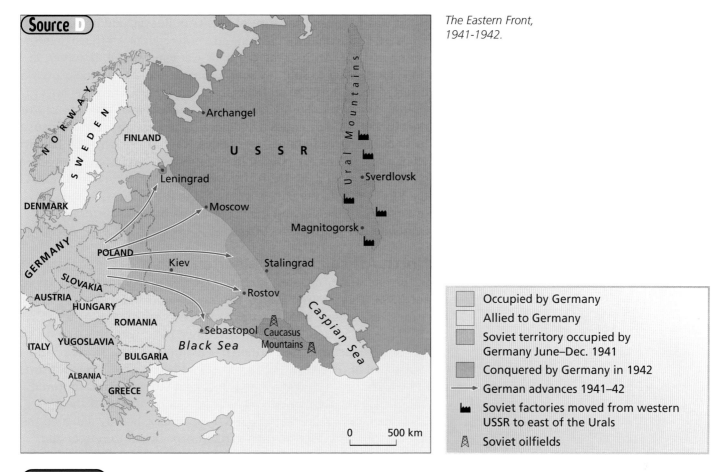

**Source D**

| | |
|---|---|
| ▢ | Occupied by Germany |
| ▢ | Allied to Germany |
| ▢ | Soviet territory occupied by Germany June–Dec. 1941 |
| ▢ | Conquered by Germany in 1942 |
| → | German advances 1941–42 |
| 🏭 | Soviet factories moved from western USSR to east of the Urals |
| ⛏ | Soviet oilfields |

> **Questions**
>
> 1 Why did the German invasion of June 1941 take Stalin by surprise?
>
> 2 How useful is **Source C** for explaining why the war on the Eastern Front was so savage?

# CHAPTER 9

# Allied victories and peace in Europe

## 'General Winter'

The winter of 1941-42 was very severe. The Germans had expected to defeat the USSR before winter set in, and they were not equipped for a winter campaign. Their advance was stopped by rain and mud, and then by snow and extremely low temperatures. German soldiers suffered from frostbite, while machinery and fuel froze. This allowed the Red Army to counter-attack in December 1941. Their Siberian troops were specially trained for such conditions. The USA also began sending supplies to the Soviet Union in November, under a Lend-Lease scheme. This was stepped up after the USA declared war on Germany. Under General Zhukov, the Red Army launched several counter-offensives (not all of them successful) from then until March 1942.

## The Battle of Stalingrad

Hitler was furious at the turn of events in Russia, and began to interfere in the military planning. He ordered a new offensive in the spring of 1942. At first, the Germans were successful. However, in June, he decided to split his southern forces into two. One army was diverted to capture the oil fields in the Caucasus. The other was to capture Stalingrad. By August, the Germans seemed about to capture the city but, as they entered Stalingrad, the Russians resisted house by house in bitter fighting. This lasted from November until January 1943. General Zhukov poured in several fresh armies and was able to outflank, surround, and defeat the German Sixth Army. In July 1943, the Russians won the Battle of Kursk, the last major German offensive in the USSR and the biggest tank battle in history. From September 1943, the Red Army was on the offensive.

## North Africa and the Mediterranean

In the end, Hitler devoted 75% of his forces to the attempt to destroy the USSR. This allowed Britain time to regroup and organise counter-offensives. In June 1941, a British offensive against the Afrika Korps had been unsuccessful. But, in November 1941, with so many German troops in Russia, Britain's Operation Crusader was at first successful in relieving Tobruk which had been under siege. However, in May 1942, Rommel defeated the British 8th Army and captured Tobruk. In August, Montgomery was put in command of the 8th Army and, during 23 October and 4 November, heavily defeated the Axis forces at El Alamein. The Afrika Korps began to retreat and, after the launch of the Anglo-American Operation Torch, the Afrika Korps surrendered in Tunisia. By May 1943, there were no Axis forces left in Africa. Axis forces were also slowly pushed out of the Balkans from 1943 onwards.

This allowed an Anglo-American invasion of Sicily in July and, by September, the Allies had begun their invasion of mainland Italy. Mussolini was overthrown and the new government declared war on

### Source A

Right until the late afternoon, we had to fight, shot for shot, against thirty-seven enemy anti-aircraft positions, manned by tenacious fighting women, until they were all destroyed.

*Extract from the report of the German 16th Panzer Division, about the fighting in Stalingrad in August 1942.*

### German Sixth Army

*Hitler refused to allow von Paulus, its commander, to organise a retreat. On 31 January 1943, with his original army of 300 000 reduced to 91 000 half-starved soldiers, von Paulus surrendered. As well as being a big blow to German morale, this defeat had destroyed much of Germany's military strength. According to Churchill, it 'tore the guts out of the German army'.*

### Source B

*Captured German troops, taken during the important battle of El Alamein.*

Germany. But German forces were sent to Italy, and mounted determined resistance until May 1945.

## The Battle of the Atlantic

Before the USA entered the war, Roosevelt finally decided to end isolationism and neutrality. Under the Lend-Lease Scheme, American military supplies were supplied to Britain, though these were carried in British ships. At first, German U-boats had great success in destroying merchant ships carrying these vital supplies before they reached Britain. However, a turning point came in April 1943, when German radio codes were broken. From May 1943, the Allies began to destroy almost 50 German submarines a month. This was achieved by using faster convoy ships, radar and asdic, and long-range aircraft. In March 1944, the Germans ended their attacks on convoys. The Battle of the Atlantic had been won by the Allies.

## D-Day

Stalin had been pressing Britain and the USA to open up a 'second front' in Europe ever since 1942. He wanted this to take the pressure off the Red Army which was facing the bulk of Hitler's armies. The Allies did begin a heavy bombing campaign against German industry and civilians in February 1942, and this intensified from 1943 onwards. But, until 1944, Britain and the USA had said they were not strong enough to invade western Europe. By then, there were 228 German and Axis divisions in the USSR, with 5250 tanks. At the same time, there were only 61 German divisions in western Europe. The Allies finally agreed to open up the second front in the spring of 1944.

Operation Overlord began on 6 June 1944, with US General Eisenhower in overall command. Over 1 million Allied troops were landed on the Normandy coast in 10 days. At the same time, the Soviet Union launched a massive offensive to prevent Hitler transferring German forces to the west. By August 1944, all German troops had been pushed out of the USSR. In the west, the Allies advanced through France, driving the Germans before them. Paris was liberated in August. In December 1944, the Battle of the Bulge slowed the Allied advance, but this last German offensive was quickly defeated.

## Germany surrenders

From early 1945, Allied bombing of Germany was stepped up. As Red Army troops entered the suburbs of Berlin, Hitler committed suicide. On 2 May, German troops in Italy surrendered and, on 8 May, Germany formally surrendered. Hitler's Third Reich was in ruins and his 1000 year empire had ended after only 12 years. The war in Europe was over.

**Source C**

*Soviet troops raise their flag over the German Reichstag, on 1 May 1945.*

**Questions**

1 Why did the German invasion of the Soviet Union begin to go wrong at the end of 1941?

2 What can you learn from **Source A** about the Russian resistance to the German attempt to capture Stalingrad?

3 Why was the German defeat at El Alamein an important turning point in the war ?

# CHAPTER 9

# Early stages of the Asian-Pacific War

## Japanese expansion after 1931

After invading Manchuria in 1931, Japan carried out further aggression against China. In 1932, it attacked Shanghai and in 1933 occupied the northern province of Jehol. Between then and 1936, two more provinces were taken over. This military expansion was in part the result of the continuing impact of the Depression. Japan was concerned that the Nationalist government of China might want to take control of important Japanese investments in the area. It was, however, also part of a clear attempt at military expansion.

## The invasion of China, 1937

In July 1937, Japan's conflict with China became more serious. In that year, Japan launched a full-scale attack on mainland China. However, Jiang Jeshi, the ruler of China, was reluctant to take strong military action against the Japanese invaders. This was because he was more concerned to crush the forces of the Chinese Communist Party in the civil war which had been raging since the 1930s.

However, the Soviet Union was concerned about the Japanese invasion of Manchuria in 1931, as it threatened Siberia. These concerns were increased when Japan signed the Anti-Comintern Pact with Nazi Germany in 1936. So, after Japan invaded China, Stalin signed a treaty with China in August 1937. As well as giving military aid to the Nationalists, Red Army divisions began to fight the Japanese in Manchuria. In August 1939, the Red Army inflicted a serious defeat on Japanese forces in Manchuria at the Battle of Khalkin-Gol. At the same time, the invasion of China was proving costly for Japan, and an increasingly large army was needed in China.

**Source B**

*The US naval base at Pearl Harbor after the Japanese surprise attack.*

## The invasion of French Indo-China

The high cost of the invasion of China led Japan to consider expanding in South-east Asia. This was in order to obtain vital supplies of oil and other raw materials. Its chance came when France was defeated by Germany in 1940, leaving its colony of Indo-China in the area vulnerable. Japan believed it would be possible to expand there without provoking war with the USA. Japan's idea was to set up its own empire, to be called the Greater East Asia Co-prosperity Sphere. However, when Japan began to invade in July 1941, the USA responded by banning vital supplies of oil, iron and aircraft to Japan, and by freezing all Japanese assets in the USA. Roosevelt said these would not be restored until Japan made peace with China.

## The attack on Pearl Harbor

Other possible sources for oil in the region were the British and Dutch colonies in South-east Asia. The Netherlands had been defeated by Germany in 1940. But Japan was not strong enough to face a combined Anglo-American naval force. So, in December 1941, the Japanese commander, General Tojo, decided on a surprise attack on the main base of the US Pacific Fleet, in order to destroy as much of it as possible. This was based at Pearl Harbor, in the US Hawaiian Islands. Some historians think the USA deliberately provoked Japan and then kept Pearl Harbor unprepared, as an attack would allow Roosevelt to enter the war against Germany. Immediately after the attack, the USA and Britain declared war on Japan, and Germany and Italy declared war on the USA. The Asian-Pacific War now became part of the Second World War.

## The early war in the Pacific

By May 1942, Japanese forces had successfully occupied large areas of the Philippines and the Dutch East Indies. Singapore and Malaya had been taken and, by August, large parts of Burma had also been occupied. They now controlled important oil and rubber reserves, and thousands of British and American troops had been captured. The important British colony of India was threatened. Japan seemed unstoppable.

**Source C**

*Japanese troops 'presenting arms to the Rising Sun', on the Burmese/Indo-Chinese border.*

**Source D**

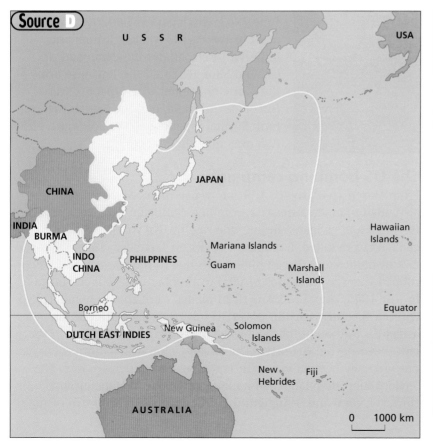

| | Area under Japanese control by 7 August 1942 |
| --- | --- |
| | Allied territory, 7 August 1942 |

*The expansion of the Japanese Empire up to August 1942.*

### Questions

1 How reliable is **Source A** for finding out about the foreign policy aims of the Japanese government in the early 1940s?

2 In what ways do historians disagree over the events leading to the Japanese attack on Pearl Harbor?

# The defeat of Japan

### The turning point

However, in May 1942, Japan suffered its first defeat at the Battle of Midway. The US Pacific Fleet sank four Japanese aircraft carriers and shot down 300 planes. Japanese naval supremacy in the region was ended, and from then on American forces, under the command of General MacArthur, began to assert increasing control of the Pacific. After fierce fighting in January and February 1943, Japanese forces were forced to withdraw from well-defended positions on Guadalcanal. In June, the USA was able to begin submarine warfare against Japanese shipping. This eventually destroyed over 75% of Japan's merchant fleet. In August, Australian forces defeated the Japanese in New Guinea.

Source A

US planes flying over the Japanese fleet during the Battle of Midway.

### 'Island Hopping'

From January 1944, Allied forces began a strategy of concentrating their attacks on Japanese-held islands which had harbours and airbases. The less-well defended islands were bypassed. The Japanese put up fierce resistance. During the battle for the Philippines island of Luzon, the USA lost over 30 000 troops, but the Japanese casualties were almost 160 000. US Admiral Nimitz continued with this strategy and, by June 1945, the Japanese had lost control of most of the Pacific islands. British and Imperial forces, under the command of General Slim, defeated the Japanese army at the Battle of Imphal. The Japanese were forced out of India, and the British then re-took Burma. Japanese control of South-east Asia was now threatened.

### The US bombing campaign

From March 1945, the USA began to use the newly-captured airfields to launch a massive bombing campaign against Japanese factories and civilians. In just one raid on Tokyo, over 83 000 civilians were killed. Firebomb attacks on Japanese cities destroyed 25% of homes and forced millions to flee to the countryside. This robbed the war-industries of vital workers and so reduced output. In July 1945, over 1500 American planes were able to bomb Tokyo without meeting resistance. On 30 July, the Allies offered Japan an armistice. Although the Japanese government was divided, in the end they rejected the offer. The Soviet Union which, until then, had not officially been at war with Japan, agreed to declare war. The Soviet Union then launched a major offensive in Manchuria. However, on 6 and 9 August, the USA decided to drop two of its new secret atomic weapons on the Japanese cities of Hiroshima and Nagasaki. In Hiroshima, at the centre of the explosion, the intense heat turned everything solid into gas. Further away, people were burnt alive, and the wind created by the explosion was so strong that many people were crushed alive. In addition, many suffered from the radioactive fall-out, which caused flesh to dissolve, internal bleeding and severe sickness. For many years afterwards, people continued to die because of the radiation, while many deformed babies were born. Over 300 000 civilians were killed and, on 14 August 1945, Japan surrendered unconditionally. The Asian-Pacific War, and the Second World War, were over.

**Atomic weapons**

*Historians are divided over why the USA decided to drop these atomic bombs in August 1945. Before August, US intelligence services had found out that the Japanese government was ready to discuss peace terms.*

**Source B**

**Source C**

It was my reaction that the scientists and others wanted to make this test because of the vast sums that had been spent on the project...

The use of this barbarous weapon at Hiroshima and Nagasaki was of no material assistance in our war against Japan. The Japanese were already defeated and were ready to surrnder because of the effective sea blockade and the successful bombing with conventional weapons.

*An extract from the memoirs of Admiral Leahy, the US Chief of Staff in 1945, concerning the American decision to drop nuclear bombs on Japan.*

*A photograph of the 'mushroom cloud' over Nagasaki following the dropping of the atomic bomb by the USA on 9 August 1945. The Japanese government surrendered soon afterwards.*

**Questions**

1 Why was the Battle of Midway so important?

2 Why did the USA adopt the method of fighting known as 'island hopping'?

3 Why, according to **Source C**, did the USA decide to drop atomic bombs on Japan in August 1945?

4 How useful is this source as evidence of American motives at this time?

# SUMMARY

## 1929–1933

- After the Depression, the League found it increasingly difficult to prevent aggression, partly because some countries tried to solve their economic problems at the expense of their weaker neighbours.
- Japan invaded the Chinese province of Manchuria in 1931, But the League was unable to take effective action, as many states were not prepared to endanger their trade and military interests.

## 1933–1939

- Hitler came to power in 1933. The 1932-33 World Disarmament Conference failed to reach agreement. In 1933, both Japan and Germany left the League.
- At first, Fascist Italy acted with Britain and France against Hitler. They blocked his attempt to take over Austria in 1934, and formed the Stresa Front in 1935. But this broke down after 1935, after Mussolini's invasion of Abyssinia. Italy began moving closer to Nazi Germany.
- In 1936, Hitler stepped up German rearmament, reoccupied the Rhineland and intervened in the Spanish Civil War. In October, Germany and Italy signed the Rome-Berlin Axis.
- Chamberlain, Prime Minister of Britain from 1937, continued the policy of appeasement. In 1938, at the Munich Conference, Germany was allowed to take the Sudetenland. Germany then invaded the rest of Czechoslovakia in 1939. But Britain and France then promised to defend Poland.

## 1939–1941

- After signing a Non-Aggression Pact with the USSR, Hitler invaded Poland in September 1939. Britain and France declared war on Germany.
- The 'Phoney War' saw little fighting. But in 1940, Nazi Blitzkrieg methods allowed Hitler to occupy Denmark, Norway, the Netherlands, Belgium and part of France. The BEF had to be evacuated from Dunkirk to avoid capture.
- Britain was on its own, but won the Battle of Britain and so prevented a German invasion. However, Italian forces inflicted early defeats on British forces in North Africa. In June 1941, Hitler launched a massive invasion of the Soviet Union.

## 1942–1945

- By the winter of 1941, the situation had started to change for the Axis powers. The Russians counter-attacked, while Italian forces suffered set-backs in North Africa and the Balkans. In December 1941, Japan attacked Pearl Harbor and Germany declared war on the USA. In early 1942, the Allies began heavy bombing of Germany. In May 1942, early Japanese successes were ended by the Battle of Midway.
- During 1943, Axis forces suffered a series of defeats in Europe, North Africa and the Pacific. Particularly important were the Battles of El Alamein and Stalingrad. In July, the Allied invasion of Italy began, and Mussolini was overthrown.
- The final stage began with the D-Day landings in June 1944. By May 1945, Hitler had committed suicide and Germany had surrendered. The war in the Pacific was ended in August, when the USA dropped two atomic bombs on Japan.

# Exam Question Practice

## Cross-referencing of sources

Study Sources A and B, which are about the Battle of Stalingrad.

How far do Sources A and B agree about the Battle of Stalingrad being a major turning point in the Second World War?

### Source A

A fierce battle for the control of [Stalingrad] was fought in the autumn of 1942. The Soviet forces launched a counter-attack in November and the German army was eventually surrounded. At the end of January 1943 the German army at Stalingrad surrendered. The Battle of Stalingrad was a crucial event. It proved that the Red Army could beat the German army. After Stalingrad, Germany was on the defensive and the war began to go against Hitler.

*An extract from a British history textbook, published in 1996.*

### Source B

We talked about everything, particularly about the fall of Stalingrad ... it wasn't possible: 'The Sixth Army! My God! They couldn't be beaten by the Soviets!'... if for some the fall of Stalingrad was a staggering blow, for others it provoked a spirit of revenge which rekindled faltering spirits. In our group, given the wide range of ages, opinion was divided. The older men were, generally speaking, defeatist, while the younger ones were determined to liberate their comrades.

*Extracts from the autobiography of a German soldier who fought on the Eastern Front. It gives the reactions of himself and his comrades on hearing of the defeat at Stalingrad.*

### Examiner's Tips

**When answering questions like this:**

◎ Remember that comparing sources does not mean just describing, copying out or re-phrasing, what the sources say or show - you must compare and contrast the sources.

◎ Remember that 'how far' means you must look for both agreements and disagreements, or similarities and differences, between the sources mentioned. For example, does one source contain extra information compared to the other?

◎ Try to point out the limitations of each source, by commenting on the type of source and what each one can and cannot show.

◎ Make sure that you make detailed, precise and clear references to all the sources mentioned. However, the references do not have to be long - a brief quotation or example (or even a reference to specific lines in written sources) will be enough.

◎ It is a good idea to get into the habit of writing answers to such questions which contain sentences like these: 'Sources A and B are similar/agree/support each other because Source A says....and Source B shows/says .... However, though Source A says.... this is not fully supported by Source B which is a primary source ...'

# CHAPTER 10

## BRITAIN AND THE SECOND WORLD WAR

**Source A**

*School children being evacuated from London. This was taken on Ealing Broadway Station in September 1939.*

**Source B**

*War damage in Balham High Road, London during the Blitz.*

**Source C**

*Women barrage balloon operators.*

*RAF pilots running to their Spitfires during the Battle of Britain.*

## Key Questions

**Why** were children evacuated from London, as shown in **Source A**, after the start of the Second World War?

**What** was evacuation like for those children who were evacuated?

**How** did people cope with the effects, as shown in **Source B**, of what was known as the 'Blitz'?

**What** contributions did women (including those operating barrage balloons as shown in **Source C**) make to Britain's eventual victory in the Second World War?

**How** important was the Battle of Britain in 1940, a scene of which is shown in **Source D**?

These are some of the issues that we will cover in this chapter. The main focus of this chapter on Britain during the Second World War will be:

• The impact of the Blitz and the experience of evacuation

• The Home Front and rationing

• The various roles of women during the war

• Censorship and propaganda

• The social and political impact of the war

# Blitz and evacuation

Source A

*Keeping watch, from the roof tops of London, for enemy aircraft. St. Paul's Cathedral can be seen in the background.*

## Black-out

*This was a series of precautions taken to make it harder for German bomb-aimers to see targets at night. Streets were not lit, cars and lorries had to drive without lights, and people had to make sure no light escaped from their houses before they switched on the lights.*

## V1s and V2s

*These were rocket-powered flying bombs. They were 'retaliation weapons' (Vergeltungswaffe), and began their attacks in June 1944. The V1s were known as 'doodlebugs' or 'buzz bombs'. About 10 000 were launched against Britain but the anti-aircraft batteries were able to shoot down about 4000 of them. Even so, there were about 20 000 civilian casualties, and large numbers of houses were destroyed. In September, Germany also began to launch V2 rockets, which flew too fast and too high to be shot down. But these were not accurate. The V1 and V2 raids continued until March 1945.*

## The fear of bombing

One of the reasons behind the British government's policy of appeasement had been fear of the impact of bombing raids on civilians. Events in 1937, such as the German bombing of Guernica during the Spanish Civil War, and the Japanese bombing of Shanghai during their invasion of China, had shown the massive and dreadful casualties civilians would suffer. There was also the added fear that gas bombs would be used, as they had been during the First World War. During the 1938 crisis over Czechoslovakia, the British government issued gas-masks. When war was declared on 3 September 1939, this was done again.

## Bombing precautions

The government also tried to protect civilians in other ways. Barrage balloons were used to stop bombers flying low, and searchlight and anti-aircraft batteries were set up. The government also provided people with air-raid shelters. 'Anderson' shelters were to be built outside and, by the time the Blitz began, over 2 million had been provided. In 1941, 'Morrison' shelters were introduced for use indoors. By the end of the year, over 500 000 had been distributed. Air-Raid Precautions (ARP) wardens were appointed to patrol the streets, and 'black-out' regulations were enforced. The ARP had been set up in 1937, and by 1939 there were almost 500 000 wardens. The ARP wardens also helped people to shelters, and gave assistance after the raids.

## The Blitz

The first air raids came in September 1940, after the Germans had failed to destroy Fighter Command in the Battle of Britain. The first target was London. These raids took place virtually every night until May 1941. Other important cities, such as Liverpool, Manchester, Sheffield, Southampton, Plymouth and Norwich were also regularly bombed. In November 1940, Coventry suffered a heavy raid in which over 550 civilians were killed. As well as docks and engineering factories, civilian housing was deliberately targeted. In London, despite the government's initial disapproval, some people just occupied the underground stations at night. Many tried to avoid the bombing by 'trekking'. This was when they left the towns and cities each evening to spend the night in the countryside. However, most people stuck to the official shelters. During 1942 and 1943, as Germany began to suffer setbacks in the war, the number of raids began to decline. However, during 1944 and 1945, although German bombers were no longer able to reach Britain, there were attacks by V1s and then V2s.

## The impact of the Blitz

In all, over 60 000 civilians were killed, and over 250 000 homes destroyed, during the Blitz. These losses were not as high as had been feared at the start of the war. They were also much less than the 600 000 civilian casualties killed by Allied bombing raids on Germany. Although there was some loss of morale at first, most people soon became determined to resist. Churchill's radio speeches helped to inspire people not to give in, although it has recently been revealed that many of these were spoken by an actor! Although there was some damage to factories, vital war production was not seriously affected.

## The evacuation

Another way the government tried to protect British citizens from the bombing was evacuation. This involved moving children from high-risk, high-population areas, such as London, to safer areas in the countryside. In September 1939, about 1.5 million of these town children were given gas masks and put on special trains which took them to their new foster homes. Many of these foster parents were shocked by the poor physical condition and health of the children who came from the poorer areas. Such children benefited from the improved diet they received in their foster homes. However, the experience was upsetting for many children, and not all foster parents were kind or understanding.

To begin with, many parents kept their children at home, and less than half the children planned were evacuated. During the 'Phoney' War, many children were brought back by their parents, but evacuation began again once the Blitz started in September 1940. By 1941, there were over 3 million evacuees. In the summer of 1944, there was another wave of evacuations. As well as school children, other categories of people evacuated included mothers and pregnant women, the under-5s and some teachers.

### Questions

1  What steps did the British government take to minimise deaths from bombing?

2  What can you learn from **Source C** about children's experiences of evacuation?

### Source B

After a heavy air raid there was the task of piecing the bodies together in preparation for burial. The stench was the worst thing about it - that and having to realise that these frightful pieces of flesh had once been living, breathing people. It became a grim satisfaction when a body was reconstructed - but there were always odd limbs which did not fit and there were too many legs. Unless we kept a firm grip on ourselves nausea was inevitable.

*An aspect of the Blitz of 1940, as remembered by a First Aid worker.*

### Morale

*One of the main German aims of the Blitz was to weaken the morale (the willingness to suffer and resist) of the British people, so that they would put pressure on the British government to make peace with Germany. The British government tried to prevent this by the use of propaganda and by understating the number of casualties. However, even in the worst-hit areas, the morale of most people was not broken - even though it was a terrifying and unforgettable experience.*

### Source C

The local ladies would walk through the mob and make a selection... The little angelic girls always went first...most girls went into the best homes. if you were like me who always looked filthier than others, your chances were pretty bleak.

*A man, after the war, describing his experiences as a boy evacuee.*

# CHAPTER 10

# The Home Front

## Local Defence Volunteers

*By the end of June 1940, there were over 1.5 million volunteers. In July, it was renamed the Home Guard, and included all males not in vital war work, except boys and pensioners. Their job was to help prevent a German invasion by guarding the coasts, roadblocks and telephone exchanges, although their weapons were limited and mostly old.*

**Source A**

*A woman working out her weekly shopping from her family's ration books.*

## Points

*Each customer was given a certain number of points, and each purchase was deducted from this points 'score'. Luxury and scarce goods, such as salmon, had higher points than other foods. Later still, clothes and furniture were also rationed.*

### The fear of invasion

As well as bombing, there were also fears in the early part of the war that Britain might soon be invaded by the Germans. As in the First World War, the government quickly took extra powers through the Emergency Powers Act of 1939. The fears of invasion increased in 1940, with the fall of France and the start of the Battle of Britain. In 1939, all men aged between the ages of 19 and 41 were conscripted into the armed forces. The minimum age was later reduced to 18. In 1940, after the evacuation of the BEF from Dunkirk, all males who had not been called up were recruited into the Local Defence Volunteers (LDV).

### The U-boat campaign

Another serious threat was posed by the German submarines which began to destroy merchant ships bringing vital supplies of equipment and food. Food shortages soon developed and there was the possibility that Britain's ability to resist might collapse because of starvation. This had been a real danger at one point during the First World War. Until 1943, the heavy losses suffered by British merchant shipping in the Battle of the Atlantic resulted in increasingly severe shortages.

### Rationing

In January 1940, the British government began a system of food rationing. This was done to ensure 'fair shares for all' when it came to allocating the foods in short supply. People had to register with their usual shopkeepers. They were then given ration books containing coupons which could be exchanged for set amounts of foods such as tea, sugar, butter, margarine, eggs and meat. At the end of 1941, as the shortages grew worse, a system based on 'points' was introduced for all tinned foods.

The government also ran various campaigns to increase food production, and to reduce waste. The 'Dig for Victory' campaign was designed to encourage people to grow food on all available spare land, including lawns, flower beds and parks. By the end of 1942, there were almost 1.5 million allotments, compared to just over 800 000 in 1939. By then, Britain's food imports were 50% less than in 1939. The Ministry of Food also gave advice on recipes involving basic foods, and on how to eat healthily. A 'Make Do and Mend' campaign encouraged people to repair clothes and materials. One result of the rationing schemes was that the fairer distribution of food actually led to an improved diet for many ordinary people. Children in particular became much healthier than they had been in the 1930s. The use of petrol was discouraged by the campaign which asked 'Is Your Journey Really Necessary?' The number of bus and train services was severely restricted.

## Censorship and propaganda

The British government, like all governments involved in a war, used censorship. The Censorship Bureau, for instance, banned all newspaper photographs of wounded soldiers, deaths resulting from air raids and houses destroyed by bombs. While this was done to maintain a high public morale, much of the censorship was for real security reasons. With a key role being played by spies, the government's efforts included the 'Careless Talk Costs Lives' campaign. However, the government did not ban people listening in to the broadcasts by 'Lord Haw-Haw' from Nazi Germany, and the BBC was not taken over. The radio was used to keep up morale by broadcasting comedy and music programmes, while cinemas showed documentaries and news films which portrayed Allied successes.

Propaganda to keep up people's spirits was carried out by the Ministry of Information. The Dunkirk withdrawal was reported as a success, although over 60 000 troops were killed, and over 100 000 vehicles had had to be abandoned. During the Battle of Britain, German losses were deliberately exaggerated. There were various poster campaigns, such as 'Your Britain. Fight for it now.' Churchill and other government ministers frequently used the radio to encourage people to support the war effort.

## Control of industry

As with the First World War, total war meant there had to be central control and planning of industrial production. Government control this time, though, was on a much greater scale. In all, over 75% of British industry was placed under direct government control. It was this which had played a big part in Britain's ability to win the Battle of Britain. In the crucial period from the end of August to early September 1940, British aircraft losses had been higher than the number of new ones being produced. However, the Ministry of Aircraft Production was able to produce over 650 more aircraft than had originally been expected. This had enabled the RAF to keep flying.

By 1943, total industrial production in Britain was over eight times higher than it had been in 1939. Ernest Bevin, a Labour Party MP, was made Minister of Labour in the wartime coalition government. He worked closely with the trade unions to keep production going. Employers were made to improve working conditions, and to provide works' canteens. At the same time, it was made illegal to strike before arbitration had been used. (This meant that both employees and employers had to present their cases to a neutral 'judge' who would try to negotiate an agreement.)

**Source B**

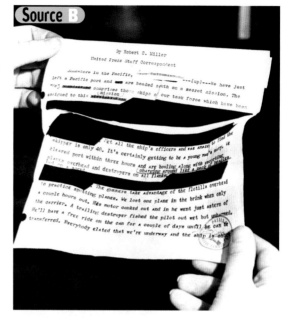

A censored notebook page from a newspaper reporter working in the Solomon Islands in the Pacific.

### Lord Haw-Haw

*His real name was William Joyce, and he was born in the USA. In 1922, he moved to England. He agreed with many of the Nazis' views and went to live in Germany before 1939. During the war, he made many radio broadcasts to Britain in an attempt to undermine the British public's confidence in their government's conduct of the war. Because he had an upper-class accent (his family was wealthy), the British public nicknamed him 'Lord Haw Haw'. After the war, he was hanged for treason.*

### Questions

1 What impact did the German U-boat campaign have on life in Britain?

2 How did government control of industry contribute to victory in the Battle of Britain?

# Women

## Recruitment

As in the First World War, women played a big part in the war effort. At the beginning of the war, women were encouraged to volunteer for the women's sections of the various armed forces, or to do essential war work. In 1941, all single women between the ages of 19 and 30 were conscripted for such work. This was the first time that any democratically elected government had taken such steps. By 1943, over 7 million women were working in industry, or involved in the various military and defence organisations. Almost 50% of women between the ages of 14 and 59 did some form of war service. Even during its final crisis year of 1944-45, Nazi Germany used far fewer women in war work than did Britain.

## Work and industry

In general, women in the Second World War worked in a much wider range of jobs than had been allowed during the First World War. Over 30 000 women worked in the Women's Land Army, doing essential agricultural work which had previously been done by men. This was especially important during the period when the Battle of the Atlantic was not going well for Britain.

Many worked in munitions factories, in order to replace the men who had been conscripted into the armed forces. Others worked in the various industries producing other vital war supplies. These included uniforms, boots and medical supplies. Although women were not allowed to work down the mines, they were used in a variety of surface jobs which had previously been 'male only'. Many women drove lorries, trams and buses, as well as working as conductresses ('clippies'). Many also worked on the railways.

In addition, large numbers of women worked in offices as administrators, clerks and secretaries. In the Civil Service, for instance, over half the jobs were taken over by women. Many also worked for the Post Office, sorting and delivering mail. Many other women joined various voluntary organisations, such as the Women's Voluntary Service (WVS). One result was that the number of women who worked in domestic service fell from over 1.2 million to less than 500 000. However, the government did not grant equal pay to working women, in case it provoked unrest from the male-dominated trade unions. Nor did the Ministry of Health provide nurseries as it said such a level of female employment would only be temporary.

## The armed forces and defence

When unmarried women were conscripted in 1941, they were given a choice. They could chose between war work in factories, the Women's Land Army or service in one of the women's sections of the armed forces. By 1944, there were about 500 000 women in

**Source A**

Two of the many women delivery pilots who flew planes from the factories to the air bases.

### Women's sections

These forces were the Women's Royal Navy Service (WRNS); the Women's Royal Airforce (WRAF); and the Women's Royal Army Corps (WRAC). Women could also chose to join the Auxiliary Territorial Service (ATS) or the Air Transport Auxiliary (ATA).

the three women's forces, and a further 600 000 involved in the ATS (Auxiliary Territorial Service) and Civil Defence organisations. In particular, almost 100 000 women acted as ARP wardens.

Generally, women in the forces undertook jobs such as radio operators, chauffeurs and clerks. About 200 women in the ATA (Air Transport Auxiliary) were trained as pilots, and flew planes from their places of production to British air bases. WRNS radio mechanics also often flew to test radios. In addition, women in the ATS worked on the many anti-aircraft batteries, including the period when the Blitz was at its heaviest. Many women were uniformed nurses in the First Aid Nursing Yeomanry (FANY) which had been set up during the First World War.

## Women in the SOE

While women in the three armed services were not allowed to take part in combat, some women did experience active service. These were the women recruited into the Special Operations Executive (SOE). A large number of women (often recruited from FANY) acted as its administrators, radio operators and signallers, forgers, translators, coding clerks, drivers and secretaries.

The SOE was the only wartime organisation to allow women to fight on equal terms with men. In 1942, it was decided to recruit and train a larger number of women field agents, in order to set up a network of radio operators and couriers in France. From 1942-44, F Section sent 39 women agents into Nazi-occupied France. All got the same training as men, including unarmed combat, weapons and plastic explosives.

One of their main tasks was to help strengthen the French resistance movement. When the Allies finally invaded in June 1944, these resistance groups were better armed and so able to attack German troops and carry out sabotage. This contributed to the success of the D-Day landings. Of this group of 39, 15 were eventually captured by the Germans and sent to concentration camps. Only two of them survived; one of them was Yvonne Baseden. Among the 12 eventually shot by the Germans were Violet Szabo, Denise Bloch and Lilian Rolfe.

## The double burden

Many of the government's propaganda campaigns were specifically aimed at women. As well as having to take the place of men in a wide variety of roles, many women were left alone to face the problems of life in wartime Britain. In addition to coping with jobs, they still had to look after the families. This was made even harder by the problems arising from evacuation, the Blitz, food shortages and rationing. Over 60 000 women were killed during the war.

**SOE**

*The SOE was set up in 1940, after the fall of France. It was first under the control of Hugh Dalton, a Labour Party minister. He was told by Churchill to get the SOE to conduct secret operations in Nazi-occupied Europe.*

**Source B**

*Odette Sansom and her daughters outside Buckingham Palace, where she had just received the George Cross for bravery. Sansom was an SOE agent who was captured in France by the Gestapo in 1943. She was tortured but refused to give any information to the Germans.*

**Questions**

1 Name 3 different types of civilian work done by women during the Second World War.

2 Why do you think the SOE allowed women to fight on equal terms (unlike the other women's sections)?

3 What was the 'double burden' faced by many women during the war?

# The social impact

## Changing attitudes

People in rural areas were often shocked by the poor condition of many of the children evacuated from the bigger cities such as London, Liverpool and Glasgow. In 1940, the government introduced the National Milk Scheme, which began to provide cheap milk for children and expectant mothers. Their ration cards also had vitamins and cod-liver oil added.

Some people became convinced that, after the war, there should be no return to the huge social inequalities which had marked the 1930s. In part, this was because everyone was affected by experiences of 'total war', such as bombing and food shortages. This attitude was reinforced by government initiatives like the 'fair shares for all' policy. Social barriers began to break down, though only to a limited extent. The troops fighting in the various theatres of the war were also increasingly determined that the government should create a 'New Britain' after the war.

## Early measures

In 1940, the Assistance Board was created to replace the old Unemployment Assistance Board. This gave help to families who had been bombed-out, to the wives and families of dead servicemen, and to old people cut off from their families because of the war. Supplementary (extra) pensions were paid out to over 1 million old people and widows. Pensions were also extended to war widows and orphans.

## The Beveridge Report

The government set up a Committee of Inquiry in 1941, under William Beveridge, a government minister, to produce a plan for a better system of social welfare. His report came out in 1942, and made several important recommendations. These were based on his belief that Britain was faced by 'five giants' which blocked social progress and which would need to be tackled if poverty was to be abolished. They were: 'Want, Disease, Ignorance, Squalor and Idleness'. To remove them, he suggested a single new insurance scheme to all cover problems such as unemployment, sickness and old age, which caused an 'interruption of earnings'. Such benefits should continue for as long as necessary, and the 'means test' should be abolished. Beveridge also argued that the benefits should be based on a minimum standard of living, below which no one should be allowed to fall. The improvement of housing was also seen as necessary.

## The impact of the Beveridge Report

At first, the wartime coalition government, refused to commit itself to carrying out the recommendations as, unlike the Labour Party, the Conservative members of the government had several reservations.

---

**'Total War'**

*This means a war with no limits or restraints, using every and any weapon against entire populations, not just the military. Thus civilians - especially those involved in the war effort in any way - become targets.*

---

**'Want, Disease, Ignorance, Squalor and Idleness'**

*By these five giants he meant: poverty, ill-health, lack of education, poor quality housing and unemployment.*

However, when the Report went on sale in December 1942, over 100 000 copies were bought by people in the first month. It went on to sell almost 650 000 copies, and became a best-seller. A special pamphlet about it was printed for troops overseas and was enthusiastically welcomed. So, in 1944, the government set up a Ministry of National Insurance to begin to prepare a new scheme of social security.

## Education

The demands of wartime production had quickly showed a serious shortage of skilled workers. A particular need, both in wartime and for post-war reconstruction, was clearly for more technical education. So, in 1944, the government began to tackle the 'giant' of 'Ignorance' with the Education Act of 1944. This made secondary education free for all children between the ages of 11 and 14. Children who passed the 11+ exam went to grammar schools, while the others went to technical or secondary modern schools. In theory, all three types of schools were to have equal importance. The government would also provide grants for those wanting to carry on their studies in higher education. Local Education Authorities were to provide subsidised school meals for as many children as possible. This was necessary because of the large numbers of working mothers. From September 1941, subsidised or free milk, and regular medical and dental inspections, were also provided.

## Health

The 'fair shares for all' rationing scheme began to improve the diets of the poorest families, as did the provision of free milk, orange juice and cod-liver oil. The new tinned foods which came from the USA as part of the Lend-Lease Scheme also helped. In 1945, the government brought in Family Allowances which were payable for each child after the first one.

In order to cope with war casualties, the government introduced the Emergency Hospital Scheme. This gave it direct charge of most hospitals. There was also a mass innoculation scheme designed to prevent epidemics breaking out because of bomb damage to water and sewerage systems, and sleeping in overcrowded bomb shelters. As a result, 'killer' diseases such as diphtheria were wiped out.

## Housing

There had already been a housing problem in Britain even before 1939. Despite attempts to improve things in the period 1918-39, over 4 million people still lived in substandard 'slum' housing. The problem was made worse by the Blitz, as over 3.5 million houses were destroyed, and the building of new houses came to a standstill. Although many of the houses destroyed in the Blitz were 'slums', there was clearly a big task ahead for the next peacetime government.

### Education Act of 1944

*Elementary education, which was already free and compulsory, was renamed 'primary education' - this now ended at age 11. In secondary education, all fees in grammar schools were abolished (although 165 'direct grant schools' were allowed to continue charging fees, but only for half their places). The government's main aims were to increase the education and skills of all those children who usually left school at 14, and to reduce the influence of wealth on educational opportunities and achievements. However, private education was allowed to continue. The government planned to raise the school leaving-age to 16. However, it was 1947 before it was raised to 15, and it did not become 16 until 1973.*

### Source A

*Pupils walking outside Bourne Secondary Modern School, in Ruislip, Middlesex in 1947. This was one of the many purpose-built secondary schools which were opened under the new Labour government after 1945.*

### Questions

1  How did 'total war' affect people's expectations?

2  What were the main points of the Beveridge Report of 1942?

3  What was the main purpose of the 1944 Education Act?

# The Political impact

### The 'People's War'

For many people, the Second World War came to be seen as a war for a better future, as well as being a war against fascism. In particular, a determination grew that there should be no return to the unemployment and poverty of the 1930s. This was one of the reasons why the Beveridge Report was greeted so enthusiastically. Many also believed that the war was partly the fault of those who had been in favour of appeasing Nazi Germany in the years after 1933.

This attitude was common amongst many members of the armed forces as well as civilians. An example of this was the 'Forces' Parliament' which was set up by servicemen in Cairo in November 1943. In a 'mock' election held in February 1944, the Labour 'candidates' secured a large majority, with the Conservatives coming a poor fourth. Although this development was quickly ended by the military authorities, it was clear that one political impact of the Second World War was that many people were moving to the left of politics. This tendency was increased by news of the various partisan groups fighting the Axis forces in Italy and the Balkans - many of these were led by communists.

### Labour and the coalition government

At first, as the war began to go increasingly in favour of the Allies, it was assumed that the wartime coalition government would continue and begin post-war reconstruction. However, the differing commitment of the Conservative and Labour Parties to carry out the Beveridge Report began to weaken the coalition and the electoral truce between the parties. In the last two years of the war, the Conservatives began to lose by-elections to the Commonwealth Party, which had been set up by a former Liberal MP. In many ways, the policies of the Commonwealth Party were in-between those of Labour and the Communist Party of Great Britain. Finally, in May 1945, the Labour Party decided it wanted to fight an election and the coalition came to an end after Germany's surrender, which was seen as virtually ending the entire war. Churchill then formed a Conservative government and announced that there would be a general election in July.

### The general election of 1945

Many people - including Churchill - assumed that the Conservatives would win the election. Churchill was a very popular wartime leader, and opinion polls showed that the Conservatives had pulled back since May 1945, when they had been 20% behind Labour, to being only 8% behind. However, the Conservative Party's pre-war record on unemployment and appeasement led many people to look for a clear break from the misery of the 1930s. This was especially true of many members of the armed forces, and their votes (made in special

### Forces Parliament

*This grew out of a debating society set up by the army authorities in Cairo, in an attempt to occupy the troops stationed in the area and those returning on leave from the war in the deserts of North Africa. In November 1943, the troops (mostly privates and junior non-commissioned officers) decided to turn it into a mock parliament. Their argument was that the war was against fascism and for democracy, and that democracy meant debate. In all, about 500 to 600 army and air force servicemen took part in these monthly debates, and they quickly divided into 'government' and 'opposition' sides. They then began to discuss and vote on 'laws'. In December 1943 and January 1944, they voted by large majorities to nationalise the distribution industry and to restrict inheritance.*

*The military authorities became increasingly alarmed and decided to close it down when the troops announced they would have a mock general election in February. However, those participating divided up into Labour, Commonwealth, Liberal and Conservative 'candidates', and the results were as follows: Labour 119, Commonwealth (close to Labour) 55, Liberals 38 and Conservative 17. In March, the new Labour 'government' announced that a law to nationalise British banks would be debated the following month. Although the commanding officer turned up to the April session and ordered it to stop, the troops voted 600 to 1 to ignore him, and the bill to nationalise the banks was passed with a huge majority. This was its last meeting, as the authorities closed it down, and the main organisers were quickly posted elsewhere.*

polling stations around the world) went heavily to Labour. The results showed a clear victory for the Labour Party, which won 393 seats compared to the Conservatives' 213 seats. The Communist Party increased its number of MPs from one to two, in part because it was associated with the role played in Hitler's defeat by the Soviet Union and its Red Army. The Commonwealth Party won one seat. In addition, three Independent Labour Party candidates were also elected; while the Liberals took 11 seats.

## Socialism and public ownership

The new Labour government, led by Clement Attlee, was committed to carrying out the Beveridge Report. It was also in favour of the nationalisation of several key industries. The Labour Party's constitution, drawn up in 1918, contained Clause 4. This said that a Labour government would nationalise factories, shops and transport in order to create a socialist Britain. In the 1945 election, Churchill had tried to frighten the voters by saying that under Labour, Britain would become a socialist state which would have total power over the lives of its citizens. Many voters were not scared by this claim, in part because several industries had already been taken into public ownership by Liberal, Conservative and National governments before 1945. These included the London Docks (1908), the Central Electricity Generating Board and the BBC (1926), London Transport (1933) and the British Overseas Airways Corporation (1939). These steps had been taken to ensure a standard service and especially to provide the massive amounts of money needed for modernisation, which private owners could not - or would not - provide. In fact, despite the hopes of many of its members and supporters, the new Labour government made it clear that any nationalisations would be for reasons of greater efficiency, not to create a socialist Britain. As a result, most of its nationalisation programme met little opposition from the Conservatives - especially as the private owners were given massive compensation payments. In 1946, the Bank of England was nationalised, and British European Airways was set up. In 1947, the coal-mines were nationalised under the National Coal Board. In 1948, British Rail was set up to take over the railways, while both the gas and the electricity industries were nationalised. All four of these industries needed huge investments in order to update equipment and even to continue functioning.

### Nationalisation

*This meant taking firms into public ownership. While many on the left of the Labour Party saw this as the first step towards creating a socialist economy, the Labour leadership made it clear that they were determined to maintain a mixed economy. This meant that while some industries would be publically-owned (mainly the public utilities, such as electricity and public transport), the bulk of companies would remain privately-owned. Most of the industries nationalised in the period 1945-51 were making losses. They were nationalised in line with the views of Herbert Morrison, a senior Labour minister. He rejected calls to put the nationalised industries under democratic workers' control, as desired by the left. Instead, public corporations were set up, each with a Chairman and a Board, which managed the industries. In many cases, the new managers were the former owners and directors. These are some of the reasons why the Conservatives did not oppose the majority of Labour's nationalisations. The nationalisation of the iron and steel industry, and of the road haulage companies, however, did meet fierce opposition from their owners and the Conservatives. Unlike the other industries, these ones were still profitable. The Labour government backed down over road haulage, but managed to push through nationalisation of steel in 1950. This industry was returned to private ownership by the Conservatives in 1953, after Labour lost the 1951 election. In all, the Labour government took about 20% of the economy into public ownership, resulting in some 10% of the workforce working in nationalised industries.*

### Questions

1 Why did the wartime coalition come to an end in May 1945?
2 Why did the Conservatives lose the 1945 election, despite Churchill's success as a wartime leader?
3 What was the main aim of the Labour government's programme of nationalisation in the years 1945-51?

# Labour and the Welfare State

**Source A**

HERE HE COMES, BOYS !
7th August, 1945. Mr. Aneurin Bevan's appointment as Minister of Health is not welcome in certain circles.

*A cartoon of 7 August 1945, showing the opposition of many doctors to the idea of a free National Health Service and possible restrictions on private medicine. Note the reference to 'Health for all', on the case carried by Aneurin Bevan, the new Minister of Health.*

## Health for all

The main item on Labour's agenda of reform was the creation of a National Health Service (NHS) which would provide health care for all, free of charge. It was intended to cover free specialist and hospital treatment, as well as local doctors, opticians and dentists. This had also been recommended by the Beveridge Report and, during the war, the coalition government had provided health care for all, even to those people who could not afford to pay. However, the two main parties disagreed on how a free health service should be arranged once the war was over.

After the July 1945 election, Aneurin Bevan became the new Minister of Health. Bevan and the Labour government faced a lot of opposition from doctors who feared they would be unable to spend time on profitable private medicine, and who resented the prospect of increased State control which might interfere in how they treated patients. Many disliked the plan to 'draft' doctors into the poorer areas which had very few doctors because most people could not afford to pay fees. Once the NHS Act was passed, the British Medical Association stepped up its opposition. With the threat of a doctors' boycott of the planned NHS, Bevan was forced to make concessions on allowing private medicine to exist within the NHS, paying doctors fees rather than salaries, and keeping medical services out of central or local government control.

**Source B**

On Monday morning you will wake up to a new Britain in a state which 'takes over' its citizens six months before they are born, providing care and free services for their birth, early years, their schooling, sickness, workless days, widowhood and retirement. All this with free doctoring, dentistry and medicine for 5 shillings (25p) out of your weekly pay packet.

*An extract from a British newspaper, published on 3 July 1948.*

## The National Health Service

5 July 1948 was known as the Appointed Day - the official date on which Labour's new 'Welfare State' began. The NHS and the National Insurance Act of 1946 (see below) both came into force. Immediately, thousands of people flocked to doctors' surgeries, and to opticians and dentists. In less than a year, over 187 million prescriptions and over 5 million pairs of glasses had been provided. At the same time, over 8 million people received dental treatment. This massive take-up was clear evidence of earlier neglect resulting from people's inability to pay for the health care they needed.

However, the demands on hospitals and the new health centres - and the costs - proved greater than expected. So, in 1949, prescription charges were imposed on some medicines; then, in 1951, on glasses and dental treatment. Although these were not for the full cost, it conflicted with the earlier aim of a free and universal system of health care. Bevan and some other junior ministers resigned in 1951, in protest at what they saw as a fundamental principle.

## National Insurance

In 1946, the Labour government also passed the National Insurance Act. This was to cover old age pensions, unemployment and sickness benefits, and maternity grants. As with the NHS, this was to be universal and not dependent on the hated means test. Instead, everyone was to pay a flat rate contribution from their wage each week. Any extra costs not covered by the insurance contributions would be met from general taxation. The new act thus offered security for all 'from cradle to grave'.

However, it soon became clear that the very poor were unable to contribute much. So, in 1948, the National Assistance Act was passed to give extra benefits to those in extreme need. Taken together, these two acts, and the NHS, did much to remove the fears many had of a return to the poverty of the 1930s. Despite some differences and criticisms, the Conservative Party accepted most of the principles set down by the Labour government.

## Housing

Labour also began to tackle the 'Giant' Squalor identified by Beveridge. During the war, over 500 000 houses had been destroyed, and new building had virtually stopped. To deal with this housing shortage, the government immediately took over military buildings and set up estates of pre-fabricated houses ('pre-fabs') to offer emergency housing. The government then directed the building trade and local councils to concentrate their resources on building good-quality council houses at subsidized rents. Within five years, despite tremendous shortages of materials, over one million new houses had been built. This was an achievement unmatched by any other West European country.

## Labour loses power

Although the Labour government's reforms brought about tremendous improvements for most people in the years after 1945, Labour was associated with the continuation of rationing and government economic controls (such as a wage restraint policy) designed to prevent inflation. A harsh winter in 1947 was followed by currency crises related to the strength of the US dollar. This led to a devaluation of the pound in 1949. Although exports were recovering from the decline caused by the war, Labour's overall majority was reduced to single figures in the general election in February 1950. In October 1951, Labour lost power. The Conservatives won a small majority, and Churchill became Prime Minister once again.

*New house building in London.*

### Labour lost power

*The February 1950 result was mainly because of electoral boundary changes, as Labour polled 13.3 million votes to the Conservatives' 12.5 million. When the Korean War broke out in June 1950, the Labour government raised income tax to increase the defence budget. This, and the introduction of further health charges, led to a split in the party. Despite this, the Labour government fought the October 1951 election on its record of achievements. However, despite winning 48.8% of the vote compared to the Conservatives' share of 48%, the small number of Liberal candidates standing meant that the Conservatives won 321 seats, while Labour dropped to 295.*

### Questions

1 Why was there opposition, such as that shown in **Source A**, to Labour's proposals to set up a National Health Service?

2 What was the 'Appointed Day'?

# SUMMARY

## 1939–1940

- As soon as the war began, the government took extra powers under the Emergency Powers Act, 1939. Most of industry was quickly placed under government control.
- All males aged 19-41 were conscripted. Later, the minimum age was reduced to 18.
- Over 1.5 million children were evacuated from the major cities, and people were provided with bomb shelters. Other precautions against bombing included the setting up of ARP units.
- After the Battle of Britain, the Blitz began as German tactics changed to concentrate on bombing industrial and civilian areas in the major cities.
- Because of German U-boat attacks, rationing was introduced. The government also began to provide free milk and vitamins, as evacuation had shown the extent of poverty in the larger towns and cities.

## 1941–1943

- Because so many men were in the armed forces, all single women aged 19-30 were conscripted. They could join one of the women's sections in the armed forces, organisations such as the ATS or the ATA, or work in factories or on the land.
- The first Blitz ended in May 1941 - by then, over 40 000 people had been killed and over 800 000 houses destroyed or damaged.
- During 1942-43, air raids continued, but were less heavy and often on less well-defended towns and cities.
- In 1942, the Beveridge Report recommended big changes to social insurance to deal with the 'five giants'. Many civilians and troops welcomed its proposals.

## 1944–1945

- The government began to carry out some reforms linked to the Beveridge Report. The Education Act of 1944 made secondary education free for children aged 11-14.
- In 1944, a Ministry of National Insurance was set up and, in 1945, the government began to pay Family Allowances.
- In 1944 and 1945, British cities were attacked by V1 flying bombs and V2 rockets. Between them, these new weapons killed or injured about 30 000 civilians. These attacks finished in March 1945, two months before the end of the war in Europe.

## 1945–1951

- In the general election of July 1945, the Labour Party won a massive 'landslide' victory, as many voters wanted a change from the poverty of the Depression of the 1930s.
- Between 1945 and 1951, the new Labour government did much to extend the Welfare State. In 1946, it passed the National Insurance Act and, in 1948, set up the National Health Service. It also nationalised several industries. Although it won the 1950 election, the Labour Party lost power to the Conservatives in 1951.

# Exam Question Practice

## Judgement or interpretation questions

Study Sources A and B below, and then answer the following question.

'The contribution made by women in Britain during the Second World War was restricted to helping with war production'. Do you agree with this statement? Use the sources and your own knowledge to explain your answer.

Source B

Source A

Members of the Women's Land Army at work during the harvest of 1942.

A recruitment poster for women munitions workers.

### Examiner's Tips

**When answering questions like this:**

◎ Make sure you do the two things the question asks you - use your own knowledge AND the sources. You will need to comment on what each of the sources suggests about women's contribution, and add what you know about the kinds of contribution women made.

◎ Don't just say 'Yes' or 'No', because the Principal Examiner will be expecting you to write a BALANCED answer. This is one which tries to look at both sides of the question ('Yes' AND 'No').

◎ Try to spend roughly the same amount of time on putting both sides, even if you have a strong view one way or the other.

◎ Make sure you deal with a range of issues/factors - you will not score high marks if you only write about one aspect.

◎ When you are using your own knowledge, try to give detailed and precise bits of information, e.g. Don't just say 'women also joined various organisations' - mention specific ones such as the WRNS, WRAF and the WRAC, and try to give supporting statistics.

◎ If you can't make a decision one way or the other, say so and show why (e.g. women did play many other important roles, but most women were involved in war work).

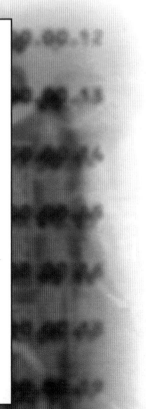

# CHAPTER 11

## THE COLD WAR 1945-1961

Soviet and American soldiers meeting on the River Elbe in Germany in May 1945.

Source B

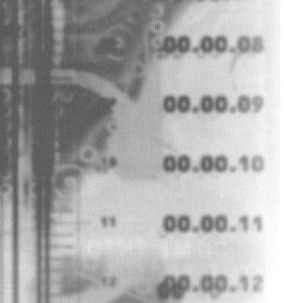

The building of the Berlin Wall, at the Brandenburg Gate, on 20 November 1961.

Source C

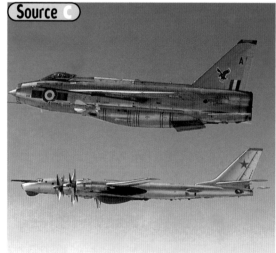

An RAF Lightning fighter intercepting a Soviet Bear reconnaissance aircraft over the North Sea.

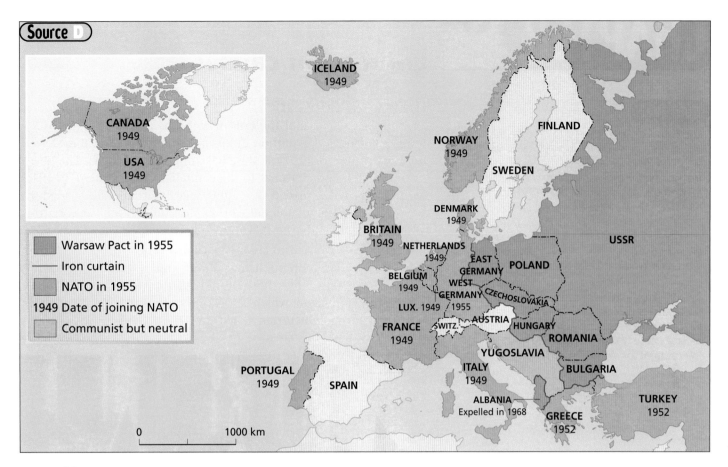

**Source D**

Legend:
- Warsaw Pact in 1955
- Iron curtain
- NATO in 1955
- 1949 Date of joining NATO
- Communist but neutral

CANADA 1949
USA 1949
ICELAND 1949
FINLAND
NORWAY 1949
SWEDEN
DENMARK 1949
BRITAIN 1949
NETHERLANDS 1949
EAST GERMANY
POLAND
USSR
BELGIUM 1949
WEST GERMANY
CZECHOSLOVAKIA
LUX. 1949 / 1955
AUSTRIA
HUNGARY
FRANCE 1949
SWITZ.
ROMANIA
YUGOSLAVIA
PORTUGAL 1949
SPAIN
ITALY 1949
BULGARIA
ALBANIA Expelled in 1968
GREECE 1952
TURKEY 1952

0     1000 km

*A map of Europe showing the iron curtain and the opposing military alliances in 1955.*

## Key Questions

**Why** did the friendship, shown in **Source A,** between the members of the Grand Alliance not last beyond the defeat of Nazi Germany?

**How** did both sides come to distrust each other so much that the building of the Berlin Wall, shown in **Source B,** took place just sixteen years after the end of the Second World War?

**What** were the reasons behind the arms race, an aspect of which is shown in **Source C,** which developed between the two sides?

**Why** did the Cold War result in Europe being divided in the way shown in **Source D**?

These are some of the issues which we will cover in this chapter. The main focus of this chapter on the Cold War will be:

- The long-term tensions which existed between the USSR and the rest of the world before 1945

- How the Cold War began to develop immediately before and just after the end of the Second World War

- The particular problems of the post-war settlement concerning Germany and Poland

- How distrust and fear led to an arms race between the two superpowers after 1945

- How the Cold War was affected by the outbreak of war in Korea

- The ways in which the Cold War developed after the end of the Korean War

# Long-term causes

## The 'Great Contest'

The long-term causes of the Cold War can be traced back to 1917 and the Bolshevik Revolution in Russia. This resulted in the creation of the world's first state based on Marxist ideas. The new Soviet Republic was a threat to the capitalist world system. In 1919, Lenin and Trotsky formed the Communist International, headed by Zinoviev, to stimulate and aid world revolution. Capitalist countries were suspicious and even fearful of this new state.

Soviet Russia also tried to create a socialist economy, in which the economy was based on public ownership and putting the needs of society as a whole above those of individuals. This was completely opposed to capitalism, which was based on private ownership and individualism. One historian called this rivalry between the two different systems the 'Great Contest'.

### Source A

*A large communist rally in Berlin in 1918. Many governments were afraid communism would spread across Europe - especially after the formation of the Communist International.*

## Early conflicts

From 1918-1921, the new Soviet state was faced with foreign military intervention in the Civil War which broke out in 1918. This included armies from the USA and Britain. From 1920-21, Poland - backed by Britain and France - attacked Russia. The Bolsheviks saw these actions as deliberate capitalist attempts to destroy their revolutionary socialist experiment. Although the Bolsheviks emerged victorious, the USA (among others) refused to recognise the Soviet government.

## Soviet weakness and isolation

By 1923, the various attempts at socialist revolution in Europe outside of Russia had all been crushed. In addition, the economy of the new Soviet state was weak. Apart from the general problems connected with the economic backwardness of Tsarist Russia, there were other serious problems. These were the result of the conflicts in which Russia had been involved since 1914: the First World War, the Revolutions of 1917, the Civil War and foreign intervention, and the Polish invasion of 1920-1921.

### Source B

The year 1917 was a momentous one in the history of the twentieth century. It was the year when the two great extra-European powers - the Soviet Union and the United States - stepped into the mainstream of history to proclaim two rival world ideologies. The United States, under President Wilson, entered the First World War not to restore the balance of power but to end the whole European state system and 'make the world safe for democracy' under a new international order. Russia, under the leadership of Lenin, had the Bolshevik Revolution, withdrew from the war and called for a 'world' revolution. There is a sense... in which it is accurate to speak of the cold war beginning in 1917.

*An extract from a history book, published in Britain in 1996.*

These military attacks were replaced by bans on trade with Russia in the early 1920s, which restricted attempts to rebuild the Russian economy. In the words of Winston Churchill, this was done to 'strangle infant Bolshevism in its cradle'. Thus, the 'Great Contest' was one-sided, as the USA had emerged economically and militarily strengthened from the First World War.

For most of the period after 1923, Soviet communism was no serious rival to world capitalism. Under Stalin, although Soviet industry expanded, agriculture suffered. After 1929, the 'Great Contest' seemed less important than the Great Depression, the rise of fascism and the threat of another world war.

## Relations in the 1930s

After Hitler came to power in Germany in 1933, relations between the USA and the USSR began to improve. In 1933, the USA at last gave official recognition to the USSR, and Stalin joined the League of Nations in 1934. However, Stalin's Great Purge in the USSR in 1935-7 strengthened anti-Soviet attitudes in the USA, which set up a Division of Russian Affairs. Later, this Division was responsible for the important Riga Axioms. The Division was headed by Charles Bohlen and George Kennan, and was much influenced by Russians opposed to the Bolsheviks. These 'Whites' tended to stress the world revolution aims of the new Soviet state.

The views of American 'hardliners', such as Kennan, seemed confirmed by Soviet actions in the period 1939-41. These included the Nazi-Soviet Non-Aggression Pact, the partition of Poland with Germany, war against Finland, and the Soviet takeover of the Baltic states (including Lithuania). Kennan's views were supported by Joseph Kennedy, the US Ambassador in London. He favoured the British foreign policy of appeasing Nazi Germany, rather than allying with the Soviet Union.

These views were opposed by Joseph Davies, US Ambassador in Moscow during 1937-1938. He believed that the USSR was interested in cooperation in order to prevent Nazi aggression in Europe. Roosevelt saw Nazi Germany as more expansionist than the USSR, and thought a weakened Soviet Union, at the end of a war with Germany, could be persuaded to drop the idea of world communism.

### Riga Axioms

*The Division of Russian Affairs (DRA) was based in Riga, the capital of Lithuania, which was also a safe refuge for 'White' Russian exiles after the Bolsheviks won the Civil War. The 'Axioms' refer to the views of those who worked in the DRA. In particular, these urged the USA to take action against the Soviet Union. Such views shaped American policy towards the USSR throughout the 1930s and 1940s.*

### Questions

1 What is meant by the term the 'Great Contest'?
2 To what extent does **Source A** support the views of **Source B**?
3 Why were other countries like Britain and the USA so hostile to the USSR?
4 How were their views affected by the Nazi rise to power in Germany?

# CHAPTER 11

## Short-term causes

**Second front**

*This did not finally happen until the D-Day landings in June 1944. Stalin suspected this was because the USA and Britain wanted the USSR to be left seriously weakened after the war. In all, about 80% of all Axis military resources were thrown against the Soviet Union.*

**Source A**

The delay in launching the second front fuelled Stalin's suspicions about Anglo-American motives.... The fear that the Western Powers might reach an agreement with Hitler behind his back lingered on until early 1945.

*An extract from a history book, published in Britain in 1995.*

### The Grand Alliance

When the USSR was attacked by Germany in June 1941, and the USA by Japan in December 1941, the USA and Britain soon joined with the Soviet Union in a Grand Alliance. They saw Hitler as a more serious and immediate threat than Stalin. One result was that the USA began to send some military supplies to the USSR under a Lend-Lease scheme.

However, from 1942 onwards, Stalin began to press the USA and Britain to take the pressure off the Soviet Union, which was facing the bulk of Hitler's armies. He wanted them to open a second front in western Europe. By June 1944, there were 228 Axis divisions on the eastern front, compared to 61 divisions in western Europe.

### The Tehran Conference

The outbreak of the Second World War seemed to end the pre-war rivalry. But disagreement over the opening of a second front, and other problems, soon began to emerge within the Grand Alliance. In particular, the Soviet Union was concerned over Roosevelt's statements on American foreign policy. He called for 'democracy and economic freedom' and similar ideas were set out in the Atlantic Charter of 1941, and the Declaration of the United Nations, 1942. The Soviet Union was also suspicious of Roosevelt's 'Open Door' policy. This was based on 'free' world trade and 'equal' access to raw materials. Stalin saw this as being designed to benefit economically advanced countries, especially the USA.

However, as the war was still continuing, the Big Three (Roosevelt, Stalin and Churchill) managed to maintain the alliance when they met at Tehran in November 1943. There was initial outline agreement that the Soviet Union could have its 1918 border with Poland restored, while Poland's western border would move further west, taking over German land. There was also agreement that no central European alliance would be allowed against the Soviet Union. These two points seemed to remove some of Stalin's main security concerns, though Churchill and Roosevelt were not in total agreement on these issues.

**Source B**

*The Soviet Union has become a danger to the free world. A new front must be created against her onward sweep. This front should be as far east as possible. A settlement must be reached on all major issues between West and East in Europe before the armies of democracy melt.*

*Part of a note written by Churchill to Roosevelt shortly after the Yalta Conference in February 1945. Churchill's main concern was to impose Western aims on the USSR before Anglo-American forces were reduced to peacetime levels.*

### The breakdown of the Grand Alliance, 1944-1945

Tensions, which finally led to the breakdown of the Grand Alliance and the start of the Cold War, began to emerge more sharply at the 1945 Big Three Conferences held at Yalta, in February, and at Potsdam in July. There were four main areas of disagreement: Germany, Poland, economic reconstruction, and nuclear weapons.

The war against Germany was still continuing when the Allies met at Yalta in February 1945, but was clearly nearly over as far as Europe was concerned. The issues which had emerged at Tehran, especially over Poland and the fate of the east European countries, now clearly had to be resolved. The Conference seemed to reach agreement on several of these issues. However, Roosevelt died in April 1945, and Vice-President Truman took a more hardline approach to the Soviet Union. In May, he abruptly ended the Lend-Lease scheme to the USSR. This was a serious blow to the war-devastated Soviet Union. At the Potsdam Conference in July 1945, the agreements reached at Yalta about Germany were revised. The Riga Axioms, put to one side during the war against Germany, now increasingly dominated American foreign policy again. Nonetheless, the Potsdam Conference did see a final acceptance of the Soviet plans for Poland. Look at the next spread for details of the agreements reached.

## The US atomic bomb

The apparent, though partial, agreements reached at Potsdam were undermined in August 1945 when the USA exploded the world's first atomic bombs on Hiroshima and Nagasaki. More significant than the bombs themselves, was the USA's refusal to share the technology with its Soviet ally. At the Yalta Conference, Roosevelt had got Stalin to promise to enter the war against Japan, once Germany was defeated. However, Truman and his Secretary of State, James Byrnes, saw the A-bomb (tested successfully on 16 July 1945) as a way of ending the war against Japan without Soviet participation, as well as keeping American casualties to a minimum. This would prevent any Soviet demands for influence in Asia, which was seen as a region vital to American interests. The Potsdam Conference was delayed until 16 July, partly in order to give Truman a new powerful negotiating tool. This policy was opposed by the US Secretary of War, Henry Stimson, who argued that the Soviet Union should be offered an atomic partnership if some concessions on eastern Europe were made. Stalin interpreted the refusal to share nuclear technology as a demonstration of American power to a seriously weakened USSR.

**Source C**

Leaders at the Potsdam Conference. Those seated, from left to right, are Attlee, Truman and Stalin, of the Britain, USA and USSR, respectively.

**Source D**

Poland has borders with the Soviet Union, but does not have any with Great Britain and the USA. I do not know whether a democratic government has been established in Greece, or whether the Belgian government is genuinely democratic. The Soviet Union was not consulted when these governments were being formed. We did not claim the right to interfere in those matters, because we realise how important Belgium and Greece are to the security of Great Britain.

An extract from a note sent by Stalin to Truman and Churchill in April 1945, stressing the importance of Poland to Soviet security. Poland was one of the main issues dividing the Allies at the conferences held in 1945.

**Questions**

1 Why, as suggested by **Source A**, was the opening of a second front an area of distrust between the USSR and its Western Allies?

2 How useful is **Source B** as evidence of Western policy during the Yalta Conference?

3 Use **Source D** and your own knowledge to explain why the future of Poland was so important to the USSR.

# The start of the Cold War

*Russian refugees returning to their town in 1944. Their wooden homes have been burned down and only the brick chimneys remain. As the USSR had suffered far greater damage than any other country, Stalin felt it was in a very vulnerable position.*

### Five Ds

*These were the agreements made about what was to be done with Germany after the war. The Five Ds were:*

- *demilitarisation (remove the armed forces)*
- *denazification (remove Nazis from power)*
- *democratisation (restore free elections and other political parties)*
- *de-industrialisation (reduce heavy industry)*
- *decentralisation (take power away from central government)*

*These were all intended to ensure Germany would not pose a threat again - especially to the USSR. However, as the Cold War deepened, several of these points were altered or even abandoned.*

## Soviet concerns

As the war came to an end, the USSR was particularly concerned about what would happen to Germany and the east European states. Since 1900, Germany had twice invaded the USSR. Poland, and eastern Europe generally, was also an issue, as the USSR had been invaded through Poland three times since 1900. Stalin was also desperate for compensation from Germany, so that the USSR could begin economic reconstruction.

## Germany

At the Yalta Conference, in February 1945, the Big Three agreed to divide Germany temporarily into four zones of occupation (run by the USA, the USSR, Britain and France). There was also outline agreement on compensation (reparations) for the damage done by Nazi Germany, especially to the USSR. At the Potsdam Conference in July 1945, Truman, the new US President, said the USA would only agree to the Soviet Union having reparations from the eastern zone of Germany. This was mainly rural and, therefore, poorer. After further discussion, it was agreed that the USSR could also have 25% of the machinery from the three western zones. But this depended on the USSR sending to the west 60% of the value of these industrial goods, in the form of raw materials (especially coal). Germany was to be run by an Allied Control Council, and the 'Five Ds' were to be carried out. It was further agreed that the capital Berlin, which was inside the Soviet zone, should also be divided into four zones.

## Poland

Poland was the largest of the east European countries. As with Germany, Stalin saw the question of Poland as a life and death question for the Soviet Union. At Yalta, it had eventually been agreed that the USSR could take parts of eastern Poland. Poland would receive land from Germany, as compensation. The Potsdam Conference, which took place after Roosevelt's death, saw a final acceptance of the Soviet plans for Poland. However, there was disagreement over how Poland should be governed, although Stalin did promise to hold free elections there.

## The Growing Divide, 1946

More serious divisions arose during 1946. In February, Kennan, from the US Division of Russian Affairs, sent a report to the American government about Soviet foreign policy. This 'Long Telegram', as it came to be called, said that the USSR was an expansionist state which would never co-operate with the USA. This view rapidly became the basis of American policy, and was the origin of the policy of 'containment' (this term was first used by Kennan), which first emerged the following year. Then, in March 1946, Winston Churchill made his famous speech claiming that an 'iron curtain' had descended across Europe. He also claimed that the Soviet Union was an expansionist state, and pointed to increasing Soviet control over the countries of eastern Europe (see map on page 222). This was an important shift away from Roosevelt's policy of attempting co-operation with the USSR.

## The Truman Doctrine

Most American officials soon came to support Kennan's views. Some who believed the USSR was willing to compromise, were forced to resign. By then, most west European countries were facing a serious economic crisis, made worse by a poor harvest in 1946 and a severe winter in 1946-1947. At the same time, communist parties in France and Italy were becoming relatively large and popular. This was because of their role in the wartime resistance movements, and the contribution made by the USSR to Hitler's defeat. In February 1947, Britain announced it would no longer be able to give economic or military aid to the Greek Royalists in their civil war against the Greek Communists. Dean Acheson, US Secretary of State, argued that if Greece went communist, then the Balkans and, ultimately, Africa and western Europe (especially France and Italy) would be undermined. This 'rotten apple' argument was based on the idea that one communist state would begin to 'spoil' its immediate neighbours. This was similar to the 'domino theory' which soon came to dominate American foreign policy in south-east Asia.

So, on 12 March 1947, Truman announced what became known as the Truman Doctrine. Though the USSR was not directly mentioned, he implied it was aggressively expansionist and therefore needed to be 'contained'. He argued that all countries had to choose between the 'freedom of the West or the subjugation of communism'. Truman then proclaimed America's readiness to assist any country resisting 'armed minorities' or 'outside pressure'. The USA had clearly abandoned 'isolationism'.

## The Marshall Plan

The USA also decided to help revive the economies of west European states, by giving loans, and helping to rebuild the German economy. This would also be good for American exports. The Marshall Plan was announced on 5 June 1947. Technically, this was also open to the Soviet Union and the east European states. But its political and economic conditions meant Stalin was unlikely to accept it. In fact, both the USA and the USSR saw it as an attempt to weaken Soviet control of eastern Europe. Early applications from Poland and Czechoslovakia were stopped by Stalin. Over the next four years, $1.7 billion was provided by the USA, and the west European economies quickly revived. The Truman Doctrine and the Marshall Plan, along with Soviet actions in eastern Europe, played a significant part in the split of Europe into two opposing camps.

**Source B**

Our policy is directed not against any country or doctrine but against hunger, poverty, desperation and chaos. Its purpose should be the revival of a working economy in the world....

*An extract from a US Department of State Bulletin, 15 June 1947, concerning the Marshall Plan.*

**Source C**

The Truman Doctrine and the Marshall Plan were always two halves of the same walnut.

*A comment made by President Truman, on the two important foreign policy initiatives begun by the USA in 1947.*

**Source D**

*The re-building of flats in Berlin in 1950, under the Marshall Plan.*

**Questions**

1 What were the main Soviet concerns after the end of the Second World War?

2 In what way does **Source C** disagree with the view of Marshall Aid put forward in **Source B**?

# CHAPTER 11

# The Cold War in Europe intensifies

### Source A

The ruling [group] of American imperialists... has taken the path of outright expansion, of enslaving the weakened capitalist states of Europe and the colonial and dependent countries...The clearest and most specific expression of the policy is provided by the Truman-Marshall Plans...Imitating the Hitlerites, the new aggressors are using blackmail and extortion.

*An extract from a speech, made in September 1947 by a leading member of the Soviet government.*

### American nuclear monopoly

*At the time, the USA believed it would take the USSR at least 20 years to develop its own atomic bomb. However, this lack of nuclear weapons did not affect Soviet policy in eastern Europe to any great degree. For instance, despite American pressure, Stalin refused to reorganise the governments of Romania and Bulgaria. In part, this was because Stalin calculated that the USA would be reluctant to use nuclear bombs in Europe.*

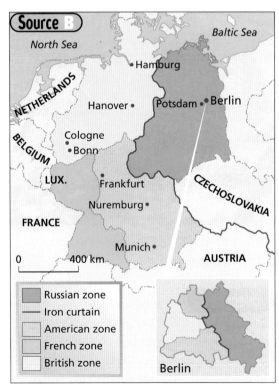

### Source B

*The division of Germany and Berlin after the Second World War.*

## The superpowers

In 1945, the USSR was only a regional power, unlike the USA, which was by then already a truly global power. In particular, the USA had the world's largest navy and airforce, as well as being the richest country in the world. By the end of the war, the Red Army was about 11 million strong, but American forces totalled almost 12 million. Because of the Soviet Union's need for rapid economic reconstruction, money had to be shifted from defence to industry. According to Khrushchev, by 1948, the Red Army had been rapidly demobilised, to under 3 million. Thus, the USA was clearly a superpower, but the Soviet Union was a much less powerful one.

## The American nuclear monopoly

The USA's long-term aims increasingly conflicted with the USSR's regional objectives. Possession of the atomic bomb was seen by Truman and his advisers as a 'negotiating tool', to force the USSR to accept America's plans for post-war Europe and the world. Stalin was very concerned about this American nuclear monopoly, and quickly authorised the development of a Soviet atomic bomb.

## The problem of Germany

During 1947-48, a crisis developed over Germany. At Potsdam, it had been agreed that Germany should be treated as one economic unit, administered jointly by the four Allies. However, the question of reparations continued to cause problems between the Soviet Union and the other allies. Stalin still wanted massive reparations to compensate for the tremendous destruction suffered by the Soviet Union. But the USA and Britain believed a revival of German industry was essential. This would allow the west European economies in general to recover. Also, the USA and Britain did not want to prop up the German economy indefinitely. In January 1947, the USA and Britain merged their two zones into what became known as Bizonia. Then, in February 1947, Britain stated that it might have to pull out of Bizonia if German heavy industry was not revived.

When the Truman Doctrine and the Marshall Plan were announced in June 1947, the USSR became even more suspicious. Stalin began to see these steps as attempting to build up the economy of a new state of West Germany. With 75% of the German population and the important industrial regions, such a state might be a military threat to the Soviet Union in the future, as it had in the past. Stalin was especially worried as it would probably be allied to an increasingly hostile USA.

The USA and Britain agreed to develop Bizonia and introduce currency reform, as first steps in the setting up of a separate West German state. France then joined its zone to Bizonia to form Trizonia. On 18 June, without consulting the Soviet Union, the West introduced a new currency, the Deutschmark, to replace the Reichsmark. On 23 June, this was extended to West Berlin.

## The Berlin Blockade and the Berlin Airlift

The Soviet Union was opposed to the idea of a separate West German state, and tried to prevent this by putting pressure on West Berlin. On 24 June, the Soviet Union cut off all road, rail and freight traffic to West Berlin. This Berlin Crisis, the Berlin Blockade, was the first open Cold War conflict between the two sides. However, it did not develop into a 'hot' war.

Instead, the Allied response was the massive Berlin Airlift, in which tons of food, fuel and other basic items were flown from Trizonia into West Berlin to supply its 2 million citizens. The Airlift lasted for almost a year, until May 1949, when the obvious failure of the Blockade finally led Stalin to call it off.

## The division of Germany

In fact, the Berlin Blockade, designed to make the West drop its idea of a separate West German state, actually speeded it up. The West saw it as an attempt by the Soviet Union to drive the Allies out of West Berlin in preparation for taking over the Western zones of Germany. The political leaders of the three west German zones had, at first, been reluctant to accept the creation of a separate West German state. Now they saw it as a way of ensuring American protection against a Soviet 'takeover'. In May 1949, the new Federal Republic of Germany was set up, and its first government began operating in September 1949. On 7 October, the USSR announced the transformation of its eastern zone into a new state, called the German Democratic Republic. This division of Germany soon came to represent the division of Europe into two mutually suspicious and hostile camps.

## The establishment of NATO

In February 1948, with the Soviet Union continuing its take-over of eastern Europe, the USA's western allies had formed the Brussels Treaty Organisation. This was a military alliance of defence against the Soviet 'threat'. In January 1949, during the Berlin Crisis, the USA joined and it became known as the North Atlantic Treaty Organisation (see the map on page 187). At this time, the USSR had no similar alliance, and was alarmed at the fact that NATO was based on the ability of the USA to launch nuclear bombs at Soviet territory. At this point, the USSR had no ally outside Europe, only the relatively poor and weak countries of eastern Europe. Although the USSR had many more soldiers in Europe than the West, NATO countries greatly increased the number of soldiers in West Germany. By 1953, the USA alone had five divisions permanently based in West Germany.

**Source C**

Some West Berliners waving at a supply plane during the Berlin Airlift.

**Questions**

1 How did the aims of the USA and the USSR differ on the future of Germany?

2 How did the Berlin Crisis of 1948-49 increase Cold War tensions?

3 What happened to Germany after the ending of the Berlin Blockade?

# The Korean War

## The impact of the Chinese Revolution, 1949

After the Berlin Crisis ended in 1949, Cold War tensions shifted from Europe to Asia. This was because, in October 1949, the Chinese Communist Party finally defeated the Nationalists in a civil war which had begun in 1927. This communist victory came just after the USSR had exploded its first atomic bomb. These two events led Republican politicians in the USA to accuse Truman of being 'soft' on communism and of having 'lost' China. In February 1950, Communist China signed a 30-year Treaty of Friendship and Mutual Assistance with the Soviet Union. These developments increased Cold War tensions and led to a 'Red Scare' and a communist witch-hunt in the USA, led by Senator McCarthy. In response, Truman ordered the National Security Council (NSC) to carry out a complete review of American Cold War policies. This was completed in April 1950.

**Source A**

[We advocate] an immediate and large-scale build-up in our military and general strength and that of our allies with the intention... that through means other than all-out war we can induce a change in the nature of the socialist system...

The United States... can strike out on a bold and massive program of rebuilding the West's defensive potential to surpass that of the Soviet world... This means virtual abandonment by the United States of trying to distinguish between national and global security.

*Extracts from the secret document NSC 68, drawn up in April 1950.*

## NSC 68

Among other things, this report recommended a big increase in American military spending, and the development of a hydrogen bomb in order to restore the USA's nuclear superiority. It also said that the policy of containment should be replaced by a more aggressive one of 'rolling back' communism. However, Truman calculated that such a big increase in government expenditure would not be popular. So the recommendations of NSC 68 were put to one side for the moment.

## Korea and the Cold War

From 1910-45, Korea was ruled by Japan. At the end of the war, Korea was temporarily divided along the 38th parallel by the USA and the USSR, for the purpose of dealing with surrendering Japanese troops. As the Cold War began, Korea became divided into a communist North and a capitalist South. This was completed in 1948. The North was ruled by Kim Il Sung, and the South by Syngman Rhee. Both wanted to reunite Korea under their control, and both were prepared to do so by military means. However, the USA did not see Korea as being vital to its interests, while Stalin was satisfied with having a communist government in control in the North, which bordered on the USSR. In the summer of 1948, Stalin withdrew all Soviet troops, and US troops were

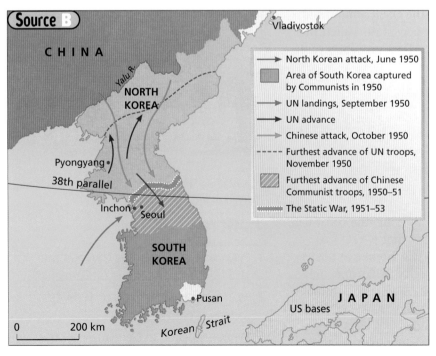

*The division of Korea in 1948 and the Korean War.*

Source B

North Korean attack, June 1950

Area of South Korea captured by Communists in 1950

UN landings, September 1950

UN advance

Chinese attack, October 1950

Furthest advance of UN troops, November 1950

Furthest advance of Chinese Communist troops, 1950–51

The Static War, 1951–53

CHINA

Vladivostok

Yalu R.

NORTH KOREA

Pyongyang

38th parallel

Inchon

Seoul

SOUTH KOREA

Pusan

Korean Strait

JAPAN

US bases

0    200 km

withdrawn in June 1949. In January 1950, the US Secretary of State, Dean Acheson, made a speech about what the USA saw as important countries in a 'Defensive Perimeter' in Asia, which the USA should defend from communist aggression. South Korea was not on the list.

## The start of the Korean War

From 1945-50, there were several military clashes between North and South. By 1950, Rhee's government had become very unpopular, and many in the South wanted re-unification with the North. Kim now believed he could achieve a quick victory, and told Stalin and Mao (leader of Communist China) of his plans. On 25 June 1950, the armies of the North invaded the South. At first, they were very successful and after only four days had captured Seoul, the capital of the South.

## The American response

Truman believed that Stalin had ordered Kim to invade, so he immediately ordered American troops and military supplies in Japan to be sent to South Korea. On 27 June, he was able to get the Security Council of the United Nations to agree to send an army to help the South. The USSR could have blocked this by using its veto, but it was absent from the meeting. This was because it was boycotting the UN in protest at the USA's refusal to give Communist China a seat at the UN. In all, 15 UN member states sent troops, including Britain. But, in reality, it was very much an American enterprise. Out of the 300 000 UN troops, 260 000 were Americans, and all were under the command of US General MacArthur, who reported to Truman, not to the UN.

### Kim Il Sung's plans

*Neither Stalin nor Mao was prepared to get involved in a direct confrontation with the USA. At first they told Kim to abandon the idea. However, Stalin eventually allowed Soviet military planners to help draw up Kim's invasion plans, as he believed the USA was unlikely to get involved.*

### Source D

From my viewpoint, foreign policy is based primarily on one consideration: the need for the USA to obtain raw materials and to preserve profitable foreign markets. Out of this comes the need to make certain that those areas of the world where there are essential raw materials are accessible to us.

*Comments made by US General Eisenhower in 1951. He later became President of the USA in 1953.*

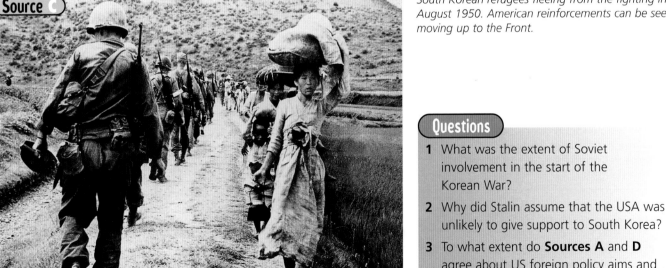

### Source C

*South Korean refugees fleeing from the fighting in August 1950. American reinforcements can be seen moving up to the Front.*

### Questions

1 What was the extent of Soviet involvement in the start of the Korean War?

2 Why did Stalin assume that the USA was unlikely to give support to South Korea?

3 To what extent do **Sources A** and **D** agree about US foreign policy aims and motives in the early 1950s?

# From war to 'thaw'

## Chinese border

*The Communist government of China, led by Mao Zedong, had only been in power for a year, and at this stage still feared the possibility of invasion by Chinese Nationalist forces based in Formosa (Taiwan). They also feared that American troops, once they were on China's border, might invade to restore Jiang Jieshi, the Nationalist leader, to power.*

## The war

At first, the Northern invasion continued to be successful. By September 1950, Kim's army had been able to push the American/UN armies back to a small coastal area around Pusan in the south-east. However, MacArthur then launched a seaborne counter-attack at Inchon, well behind the North Koreans' lines. This allowed the American/UN forces at Pusan to break out. By October, the North Koreans had been pushed back over the border. Truman then decided to follow the NSC 68 recommendations about 'rolling back' communism. So, MacArthur was ordered to cross the 38th parallel.

### Source A

*A Chinese woodcut of 1951, showing North Korean and Chinese soldiers joining forces before attempting to halt the US army's advance.*

The North Korean capital, Pyongyang, was quickly captured, and by the end of October MacArthur's armies were nearing the Yalu River. This was the border between North Korea and China. Mao warned the USA that if MacArthur continued his advance, a Chinese army would be sent to help the North. The USA decided to ignore this threat, and MacArthur pushed on. So, on 25 October, 250 000 Chinese troops moved into North Korea.

## Stalemate

At first, the combined North Korean-Chinese forces had several victories. By January 1951, the American/UN forces had been pushed back over the 38th parallel and Seoul was re-captured.

For a time, the USA considered dropping atomic bombs on China. After strong protests by Britain, this idea was dropped. In February and March, two American/UN counter-attacks succeeded in pushing the North Koreans and Chinese forces back across the border. In April, though, MacArthur criticised Truman's policies and was sacked (Source C). Large Chinese offensives in April and May were unsuccessful, and by early summer the two sides in the Korean War had reached stalemate.

## The cease-fire

Talks for a truce began in July 1951 but, although they continued until 1953, failed to reach agreement. Although the USA was able to develop its hydrogen bomb in 1952 (a much more powerful bomb than the atomic bomb), the USSR and China would not be bullied. In 1952, Truman was defeated by Eisenhower, who became

### Source B

Had [the Chinese] intervened in the first or second months it would have been decisive, [but] we are no longer fearful of their intervention. Now that we have bases for our Air Force in Korea, there would be the greatest slaughter.

*Comments made by General MacArthur in October 1950. Like many US officials, he underestimated the concerns of the Chinese government and its willingness to take action over developments in Korea.*

President in January 1953. He developed a new foreign policy known as the 'New Look', and at first threatened to use the hydrogen bomb if a truce was not signed. Then, in March, Stalin died and both superpowers became willing to negotiate over their Cold War differences. An armistice was signed on 27 July 1953. This was despite the fact that, in the same month, the Soviet Union successfully tested its own hydrogen bomb. The result was that, after a three-year war in which over 10 million people had been killed or injured, Korea remained divided roughly along the 38th parallel. Because of the Cold War, the division of Korea continued, and no formal peace treaty has yet been signed.

## The thaw

Even before Stalin's death, the USSR had attempted to limit the nuclear arms race by organising several 'peace campaigns' in western Europe. This had had much to do with the tremendous amount of money which the Soviet Union needed to spend on nuclear weapons just to stop falling too far behind the USA. Stalin had also suggested that Germany and central Europe should demilitarise and be neutral. In March 1952, in the 'Stalin Notes', he said that the USSR would accept the reunification of Germany if it remained neutral.

Though these suggestions failed, the new collective Soviet leadership which took over in 1953 decided to continue attempts to 'thaw' Cold War tensions, which had been increased by the Korean War. One immediate result was Soviet pressure on North Korea to sign an armistice. At the same time, despite Eisenhower's adoption of his 'New Look' policy which called for the 'rolling back' of communism, and the idea of 'brinkmanship', he too was prepared to reduce tensions. In practice, his 'New Look' was not much different from Truman's policy of 'containment'. This was partly because he believed a nuclear war between the two superpowers would be an awful disaster. By 1952, the USA had developed the hydrogen bomb, which began the thermonuclear age. By 1953, the USSR had matched it.

### Source C

For a long time there had been tension between Truman and MacArthur. This now reached breaking point. On 24 March [1951] MacArthur made a public statement criticising the idea of a deal with the Chinese. Truman was annoyed when he heard this. MacArthur... sent a message to an American politician explaining his views that America should keep fighting until the Chinese were defeated. Truman was very angry that a general was trying to control the war, instead of obeying his orders, and in April MacArthur was dismissed.

*An extract from a history textbook, published in Britain in 1998.*

### Brinkmanship

*This was a policy associated with J. F. Dulles, appointed as US Secretary of State in 1952 by Eisenhower. By it, Dulles meant that the USA should be more aggressive and confrontational towards the USSR and Communist China - up to and including the use of nuclear weapons. This was based on his belief that the USA's big nuclear superiority would force the Soviet bloc to make concessions. The 1952 US presidential election had included promises to 'liberate' eastern Europe, and a commitment to use nuclear weapons 'when necessary'.*

### Questions

1  Why did Communist China become involved in the Korean War?

2  How useful is **Source C** for understanding why MacArthur was dismissed in April 1951?

3  Why were both sides in the Cold War keen to reduce tensions between them in the early 1950s?

# Peaceful coexistence and crisis

We communists believe that the ideas of communism will be victorious throughout the world just as they have been in China and in many states. Many will probably disagree with us. It is their right to think so. We may argue, we may disagree with each other. The main thing is to argue without resort to arms to prove that one is right.

*An extract from a speech by Khrushchev in 1959. It gives his view of 'peaceful coexistence' between the communist and capitalist blocs.*

## The continuing problem of Germany

The German question had continued to be a Cold War problem, despite the end of the Berlin Crisis of 1948-49. The new Soviet leaders, such as Malenkov and Khrushchev, decided to continue Stalin's German policy. This was because they felt a united but neutral Germany was better than the tensions caused by its continued division. An offer in 1954 of reunification in return for German neutrality was again rejected, as the West did not trust Soviet motives.

Soviet concerns were increased in May 1955, when West Germany was allowed to join NATO and to rearm. One immediate result was that the USSR decided at last to form its own military alliance. Shortly after Germany became a member of NATO, and six years after the formation of NATO, the Soviet Union announced the creation of the Warsaw Pact Organisation.

## 'Peaceful coexistence'

By then, a power struggle in the USSR had ended with the emergence of Khrushchev as the main leader. He soon became closely associated with the policy of 'peaceful coexistence'. This had been followed, on and off, by Soviet governments since 1921. Khrushchev decided to show his willingness to negotiate by quickly agreeing to pull out all Soviet troops from Austria (which, like Germany, had been divided into Allied zones), if it remained neutral.

## The Geneva Summit

In July 1955, the first of several summit meetings took place at Geneva. This was between the Big Four (the USA, the USSR, Britain and France), and was the first such meeting since the Potsdam Conference in July 1945. Though no significant agreements were reached, this Geneva Summit was important for the friendly atmosphere, which became known as the 'spirit of Geneva'. However, Soviet proposals on disarmament, control of nuclear weapons and Germany were again rejected. Khrushchev also rejected Eisenhower's 'Open Skies' proposal, which would have allowed each side to fly over the other side's military sites.

## The Second Berlin Crisis

A second crisis over Berlin broke out in November 1958, when Khrushchev issued the first of several Berlin ultimatums. He had been made more confident about Soviet strength by the successful launch of Sputnik (the world's first space satellite); but he was also facing increasing criticism from other Soviet leaders. So, on 27 November 1958, he threatened to sign a separate treaty with East Germany and to end the division of Berlin into four sectors if the USA would not agree to Berlin becoming a demilitarised and

*American and Russian tanks facing each other across a Berlin border crossing in 1959.*

neutral area. This was partly due to pressure from the East German leader to do something about the influence of prosperous west Berlin. At first, Khrushchev gave the West six months, but this was later extended and negotiations continued. In an attempt to break the deadlock, Eisenhower invited Khrushchev to the USA for more talks. These took place in September 1959 at Camp David and went well. Khrushchev withdrew his ultimatum, and the two leaders agreed to another summit in Paris.

## The U-2 Incident

However, by the time the Paris Summit took place in May 1960, the situation had changed. American spy-planes (U-2s) had flown over the USSR and had discovered how far it was behind the USA as regards numbers of Inter-Continental Ballistic Missiles (ICBMs). Then, on 1 May 1960, the USSR announced that a Soviet missile had shot down a U-2, and that they had captured its pilot. Eisenhower was embarrassed as he had always denied that the USA was flying spy-planes over the USSR. He refused to apologise and the summit ended in stalemate.

## The Berlin Wall

One result of this increased tension over Berlin was that thousands of East Germans began to migrate to the West through west Berlin. By 1959, about 200 000 were leaving every year. As many of them were skilled workers, this soon began to hit the East German economy. In 1960, Khrushchev came under increasing pressure from the East German government to take action. He believed that Kennedy, the newly-elected US President, could be persuaded to compromise. However, at their first meeting at the Vienna Summit in June 1961, Kennedy would not budge on the Berlin issue.

So Khrushchev announced another ultimatum, which raised tensions and led to even more East Germans rushing to the West. The Warsaw Pact then instructed the East German government to secure its borders with the West. In August 1961, work began to build the Berlin Wall. It was a concrete symbol of Cold War divisions, and remained until 1989.

### Questions

1 What was the U-2 Incident in 1960, and how did it affect Cold War tensions between the USA and the Soviet Union?

2 Why did a new crisis break out over Berlin in 1958, a scene from which is shown in **Source B**?

3 What can you learn from **Source C** about the effects of the Berlin Wall on the lives of Berlin residents?

### ICBMs

*These are long-range missiles, which are capable of delivering nuclear warheads across continents. Although they were first tested by the USSR in 1957, as part of their 'Sputnik' programme, the USA had already been developing their own. Immediately after 1957, the USA began testing and building their own ICBMs and soon had a massive lead over the USSR. However, US governments claimed throughout the late 1950s and the 1960s that there was a 'missile gap' between the two superpowers and that the USA was behind. Even though both governments knew this was not true, this claim was used to justify a big increase in American defence spending in the early 1960s.*

### Source C

*Parents lifting up babies to show them to relatives across the Berlin Wall, 1961.*

# SUMMARY

## 1943–1945

- In 1943, the Big Three (the USA, the USSR and Britain) met at the Tehran Conference. Despite some disagreements, there was common ground.
- There were greater differences at the Yalta Conference in February 1945. These widened at the Potsdam Conference in July, when Truman replaced Roosevelt as President of the USA, and the USA dropped atomic bombs on Japan. It was agreed to divide Germany temporarily into four Allied zones.

## 1946–1947

- In March 1946, Churchill made his 'iron curtain' speech. In January 1947, the USA and Britain merged their German zones to form Bizonia.
- In March, the USA announced the Truman Doctrine, to 'contain' communism, and the Marshall Plan to rebuild western economies. Massive American aid to western European countries soon made them much wealthier than those in eastern Europe.

## 1948–1949

- In June 1948, France joined its German zone to Bizonia to form Trizonia, and a new currency was introduced by the West without consulting the USSR. Stalin began the Berlin Blockade, which was met by the West with the Berlin Airlift.
- In April 1949, the West formed NATO and the Berlin Blockade was called off. The new state of West Germany was then set up.
- In August, the US nuclear monopoly ended when the USSR exploded its own atomic bomb. In October, the Chinese Communists came to power.

## 1950–1953

- In January 1950, Dean Acheson (US Secretary of State) made his 'Defence Perimeter' speech. Korea, which had been divided after 1945 into North and South, was not mentioned. In June, North Korea invaded the South, so beginning the Korean War.
- The USA got the UN to agree to send troops to help the South. When these troops advanced to the Chinese border, China sent an army in to help the North.
- By 1951, a stalemate was reached. In 1952, the USA exploded its first hydrogen bomb. In 1953, after Eisenhower became President and Stalin died, an armistice ended the fighting. Shortly after, the USSR exploded its own hydrogen bomb.

## 1954–1961

- After Stalin's death, the Soviet leaders and Eisenhower tried to reduce Cold War tensions (the 'thaw'). In 1955, Khrushchev became the main Soviet leader, and followed a policy of 'peaceful coexistence'.
- The 'thaw' slowed when West Germany was allowed to join NATO. As a result, the USSR set up the Warsaw Pact Organisation as a rival military alliance in 1955.
- After the Geneva Summit in July 1955, relations seemed to improve again. But in 1958, a new crisis arose over Germany and Berlin. The Camp David meeting in September 1959 was a success, but the U-2 Incident ended the Paris Summit in May 1960. The Vienna Summit in June 1961 also failed. One result was the building of the Berlin Wall.

# Exam Question Practice

## Explanation/analysis questions

Study Source A below, which is about the introduction by the West of a new currency for the three western zones of Germany in 1948, then answer the following question:

Why was the question of Germany such an important factor in the Cold War during the period 1945 to 1961? **(12)**

---

**Source A**

[Western currency reform] is against the wishes and interests of the German people and in the interests of the American, British and French [capitalists]...the separate currency reform completes the splitting of Germany. It is a breach of the Potsdam decisions and the control mechanism for Germany which [saw] the treatment of Germany as an economic whole.... The American, French and British... in the western zones are supported in their policy of splitting Germany by the big German capitalists and [those] who helped fascism to power and prepared the Second World War

---

*A proclamation by Marshal Sokolovsky, Soviet Military Governor of Berlin, 18 June 1948.*

## Examiner's Tips

**When answering questions like this:**

◎ Remember you are being asked to explain something, so don't just describe the tensions and problems over Germany from 1945-61, as this will not answer the question - even if many of the facts you give are accurate and relevant. You must show the examiner that you are aware of reasons/causes, as well as knowing the facts.

◎ Make sure you try to give a number of different reasons to show both East and West's concerns over the future of Germany - and make sure you can give one or two precise examples to illustrate the reasons you have given. If you just list several different reasons without giving supporting facts, you will not score the higher marks.

◎ Check the number of marks available. Such questions often carry high marks, so you will find it helpful to do a rough plan first - that way, you can check to see you are giving several different reasons.

◎ Try to see if you can sort the reasons out into more/less important ones where this is possible/relevant.

# CHAPTER 12

## CUBA AND VIETNAM: COLD WAR 'HOTSPOTS' 1962-1975

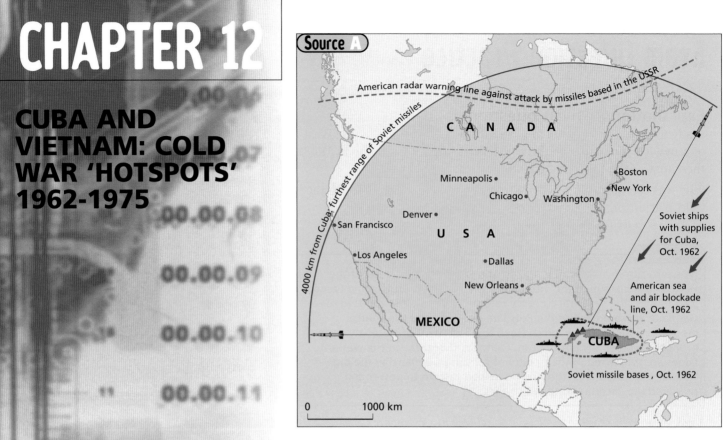

Source A

American radar warning line against attack by missiles based in the USSR

4000 km from Cuba: furthest range of Soviet missiles

C A N A D A

Minneapolis •

Boston •
New York •

Chicago • Washington •

Denver •

San Francisco •

U S A

Los Angeles •

• Dallas

New Orleans •

Soviet ships with supplies for Cuba, Oct. 1962

American sea and air blockade line, Oct. 1962

MEXICO

CUBA

Soviet missile bases, Oct. 1962

0        1000 km

*A map of Cuba showing the American blockade, and the range of Soviet missiles based on Cuba.*

Source B

*Some of the Vietnamese civilians killed by US troops in the My Lai massacre in 1968. This photograph was not published until 1969.*

Source C

*The last US citizens and their South Vietnamese supporters land on a US aircraft carrier after fleeing Saigon by helicopter in 1975.*

## Key Questions

**How** did a small island like Cuba, shown in **Source A**, come to be the focus of one of the most serious Cold War crises?

**Why** did American troops massacre Vietnamese civilians as shown in **Source B**?

**Why** was the world's most powerful state forced to leave Vietnam in the circumstances shown in **Source C**?

These are some of the issues which we will cover in this chapter. The main focus of this chapter on Cold War 'hotspots' will be:

- How Cuba became an important issue in the Cold War
- The development of the Cuban Missile Crisis
- The impact of the Cuban Missile Crisis on the Cold War
- How the USA became involved in a war in Vietnam
- The nature of the Vietnam War
- Why the USA was finally forced to withdraw from Vietnam

# Cuba and the Cold War

If a nation shows that it knows how to act with reasonable efficiency and decency in social and political matters, if it keeps order and pays its obligations, it need fear no intervention from the United States. Chronic wrong-doing... may... ultimately require intervention by some civilised nation, and in the western hemisphere the adherence of the United States to the Monroe Doctrine may force the United States, however reluctantly... to the exercise of an international police power.

*An extract from the statement made by President Theodore Roosevelt in 1904 which became known as the 'Roosevelt Corollary'.*

## The Monroe Doctrine

The USA always saw the American continent as its sphere of influence. In 1823, the Monroe Doctrine made it clear that the USA would not tolerate the presence of any European nation in its 'backyard'. In 1898, the USA fought a war against Spain, which had several colonies in Latin America and the Caribbean. The USA won the war, occupied Cuba, Puerto Rico and Panama, and made the Dominican Republic its 'protectorate'.

In 1904, Theodore Roosevelt, the US President, issued the Roosevelt Corollary. This said that American intervention in the region, to protect private property, American lives or to maintain order, would be justified. During the 1920s and 1930s, there were several military interventions in the Americas by the USA to protect American interests. At the same time, American investments in the region were greatly increased. By 1939, under the 'Good Neighbour' policy, $3 billion had been invested.

**Source B**

*A photograph from the early 1950s showing signs of American investment in Cuba. The large skyscraper is the Havana Hilton Hotel.*

## The impact of the Cold War

As soon as the Cold War began, the USA took steps to prevent any communist or pro-communist government coming to power in the region. In 1947, the USA signed the Rio Pact with the countries of Latin America and, in 1948, set up the Organisation of American States (OAS). The Charter of the OAS said that 'international communism' was incompatible with 'American freedom'.

However, in 1954, the USA failed to get the OAS to agree to take action in Guatemala. There a left-of-centre government, elected in 1951, was carrying out land reform which involved the nationalisation (with compensation) of undeveloped land owned by American companies. So, instead, Eisenhower authorised the CIA to take covert action. This brought about the overthrow of the Guatemalan government, and its replacement by a military dictatorship friendly to the USA.

## Cuba before 1956

After the Spanish-American War of 1898, Cuba was occupied by American troops but, in 1901, the USA allowed Cuba to draw up a constitution. However, the USA insisted that this include the Platt Amendment. This said the USA had the right to 'oversee' the Cuban economy, intervene in Cuba's internal affairs and to veto any international agreements. Although this was ended by Roosevelt in 1933, the Cuban economy was by then highly dependent on the sale of sugar and tobacco to the USA.

From 1934, Cuba was run by a right-wing military dictator, General Fulgencio Batista, who was supported by the USA. During his rule, there was increasing American control of both the economy and internal politics. Many Cubans opposed him and, on 26 July 1953, a small group of revolutionaries led by Fidel Castro, attacked the army's Moncada Barracks. The attack failed and Castro was imprisoned. On his early release in 1954, he went into exile in Mexico. In 1955, he formed the 26 July Movement which was later joined by Ernesto 'Che' Guevara, a young Argentine doctor and revolutionary.

## Castro's Revolution

In 1956, Castro and Guevara led a small group to Cuba to overthrow Batista. At this stage, most of the revolutionaries were middle-class liberal reformers and had no connection to the Cuban Communist Party. After two years of guerrilla warfare, Batista fled from Cuba. This allowed Castro's forces to enter Havana on 1 January 1959. Cuba's new President was Urrutia, with Cardona as Prime Minister. However, real power rested with Castro who was Commander-in-Chief of the armed forces. In February, Cardona resigned in protest at his lack of real power. His place was taken by Castro.

**CIA**

*These initials stand for the Central Intelligence Agency, the US secret service, set up at the end of the Second World War, in 1947. Its main activities were connected to 'containing' communism around the world. This covered a variety of activities, including: spying; training and arming anti-communist forces; organising coups against governments seen as being too sympathetic to communism or socialism; and even the assassination of left-wing leaders. It reported to the National Security Council, but did not have to account for its budget. The Soviet equivalent was the KGB.*

**Source C**

I believe there is no country in the world...whose economic colonisation, humiliation and exploitation were worse than in Cuba, partly as a consequence of US policy during the Batista regime. I believe that, without being aware of it, we conceived and created the Castro movement, starting from scratch.

*Comments made by US President Kennedy in 1963, after the Cuban Missile Crisis.*

**Questions**

1 What were the implications of the Monroe Doctrine and the Roosevelt Corollary for American foreign policy in the Americas?

2 How useful is **Source C** as evidence of American exploitation of Cuba before Castro's revolution in 1959?

# Growing tensions over Cuba

## American concerns

At first, Castro hoped for help from the USA which was the main purchaser of sugar and tobacco, Cuba's largest exports. Although Vice-President Nixon agreed to meet him at the UN in April 1959, Eisenhower refused to discuss the question of American aid. American hostility increased in May, when Castro announced his land reform programme under which foreigners would no longer be able to own land in Cuba. Then, in September 1959, Castro declared Cuba's neutrality in the Cold War.

Tension increased in 1960 when American-owned oil refineries in Cuba refused to process Soviet crude oil which was cheaper than the oil usually bought. Castro then nationalised the American companies. He also signed a trade agreement with the USSR. In reply, Eisenhower first suspended and then, in December, completely ended the sugar quota (an agreement on the quantity of sugar that the USA would guarantee to buy from Cuba). Castro's response was to nationalise all American companies, so the USA placed a ban on almost all trade with Cuba. The USSR then agreed to buy two million tons of Cuba's sugar for the next four years. Castro then signed trade agreements with most of the countries of the Soviet bloc. In January 1961, the USA broke off all diplomatic relations with Cuba.

## The Bay of Pigs

By 1961, Eisenhower had drawn up plans for US-backed Cuban exiles to invade Cuba. They were already bombing Cuba and burning sugar plantations. These invasion plans were put into operation by Kennedy, the newly-elected US President. On 15 April, CIA pilots helped the exiles bomb Cuban air bases. Castro immediately announced Cuba would become socialist. On 17 April, about 1400 exiles landed in the Bay of Pigs. Although no American troops were involved, the USA provided transport, weapons and military advisers. However, the exiles were quickly defeated, and 1179 were captured. To get them back, the USA had to give $53 million worth of aid in the form of baby food, medicines and medical equipment. Despite this humiliation, Kennedy ordered the CIA to continue with sabotage and its attempts to overthrow or assassinate Castro.

## The 'missile gap'

After the Bay of Pigs and the continued CIA campaigns, Castro was convinced that the USA would soon invade again. In fact, in

### Source A

In 1959 and 1960, Castro attempted to get American aid for the development of Cuba, but was turned down. Instead, Eisenhower reduced the amount of Cuban sugar bought by the USA by 95%. This meant ruin for Cuba. Only then did Castro turn to the Soviet Union in 1960. The Soviet Union agreed to buy one million tonnes of Cuban sugar every year. This tied the two countries closely together.

*An extract from a history textbook, published in Britain in 1999.*

### Source B

*Some of the American-backed Cubans opposed to Castro, captured after the Bay of Pigs incident in 1961.*

November 1961, Kennedy did authorise another attempt to overthrow Castro. For protection, Castro appealed to Khrushchev for more Soviet weapons. From May 1962, the USSR greatly increased its deliveries of tanks and military aircraft to Cuba. The number of Soviet troops stationed there rose to 42 000.

However, Castro's request came at a time when the USSR was becoming increasingly concerned at the 'missile gap' resulting from the USA's vast superiority in long-range weapons. In particular, Khrushchev was worried by the American missiles stationed in Italy and in Turkey on the Black Sea coast near to the USSR.

## Soviet missiles

Khrushchev thought that by placing Soviet missiles on Cuba, which was only 90 miles from Florida, he would balance the threat of the American missiles in Turkey, as well as giving Castro the protection he was demanding. So, in September 1962, Soviet technicians began to install and equip missile sites in Cuba.

On 11 September, Kennedy warned Khrushchev that the USA would prevent the installation of Soviet nuclear weapons on Cuba by 'whatever means might be necessary'. Khrushchev replied that the missiles would not be capable of hitting the USA. However, on 14 October, an American U-2 spy plane flew over the sites and took photographs which showed that the USSR had sent intermediate-range (IRBM) as well as short-range missiles. The IRBMs had a range of over 1000 miles and so could reach most major American cities (see map on page 204). However, the photographs also showed that the missiles had not yet been made ready.

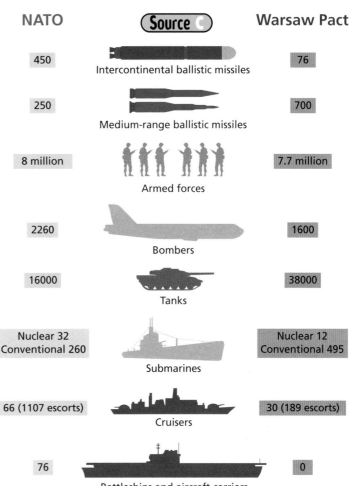

**Source C**

| NATO | | Warsaw Pact |
|---|---|---|
| 450 | Intercontinental ballistic missiles | 76 |
| 250 | Medium-range ballistic missiles | 700 |
| 8 million | Armed forces | 7.7 million |
| 2260 | Bombers | 1600 |
| 16000 | Tanks | 38000 |
| Nuclear 32 Conventional 260 | Submarines | Nuclear 12 Conventional 495 |
| 66 (1107 escorts) | Cruisers | 30 (189 escorts) |
| 76 | Battleships and aircraft carriers | 0 |

*The relative strengths of the two Alliances in 1963.*

**Source D**

*A photograph taken by a US spy-plane on 24 October 1962, showing evidence of a missile base being built on Cuba.*

### Questions

1  What was the USA trying to achieve by the Bay of Pigs incident, referred to in **Source B**?
2  How did the information given in **Source C** contribute to Khrushchev's decision to install Soviet missiles on Cuba?
3  Why was Castro prepared to allow Khrushchev to install Soviet missiles on Cuba?

# The Cuban Missile Crisis

## Source A

A US destroyer (in the foreground) shadowing a Soviet supply ship as part of the 'quarantine' imposed by the USA in October 1962.

## Source B

You are worried over Cuba. You say that it worries you because it lies 90 miles across the sea from the shores of the United States. However, Turkey lies next to us. You have stationed devastating rocket weapons in Turkey, literally right next to us. This is why I make this proposal: We agree to remove the weapons from Cuba. We agree to this and to state this commitment in the United Nations. Your representatives will make a statement that the United States, on its part, will evacuate its similar weapons from Turkey.

An extract from Khrushchev's letter of 27 October sent to Kennedy.

## Jupiter missiles

These missiles were removed from Turkey in April 1963. However, the USA had already decided to remove them before the Cuban Missile Crisis. This was because such land-based missiles had been made obsolete by the development of Submarine-Launched Ballistic Missiles (SLBMs), which were much more difficult to detect and destroy.

## The crisis

For six days, a few members of the US government met to discuss what the USA should do. This Executive Committee of the National Security Council (ExComm) considered several options, which included invading Cuba. None of the USA's allies, including Britain, was consulted or even informed until 21 October, when Kennedy had already decided. On 22 October, the USA announced a naval blockade or 'quarantine' of Cuba. This would involve stopping and searching all ships heading for the island.

Although the USSR declared that this was against international law and that they would not comply, on 24 October, 18 Soviet ships stopped and turned round before reaching the limit set by the USA. The USA then increased the risk of a nuclear Third World War by stating that if the Soviet missiles were not removed at once, it would invade Cuba. The USA then began to prepare for air-strikes against the missile sites. Castro, and some Soviet generals, urged Khrushchev to launch some missiles to prevent the American invasion.

## The compromise

Khrushchev, however, refused to do so. Instead, on 26 October, he sent Kennedy a letter, offering to withdraw all Soviet missiles if the USA would promise not to invade Cuba. Then, on 27 October, without having had a response from Kennedy, Khrushchev sent a second letter. This time, he offered to remove the Soviet missiles if the USA would remove their Jupiter missiles from Turkey. He also suggested this be supervised by the UN.

This proposal presented problems for the USA, as they had never publicly admitted they had placed missiles in Turkey. So Kennedy decided to ignore the second letter, and gave a commitment not to invade Cuba, provided the missiles were removed. However, Robert Kennedy, the President's brother and Attorney General, was instructed to give an unofficial ultimatum and offer to the Soviet Ambassador. This said that if the USSR had not promised by

28 October to remove the missiles, the USA would attack and destroy them. The offer was that once the missiles had gone, then the USA would soon remove theirs from Turkey. However, Kennedy said that all this (including the deal over Cuba) would have to be kept secret. Khrushchev accepted this deal, even though it seemed to the world that the USSR had been defeated. After what proved to be the most serious 13 days in the entire Cold War, the crisis was over.

## The 'hot line' and the Test Ban Treaty

Both sides had been shocked at how close the world had come to a nuclear war. Once the Cuban crisis was over, the two leaders agreed to set up a telephone 'hot line' between the White House and the Kremlin. This was so that in any future Cold War crisis they could communicate quickly and directly. The line was in operation by June 1963. Although the Cold War continued, tensions were never as high as they had been in October 1962.

The two sides also tried to reduce the nuclear arms race. In August 1963, they signed a Nuclear Test Ban Treaty to limit the testing of nuclear devices. However, it did not limit or reduce the building and deployment of such weapons. In a separate arrangement, the USA also agreed to sell the Soviet Union surplus grain worth $250 million.

## The impact of the Cuban crisis

Although Khrushchev had got the USA to give an unofficial promise not to invade Cuba again, many leading Soviet Communists were unhappy at the USSR's public climb-down. Khrushchev's handling of the Cuban Missile Crisis played an important part in his downfall in 1964. At the same time, the USSR's apparent defeat convinced the Chinese Communists that the Soviet Union under Khrushchev would never stand up to American aggression. This helped widen the split in the world communist movement. Finally, the USA's refusal to consult its NATO allies, even though a nuclear war would also have involved them, led to great concern. Later, de Gaulle decided to withdraw France from membership of NATO.

**Source C**

*Khrushchev sitting in the garden of his country home in 1967, after being removed from power in 1964.*

### Questions

1 Why did the USA find it difficult to respond publicly to Khrushchev's second letter, part of which is given in **Source B**?
2 What were the immediate results of the Cuban Missile Crisis?

# Involvement in Vietnam

## Vietnam before 1946

By the time the Cuban Missile Crisis was over, the USA had begun to get involved in another Cold War conflict. This was in the south-east Asian country of Vietnam. Before the Second World War, Vietnam had been part of the French colony of Indo-China. However, an increasing number of Vietnamese had begun to demand independence. During the war, the Japanese drove the French out and occupied Vietnam. Some Vietnamese nationalists then set up the League for Vietnamese Independence - the Viet Minh. They were led by a Communist called Ho Chi Minh. Under his leadership, the Viet Minh fought a guerrilla war against the Japanese invaders in order to drive them out and become independent. By August 1945, when the Second World War ended, the Viet Minh were in control of the north of Vietnam. In September 1945, Ho Chi Minh declared Vietnam's independence.

## The return of the French

The French, however, wanted to rule Vietnam again. In 1946, war broke out between the French and the Viet Minh. At first, the USA did not back France's wish to regain their colony. But when the Cold War began, their attitude to the Viet Minh changed, particularly after 1949, when the Communists took power in China. In 1950, the USA began to give massive financial aid to help the French fight the Viet Minh, who soon began to receive aid from Mao's Communist China. Despite American aid, the French continued to do badly in the war. In 1954, they suffered a big defeat at the battle of Dien Bien Phu and decided to pull out of Vietnam.

**Source A**

*Vietnam after the Second World War.*

## The division of Vietnam

Peace talks were held in Geneva between the USA, the USSR, France, Britain and China about what should happen to Vietnam. It was decided that Vietnam should be temporarily divided into North and South along the 17th parallel, and that elections should be held in 1956 to decide on its future government. Ho Chi Minh, who was in control of the north, agreed to this because he believed the Viet Minh were popular enough to win the elections in both the North and the South.

## The growth of American involvement

However, President Truman then decided not to sign these Geneva Agreements. This was because of the USA's belief in the Domino Theory. In 1954, in order to stop Vietnam from becoming communist, the USA sent advisers to South Vietnam to persuade people not to vote for Ho Chi Minh in the 1956 elections. In 1955, Ngo Dihn Diem became President of South Vietnam. He was strongly anti-communist and so was supported by the USA, but he was also undemocratic and corrupt. In 1956, he refused to hold the reunification elections which had been part of the Geneva Agreements. He then rigged a referendum to show that the people of South Vietnam supported him and his actions. The USA went along with this as they believed that the Communists would have won the reunification elections.

## The Viet Cong

Ho Chi Minh was angry that the elections had been cancelled. Meanwhile, Diem began to rule South Vietnam more and more as a dictator. Diem, who was a Roman Catholic, gave the best jobs to his relatives, and did nothing to solve the problems of the peasants - the majority of whom were Buddhists. Over the next three years, the number of South Vietnamese opposed to Diem's rule increased. In 1959, the government of North Vietnam decided to encourage a nationalist revolution in the South. In 1960, various groups opposed to Diem joined to form the National Liberation Front. This NLF was also known as the Viet Cong. It contained many Communists and promised land reform, reunification with the North and complete independence. The NLF launched a guerrilla war against Diem, which included sabotage and terrorist attacks against government officials. The government of North Vietnam then gave aid to the NLF.

## American involvement under Kennedy

President Eisenhower increased the amount of American financial and military aid to Diem's government in the South. Kennedy, who became the next President of the USA in 1961, also believed in the Domino Theory and the need to 'contain' communism. He increased American assistance even more. By 1963, there were over 16 000 US military 'advisers' in South Vietnam, and financial aid had increased by over 300% since 1960. Kennedy also sanctioned the 'strategic hamlets' programme, which involved putting peasants into fortified villages in order to prevent contact with the Viet Cong. However, this policy was unsuccessful and only increased the opposition to Diem. At the same time, Diem's intolerant attitude to the Buddhists and his favouritism to Catholics, led several Buddhist monks to protest by setting themselves on fire. Diem's dictatorial rule, his refusal to carry out any reforms and the mounting protests, led the USA to look for another leader in the South. In November 1963, with the backing of the CIA, a group of army generals overthrew Diem in a coup. Later, he and his brother were murdered by the generals. Later that same month, Kennedy was himself assassinated in the USA.

**Source B**

It was generally agreed that if an election had been held, Ho Chi Minh would have been elected Premier....At the time of the fighting [1954], possibly 80% of the population would have voted for the Communist leader.

*An extract from President Eisenhower's memoirs, written after the USA had become heavily involved in the Vietnam War.*

**Source C**

*A Viet Cong unit being briefed before an attack on a US fire base in South Vietnam.*

**Questions**

1  Why did the USA get involved in Vietnam?

2  Explain the popularity of the Viet Minh and the Viet Cong.

3  What can you learn about the Viet Cong from **Source C**?

# CHAPTER 12

# Escalation of the Vietnam War

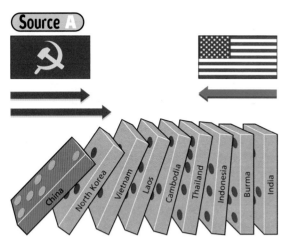

The Domino Theory.

American troops at rest in a forest in South Vietnam. Note the damage done by the chemical defoliants used by the US armed forces.

## Chemical defoliants

*These included 'Agent Orange' and were dropped to strip the leaves off the trees in the jungles, so that Viet Cong and North Vietnamese troops could be seen more easily from the air. 'Agent Blue' was dropped on fields in order to reduce the food available for the Viet Cong. Millions of gallons were dropped, and this resulted in thousands of deformed babies being born.*

## Johnson and escalation

When Kennedy was assassinated in 1963, he was replaced by Vice-President Johnson. Johnson was even more willing than Kennedy had been to escalate American involvement in the war in Vietnam. By then, the Viet Cong were in control of more than half of the countryside of South Vietnam. Johnson believed in the Domino Theory, and was especially determined to counter the presence of North Vietnamese troops in the South. These were sent to the South in 1964 to help the Viet Cong.

## The Gulf of Tonkin Incident

In August 1964, a US destroyer, which was close to the North Vietnamese coast, was attacked by some North Vietnamese ships in the Gulf of Tonkin. Although no serious damage was done, Johnson used the Incident as an opportunity to order the bombing of North Vietnam's naval bases. Yet no state of war had been officially declared. He then persuaded the US Congress to pass the 'Tonkin Resolution'. This gave him the power to 'take all necessary steps, including the use of armed force' to defend South Vietnam. In the November 1964 presidential elections, Johnson said he would not let south-east Asia 'go the way China went'.

## Operation Rolling Thunder

For several years, Johnson had favoured sending a large US army to South Vietnam. After the Tonkin Resolution, he no longer had to consult Congress on the next steps. By March 1965, US bombers were regularly attacking targets in the North in a massive bombing campaign known as 'Operation Rolling Thunder'. In July, Johnson sent in 180 000 American troops. The conflict between the USA and the Viet Cong had escalated into a war between the USA and the North. By 1968, Johnson had increased the number of American troops in the South to 540 000.

## American tactics

Although the arrival of such large numbers of American troops prevented the defeat of the South, they were unable to crush the Viet Cong. The USA responded in several ways. Firstly, the bombing of North Vietnam, and of Viet Cong-controlled areas in the South, was repeatedly stepped up. According to some estimates, more bombs were dropped on North Vietnam in three years than the combined total dropped on Germany, Italy and Japan during the whole of the Second World War.

Secondly, the USA made great use of napalm, chemical defoliants and anti-personnel bombs. These, in addition to the heavy conventional bombing, caused many civilian casualties. In 1965, about 100 000 civilians in the South were killed. By 1968, the figure had risen to over 300 000. This led to mounting opposition from South Vietnamese peasants to the USA and the government of the South, and increased support for the Viet Cong and the North. Finally, on the ground, American troops followed a policy known as 'search and destroy'. This involved destroying the villages from which the Viet Cong seemed to be operating. As well as killing the Viet Cong, this strategy was aimed at frightening civilians in these villages into moving to areas controlled by the government of South Vietnam. It was then assumed that anyone staying behind was a Viet Cong suspect who could be treated accordingly.

**Source D**

### The Tet Offensive

The failure of such tactics was made clear in January 1968. During the Tet (New Year) religious celebrations, the Viet Cong and North Vietnamese troops launched a massive attack against many towns and US military bases in the South. This failed to spark off a rebellion in the South as the Viet Cong had hoped and, after three months of heavy fighting, this Tet Offensive was defeated. By March 1968, over 50 000 Communist troops had been killed and most of the areas gained had been recaptured. However, the size of the offensive showed that the USA was wrong to claim that it was close to victory in the war in Vietnam.

**Questions**

1 What were the main ideas behind the Domino Theory referred to in **Source A**?

2 What can you learn about American tactics during the Vietnam War from **Sources B**, **C** and **D**?

3 Why, despite the use of such tactics, was the USA not more successful?

**Source C**

We didn't look at the Vietnamese as human beings. They were sub-human. To kill them would be easy for you. If you continued this process you didn't have any bad feelings about it because they were a sub-human species. We used terms like 'gooks' and 'zipperheads' and we had to kill different insects every day and they would say 'There's a gook, step on it and squash it'.

*A US marine talking about the training he received in the 1960s, before being sent to Vietnam.*

*American soldiers carrying out a 'search and destroy' mission in a South Vietnamese village.*

**Source E**

The US Command's Director of Combat Operations, Brigadier General John Chasson, confirmed the Embassy's assessment of the continuing Viet Cong threat [that 'They have shown they are still capable of presenting a real military challenge']. 'I must confess the VC surprised us with their attack', he said. 'It was surprisingly well co-ordinated, surprisingly impressive and launched with a surprising amount of audacity'....
He described the enemy offensive as very successful.

*An extract from the* Sunday Times, *4 February 1968, about the impact of the Tet Offensive.*

# The USA looks for a way out

## A turning point

In fact, the Tet Offensive turned out to be an important turning point in the war. It caused many of Johnson's advisers to think that a Communist victory could not be prevented. Johnson scaled down US bombing, and called for peace talks. North Vietnam agreed and the first peace talks took place in Paris in May 1968. The Tet Offensive, and the number of American troops killed, also increased opposition to the war in the USA itself. In March 1968, Johnson announced he would not be standing as the Democratic candidate in the November presidential elections. However, the peace talks did not make much progress. In October 1968, Johnson temporarily halted American bombing of the North to help the talks along.

## Nixon and the search for peace

The Republicans won the November elections, and the new President of the USA was Richard Nixon. He took over in January 1969, and was determined to end the war. By then, opposition to American tactics in Vietnam had led to large anti-war movements in the USA and across the world. By 1969, the war was costing the USA $28 billion a year, and over 300 American soldiers were being killed every day.

**Source B**

National Guardsmen began moving across the common... They began firing tear gas. The students picked it up and threw it back at them... At roughly a quarter to one, the Kent State students around Hayworth Hall... began to throw rocks at the Guardsmen... The Guardsmen again responded with tear gas... and then there were several volleys of automatic weapons fire... at least three of the students were dead.

*An extract describing the shooting of four anti-war students in 1970, taken from a book published in Australia in 1985. The writer, a reporter, was there at the time.*

**Source C**

*The body of one of the anti-war students, protesting against American involvement in Vietnam, shot by the National Guard at Kent State University in Ohio in 1970.*

## Nixon and 'Vietnamisation'

Nixon decided that the bulk of the fighting should be done by South Vietnamese troops, to allow American troops to withdraw gradually from Vietnam. American financial aid for the South, though, would continue. Between April 1969 and the beginning of 1971, Nixon reduced the number of American troops from 543 000 to 157 000.

The policy of 'Vietnamisation', however, also included increased bombing of the Ho Chi Minh trail. This was to prevent fresh supplies of troops and equipment reaching the Viet Cong from the North. Although this involved the USA bombing parts of Laos and Cambodia, through which parts of the Trail ran, it had little impact on the fighting capabilities of the Viet Cong. This was despite the fact that the USA dropped over 500 000 tonnes of explosives on Cambodia in the years 1969-73. In the end, its main achievement was to increase support for the communist guerrillas in those two countries as well.

## The My Lai massacre

By then, however, the USA had been shocked by the exposure, in 1969, of the My Lai massacre. This occurred when an American 'search and destroy' mission, led by Lieutenant Calley, massacred over 400 civilians, in May 1968, in the small village of My Lai. Eventually, Calley was sentenced to 20 years' imprisonment for the murder of 109 civilians. He was released after serving only five years. This incident increased opposition to the war, especially when it was revealed that it was not an isolated event.

## The 'China card'

Nixon tried to agree an end to the war in several ways. He suggested to the North Vietnamese government that they should pull out all their troops from the South at the same time as the USA withdrew theirs, and threatened to launch a massive bombing campaign on the North if they did not agree. Although the North refused, Nixon did not carry out his threat. He did, however, try to persuade the USSR and China to put pressure on the North to agree to his proposals.

When this did not work, Henry Kissinger, his adviser, suggested making use of the hostility between China and the USSR. Although China was giving some limited aid to the North, it was unhappy at the closer relations the North had with the Soviet Union. Kissinger saw that a deal with China could help put pressure on both the USSR and North Vietnam. As China was not a world power, he did not see this as harming American interests. So, in 1971, Nixon visited Communist China and also allowed it to join the UN. In February 1972, Nixon agreed to withdraw American troops from Nationalist Taiwan and to support Chinese reunification, if China would help the USA get out of Vietnam without 'losing face'.

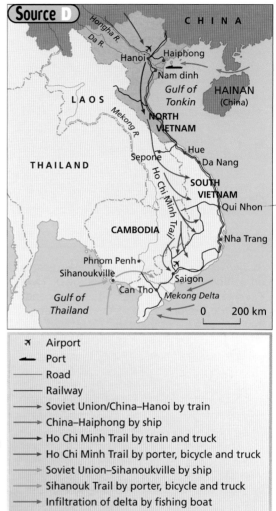

**Source D**

The Viet Cong supply routes.

Key:
- ✈ Airport
- Port
- Road
- Railway
- → Soviet Union/China–Hanoi by train
- → China–Haiphong by ship
- → Ho Chi Minh Trail by train and truck
- → Ho Chi Minh Trail by porter, bicycle and truck
- → Soviet Union–Sihanoukville by ship
- → Sihanouk Trail by porter, bicycle and truck
- → Infiltration of delta by fishing boat

**Source E**

We ran through My Lai herding men, women, children and babies into the centre of the village. Lieutenant Calley came over and said, 'You know what to do with them, don't you?' And I said, 'Yes,' and he left and came back about ten minutes later, and said, 'How come you ain't killed them yet?'.... We huddled the villagers up. We made them squat down. I fired about four clips-worth of bullets into the group... The mothers were hugging their children. Well, we kept on firing.

*Extracts from the account, given by a soldier of 'Charlie Company', of his part in the My Lai massacre.*

## Questions

1 What was the main aim of Nixon's policy of 'Vietnamisation'?

2 What impact did events like those referred to in **Sources B, C** and **E** have on the American people?

# Why the USA was forced to withdraw from Vietnam

## Linkage and Détente

*'Linkage' refers to the idea of offering concessions in areas seen as being important by one superpower, in return for equally important concessions by the other superpower. This policy began to ease Cold War tensions, and this relaxation gradually led to an improvement in relations between the USA and the USSR. This easing of tensions came to be known as 'détente'. One aspect of this was a greater willingness by the two sides to tolerate the continued existence of two very different social and political systems in the world.*

## Source A

At 12.30pm... 23 January 1973, the agreement on ending the war...was initialled by Dr. Henry Kissinger on behalf of the United States and by Le Doc Tho on behalf of the Democratic Republic of [North] Vietnam...

Throughout these negotiations we have been in the closest consultation with President Thieu and other representatives of the Republic of [South] Vietnam. This settlement meets the goals and has the full support of President Thieu.

The United States will continue to recognise the Government of the Republic of Vietnam as the sole legitimate government of South Vietnam. We shall continue to aid South Vietnam within the terms of the agreement...

*Part of President Nixon's 'Broadcast to the Nation', on 23 January 1973, announcing the end of the USA's involvement in the Vietnam War.*

## Source B

In 1973, President Nixon secretly promised to intervene, if need be, to protect South Vietnam. Is an American's word reliable these days?

*An extract from President Thieu's resignation speech in April 1975, just before the collapse of his government in South Vietnam.*

## Cease-fire and withdrawal

This plan was weakened by Nixon's involvement in a scandal at home and by the US Congress's refusal at first to give official recognition to Communist China. However, the closer relations between the USA and China worried the Soviet government. Kissinger then suggested that if the USSR helped the USA get out of the Vietnam War, the USA would accept its control of eastern Europe and provide financial and technical assistance. Kissinger called this policy 'linkage' and it helped develop an improvement in Cold War relations known as 'détente'.

While these negotiations were going on, the North launched a large and successful offensive in the South. Congress refused to allow Nixon to send American troops into Cambodia in order to put more pressure on the North, and ordered him to stop the bombing of Cambodia. So, on 27 January 1973, the USA and the North agreed a cease-fire. Once it was signed, the USA began to withdraw its remaining troops, but promised $1 billion of American aid for the South.

## Reunification of Vietnam

Although American troops had gone, the war itself was not ended. Fighting soon began between the Communists and the government of South Vietnam. In March 1975, the North launched another massive offensive. Without the benefit of American air power or troops, the forces of the South soon began to disintegrate. The Communists took control of Saigon, the capital of the South, on 29 April 1975. Saigon was later renamed Ho Chi Minh City and Vietnam had a single government. By then, however, over 2.5 million Vietnamese had been killed, and over 1.5 million injured.

## Why the USA failed in Vietnam

There were several reasons why the world's most powerful nation was forced to withdraw from the war in Vietnam. To begin with, the Viet Cong and the North Vietnamese troops had had years of experience of fighting a guerrilla war in the jungles of Vietnam. Since 1943, they had fought the Japanese and then the French, and had learned how to make booby traps. The main types of booby traps used by the Viet Cong included mines, grenades attached to trip wires below the surface of streams, sharpened bamboo stakes (known as punji stakes) in pits or attached to trip wires connected to trees, and the use of poisonous snakes. The Viet Cong also built thousands of miles of tunnels in which to hide. These too were full of booby traps to kill any US soldiers who discovered and entered them. This all produced constant fear amongst US soldiers and meant they could never relax. American troops, many of whom were very young (the average age was 19), were not used to these conditions, and had only experienced traditional warfare as used in Korea.

The Viet Cong often had the support of the local people, though sometimes they also forced peasants to help them. On the other hand, the government of South Vietnam was corrupt and unpopular, and many Vietnamese resented the presence and actions of the US military. The Communists were also strongly committed to their ideals, while American soldiers were often unhappy at being involved. This resulted in low American morale. Many US soldiers took drugs, and some shot their officers, or threw fragmentation grenades into their tents, which was known as 'fragging'.

Drugs were cheap and plentiful in Vietnam, and an increasing number of US soldiers turned to them in order to escape the nightmare of Vietnam. As early as 1970, it was estimated that 58% of US soldiers used marijuana, while 22% used heroin. By 1971, over 20 000 were being treated for serious drug problems. This was four times the number being treated for combat wounds. The 'fragging' of officers (usually those who insisted on their troops fighting the enemy) had been virtually unknown before the Tet Offensive of 1968. However, in 1970, there were 378 recorded instances of 'fragging', and in the period 1969-71, the official number of such incidents was 730, with 83 officers killed. However, many US soldiers often simply refused to fight. In 1971, there were 35 separate instances of this in just one US division in Vietnam. Desertions also became increasingly common. The rate doubled twice in the period 1969-71, compared to 1966-68. Overall, the total number of desertions in the period 1960-73 was over 500 000 out of about 10 million men drafted - a ratio of 1 in 20.

Finally, there was the problem of anti-war protest movements in the USA. Many young men refused to be conscripted ('drafted'). Some went to prison, others escaped by going abroad. As television brought more and more horrific pictures into people's homes, and the American casualties rose, opposition to the war increased. In all, the number of US soldiers killed in Vietnam was almost 57 000, with about 270 000 wounded. This compared to losses for the South Vietnamese army of 137 000, over 750 000 for North Vietnam and over 1 million for the Viet Cong. The financial cost of the war was also tremendous. As early as 1967, it was calculated that it cost the USA $400 000 to kill one Viet Cong guerrilla. This included the use of 75 bombs and 400 shells! By then, the war was already costing the USA at least $28 billion a year. This level of spending continued right through to 1973. One result was that American governments spent relatively little on dealing with the poverty and welfare needs of their own citizens. Even after the USA had decided to withdraw, in 1973, it still promised President Thieu $1 billion in military aid.

**Source C**

By every conceivable indicator, our army that now remains in Vietnam is in a state approaching collapse with individual units avoiding or having refused combat, murdering their officers or non-commissioned officers, drug-ridden and dispirited where not near mutinous.

*Comments made by a US marine colonel, as early as 1971, about the breakdown of morale and discipline of US soldiers.*

**Source D**

I'm inclined to believe the war would have ended just about when it did, even if there had been no protest and if I had not campaigned, because they didn't end it on policy finally: they just ended it because they were losing it, and... the soldiers wouldn't fight.

*Comments made by US Senator Eugene McCarthy about the USA's decision to pull out of Vietnam. In 1968, McCarthy had been one of the main leaders of the American anti-war movement.*

**Questions**

1 To what extent do **Sources A** and **B** agree?

2 How useful is **Source C** for finding out about the low morale of US soldiers in Vietnam?

3 Using **Source D** and your own knowledge, explain how important the anti-war movement in the USA was in leading the government to withdraw from Vietnam.

# SUMMARY

## 1945–1954

- In Vietnam, which was part of French Indo-China, the Viet Minh was formed to fight the Japanese invaders. The French returned to Indo-China in 1946. The Viet Minh fought a guerrilla war and, despite American aid, the French were defeated in 1954 and left.
- The Geneva Agreements temporarily divided Vietnam into North (communist) and South (anti-communist).

## 1954–1963

- As part of the Cold War and because of its belief in the Domino Theory, the USA increased its aid to South Vietnam.
- When the South refused to hold the promised reunification elections in 1956, the NLF (Viet Cong) was set up and began a guerrilla war in the South.
- In Cuba, Castro began his guerrilla war against Batista's government. In 1959, Batista fled and Castro quickly became the leader of Cuba.
- Castro's policies soon angered the USA, which broke off diplomatic relations and imposed a ban on trade with Cuba. In 1961, Kennedy's Bay of Pigs attempt to overthrow Castro failed.
- A serious crisis arose in 1962, when the USA discovered that the USSR was planning to install missiles on Cuba. In the end, Khrushchev withdrew the missiles, in return for Kennedy promising not to invade Cuba and to withdraw American missiles based in Turkey. In 1963, the USA and USSR set up a 'hot line' and signed a Nuclear Test Ban Treaty.
- In Vietnam, Kennedy increased the amount of American finance and military advisers for the South, but with little success.

## 1964–1968

- Under Johnson, American involvement in Vietnam 'escalated'. The Gulf of Tonkin Incident led to American bombing of North Vietnam (Operation Rolling Thunder) and of the Ho Chi Minh Trail in 1965.
- By 1968, there were 540 000 US soldiers in South Vietnam, but these failed to defeat the Viet Cong. The Tet Offensive in 1968, though defeated, showed the growing strength of the Viet Cong.
- The My Lai massacre and the USA's use of napalm and Agent Orange increased opposition to the war in the USA. Johnson decided not to stand for re-election.

## 1969–1973

- Nixon, the new President, began the policy of 'Vietnamisation' as a first step to ending direct American involvement. But he also stepped up American bombing, which spread to Laos and Cambodia.
- Ceasefire talks in Paris in 1973 resulted in the USA agreeing to withdraw from Vietnam.

## 1973–1975

- Fighting between the North and the South resumed and, in 1975, the North defeated the South. The last American 'advisers' left and the war ended. Once in control, the Communists re-united Vietnam.

# Exam Question Practice

## Usefulness of sources

Study Sources A and B below, which are about opposition in the USA to the continued involvement in the Vietnam War.

How useful are these sources as historical evidence about why the USA was forced to withdraw from the Vietnam War in 1973?

Source A

American news photographers filming Vietnamese children fleeing after a napalm attack on their village.

Source B

Protestors at an anti-war demonstration in the USA.

### Examiner's Tips

**When answering questions like this:**

◎ Remember that no source will be totally useless, even if it is biased.

◎ Don't forget to look for any helpful information given by the Principal Examiner about the sources (e.g. Who produced the source? Why? When?). You should try to show how this information affects the value of the source(s).

◎ Try to give a balanced answer, i.e. say how each source is and is not useful in relation to the issue in question - all sources will have some use as well as problems.

◎ Remember that to decide on the usefulness of the information given by a source, you will need to use your own knowledge to decide if the information provided is accurate and/or sufficient. In particular, show what you know about other reasons for the American withdrawal not provided by the sources.

◎ Remember to deal with all the sources mentioned in the question - if you leave any out, you will not be able to score high marks.

# CHAPTER 13

## THE USSR AND EASTERN EUROPE, 1945-1991

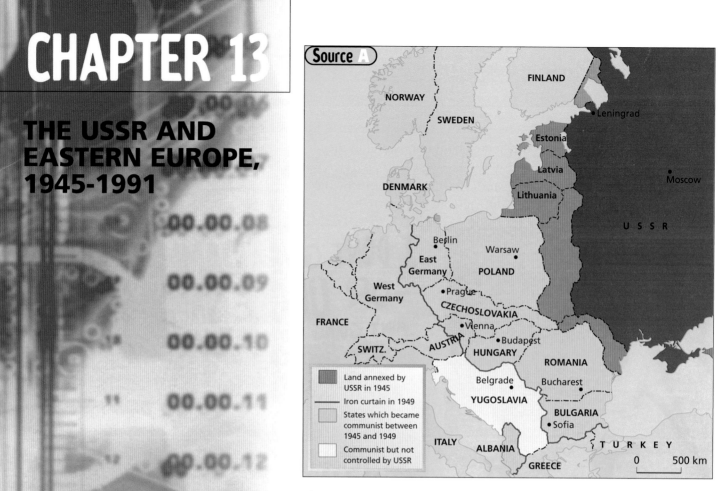

**Source A**

The communist take-over of central and eastern Europe.

**Source B**

Soviet tanks in the centre of Budapest during the suppression of the Hungarian Rising, 5 November 1956.

*Germans stand on the Berlin Wall at the Brandenburg Gate to celebrate the end of the Cold War.*

## Key Questions

**What** were Stalin's aims after the Second World War?

**Why** did the Soviet Union feel it necessary to extend its control over the countries of eastern Europe, as shown in **Source A**?

**What** impact did scenes like the one shown in **Source B** have on the Cold War?

**How** did the collapse of the 'Iron Curtain', symbolised by the events in **Source C**, come about?

These are some of the issues which we will cover in this chapter. The main focus of this chapter on the USSR and eastern Europe will be:

- The problems facing the Soviet Union at the end of the Second World War
- The Soviet take-over of the countries of eastern Europe in the late 1940s
- The problems facing Soviet control in the 1950s
- The growth of political unrest in eastern Europe after 1960
- The collapse of the Soviet bloc and the end of the Cold War

# The impact of the Second World War

## War devastation

The USSR suffered dreadful human and material destruction following the German invasion of 1941. Estimates vary as to the number of Soviet lives lost during the Great Patriotic War, at somewhere between 25 and 28 million. Of these, about 9 million were military personnel and the rest were civilians. Millions died from bombing, hunger, forced labour, reprisals for partisan activities or 'special actions' against Jews and Communists.

In addition, there was great economic destruction. In all, about 25% of all factories, mines and transport facilities were lost. In some of the occupied areas, the percentage was more than 50%. This was because Nazi Germany stripped the Soviet factories of machinery which was then sent back to Germany. After 1943, as the German forces began to retreat, they systematically destroyed all industrial equipment and agricultural produce that they could not take with them. As a result, many of the gains made under the Five-Year Plans had been wiped out.

## Economic reconstruction

As the Red Army, from mid-1944, began to recover Soviet territory which had previously been occupied by the Germans, Stalin became increasingly aware of how much damage the USSR had suffered. When the USA immediately stopped the Lend-Lease aid to the USSR as soon as the fighting in Europe ended in May 1945, Stalin concluded that the Soviet Union would have to carry out economic reconstruction on its own.

Stalin's first attempt to deal with these serious economic problems rested on the continuation of central planning. He outlined a 15-year recovery programme and, in March 1946, he announced the Fourth Five-Year Plan. Although over 2.5 million homeless people were rehoused in less than nine months, the main focus of this Plan was on rebuilding heavy industry and reviving agriculture. As the factories and mines which had survived came back into production, and the war industries shifted to peace-time production, Soviet industry began to revive. By 1950, Stalin was claiming that the targets of the Fourth Five-Year Plan had already been exceeded and that production levels were equal to or higher than those for 1940. While this was an exaggeration, the Fifth Five-

**Source A**

25 million people killed

25 million homes destroyed

31,000 factories destroyed

84,000 schools destroyed

10.5 million displaced people (refugees)

17 million cattle killed

100,000 collective or state farms partially or completely destroyed

*Soviet losses and damage during the Great Patriotic War.*

**Source B**

One of the commonest sights in the Russian countryside in the latter part of the war was a row of... brick chimneys, blackened by fire and surrounded by the ashes of what had been a peasant's [wooden] home. Many a village ceased to exist, and many a large town was practically raised to the ground.

*Part of an account, given by a British visitor to the Soviet Union in 1943, of the war damage suffered by the USSR during the Second World War.*

Year Plan which ran from 1951-55, had made significant improvements by the time Stalin died in 1953. In addition, the harsh pre-war labour codes were not used and, by 1952, real wages were higher than they had been in 1940. Agriculture also improved after a serious drought in 1946, but more slowly than industry. In 1947, rationing was ended and, by 1950, State meat purchases were back to the pre-war levels of 1940. However, the grain harvest in 1950 was about 15% below the 1940 figure.

## Political control

As well as concentrating on economic reconstruction after the war, Stalin was also determined to maintain his political power. He remained deeply suspicious of any potential rivals, and took action to safeguard his dominance. High-ranking Red Army officers soon lost their influence and positions. Those affected included Marshal Zhukov, who lost his place on the Central Committee. From 1945 to 1953, there were hardly any promotions to the higher ranks in the armed forces. In August 1946, the system of political commissars (officials) in the army was re-introduced in order to limit the independence of army officers.

Stalin was also determined to maintain his control over the Communist Party. Once he had brought the military under control, Stalin began to exclude leading Party members from the decision-making process. He by-passed both the Politburo and the Central Committee and instead met with small sub-committees made up of those he happened to trust at the time. In fact, the full Central Committee did not meet until the Nineteenth Party Congress in October 1952, which itself had been delayed for five years. He also continued with his 'cult of personality'.

## Purges

Beria remained in control of the NKVD (the secret police) and helped Stalin in his attempts to remain supreme. However, in 1946, Stalin removed Beria's control of the secret police and passed it over to a new ministry of State security. From 1946-48, the USSR experienced another period of repression; mostly, though, this affected the sciences and culture. This was led by Zhdanov, and the period became known as the Zhdanovshchina ('The time of Zhdanov'). Although Zhdanov died in August 1948, this repression still continued. In July 1949, Stalin had over 1000 leading Party and administrative officials in Leningrad arrested. Many of these were executed in what became known as the 'Leningrad Affair'. Stalin also made frequent personnel changes at the top of the Party and State bodies, especially as he began to suffer increasingly bad health.

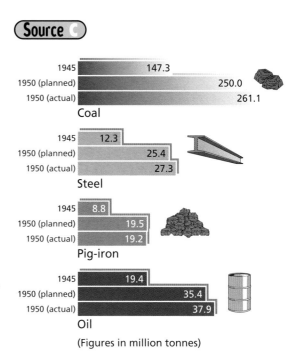

**Source C**

| | |
|---|---|
| 1945 | 147.3 |
| 1950 (planned) | 250.0 |
| 1950 (actual) | 261.1 |

Coal

| | |
|---|---|
| 1945 | 12.3 |
| 1950 (planned) | 25.4 |
| 1950 (actual) | 27.3 |

Steel

| | |
|---|---|
| 1945 | 8.8 |
| 1950 (planned) | 19.5 |
| 1950 (actual) | 19.2 |

Pig-iron

| | |
|---|---|
| 1945 | 19.4 |
| 1950 (planned) | 35.4 |
| 1950 (actual) | 37.9 |

Oil

(Figures in million tonnes)

*Production under the Fourth Five-Year Plan, 1946-50, according to official Soviet statistics.*

**Questions**

1 How did Stalin attempt the economic reconstruction of the Soviet Union after the Second World War?

2 According to **Source C**, by how much did steel production increase from 1945 to 1950?

3 How reliable is **Source C** as evidence of the economic reconstruction achieved by 1950?

4 What steps did Stalin take to preserve his own power within the USSR?

# The Soviet take-over of eastern Europe

## The Soviet quest for reparations and loans

As well as attempting to revive the Soviet economy by relying on the USSR's own resources, Stalin also looked for other sources. The main source he had in mind was Germany, which he believed should be made to pay massive reparations (compensation) to the Soviet Union. In 1943, at the Tehran Conference, there had been agreement in principle by the Big Three that the Soviet Union should receive compensation after the war. Stalin and the Soviet leadership believed this was only fair as the USSR had made by far the biggest contribution to the defeat of Nazi Germany. Over 10 million Germans had been killed on the Eastern Front. This was 80% of Germany's total losses. As a result of this, the Soviet Union had suffered far more than Britain and especially the USA, neither of which had been invaded. However, it became increasingly clear in the years 1945-47 that the USA and Britain had changed their minds on the question of German reparations.

Stalin had also hoped that, after the war, the USA would give the USSR massive loans to help rebuild its economy. But it soon became clear that this would only happen if Stalin allowed capitalist firms and market forces to operate in the USSR. Although, initially, Stalin had hoped for funds from the Marshall Plan which the USA announced in 1947, this became impossible as the Cold War began to develop. It thus became clear that any compensation for the Soviet Union would have to come from its zone in east Germany and from those east European states which had fought on the side of Nazi Germany.

## Eastern Europe

However, Stalin was not only interested in the states of eastern Europe for compensation and resources with which to rebuild the Soviet economy. He also saw these states as being vitally important for the future security of the USSR. Stalin was determined that the Soviet Union would never again be invaded. Before the war, these east European states (apart from Czechoslovakia) had been ruled by undemocratic right-wing regimes. Of these, Hungary and Romania had fought on the side of Nazi Germany. A particular concern was that Poland, the largest of these states, had twice been used by Germany as a route into Russia since 1900, and that Poland itself had invaded Russia in 1920. He thus believed that it was essential to control these states, or at least to ensure that they were ruled by governments which would be friendly to the USSR.

This question had bothered the Soviet leadership even during the Second World War, when the Grand Alliance still seemed strong. After the Tehran Conference in 1943, Churchill and Stalin met in Moscow in October 1944. There they made the informal

### Source A

The following circumstances should not be forgotten. The Germans made their invasion of the USSR through Finland, Poland, Romania, Bulgaria, and Hungary..... Governments hostile to the Soviet Union existed in those countries...the Soviet Union's loss of life has been several times greater than that of Britain and the United States put together. And so what can be surprising about the fact that the Soviet Union, anxious for its future safety, is trying to see to it that governments loyal to the Soviet Union should exist in these countries? How can anyone who has not taken leave of his senses describe these peaceful hopes of the Soviet Union as expansionist?

*Stalin's reply to Churchill's 'iron curtain' speech of March 1946 (see the next spread), which criticised the Soviet take-over in eastern Europe.*

### Source B

We must understand that Russia is just as frightened of attack by the Western Alliance as we are of attack by the USSR. Part of her overall security is the belt of nations in eastern Europe.

*An extract from the memoirs of Field Marshal Montgomery, published in 1958, at the height of the Cold War.*

'percentages agreement' concerning influence in south-eastern and eastern Europe. Although Roosevelt had not been present, he had been told about it afterwards and had made no objections.

## The Red Army in eastern Europe

The USSR had begun to act on this 'percentages agreement' during the remainder of 1944, as the Red Army pushed the Germans out of eastern Europe. Once a country had been liberated from German control, the Red Army set up anti-fascist coalition governments. Stalin then insisted that the local Communist parties be given a major role in such governments. This security issue became especially important after 1945, as the destruction the USSR suffered during the war meant that the Red Army was quickly reduced in order to allow as rapid an economic reconstruction as possible. In 1945, the Red Army was about 11 million strong, and American forces were almost 12 million. However, within a short time, the Red Army had been reduced to under 3 million. Although the USA also demobilised a large part of its army, the USSR remained worried by the American monopoly of nuclear weapons which was not ended until 1949.

## The impact of the Cold War

As Cold War tensions began to emerge after 1945, the USSR began to insist that the Communist parties in eastern Europe be given an even greater share of power. As early as March 1946, Churchill was talking about an 'iron curtain' dividing Europe into a capitalist west and a communist east. Stalin then stepped up his demands, and became even more insistent after the announcement of the Truman Doctrine and the Marshall Plan in 1947. Stalin increasingly came to see Europe as being divided into two hostile camps and so saw greater control of eastern Europe as essential for Soviet security. In particular, these countries were seen as acting as a buffer zone between the USSR and Germany, in case of any future invasion. Over the next three years, the Communist-dominated governments in eastern Europe began to nationalise industry and the land. At the same time, opposition parties were increasingly restricted and elections were rigged. By 1948, Soviet control was virtually complete, with only Yugoslavia under Tito remaining independent. The actual speed and process of the Soviet take-over, however, varied from country to country.

**Percentages agreement**

This agreement concerned the 'spheres of influence' in eastern Europe at the end of the war. The percentage ratios for Britain and the USSR, respectively, were agreed as follows: Romania - 10:90; Greece - 90:10; Bulgaria - 25:75; Hungary - 25:75; Yugoslavia - 50:50. When the Cold War began, it became clear that Stalin intended to impose political control (and Soviet-style economic and social systems) on those countries in the Soviet sphere.

**Source C**

Red Army occupation troops, marching through the Brandenburg Gate in East Berlin on 23 February 1949. The march was to celebrate the 31st anniversary of the foundation of the Red Army.

**Questions**

1 Why do you think the USA and Britain
a agreed that the USSR should receive compensation from Germany?
b later decided not to pay any compensation from the German zones they controlled?

2 Study **Sources A** and **B**. Which one do you think is more useful for finding out about the Soviet Union's reasons for wanting to control the countries of eastern Europe?

# The Iron Curtain 1945-1953

## The Soviet take-over

In **Bulgaria**, the Communists dominated the Fatherland Front, which was a coalition of left and centre parties. The Bulgarian Communists ignored the promises Stalin had given to the USA and Britain about allowing representatives of the opposition to have seats in the government. After elections in October 1946, the Communists had almost total control, and began to restrict the activities of the main opposition parties.

In **Hungary**, the right-of-centre Smallholders' Party (KGP) won elections held in October 1945, and formed a government headed by Ferenc Nagy. He faced opposition from an alliance of the Communist, Social Democrat and National Peasants' parties. In March 1946, he was forced to form a coalition government. Demonstrations against the government's economic policies led the KGP ministers to resign. The security forces, which were under the control of a Communist minister, then closed down the opposition parties and arrested leading members of the KGP. By the summer of 1947, Nagy had been forced to resign. New elections held on 31 August 1947, resulted in a Communist victory.

In **Poland**, the Peasants' Party was the main opposition and was led by Mikolajczyk, who was also Deputy Prime Minister. He was not keen on cooperating with the Polish Communists, so elections which had been promised for February 1946 were postponed until January 1947. These elections were manipulated by the Communists so that the Peasants' Party won only a handful of seats. The Communists then strengthened their control over government bodies.

In **Romania**, a Communist government, headed by Dr. Petra Groza, was recognised by the West after representatives of the National Peasants and the Liberals were included. However, the government was increasingly by-passed by the Soviet authorities. After a heated campaign and vote-rigging, the Communists and their allies won virtually all the seats in the elections held in November 1946. During 1947, the opposition parties were closed down and, on 30 December 1947, the King abdicated and Romania became a People's Republic.

The last east European state to come under Communist control was **Czechoslovakia**. Unlike the other states, this had been a democracy before the war. In free elections held in May 1946, the Communists had won 38% of the vote, and had become part of a coalition government. However, when a serious economic crisis developed in the summer of 1947, the Communists began to put pressure on the non-Communist members of the coalition by calling for more radical policies. When the Communist Minister of

---

**Source A**

From Stettin in the Baltic, to Trieste in the Adriatic, an iron curtain has descended across the continent. Behind that line lie all the capitals of the ancient states of central and eastern Europe... All these famous cities lie in the Soviet sphere, and all are subject to a high and increasing control from Moscow. The Russian-dominated Polish government has been encouraged to make enormous and wrongful inroads upon Germany...

*An extract from Winston Churchill's famous 'iron curtain' speech, delivered at Fulton, Missouri, in the USA in March 1946. The iron curtain was an imaginary wall of secrecy between the Soviet Union and western Europe. It was first used by the leading Nazi, Joseph Goebbels in February 1945.*

**Source B**

At Yalta we had agreed that the present Polish government was to be reconstructed. Anyone with common sense can see that this means the present Communist government is to form the basis of the new one. No other understanding of the Yalta Agreement is possible.

*A comment made by Stalin in 1945, following disagreements over the composition of the new Polish government.*

the Interior began appointing pro-Communist police chiefs, most non-Communists resigned from the coalition government on 24 February 1948. The Communists then organised huge demonstrations and a general strike. Gottwald, the leader of the Czech Communist Party, became Prime Minister and replaced those who had resigned with Communist ministers. New elections resulted in the Communists and their allies winning 66% of the vote. Benes, the non-Communist President, was then replaced.

## Cominform and 'Two Camps'

Soviet control of eastern Europe was increased in September 1947, when the Communist parties of these states agreed to set up the Communist Information Bureau (Cominform). It was intended to keep the Communist parties in Europe under Moscow's control. At its first Conference, Zhdanov made a speech in which he talked of the world being divided into 'two opposing camps'. This was the Soviet response to the Truman Doctrine and the Marshall Plan. According to Zhdanov, these policies were attempts by the USA to increase its power and to prepare for an invasion of the USSR. When Tito in Yugoslavia (who had already ignored Stalin's instructions not to form a Communist government there as it broke his 'percentages agreement' with Churchill) tried to form separate trade agreements with Romania and Hungary in late 1947/early 1948, Stalin tried to arrange his downfall. When this failed, Yugoslavia was expelled from Cominform, and Stalin began an extensive purge of 'Titoists' in the Communist parties of eastern Europe. In 1949, the Council for Mutual Economic Assistance (Comecon) was set up. This was seen as the Soviet version of the Marshall Plan, and was intended to co-ordinate the economic policies of the east European states with those of the USSR.

## The death of Stalin

After 1949, the eastern European economies did begin to recover but, without the massive American aid which was given to western Europe, this recovery was much slower and more limited - especially as most of these countries had been mainly agricultural before the war.

Within the USSR, Stalin still ruled with an iron hand, and at times continued to order purges of those he feared were rivals. By 1952, he was largely isolated and, in January 1953, seemed about to launch another purge. However, before this one could develop, he suffered a stroke and died on 5 March 1953. Although Beria, the head of the KGB, expected to take over, there was at first no obvious successor.

**Cominform**

*This was designed to control and coordinate the different Communist governments of eastern Europe and the Communist parties in western Europe. Its HQ was originally in Belgrade, the capital of Yugoslavia, but was moved to Bucharest in Romania in 1948 when Tito was expelled from Cominform for not following Stalin's orders. It was abolished by Khrushchev in 1956.*

**two opposing camps**

*According to Zhdanov, the post-war world was now divided into two camps: the Soviet-led anti-imperialist and democratic camp, and the US-led imperialist and anti-democratic camp. He argued that the existence of the Soviet bloc was the only thing preventing American domination of the whole of Europe, and that only the Soviet Union was trying to preserve world peace.*

**Comecon**

*As well as coordinating industrial development and trade between the USSR and its satellite countries in eastern Europe, Comecon was designed to prevent trade with the West. At first, the USSR insisted on terms of trade advantageous to its own economy, especially as regards raw materials needed for post-war reconstruction. Later, under Khrushchev, the terms were made more equal and, in 1964, a Bank for Socialist Countries was set up.*

**Questions**

1 What steps did the Soviet Union and local communists use to get the kind of governments they wanted in eastern Europe?

2 How did the Truman Doctrine and the Marshall Plan contribute to a hardening of Cold War attitudes in the Soviet bloc?

3 What can we learn from Stalin's response to Tito about Stalin's aims for eastern Europe?

# Reform from above, 1953-56

## Changes in the USSR

When Stalin died in March 1953, the CPSU (Communist Party of the Soviet Union) decided to have a collective leadership and to end the system of purges associated with Stalin's rule. At first, Georgi Malenkov was both Prime Minister and General Secretary of the CPSU, but then Nikita Khrushchev took over the latter post. The other main leaders were Molotov, Bulganin and Kaganovitch. Although Beria at first remained one of the leaders, the others were determined to prevent any new terror. So, in December 1953, Beria was quickly arrested and executed in what proved to be the last political execution of a member of the CPSU.

## Khrushchev's reforms

By the end of 1955, however, Khrushchev had used his control of the Party machine to become the most important leader. He was determined to carry out economic and political reforms. In particular, he tried to improve living standards by modernising the Soviet economy. In industry, he tried to reduce central control by setting up over 100 regional economic councils (sovnarkhozy). These were to encourage local decision-making and initiative. At the same time, controls on workers were relaxed, and the working day was reduced to 7 hours. In agriculture, Khrushchev tried to increase food production by the Virgin Lands Scheme, and by merging collective farms to make bigger and more efficient ones.

As regards politics, Khrushchev was one of many communists who wanted to relax the strict system set up under Stalin, although he did not want direct criticism of the goal of communism itself. In February 1956, at the 20th Party Congress, he made a 'secret speech' in which he attacked Stalin for the crimes during the Great Purge and Terror, and for his 'cult of personality'.

In the USSR, this led to a limited process of 'de-Stalinisation', in which some of the restrictions associated with Stalin were relaxed. In particular, writers and artists were allowed to openly refer to the purges and the gulag. At the same time, many gulag prisoners were released.

### Virgin Lands Scheme

*This scheme was based on increasing agricultural production by ploughing up large areas of land which had not been farmed before. About 13 million hectares of land were cultivated, much of it in remote areas of the USSR. Khrushchev hoped that an extra 20 million tonnes of grain would be produced, which would solve the long-term problem of food production in just a few years. However, the plan was rushed, with too little fertiliser used, and the climate in some of these areas meant the crops often failed. Khrushchev also failed to take into account the greater costs and problems associated with transporting the crops over much greater distances. By 1960, the scheme was already showing signs of failure. The low harvest in 1963 forced the USSR to buy grain from the west, including the USA.*

**Source A**

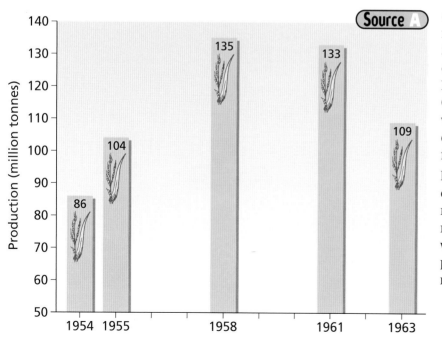

*Grain production under the Virgin Lands Scheme.*

## The effect of Khrushchev's secret speech

Khrushchev's secret speech, soon became known in eastern Europe. Many communists and non-communists who wanted to reduce Soviet control thought that a reduction would now be tolerated, while reform communists believed that they would be allowed to liberalise the strict 'Stalinist' systems which had been imposed on their countries. Many in eastern Europe had been excited by the fact that the new Soviet leadership was trying to improve relations with Tito's Yugoslavia, which had resisted Stalin's attempts to impose Soviet control and had followed its own 'road to socialism'. They had also been encouraged by Khrushchev's dissolution of Cominform in the same month, which seemed to signal a loosening of Soviet control over eastern Europe.

## Reform in Poland

The death of Stalin, in 1953, had already led to trouble in East Germany, where workers had demonstrated and then rioted against the strict Soviet controls. These had been so serious that Soviet forces had had to help the East German security forces restore order. The first east European country to react to Khrushchev's speech was Poland. There, workers' protests against increased work targets had developed into a serious riot at Poznan in June 1956. Reform communists in the Polish United Workers' Party (PUWP), led by Gomulka, persuaded the Communist government to begin a programme of reform and liberalisation. At first, because of the Cold War, the Soviet leaders were worried about the possible consequences of a Poland independent of Soviet control. In October, Soviet leaders met Gomulka in Warsaw, while Red Army troops in Poland held military manoeuvres. However, Gomulka assured the USSR that Poland would not leave the Warsaw Pact and that the communist framework would not be abandoned. Khrushchev finally decided that Gomulka could be trusted and that no military intervention was necessary to safeguard Soviet security.

At first, Gomulka was able to do much to improve the situation in Poland. The previous system under which Poland had to supply coal to the USSR at one tenth of the world price was ended, and the requirement to pay for the cost of Soviet troops stationed in Poland ceased. In addition, Khrushchev cancelled a debt of 2 billion roubles to the Soviet Union, and agreed new credits for Poland. Gomulka also ended the programme of collectivisation, and most agricultural land eventually returned to private ownership. However, many reform communists were disappointed when Gomulka rejected economic reforms which would have given factories and workers considerable freedom from central State control.

### Source B

Stalin acted not through persuasion, but by imposing his concepts and demanding absolute submission to his opinion.... Mass arrests and deportations of thousands of people, execution without trial, created conditions of insecurity, fear and even desperation.... A situation was created where one could not express one's own will...

Stalin had completely lost consciousness of reality; he demonstrated his suspicion and haughtiness not only in relation to individuals in the USSR but in relation to whole parties and nations.

*Some extracts from Khrushchev's 'secret speech', February 1956.*

### Gomulka

*Wladyslaw Gomulka had been the leader of the Polish Communist Party but had been imprisoned during the east European purges ordered by Stalin in the late 1940s. At the time of the Poznan riot (in which 75 people were killed after troops were called in to suppress the protest), he had only recently been released and rehabilitated, following Stalin's death in March 1953. Like several reform communists, Gomulka began stressing the 'Polish path to Socialism'. Such communists resented the degree of Soviet control and wanted to reassert national independence. However, he and his supporters stressed their commitment to the Warsaw Pact which had been set up in 1955.*

### Questions

1 Why did the Virgin Lands scheme, as shown in **Source A**, fail to produce the results it was designed to achieve?

2 What impact did Khrushchev's 'secret speech' have in Poland?

# CHAPTER 13

# Crises in eastern Europe 1956-1968

## The Hungarian Revolt 1956

The situation which developed in Hungary, however, became much more serious. Encouraged by Gomulka's success in Poland, a massive illegal demonstration in support of the Polish reform communists took place in Budapest on 23 October. This developed into a riot and security forces opened fire on the demonstrators. Soon, an armed revolt broke out and the Hungarian government - headed by Rakosi, who was a strict Stalinist - called in Soviet troops for assistance. At first, Khrushchev hoped a solution along Gomulka's lines in Poland would end the unrest. So Rakosi was forced to resign in July, and was replaced by Erno Gero. However, he was seen by many in Hungary as just another Stalinist and the unrest continued. On 24 October, Imre Nagy, a reform communist who had been expelled from the Communist Party by Rakosi in 1955, was allowed to form a new government.

However, many Soviet leaders became extremely concerned when Nagy allowed the formation of opposition political parties. These worries were increased by signs that some reformers were thinking of taking Hungary out of the Warsaw Pact. Despite talks in which Nagy assured the USSR that this would not happen, on 1 November, Nagy announced that Hungary would become neutral and leave the Warsaw Pact. Although he said Hungary would remain friendly with the USSR, Khrushchev now became convinced that an armed invasion was necessary in order to maintain the USSR's security buffer zone.

On 4 November, Soviet forces invaded and, after some fierce fighting, a new pro-Soviet government was installed. A purge followed, with many being expelled from Party and State jobs. Nagy was flown to the USSR where, in 1958, he was executed. Once the situation had settled down, Khrushchev allowed the new Hungarian leader, Janos Kadar, to implement several of the reforms previously promised by Nagy.

## The fall of Khrushchev

Many Soviet leaders became increasingly concerned about Khrushchev's political and economic reforms, and his conduct of foreign affairs. The Berlin Crisis of 1961 (see page 201) was followed by the Cuban Missile Crisis in 1962 (see page 201). In both cases, Khrushchev's risk-taking had failed to deliver any significant improvements in Soviet security. In October 1964, his opponents persuaded the majority of the Central Committee to remove Khrushchev from power. He was forced to retire and, at first, power was shared between Leonid Brezhnev (the new First Secretary of the CPSU) and Alexei Kosygin, the new Premier (Prime Minister). In particular, the new Soviet leadership was determined to end the de-Stalinisation and liberalism associated with Khrushchev.

## Czechoslovakia and the 'Prague Spring' 1968

After the Soviet invasion of Hungary in 1956, there was little political unrest in eastern Europe. However, economic problems in Czechoslovakia in the mid-1960s eventually led to political protests. At first, these mostly involved students who wanted political reforms such as freedom of speech and a free press. Their demonstrations in 1966 soon led to public criticism of Soviet control of the economy. In January 1968, Antonin Novotny, the hardline Stalinist ruler, was replaced by the reform communist Alexander Dubcek.

Dubcek was the new First Secretary of the Czech Communist Party and, in April 1968, he announced his 'Action Programme'. This was a series of political and economic reforms designed to achieve 'socialism with a human face'. However, this 'Prague Spring' alarmed the hardliners in the Czech Communist Party and in the other Communist parties in Eastern Europe. It also worried Brezhnev in the USSR, especially as it came on top of recent problems with Albania and Romania. In July, the leaders of five Warsaw Pact countries met to discuss the situation and on 15 July, they sent an open letter to the Czech Communist Party. This 'Warsaw Letter' stressed their security concerns about Dubcek's Action Programme. Although Dubcek made it clear he had no intention of taking his country out of the Warsaw Pact, he insisted on continuing his reforms. However, on 3 August, Soviet and Warsaw Pact pressure led Dubcek to sign a joint 'Bratislava Declaration' which confirmed a commitment to 'defend' socialism in eastern Europe.

## The Warsaw Pact invasion

Despite this, the demand for more reforms continued, and the leaders of East Germany and Poland urged Brezhnev to take action. So, on 20 August, forces from the USSR and the four other signatories of the Warsaw Letter crossed into Czechoslovakia to 'restore order'. They met only passive resistance. Dubcek and several other Czech Communist leaders were arrested and taken to Moscow. On 27 August, Dubcek agreed in a joint statement to end the Prague Spring and return to pre-1968 methods of rule. In November 1968, Brezhnev issued what became known as the 'Brezhnev Doctrine'. This stated that the independence of the east European states was limited by their duties to the security of the USSR and the other Warsaw Pact countries, and to their own 'socialist systems'.

**Dubcek**

*Alexander Dubcek led a group of reform communists who wanted to democratise Czechoslovakia's political system and to modernise the economy. His plan for building 'Socialism with a human face' included reducing censorship and the powers of the secret police, and allowing free discussion and criticism in the press and on television. These moves were supported by many people, including students, artists and writers. Together these reforms became known as the 'Prague Spring'. Dubcek was determined to stress the fact that these reforms were not about ending communism in Czechoslovakia, and that he had no intention of leaving the Warsaw Pact. After the Warsaw Pact invasion, he was removed from power, and ended up as a forestry worker. In 1989, after the collapse of the eastern European Communist governments, he became the new President of the Czech Republic.*

**Source C**

*Czech protestors surrounding a Soviet tank in Prague, August 1968.*

**Questions**

1 What does **Source B** tell us about the rebels fighting against the Soviet forces in 1956?

2 What was the 'Brezhnev Doctrine' and why was it issued?

# Gorbachev and reform

## Poland, 1980-85

*Lech Walesa, the main leader of Solidarity, in Gdansk.*

A new crisis broke out in eastern Europe in Poland in 1980. During the 1960s and 1970s, the Polish economy stagnated and, in 1970, strikes forced Gomulka to resign. A large increase in food prices in July 1980 caused widespread unrest and strikes. In Gdansk, an unofficial and independent trade union, called Solidarity, was set up by the strikers in August. One of its main leaders was Lech Walesa, and Solidarity soon had 9 million members. As well as improved wages and working conditions, Solidarity soon began to demand political freedoms. Edward Gierck, the Communist leader, was forced to resign and, in November, the Polish Supreme Court ruled that Solidarity was legal. Between December 1980 and March 1981, the Soviet leaders, who still saw Poland as a vital part of the Warsaw Pact, discussed whether a military invasion would be necessary to preserve Communist rule in Poland and Soviet security. The USSR still felt vulnerable in Europe, even though their Red Army totalled 3.7 million compared to the USA's 2 million. This was because differences with China meant the majority of Soviet forces (44 divisions) were deployed on the Sino-Soviet border, compared to the 31 divisions in eastern Europe. However, they decided instead to pressurise the Polish Communists into taking steps to destroy Solidarity. General Jaruzelski became the new Prime Minister and held talks with the Solidarity leaders. These failed and, in December 1981, he imposed martial law. Using emergency powers, Solidarity was banned, its leaders were arrested, and many supporters lost their jobs. However, these actions did not destroy Solidarity. Instead, many Communists resigned from the Party and, in November 1982, Walesa was released.

*Polish soldiers in Gdansk on 31 August 1982, during the period of martial law imposed to crush the Solidarity movement.*

## The rise of Gorbachev

Although one of the reasons why Khrushchev was removed from power was the failure of his economic policies, the Soviet economy was stagnating by the 1970s. Brezhnev, who had soon emerged as the main leader, was not in favour of economic reforms, and spent huge amounts of money on trying to catch up on the USA's lead in nuclear weapons. In 1982, Brezhnev died but, for many years before then, no serious attempts to reform the economy had been made. Between 1982 and 1985, the USSR was ruled by two leaders, both old and sick. Yuri Andropov was in favour of reform but died in 1984, before he had achieved any significant reforms. His successor, Konstantin Chernenko, was against reform and died in March 1985.

He was succeeded by Mikhail Gorbachev, who had been promoted by Andropov and was determined to carry out reforms. His main policies were 'perestroika', 'glasnost' and 'demokratizatsiya'. This resulted in a series of reforms designed to modernise the Soviet economy to reverse stagnation, and to allow greater political freedoms for the Soviet people. These included the right to more information and the opportunity to criticise government policies and Communist officials. However, these met great opposition from the hardliners in the Party, and such people used their power to block many of Gorbachev's attempts at reform.

## Gorbachev and eastern Europe

Gorbachev also applied his reforms to foreign affairs. In particular, he followed what he called his 'New Thinking', which was based on the belief that the Soviet economy was being destroyed by the attempt to compete with the USA in the nuclear arms race. In a series of four summit meetings with President Reagan of the USA between 1985 and 1988, Gorbachev proposed important cuts in both nuclear and conventional forces. He also said that foreign affairs should be founded on human rights and democracy. While these ideas were unpopular with many Soviet and east European leaders, they appealed to many people in eastern Europe.

In March 1985, Gorbachev also stated that the USSR was abandoning the Brezhnev Doctrine of 1968. Soviet troops would no longer be sent into any east European country either to defend unpopular rulers or to crush protests. Instead, he urged the leaders of eastern Europe to follow his reform policies.

### Questions

1 Why did the USSR put pressure on the Polish government to stop Solidarity?

2 How useful is **Source C** as evidence of Gorbachev's foreign policy beliefs?

### Perestroika

*This means 'restructuring' and refers to Gorbachev's attempts to modernise the Soviet economy and improve its productivity. His main ideas involved reducing central controls, and allowing factories which operated profitably to give bonuses to management and workers. The word soon came to stand for all his plans to modernise the USSR.*

### Glasnost

*This means 'openness', and by it Gorbachev meant that mistakes should be acknowledged and that people should be allowed to criticise the government and the ruling Communist Party in the media. He also said that all documents should be open to historians, so that there would be no 'blank pages' in the history of the Soviet Union. As a result, many details emerged about past actions, including Stalin's purges. This led to many of his victims (including Zinoviev, Kamenev and Bukharin) being rehabilitated. A commission was still looking into Trotsky's case when the USSR collapsed in 1991.*

### Demokratizatsiya

*This refers to Gorbachev's attempts to make the Soviet political system more democratic. He tried to make the government more independent from Party control, and also allowed the formation of political clubs and organisations. In addition, he reformed the electoral system so that people had more choice. As a result, many local Communist bosses and administrators lost their seats. In 1990, free elections were held in which non-communist groups were able to offer candidates.*

### Source C

Force or the threat of force neither can be nor should be instruments of foreign policy. The principle of the freedom of choice is mandatory [compulsory]. Refusal to recognise this principle will have serious consequences for world peace. To deny a nation the choice, regardless of any excuse, is to upset the unstable balance that has been achieved. Freedom of choice is a universal principle. It knows no exception.

*Part of a speech made to the United Nations by Gorbachev on 7 December 1987.*

# The end of the Cold War

## The collapse of eastern Europe

By 1988, Gorbachev's policies were beginning to have a real effect in the east European states. In Poland, Solidarity, which had been banned since 1981, was legalised in January 1989. In April, the government agreed on a package of economic and political reforms which included elections to be held in June. Solidarity stood in these elections and won a clear majority. In August, the new Polish Parliament elected the first non-communist Prime Minister to hold power in eastern Europe for over 40 years. In Hungary, reform communists had been carrying out their own Gorbachev-style policies for several years. This increased after 1985 and, in 1989, the government agreed to hold multi-party elections. Gorbachev accepted these developments.

It was events in East Germany which really brought about the collapse of the Iron Curtain and the Soviet bloc in eastern Europe. When Hungary decided, in August 1989, to open its borders with Austria, thousands of East Germans began to leave via Hungary. In October, Gorbachev made it clear to Honecker, the East German ruler, that he would get no help from the USSR. Instead, he urged him to implement reforms. This led to widespread demonstrations calling for democracy. On 18 October, Honecker resigned as leader of the Communist Party and was replaced by Egon Krenze. However, the demonstrations grew bigger; on 4 November, over 500 000 demonstrated in East Berlin. Gorbachev then told the East German government that the Soviet Union could no longer afford to subsidise the economy of the GDR, and instead urged Krenz to form closer ties with West Germany. On 7 November, the GDR government resigned and, on 8 November, Krenz decided to open the Berlin Wall.

These events in East Germany then inspired mass protests in Czechoslovakia and Bulgaria. In both countries, the Communist governments resigned, and multi-party elections were held. In Czechoslovakia, the Chairman of the new federal parliament was Alexander Dubcek. The one exception to these peaceful revolutions was Romania, where the Communist leader, Ceaucescu, tried to use the security forces to suppress the demonstrations. Gorbachev refused to intervene, and the Romanian army turned against Ceaucescu, who was later executed, along with his wife.

## Source A

The time is ripe for abandoning views on foreign policy which are influenced by an imperial standpoint... It is possible to suppress, compel, bribe, break or blast, but only for a certain period. From the point of view of long-term big politics, no-one will be able to subordinate others. That is why only one thing - relations of equality - remains...

*Comments made by Gorbachev in 1987. These comments encouraged many in eastern Europe to take steps to end Soviet domination of their countries.*

## Source B

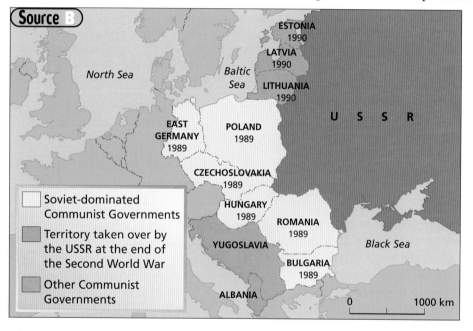

*The collapse of the Communist regimes in eastern Europe. The dates show when the Communist governments fell.*

## Source C

For most west Europeans now alive, the world has always ended at the East German border and the Wall; beyond lay darkness... The opening of the frontiers declares that the world has no edge any more. Europe is becoming once more round and whole.

*An extract from an article in the Independent newspaper, about the events in eastern Europe in November 1989.*

## The end of the Cold War

Gorbachev had hoped that the new governments in eastern Europe would be composed of reform communists or socialists which would remain friendly to the USSR. In December 1989, Gorbachev and President Bush of the USA met at the Malta Summit and officially declared that the Cold War was over. The USSR was, however, worried about the future of Germany and the possibility of NATO being able to extend its membership up to the Soviet border. In the end, though, the USSR was desperate for American aid and was forced to accept German reunification and its membership of NATO on 3 October 1990. In July 1991, the Warsaw Pact was dissolved, even though NATO remained in existence.

Gorbachev's concessions in eastern Europe, over the Warsaw Pact and on nuclear weapons, as well as his reforms in the USSR, finally led his opponents to launch a coup against him in August 1991. This failed and, although Gorbachev remained as President of the Soviet Union, real power passed increasingly to Boris Yeltsin, the newly-elected President of the Russian Republic. Yeltsin had been the Communist in charge of Moscow and had begun to introduce changes. At first, he had supported Gorbachev's reforms but, in 1987, he lost his positions when he tried to push Gorbachev into making reforms too quickly. In May 1990, elections were held in the different Soviet republics, which had just been given more powers. Within a month of being elected as President of Russia, Yeltsin broke with Gorbachev and left the Communist Party. He then allied with those who wanted to end all Communist influence in the USSR. In 1991, Yeltsin restricted the Communist newspapers and stopped the Party from organising in factories.

**Source D**

*Boris Yeltsin, and some of his supporters, holding a rally in Moscow on 19 August 1991. By then, evidence was mounting that the attempted coup against Gorbachev was collapsing.*

Russia was by far the biggest of the Soviet republics and, in December 1991, Russia, Belorussia and the Ukraine formed the Commonwealth of Independent States (CIS). On 25 December, Gorbachev resigned and the Soviet Union was formally dissolved. This ended the 'great contest' and the Cold War, leaving the USA as the world's only superpower.

### Questions

1 What aspect of Soviet foreign policy did Gorbachev seem to be abandoning in **Source A**?

2 Why were many Communists concerned about Gorbachev's reforms and foreign policy in the late 1980s and early 1990s?

3 How did the events shown in **Sources B** and **D** contribute to the end of the Cold War?

# SUMMARY

## 1945–1953

- After the Second World War, Stalin reasserted his political control. He also began to rebuild the Soviet economy by returning to the use of Five-Year Plans.
- He was determined to establish a security buffer zone along the USSR's western borders. In addition, he was desperate for reparations in order to begin the reconstruction of the USSR's war-damaged economy. As a result of the deepening Cold War, in the years 1945-48, the Soviet Union helped the Communist parties in the east European states establish one-party systems.
- Stalin was also determined to make these Communist parties follow the Soviet line. After Tito of Yugoslavia rejected Stalin's orders and broke away from Soviet control, Stalin ordered a purge of the other Communist parties.

## 1953–1964

- After Stalin's death, the leaders of the CPSU at first decided to share power so that no one person could have supreme control. However, by 1955, Khrushchev had emerged as the main leader.
- Khrushchev introduced political reforms to liberalise life in the USSR, and also tried to modernise the economy. In 1956, he made a speech condemning Stalin's purges and show trials, and began a process of 'limited de-Stalinisation'.
- Khrushchev's reforms and his 'secret speech' led many east European 'satellites' to think they could end Soviet domination. Though changes were allowed in Poland, Soviet forces invaded Hungary in 1956 to crush a large-scale revolt.

## 1964–1985

- After Khrushchev was forced to resign in 1964, he was replaced by Brezhnev and Kosygin. They ended many of his reforms and ruled in a more 'Stalinist' way. When Dubcek, the leader of Czechoslovakia tried to liberalise politics in 1968, Brezhnev soon got the forces of the Warsaw Pact to invade in order to stop the reforms. He then issued the 'Brezhnev Doctrine'.
- After 1964, the Soviet economy began to slow down and then stagnate. In part, this was due to the tremendous resources put into the arms race with the USA. Trouble in Poland began in 1980, when millions of workers joined an unofficial union known as 'Solidarity'.

## 1985–1991

- In 1985, Gorbachev became the new leader of the USSR. He wanted to modernise the Soviet economy, and to make the political system more democratic. Because of the high costs of the arms race, Gorbachev decided to push for arms reduction talks with the USA. He also made it clear that the USSR would no longer intervene in the affairs of the east European states.
- Political and economic reforms in Poland and Hungary soon sparked off demands for change in the other Soviet-bloc states. Events in East Germany in 1989 were soon followed by free elections in Czechoslovakia and Bulgaria. After some fierce fighting, the Communist leader of Romania was also overthrown.
- An attempted coup in 1991 by those in the CPSU opposed to Gorbachev, failed. Yeltsin, the leader of the Russian Republic, then brought about the break-up of the Soviet Union and Gorbachev resigned. This marked the end of the Cold War.

# Exam Question Practice

## Source sufficiency

Study Sources A and B below, and then answer the following question:

Do Sources A and B provide enough information to explain why the Soviet Union decided to crush the Hungarian Revolt of 1956?

**Source A**

Armed Hungarian Nationalists during street fighting in Budapest, November 1956.

**Source B**

We could not overlook the fact that Hungary is a neighbour of the Soviet Union. A victory of the reactionary forces would have converted that country into a new jumping-off ground for an aggressive war not only against the Soviet Union but also against the other countries of eastern Europe.

*An extract from the speech made by Shepilov, the Soviet Foreign Minister, when explaining the Soviet invasion of Hungary to the UN on 19 November 1956.*

### Examiner's Tips

**When answering questions like this:**

◎ Make sure that you use both the sources mentioned.

◎ Try to comment on the content of the sources AND any possible problems of reliability.

◎ Don't forget to also use your own knowledge of the topic - otherwise, you will not be able to comment fully on the amount of information provided by the sources.

◎ Remember, when using your own knowledge to give facts not contained in the sources, you will need to try to explain how the missing factors/events are important in understanding the topic. If you don't, you will not score high marks.

# CHAPTER 14

## CONFLICT IN THE MIDDLE EAST

Two Jewish refugee ships from Bulgaria in the Palestinian port of Haifa, 2 October 1947. The British authorities sent both ships on to Cyprus. British troops can be seen boarding the ships.

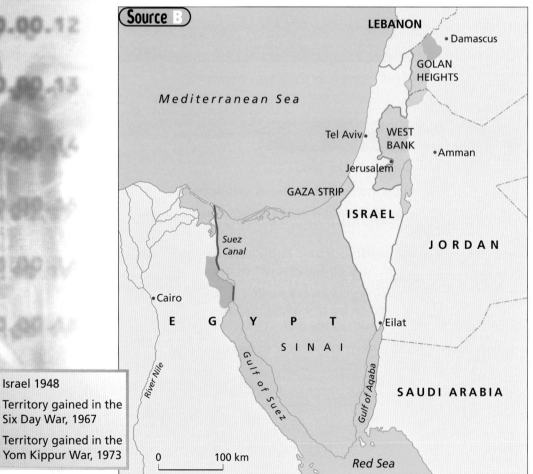

The expansion of Israel, 1948-1973.

*Palestinian protestors and Israeli soldiers, in Jerusalem in 2000.*

### Key Questions

**Why** were would-be Jewish settlers turned away from Palestine (the land they regarded as their homeland) by the British authorities as shown in **Source A**?

**Why** has Israel taken Arab territories, as shown in **Source B** in the years since 1948?

**Why** are protests such as the one in **Source C** still taking place?

These are some of the issues which we will cover in this chapter. The main focus of this chapter on conflict in the Middle East will be:

- The background to the problems in Palestine in 1947

- The first Arab-Israeli war and the creation of Israel

- How the Arab-Israeli conflict developed in the 1950s and 1960s

- The problems arising from the number of Palestinian refugees

- Why the Palestine Liberation Organisation turned to the use of terror in its struggle against the Israeli takeover of Palestine

- The importance of the Yom Kippur War in 1973

- The search for peace after 1973

# Palestine and the Jewish people

## The background

Part of the background to the conflict in the Middle East between the Arab states and Israel lies in the history of the Jewish people after the Roman occupation in 63 BC of Palestine, or what is now known as Israel. Many Jews objected to Roman rule and there were two failed revolts, which resulted in many Jews leaving Palestine. This became known as the diaspora. The descendants of most of these Jewish refugees ended up in Christian Europe. During the Middle Ages, Jewish communities in western Europe were frequently attacked and their property was stolen. Many returned to live in the Islamic states of North Africa and the Middle East, while others moved to eastern Europe, where most of them settled in areas under the control of the Russian Tsar.

However, many Jews chose to stay after the Roman occupation, even when the country was conquered by the Arabs in the seventh century and Islam became the official religion. In general, the main disadvantage experienced by Jews in the Middle East was that they had to pay extra taxes. Some Jews eventually converted to Islam.

## Anti-Semitism during the nineteenth century

During the first half of the nineteenth century, many laws which discriminated against Jews were abolished in western Europe, but violent attacks (known as pogroms) and discrimination continued in the Russian Empire. This led many Jews to move to western Europe in order to escape from poverty and violence. Some tried to mix in (assimilate) with their non-Jewish neighbours, and began to abandon parts of their religion's practices. They hoped this would help reduce the 'anti-Semitism' which had been directed against Jews for centuries. But others rejected assimilation and stuck to the strict observance of their religion. During the late 1880s, persecution and prejudice against Jews reappeared in Germany, Austria and France, and a new wave of violence against Jews broke out in Tsarist Russia.

## Zionism

Many Jews decided to emigrate to the USA, but a much smaller number came to believe that Jews would always be persecuted and should, therefore, establish their own state. These became known as Zionists, and they at first considered several possibilities, including parts of Africa and Latin America. Eventually, though, they settled on the idea of returning to Palestine. From 1881-91, over 10 000 Zionist settlers moved there.

The degree of anti-Jewish sentiments, even in the more tolerant areas of western Europe, was shown in 1894 by the 'Dreyfus Affair' in France. Dreyfus, a Jewish officer in the French army, was found guilty of being a traitor on what later turned out to be false evidence given by an anti-Semitic officer. What shocked many Jews

### Diaspora

*This means the dispersal of the Jews which followed after the Romans deported or enslaved many Jews after their revolt in AD 135. Many more then decided to emigrate in the years that followed. While many decided to head for Europe, a large number stayed in the Middle East. A large proportion simply stayed in Palestine. Some even converted to Christianity or Islam in the following centuries.*

### Anti-Semitism

*This term refers to anti-Jewish prejudice, discrimination and persecution. During the Middle Ages, many Christians - including rulers and Church leaders - blamed all Jews for the crucifiction of Christ. Also, because of discrimination in employment, some Jews became money-lenders - something that Christians were forbidden to do. Although many Christian landowners borrowed from such money-lenders, this often increased hatred of all Jews. Such prejudices increased in nineteenth-century Europe as a result of rising nationalism and the appearance of racial 'theories' which said that Jews were an inferior and alien race.*

was how much racial abuse appeared as a result of his trial. After witnessing this anti-Semitism, a Jewish journalist, Theodor Herzl, wrote a book calling for the establishment of a separate Jewish state.

Soon the Zionists were led by Herzl, who persuaded the first Zionist Conference in 1897 to support the Palestine option. However, he failed to persuade the Ottoman (Turkish) Empire to give the Zionists part of Palestine.

## The First World War

Herzl died in 1904 and was succeeded by Chaim Weizmann. He, too, failed to persuade the Turkish rulers of Palestine to agree to the formation of a separate Jewish state. When Turkey joined forces with Germany in the First World War, Britain persuaded the Arab subjects of the Ottoman Empire to rise in revolt against their Turkish rulers by promising them independence after the war. One of the key roles in this was taken by Sir Henry McMahon, the British High Commissioner for Egypt. In January 1916, after discussions which had begun in July 1915, he wrote to Sherif Hussein of Mecca, the leading Arab nationalist, promising that the British government supported the idea of independence for all Arabs 'when the situation allows'.

However, in May 1916, Britain and France secretly drew up the Sykes-Picot Plan. This agreed to divide the Middle East up between them when the war was over, with Britain having Palestine, and what eventually became Jordan and Iraq. The French were to have what became Lebanon and Syria. Even Tsarist Russia and Italy were to have parts. However, after the November 1917 Revolution, the Bolsheviks published the details of the Plan, which caused much anger amongst Arab nationalists.

Weizmann then won the sympathy of Arthur Balfour by pointing out how a Zionist settler state would help defend European control of the area. In December 1916, Balfour became the British Foreign Secretary and persuaded the rest of the government that support for Zionism would help bring the USA (which had an influential Jewish community) into the war on Britain's side. Balfour then sent a letter to Lord Rothschild (the leading British Jew), on 2 November 1917, promising vague support for a 'national home' for Jewish people in Palestine. This letter became known as the Balfour Declaration.

## Questions

1  What was 'Zionism'?
2  How did the Balfour Declaration of 1917, shown in **Source C**, conflict with the promises made in 1915-16 by McMahon to the Arab leaders?

**Source A**

If His Majesty the Sultan were to give us Palestine, we could undertake to regulate Turkey's finances. For Europe, we would constitute a bulwark against Asia down there. We would be the advance post of civilisation against barbarism. As a neutral state, we would remain in constant touch with all of Europe, which would guarantee our existence.

*An extract from The Jewish State, written by Theodor Herzl in 1896. By this time, most Zionists had decided they should set up their own state in Palestine.*

**Source B**

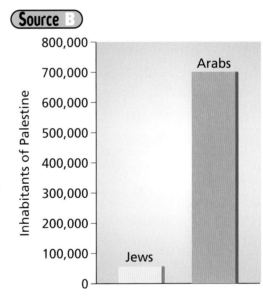

*The number of Jewish and Arab inhabitants of Palestine in 1918, according to an official British census.*

**Source C**

His Majesty's Government views with favour the establishment in Palestine of a national home for the Jewish people, and will use their best endeavours to facilitate [make easy] the achievement of this object, it being clearly understood that nothing shall be done which may prejudice [harm] the civil and religious rights of existing non-Jewish communities in Palestine,...

*An extract from the Balfour Declaration, 2 November 1917.*

# Tensions between Jews and Arabs

## Jewish immigration to Palestine after 1918

After the war, the peace treaty with Turkey confirmed British and French control of the Arab provinces in the Middle East, though technically their authority was based on League of Nations mandates (licences). The Arab leaders were furious that the promises made by Britain had been so clearly broken. Anger increased during the 1920s, as the British government allowed large numbers of Jewish immigrants to settle in Palestine. This immigration rose considerably after 1924 when Republican governments began to restrict immigration into the USA. The British also allowed the Jews in Palestine to set up their own administrative organisations. Overall, there was the Jewish Agency (first called the Zionist Executive), while the Histadrut organised the workers and cooperatives. In addition, the Jews were allowed, unofficially, to set up their own armed force, which was called the Haganah.

This Jewish immigration was accepted at first by most Palestinian Arabs, but as more and more land was bought up by Zionist groups, opposition grew. At times during the 1920s, this erupted into violence. Jewish immigration to Palestine increased even further after 1933, as many tried to escape Nazi persecution after Hitler became Chancellor of Germany. As a result, the Jewish population in Palestine had almost doubled by 1936.

**Source A**

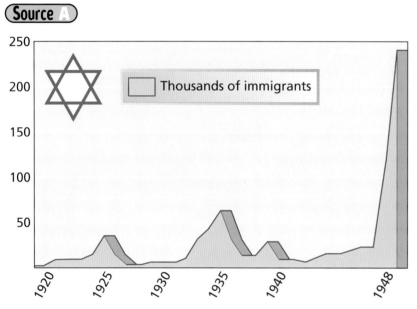

Jewish immigration into Palestine from 1918-48.

## The Arab Revolt, 1936-39

Palestinian leaders called for an end to further immigration and, in May 1936, Arabs rose in revolt against British control. A guerrilla war developed, in which Jewish farms were attacked but, by 1939, the British had defeated the Palestinians. They were then disarmed, but the unofficial Zionist organisations were allowed to keep their weapons - including a more violent group known as the Irgun Zvai Leumi. This put them in a much stronger position than they had been before the Arab revolt.

However, during this Arab revolt, the British government began to change its attitude to the Zionist project. In May 1939, a White Paper stated that Britain did not support the idea of a separate Jewish state or the partition of Palestine. Instead, it called for a united Palestine, with protection of the rights of both Jews and Arabs, and said that only another 75 000 Jewish settlers would be allowed into Palestine over the next five years. After that, there would be no further immigration. This was accepted by most Arab

**Source B**

There is no common ground between the Jews and the Arabs. They differ in religion and in language. Their cultural and social life, their ways of thought and conduct, are as incompatible as their national aspirations.... Neither Arab nor Jew has any sense of service to a single state.... The National Home cannot be half-national.

An extract from the Peel Commission's report of 1937, published while the Arab Revolt was still going on. At this stage, Britain suggested splitting Palestine in two, with a British buffer zone between the Arab and Jewish parts. Later, in 1939, the Macdonald Report recommended restricting Jewish immigration for five years, and only allowing more after that if the Palestinian Arabs agreed.

leaders, but was rejected by the Zionist organisations. However, the start of the Second World War in 1939 prevented this plan from being put into effect.

## The impact of the Second World War

The discovery of the Nazis' attempted genocide of the Jewish people led to great sympathy for the 100 000 or so who had survived the Holocaust. At the same time, the Arab cause had been weakened by the attempts of some Arab leaders to get help from Hitler in order to achieve independence. In fact, some Zionist groups (the Irgun and the Lehi) had also tried to do a deal with Hitler by offering to attack the British in return for the release of all Jews in the extermination camps. After the war, the USA put great pressure on Britain to let the Holocaust survivors go to Palestine immediately. When Britain hesitated, for fear of provoking another Arab revolt (and so risking its control of the Suez Canal and access to oil), the Haganah joined forces with the more extremist Zionist groups in October 1945, in order to fight a guerrilla war against the British.

## The UN and partition

On 26 July 1946, the Irgun planted a bomb in the King David Hotel, Jerusalem, which was being used as the British HQ. The bomb killed 91 people. During the next year, over 150 British soldiers, policemen and officials were killed by Jewish extremists, including the Stern Gang. The new Labour government in Britain favoured the idea of Arabs and Jews sharing power in an independent Palestine and, in July 1947, in order not to antagonise the Arabs, forced a ship (the Exodus) containing 4000 Jewish refugees to return to Germany. When the British authorities executed three Irgun fighters, two captured British sergeants were hanged.

By 1947, ruling Palestine was costing Britain over £40 million a year, at a time when its post-war economy was in decline. So, in February 1947, Britain announced it would hand the problem of Palestine over to the United Nations. The UN set up a commission in May and its report, which recommended dividing Palestine into two separate states, was accepted by the General Assembly of the UN on 29 November.

The UN proposals for the partitioning of Palestine in 1947.

### Questions

1 Use **Source A** and the information in this unit to explain why there was an Arab revolt in 1936?

2 Why did Britain attempt to restrict Jewish immigration into Palestine after the Second World War?

3 Why did the UN make the decision to divide Palestine into two separate states?

# From Palestine to Israel

## The first Arab-Israeli war, 1948-49

The Zionists, led by David Ben-Gurion, accepted the UN plan and, on 14 May 1948, the last British troops left Palestine. On that day, at a special conference, Ben-Gurion announced the birth of the state of Israel. He became Defence Minister and Prime Minister. However, the Arabs had rejected the UN plan, which gave over half the land of Palestine to the new Jewish state, even though Jews made up less than one-third of the population. After the plan was first announced, communal violence between Jews and Palestinian Arabs increased. The worst incident was at the small village of Deir Yassin, when Zionist extremists murdered several hundred Arabs.

As soon as Ben-Gurion announced the state of Israel, it was attacked by a combined Arab force of 30 000, made up of soldiers from Transjordan, Egypt, Iraq, Syria and the Lebanon. Although they outnumbered the Israeli army, the Arab forces were divided and badly led. In particular, the King of Transjordan, who in theory was the overall leader, was only interested in gaining control of Jerusalem and the West Bank. As a result, this initial Arab invasion was defeated, and both the Soviet Union and the USA expressed support for Israel. In June, the UN arranged a truce, during which Israel received massive arms shipments.

When fighting resumed in July, Israeli forces inflicted several defeats on Arab forces. On 24 February 1949, Israel and Egypt signed an armistice and the other states soon followed Egypt's lead. By then, the Israelis had annexed almost the whole of what had been Palestine.

## The Palestinian refugees

When the UN drew up its partition plan for Palestine in 1947, there were about 900 000 Palestinian Arabs living in what became Israel. As violence between Arabs and Zionists turned into war in 1948, 725 000 Arabs fled from Israeli-held territory to the surrounding Arab states. In fact, their departure began in December 1947, when the wealthier or more educated Palestinians decided there would be no future for them in a Jewish state. Then, in March 1948, with the Jewish military position looking weak, Zionist leaders decided that Palestinian villages should be disarmed or destroyed if there was evidence that they were supporting the Arab forces. They also decided that Arabs should be expelled from mixed areas in the more important towns. From April, the Haganah began to put this into effect, and many villages were destroyed and their inhabitants expelled. When Irgun and Lehi fighters massacred the inhabitants of Deir Yassin on 9 April, ordinary Palestinians panicked and began to flee in large numbers. As the war came to an end, Israel's forces 'cleared' many of the Arab villages close to its new borders. As soon as the war ended, Jewish settlers took over the houses and land vacated by Palestinians. By the middle of 1949, this process

### Source A

The affair at Deir Yassin had tremendous effects. The press and radio spread the news everywhere among the Arabs as well as the Jews. In this way a general terror was built up among the Arabs. Driven by fear, the Arabs left their homes to find shelter among their kin. First isolated farms, then villages, and, in the end, whole towns were evacuated.

*An extract from a report, made in 1950, by a Red Cross official who had visited Deir Yassin.*

### Source B

I do not accept that we should encourage their return [Palestinian refugees]. I believe we should prevent their return. We must settle Jaffa. Jaffa will become a Jewish city. We must prevent at all costs their return.

*Comments made by David Ben-Gurion, the new Prime Minister of Israel, on 16 June 1948. He said this during an Israeli cabinet meeting which was discussing what to do about the Palestinian refugees.*

was virtually complete and Israeli leaders had decided that the return of these Palestinians would threaten Israel's security.

## The second Arab-Israeli war, 1956

After the war, tensions remained high, as the Arab states wanted revenge for their defeat, and were angered by the plight of the Palestinian refugees. In Egypt, the Arab defeat led to the emergence of Gamal Abdul Nasser as the new military leader. When he signed an arms deal with Czechoslovakia in 1955, Israel and the West became concerned that Nasser was allowing the USSR to gain a foothold in the Middle East. When the USA blocked a loan they had promised to help Egypt build the Aswan Dam, Nasser turned to the USSR. As well as financial aid, the USSR sent military advisers, and Egypt, Syria and Jordan announced a joint military agreement.

Nasser also decided to help pay for the dam by nationalising the Suez Canal, which was still owned by Britain and France. These two countries then secretly invited Israel to help them plan an attack on Egypt. At Sevres, it was agreed that Israel would invade Egypt, while Britain and France would send troops which, in theory, would attempt to separate the two sides. The hope was that this would lead to Nasser's downfall and allow Britain and France to retake the Suez Canal. On 29 October 1956, Israel attacked Egypt and, by 5 November, had captured the Sinai peninsula. On that day, British and French forces landed around the Canal.

However, both the USA and the USSR, as well as the UN, condemned this aggression and, after financial and even military threats, Britain, France and Israel were forced to pull out. A UN Emergency Force (UNEF) was then sent to the Sinai to keep the peace between Egypt and Israel. Although later both Israel and France admitted they had planned the attack together, the British government denied any involvement for many years.

**Suez Canal**

*One of the concerns of Britain and France was that Nasser might use control of the Suez Canal to cut off oil supplies which came from the Middle East to Europe via the Canal and the Mediterranean. As well as taking back the Canal, the plan would allow Israeli forces to destroy the camps of Palestinian fighters which operated from parts of Egypt.*

**Source C**

*Some of the French soldiers who landed by the Suez Canal in November 1956. The ship in the background was one of many then sunk by Nasser to block the Suez Canal to shipping.*

**Source D**

*One of the many protests in London against the British government's involvement and policy in the Suez Crisis.*

**Questions**

1  What effect did the massacre at Deir Yassin have on many Palestinians?

2  What was the outcome of the 1956 war, which is referred to in **Sources C** and **D**?

# The continuing conflict

## Source A

Under no circumstances will we allow the Israeli flag to pass through the Gulf of Aqaba... The issue now at hand is not the Gulf of Aqaba, the Straits of Tiran, or the withdrawal of the United Nations forces, but the rights of the Palestinian people. It is the aggression which took place in Palestine in 1948 with the collaboration of Britain and the United States of America.

*Extracts from speeches made by President Nasser of Egypt during May 1967.*

## The background to the third Arab-Israeli war

After 1956, Nasser became a hero in the Arab world and, in 1958, Egypt and Syria merged together to form the United Arab Republic (UAR). Nasser hoped it would be the first step towards uniting the whole Arab world, and one of its main aims was to destroy the state of Israel. However, the UAR fell apart in 1961 because of increasing differences. By the mid-1960s, Syria was accusing Nasser of going 'soft' on Israel. Syria also allowed Palestinian guerrillas to operate across its border with Israel. The number of guerrilla raids and Israeli reprisals had increased significantly by 1966. This put pressure on Nasser to take action.

In 1967, Nasser began to make speeches which talked of destroying Israel and, on 15 May - after several serious clashes on the Israeli-Syrian border, Egyptian troops were stationed on the border with Israel, in an attempt to prevent an Israeli attack on Syria. On 18 May, Nasser ordered the UNEF to leave the Sinai peninsula and, on 22 May, he closed the Gulf of Aqaba to Israeli ships. At the same time, other Arab states bordering Israel began to move their troops into the border areas.

## Source B

*Egyptian prisoners passing advancing Israeli soldiers in June 1967.*

## The Six Day War, June 1967

Israel, however, was not intimidated, especially as discussions with the USA had resulted in assurances that there would be no pressure on Israel to show 'restraint'. This changed American attitude was due to the fact that, by the 1960s, the development of the Cold War had resulted in American support for Israel, while the USSR backed several of the Arab states. So, on 5 June 1967, Israel launched a surprise pre-emptive attack on Egypt's air force, which destroyed most of its planes while they were still on the ground. This destruction of the Egyptian airforce remained unknown to Syria and Jordan until after they had immediately entered this third Arab-Israeli war on Egypt's side. The Israelis, having established control of the skies by the end of the first day, quickly defeated Egyptian and Jordanian land forces and conquered the Sinai peninsula, the Gaza strip and the West Bank. On 9 June, Israeli forces successfully attacked the Golan Heights in Syria. On 10 June, Israel agreed to a cease-fire and what became known as the Six Day War ended.

## UN Resolution 242

After the war, the USA maintained its support for Israel by not joining with those countries which called for Israel to withdraw from the Arab lands it had conquered in 1967. Instead, the USA persuaded the UN Security Council to pass Resolution 242. This said Israel should give back the newly occupied territory, provided the Arab states made a lasting peace with Israel which accepted its right to exist.

However, the Arab states rejected the idea of recognising the existence of Israel or of making a permanent peace. In part, this was because the Israeli occupation of the West Bank had created another 350 000 Palestinian refugees. From 1969-70, a 'War of Attrition' took place between Egypt and Israel, with Egypt regularly shelling Israeli forces occupying the Sinai, while Israel carried out air raids against Egypt. A cease-fire was agreed in August 1970. Later that year, Anwar Sadat replaced Nasser as leader of Egypt. In February 1971, he offered a permanent peace with Israel, in return for an Israeli withdrawal from Sinai. When this was rejected, Sadat turned to the USSR for military aid (in particular, surface-to-air missiles or SAMs), believing this would force Israel to negotiate. Then, in April 1973, Moshe Dayan, the Israeli Defence Minister, made a speech which made it clear that Israel now regarded the Suez Canal as part of its permanent borders. Sadat became convinced that war was necessary.

## The fourth Arab-Israeli war, 1973

On 6 October, the Jewish religious holiday of Yom Kippur, Egyptian forces crossed the Suez Canal and recaptured much of the Sinai peninsula. At the same time, Syrian forces attacked and retook the Golan Heights. During this Yom Kippur War, the USA and USSR continued to supply their respective allies with weapons. After several serious defeats, by 10 October, Israel was able to launch a successful counter-offensive against the Syrians. This victory allowed them to deal with Egypt. On 14 October, Israel won a decisive victory and was able to cross the Suez Canal and began to move on Cairo.

However, the rich oil-producing Arab states used a powerful new weapon - oil. The Organisation of Petroleum Exporting Countries (OPEC) increased the price of oil by 70%, and placed a complete ban on the export of oil to all countries which supported Israel. This worried many Western countries, and the USA in particular. As a result, pressure was put on Israel to agree a cease-fire, and the Yom Kippur War ended on 26 October 1973. Although Israel had won some major victories, the Arab states had been able to inflict some serious losses early on. This improved the morale of the Arab armies, and shattered the Israeli reputation of invincibility. The unexpected attack and the number of Israeli casualties led to a political crisis in Israel, and eventually forced the resignation of Dayan and Golda Meir, the Prime Minister.

## Peace

After the Yom Kippur War, the USA was determined to establish better relations with the oil-producing Arab states. A key role in this was played by Henry Kissinger, the US Secretary of State. At the same time, one effect of the war was to make both Israel and Egypt realise that any lasting peace would only come about if they both made some concessions.

> ### Source C
> i  Withdrawal of Israel from the occupied territories.
> ii  Acknowledgement of the sovereignty and territorial integrity and political independence of every state in the Middle East.
> iii  A just settlement to the refugee problem.

*The main points of Resolution 242, adopted by the UN in November 1967.*

### Source D

*Israeli artillery firing into Syria from the Golan Heights during the fighting in 1973. Israeli had taken the Heights from Syria in the 1967 war.*

### Questions

1  What 'aggression' in 1948 was Nasser referring to in **Source A**?

2  Identify the 'occupied territories' mentioned in **Source C**.

3  Why did neither the Six Day War nor the Yom Kippur War succeed in bringing the conflict to an end?

4  What role did the USA play in Arab-Israeli relations, 1967-1973? What influenced American decisions at each stage?

# The Palestinians

*A Palestinian refugee talking about her son, who had just been killed in a PLO raid on Israel.*

**al-Fatah**

*Al-Fatah means 'victory' in Arabic. It soon became the largest of the Palestinian guerrilla groups. After the 1967 war, the original leadership of the Palestine Liberation Organisation (PLO) was discredited and, in 1969, the leader of al-Fatah, Yasser Arafat, became Chairman of the PLO. However, the organisation of the PLO was very loose, and not all Palestinian groups joined. One of the main ones which did not was the Popular Front for the Liberation of Palestine (PFLP), which was led by George Habash, a Christian Palestinian, and which was based in Syria. The PFLP adopted a more left-wing policy, and soon lost faith in the willingness of Arab governments to fight for the liberation of Palestine.*

## The Palestinian refugees and the Arab response

The question of peace in the Middle East was complicated by the plight of the Palestinian refugees. Neighbouring Arab states did not want the Palestinian refugees to settle as permanent citizens. So, instead, the refugees were placed in temporary refugee camps where conditions were poor. The UN tried unsuccessfully to persuade Israel to allow them to return, but a few of those who had done so had carried out attacks on Jewish people. As a result, Israeli forces saw all such 'infiltrators' as a threat. From 1948-1956, almost 5000 were killed by the Israeli army.

In 1949, the UN Relief Works Agency (UNRWA) began to look after the needs of the refugee camps, as some Arab governments saw the poverty of the refugees as a good propaganda weapon in their struggle against Israel. As the years went by, the population of these camps increased as more and more children were born. At first, most Palestinians hoped that the Arab states would destroy Israel so that they could return to their homes. Nasser's Egypt, in particular, seemed their most likely saviour.

## The PLO

However, some Palestinians became impatient and began to form their own organisations. One of these was al-Fatah, set up in 1957 by Yasser Arafat. During the 1960s, this became an increasingly active fighting force. In 1964, the Arab states set up an organisation for the Palestinians called the Palestine Liberation Organisation (PLO). According to the Palestinian National Charter, the aim of the PLO was to expel all Jews who had settled since 1918, and to destroy the state of Israel. At first, it was controlled

**Source B**

*PLO guerrillas undergoing training for raids against Israel.*

by the Arab states but, after their defeat in the Six Day War in 1967, PLO leaders began to believe they would have to rely on their own efforts. By 1969, al-Fatah had grown in size and had become the largest group in the PLO, with its main base in Jordan.

When attempts at waging guerrilla warfare against Israeli armed forces were unsuccessful, the various groups of the PLO turned to terrorism against Israeli civilians and to hijacking airliners. But Jordan's government became concerned about the growing influence of the PLO and, in September 1970, the Jordanian army attacked PLO bases there. The PLO later called this event 'Black September' because of the heavy casualties it suffered. After a cease-fire, fighting flared up again in 1971 and the PLO was expelled from Jordan. The PLO then based itself in Lebanon, where it continued to carry out raids in Israel. In 1972, a PLO group called Black September killed 11 Israeli athletes at the Olympic Games in Munich. In 1974, the Arab League recognised the PLO as the 'sole legitimate representative of the Palestinian people'. Later that year, Arafat was invited to speak to the UN.

*Yasser Arafat, leader of the PLO, addressing the United Nations on 12 November 1974.*

## First steps to peace

In 1977, Jimmy Carter became President of the USA. He wanted to secure peace in the Middle East, at least in part to limit the growing influence of the USSR in the region. In the same year, Menachem Begin became Prime Minister in Israel. He was prepared to make a deal with Egypt over the Sinai. Despite the opposition of Syria and the PLO, Sadat, the Egyptian President, flew to Jerusalem for discussions in November 1977. In September 1978, Sadat and Begin flew to the USA to have talks with Carter at Camp David. The Camp David Agreement resulted in Egypt accepting the existence of Israel, in return for Israel pulling out of Sinai. Both sides also agreed to give limited powers (autonomy) to the West Bank and Gaza. However, the PLO refused to accept this, and no other Arab state was prepared to make a formal peace with Israel. Although the Camp David Agreement ended 30 years of war and hostility between Egypt and Israel, Carter had hoped it would soon be followed by a general peace between the rest of the Arab countries and Israel. In fact, Arab leaders strongly criticised Sadat for making the Agreement, and for signing an official peace treaty with Israel on 26 March 1979. For many years, Egypt was isolated from most of these states, as they believed Sadat had betrayed the Palestinians. In October 1981, Sadat was assassinated by some of his own soldiers who saw him as having disgraced Arabs and Islam by signing a deal with Israel.

Meanwhile, Begin began to greatly increase the number of Jewish settlements in the West Bank.

### Questions

1. What led some Palestinians to set up their own organisations in order to fight for their return to Palestine?

2. What were the results of the event in Jordan which became known as 'Black September'?

3. What were the effects of the Camp David Agreement?

# The search for peace

## The Intifada

The Camp David Agreement deprived the PLO of an important ally, which made Israel feel free to take action against the PLO. In March 1978, Israeli forces briefly invaded south Lebanon in order to destroy PLO bases and weaken Syrian influence there. In June 1982, the Israelis invaded Lebanon a second time. By August, the PLO had been forced to flee to Tunisia but, after three years of war, the Syrians were stronger than ever in Lebanon. Although Arafat survived an attempt in 1983 to replace him as leader, he began to think a change in tactics was necessary as the use of force had brought little success. During 1985 and 1986, talks took place between the USA and the PLO on the basis of UN Resolution 242, but these broke down because of continuing divisions within the PLO.

### Source A

...the victims were men, women, and children of all ages, from the very old to the very young, even babies in arms. They were killed in every possible way. The lucky ones were shot, singly or in groups. Others were strangled or had their throats slit. They were mutilated, before or after death...

*An extract from an article by a British war journalist, written in 1982, after the massacre of over 1000 Palestinian refugees in Lebanon, following the Israeli invasion. The massacres took place in the Sabra and Chatila refugee camps, and were carried out by the Lebanese Christian Militia, which was allied to Israel.*

### Source B

*Israeli forces invading Lebanon in 1982.*

### Intifada

*This is an Arabic term which means 'uprising' or 'shaking off'. It began in the occupied territories and, in the beginning, was a form of civil disobedience. Because many of the leaders were students, the Israeli authorities closed colleges and schools. However, soon the protests turned to riots in many places, with Palestinian youths throwing stones and petrol bombs at Israeli soldiers. The Israeli response (according to their Defence Minister, it was 'force, might and beatings') only increased the resistance to the continued Israeli occupation.*

In late 1987, young Palestinians in the West Bank and Gaza began an uprising, known as the Intifada, against the Israeli authorities. Thousands of young Palestinians marched in demonstrations and threw stones at Israeli troops. The harshness of Israeli attempts to crush this uprising won much support for the Palestinians across the world. This persuaded Arafat, in December 1988, to accept UN Resolution 242, in order to get American support for the West Bank and Gaza coming under Palestinian control.

## The Israeli response

The 1988 Israeli election produced a stalemate between Labour and Likud, the two biggest parties, which resulted in an uneasy coalition. While many Israelis, including most of the Labour Party, welcomed Arafat's major change of policy, many others, including the Likud Party, dismissed this as a trick. The USA, which was unhappy about the degree of Israeli repression, urged Israel to make a deal with the PLO - especially as, in July, Jordan had given up its claim to the West Bank. However, when the Gulf War broke out in 1991, following Iraq's invasion of Kuwait, Arafat backed Iraq.

The USA, greatly strengthened in the Middle East by its victory in the Gulf War, began to put pressure on Israel to make some concessions to the Palestinians. In October 1991, the US President, George Bush and US Secretary of State, James Baker, finally persuaded Israel to meet Arafat in Madrid. The Israeli Prime Minister, Yitzhak Shamir, refused to compromise but, in June 1992, the Labour Party won the election. Yitzhak Rabin, was prepared to do a deal with Arafat, especially as more and more Palestinians were joining extreme terrorist groups such as Hezbollah and Hamas.

## The Oslo Accords

While talks continued in Madrid, secret discussions took place in Oslo and, on 30 August 1993, agreement on terms was reached. On 13 September, these were publicly agreed in Washington. This gave the Palestinians control, via a Palestinian Authority, over many of the ordinary decisions in the West Bank and Gaza, but did not solve the question of Jewish settlements there or control of Jerusalem. Although Israeli troops remained, an armed Palestinian police force was set up. This came into force in May 1994. In July, Jordan and Israel signed a peace treaty. A new agreement (Oslo II) was made in September 1995 which extended the power of the Palestinian Authority. In January 1996, Arafat was elected as its President.

However, two months before, Rabin had been assassinated by a Jewish extremist who, like many, believed the Oslo Accords gave too much away. Continued Palestinian terrorist attacks led to the defeat of Labour in the 1996 election. Binyamin Netanyahu, the new Likud Prime Minister, was opposed to the idea of a separate Palestinian state and failed to carry out all that had been agreed in the Oslo II Accords. This led to more violence between Jews and Palestinians.

### Gulf War

*This began in January 1991, when an American-led coalition of countries (including Britain) launched an attack on Iraq. In 1990, Iraq had invaded and occupied the important oil-producing state of Kuwait. Because the PLO backed Iraq, many of the wealthy Arab Gulf states, such as Saudi Arabia, stopped giving money to the PLO after the war ended in February 1991. At the same time, over 400 000 Palestinian refugees were expelled from Kuwait when its wealthy rulers returned. This all put pressure on Arafat to do a deal with Israel.*

### Source C

Let us call the agreement [the Oslo Accords] by its real name: a Palestinian surrender. The PLO has ended the Intifada, even though Israel remains in occupation of the West Bank and Gaza. There is nothing in the document to suggest that Israel will give up its violence against Palestinians or compensate its victims. Israeli troops will redeploy, not totally withdraw. Israeli settlers will remain and live under different laws.

*Comments made in late 1993 by a PLO member who opposed Arafat's leadership and the Oslo Accords.*

### Source D

*Rabin and Arafat shaking hands after the Oslo II Agreement, on 28 September 1995. US President Clinton is standing between them.*

### Questions

1 Why were some Palestinians, like the one in **Source C**, unhappy about the Oslo Accords?

2 Look back over the chapter and identify the main factors that have made peace in the Middle East so difficult. For each factor select one specific example to show how it contributed to the conflict.

# SUMMARY

## 1917–1947

- In 1917, the Balfour Declaration seemed to promise British support for a Jewish homeland in Palestine. This was despite the fact that, in 1916, Britain had promised Arab nationalists independence if they attacked the Turks.
- After the war, Britain and France took over the Arab states which had been ruled by the Turkish Empire. Britain was in charge of Palestine and, during the 1920s and 1930s, allowed many Jews to settle there. An armed Arab revolt from 1936-39 against the number of Jewish settlers and the amount of land they were buying up, was defeated by Britain.
- By 1945, Britain had decided against a separate Jewish state. This led to terrorist attacks by Jewish extremists. In 1947, Britain handed the problem of Palestine over to the UN.

## 1948–1956

- The UN decided to partition Palestine into separate Jewish and Palestinian states. This was rejected by the Palestinians. When British troops left in May 1948, a war broke out between the new state of Israel and several Arab countries. Although outnumbered, by 1949, Israel had defeated the Arab forces, and had taken over most of the areas earlier awarded to the Palestinians by the UN plan. Over 700 000 Palestinians became refugees.
- A second Arab-Israeli war broke out in 1956 over the Suez Crisis. Although the Israelis were victorious, the USA and USSR forced Britain and France to withdraw, and Israel had to give back the land it had occupied.

## 1967–1973

- Arab states, led by Egypt, were determined to destroy the state of Israel, and began to build up their armaments. But, in June 1967, the Israelis launched the surprise Six Day War. The Arab forces were again defeated, this time, because of American support, Israel held on to captured land. This third Arab defeat led the newly formed PLO to resort to terrorist attacks.
- In October 1973, Egypt and Syria launched the Yom Kippur War against Israel. Israeli forces were eventually able to push the Arab armies back. Arab oil-producers then banned oil sales to countries supporting Israel, and greatly increased the price of oil. This led the USA to put pressure on Israel to make some concessions to the Palestinians.

## 1974–1996

- After the Yom Kippur War, Egypt decided to seek peace with Israel and, in 1978, the Camp David Agreement was signed between these two countries. Israel then began to attack PLO bases in Lebanon and, in 1982, invaded it.
- In 1988, young Palestinians began the Intifada. The violence of Israeli soldiers increased world support for the Palestinian cause. In December, the PLO accepted the existence of Israel and renounced terrorism.
- This was unpopular with many Arabs, but peace talks finally led to the Oslo Accord in 1993. Israel agreed to give the Palestinian Authority limited powers in parts of the West Bank and Gaza. These powers were increased in 1995, but disputes over Jewish settlements and Palestinian terrorist attacks continue.

# Exam Question Practice

## Descriptive essay

Study Sources A and B, which are about the Arab-Israeli conflict in the years 1947-1967.

Using Sources A and B, and your own knowledge, describe how the conflict between Israel and its Arab neighbours developed in the period 1947-1967.

**Source A**

*Palestinian Arab fighters guarding a village from possible Zionist attack in 1948.*

**Source B**

Under no circumstances will we allow the Israeli flag to pass through the Gulf of Aqaba.

The issue now at hand is not the Gulf of Aqaba, the Straits of Tiran, or the withdrawal of the United Nations forces, but the rights of the Palestinian people. It is the aggression which took place in Palestine in 1948 with the collaboration of Britain and the United States of America.

*Extracts from a speech by Nasser, the President of Egypt, in May 1967.*

## Examiner's Tips

**When answering questions like this:**

◎ Make sure you stick to the period specified in the question - you will not get marks if you write about events after 1967.

◎ Remember to use both of the sources AND your own knowledge - if you only use the sources OR your own knowledge, you will only get half marks at most.

◎ Do not make the mistake of only writing about one aspect - such as the conflict between Egypt and Israel. You will also need to comment on Israel's relations with Syria and Jordan, and the problem of the Palestinians.

◎ Because you will be expected to write about several different aspects in an essay, it is always a good idea to do a rough plan first, to make sure you cover a range of points.

◎ Finally, make sure the information you give is as precise as possible, e.g. dates, names, etc - vague or generalised knowledge will not get you the highest marks.

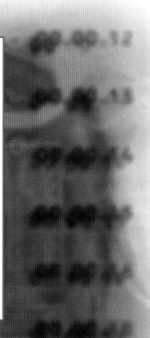

# CHAPTER 15

## SOUTH AFRICA

A white policeman checking the pass book of a black South African in 1960.

A common road sign in Johannesburg in 1956.

South African police beating black women protestors in Durban in 1959.

**Source D**

*A black shanty town near Cape Town in 1979.*

**Source E**

*Nelson and Winnie Mandela on Nelson Mandela's release from prison in 1990.*

## Key Questions

**Why** were the majority of people treated like foreigners in South Africa (**Source B**), requiring pass books like that being checked in **Source A**?

**Why** did black South Africans become involved in protests from the 1950s to the 1980s, such as that shown in **Source C**?

**Why** did South Africa, which was one of the wealthiest countries in the world, have many poor areas, such as **Source D**?

**How** did South Africa come to have a black President (the man shown in **Source E**) by 1994?

These are some of the issues which we will cover in this chapter. The main focus of this chapter on South Africa will be:

- The background to racism and apartheid in South Africa before 1910
- The main developments in South Africa from 1910-1948
- How the (Purified) National Party developed an apartheid state after 1948
- The way apartheid affected the different ethnic groups in South Africa
- Why opposition to apartheid began to grow in South Africa in the 1950s and 1960s
- The growth of opposition in the rest of the world
- Attempts to reform apartheid in the 1980s, as protests mounted
- The collapse of apartheid and the transition to majority rule

# The background to racism in South Africa

*Boer settlers in the nineteenth century.*

### The early settlers

The first people to live in what became South Africa were the Khoikhoi (who were herdsmen) and the San (who were hunter-gatherers). These were black Africans, collectively referred to as the Khoisan. In the seventeenth century, white Europeans began to move into the area around the Cape of Good Hope. Most of them were Dutch traders of the Dutch East India Company and, at first, there was much co-operation between them and the Khoisan. But trouble began when the Dutch wanted more and more land so that they could become wealthy farmers. Many of the Khoikhoi became servants, while the resistance of the San led to them being persecuted and killed.

Soon the Dutch farmers, known as Boers, began to move east from the Cape in their search for more land. Here they came up against the Xhosa people who were mainly farmers and were more able to defend their land. During the Napoleonic Wars in the nineteenth century, Britain took the Cape Colony from the Dutch (France's ally). Although at first Britain imposed strict controls on the Khoikhoi, these were later repealed. The Dutch did not like being under British rule and, from 1835, they began to leave the Cape in what became known as the Great Trek.

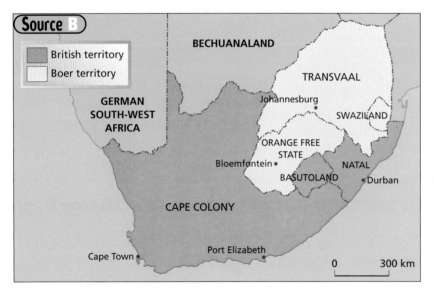

British territory
Boer territory

BECHUANALAND

TRANSVAAL

GERMAN SOUTH-WEST AFRICA

Johannesburg

SWAZILAND

ORANGE FREE STATE

Bloemfontein

NATAL

BASUTOLAND

Durban

CAPE COLONY

Cape Town

Port Elizabeth

0    300 km

*The division of southern Africa.*

### Britain and the Boer Republics

These 'Voortrekkers' wanted to maintain their own language (Afrikaans) and customs and, after many battles with various African kingdoms, they established new farming communities in Natal. From 1842, Britain tried to gain control of these areas but the Voortrekkers simply moved further east. In 1852 and 1854 respectively, Britain signed treaties with the Boers, allowing them to set up two new Boer republics, known as the Orange Free State and the Transvaal.

In 1867, diamonds were discovered in the Orange Free State and, in 1871, gold was discovered in the Transvaal. As the Boers were not at first interested in exploiting these mineral resources, the mining industries soon came under the control of British companies. Many of these were owned by Cecil Rhodes. The British government wanted to control these mines and were concerned the Boers might use the immense profits to establish complete independence. To prevent this, they decided to join the two Dutch provinces to the British ones of the Cape Colony and Natal. In 1871, the diamond fields were made part of the Cape Colony and, in 1877, the Transvaal was taken over.

**Cecil Rhodes**

*He had made a fortune in diamonds as a young man and was an outright British imperialist, believing that as much of Africa as possible should be made part of the British Empire. In 1890, he became the Prime Minister of Cape Colony, and from 1890-96 his private company seized a great tract of land which was then called Rhodesia.*

## The Boer Wars

The Boer republics were determined to resist this British take-over. As a result, the British were faced with two Boer Wars. The first one lasted from 1880-81 and a Second Boer War began in 1899. This was a much more serious war, during which the British forces faced determined guerrilla warfare from the Boers. The British, led by General Kitchener, responded with a 'scorched-earth' policy in which Boer farms and crops were deliberately destroyed. Boer women and children were also put into concentration camps, in which 25 000 died because of the bad conditions. Although the Boers were finally defeated in 1902, the methods used by the British resulted in long-term bitterness.

## Segregation under the British, 1902-10

At first, the British High Commissioner of South Africa, Lord Milner, tried to break down divisions between the Boers and the British by following a policy of 'Anglicisation'. He tried unsuccessfully to encourage large numbers of British to come to South Africa in order to make the Boers a minority white group. He also insisted that only English could be used in schools, thus angering the Boers.

In 1905, the Liberals came to power in Britain, replacing the Conservative Party. The Liberals had mainly opposed the Boer Wars and, after 1906, decided that co-operation with the Boer majority would be a better policy.

**Source C**

A picture of a British concentration camp during the Boer War, published in a French journal in 1901.

**Source D**

The Liberals had been opposed to the use of force in the Anglo-Boer War and were ashamed of the use of concentration camps and the wholesale destruction of Boer farms. They also knew that, as the Afrikaners were in a majority, they would dominate any future government. The British, therefore, tried to placate [please] the Afrikaners...

*An extract from a school textbook, published in Britain in 1997.*

In 1905, a commission set up by Lord Milner, had reported in favour of segregation of the races, which was supported by the Boers.

**Questions**

1 What is meant by the term 'segregation'?
2 Why, according to the writer of **Source C**, did the Liberal government in Britain try to appease the Boers after 1905?

**Segregation**

*The Boers had imposed segregation (separation) of the races from the early nineteenth century. The 'Hottentot Codes', for example, had forced all adult Khoikhoi to carry passes, and all their children to work on white farms. When the British authorities abolished these Codes, many Boers became 'Voortrekkers' ('those who travelled away') so that they could continue their policy of segregation. Mining companies and the white administrators also liked segregation, as it allowed them to enforce a system based on using male migrant workers who, when they were not working in the mines, were housed in compounds away from whites. Lord Milner set up the South African Native Affairs Commission to investigate the question of segregation. The Commission's report came out in 1905, and supported segregation.*

# The creation of South Africa

## The Union of South Africa, 1910-23

In 1910, the Boer republics became part of the British colony known as the Union of South Africa. To please the Boers, the Liberals agreed that the methods used to segregate blacks and whites in the Boer republics would become part of the Constitution of this new Union of South Africa. The Liberals also agreed to give greater weight to rural votes, thus ensuring that the Boers would have political control. In addition, each of the four states was allowed to keep the voting system which had existed before 1910. This meant that non-whites in the Cape could vote, provided they owned sufficient property. In the other three states, all non-whites were denied the vote. This was despite the fact that, during the Boer War, Britain had promised non-whites they would be given political rights if the Boers were defeated. From 1911-1923, several Acts were passed which extended the policies of segregation and discrimination.

These acts included the Mines and Works Act (1911) which excluded non-whites from many jobs. It also made it legal to pay blacks lower wages than whites for the same job. In 1913, the Native Land Act stopped virtually all blacks from owning land - apart from those living in a few 'native' reserves which together made up about 7% of the land total. Before 1913, many black South Africans had been share-croppers on white-owned land. Under this system, they farmed the land and then gave a share of the crop to the white owners as rent. The 1913 Land Act banned this practice and, as a result, many blacks were evicted. This caused great hardship and suffering. Finally, in 1923, the Urban Areas Act created special areas, well away from the city centres where whites lived, in which black people could be forced to live.

## Segregation increases, 1924-39

In 1924, General Hertzog, the leader of the Nationalist Party, became Prime Minister of South Africa. He was determined to bring in extra segregationist laws and to promote Afrikaner interests. In particular, he restored the use of Afrikaans, and, in 1924, the Industrial Conciliation Act made it illegal for blacks to take part in trade-union activity by barring the involvement of any 'pass bearer'. In the same year, several unskilled jobs were reserved for whites. In 1926, he passed the Colour Bar Act which prevented non-whites from doing skilled or semi-skilled jobs in the mines. In 1927, the Immorality Act made sex between whites and blacks illegal. During the Depression, the Nationalist Party joined up with the opposition South African Party (led by General Smuts) to form a coalition known as the United Party, which ruled South Africa from 1933 until 1948. As unemployment rose, blacks were sacked and even more jobs became 'white only'. In 1936, this coalition also took away the voting rights of most non-whites in the Cape. In the same

### Source A

They were wandering around the roads in the cold winter with everything they owned.... Mrs Kgobadi's child was sick. She had to be put in the ox-wagon which bumped along the road... two days later the child died... Late that night the poor young mother and father had to dig a grave where no-one could see them. They had to bury their child in a stolen grave.

*An extract from a book written by a black journalist and published in 1916. The extract describes the problems faced by a share-cropper's family which had been evicted after the Land Act of 1913.*

### Nationalist Party

*This party was founded in 1914 by General B. M. Hertzog, in order to preserve and increase the interests and privileges of Afrikaners. Its main strength was in rural areas and it was particularly committed to the maintenance and extension of segregation.*

year, another Land Act removed almost all rights of black people to rent property or run businesses, as well as own farmland.

## The impact of the Second World War

When war broke out in 1939, the United Party coalition split. Smuts wanted South Africa to fight on Britain's side, while Hertzog was opposed. Hertzog was outvoted and resigned. Smuts then became Prime Minister and the new leader of the United Party. Almost 200 000 whites then joined the army. This created a labour shortage, which was filled by black workers who migrated to the towns in great numbers in order to be nearer to the factories they worked in. Many industrialists saw this as economic sense and, in 1942, pass-law enforcement was relaxed. In 1944, a Health Commission recommended the setting up of a health-care programme that would be open to both blacks and whites. Some liberal members of the South African government even suggested that segregation should be ended. However, blacks still suffered from low wages and bad housing.

Because they were thrown together in large numbers, some began to join unions and to protest against their unequal treatment. Between 1940 and 1945, there were many strikes, as well as rent and bus boycotts. These developments worried many whites who supported segregation and discrimination. After the war, many returning white soldiers found it hard to find jobs. In addition, because the wages of blacks were so low, large unofficial squatter camps were thrown up in and around the major industrial towns and cities. In Johannesburg alone, there were over 90 000 black squatters. All these wartime developments led many white people to want a much stricter enforcement of segregation.

**Pass Laws**

*Before 1828, black people in the Cape had been forced to carry passes in order to work on white-owned farms. Although they were abolished by the British authorities, they had gradually been re-introduced and, by 1910, blacks needed a variety of passes for travel, work, residence and any curfew. If they were unable to produce them when asked by officials, they were punished. As a result, these passes were hated by blacks.*

**Source B**

| Year | Strikes | Whites | Blacks | Man-days lost |
|------|---------|--------|--------|---------------|
| 1940 | 24 | 1200 | 700 | 6500 |
| 1941 | 35 | 700 | 4800 | 23200 |
| 1942 | 58 | 1300 | 12800 | 49500 |
| 1943 | 52 | 1800 | 7400 | 47700 |
| 1944 | 52 | 200 | 12000 | 62700 |
| 1945 | 63 | 1500 | 14700 | 91100 |

*A table from the Rand Daily Mail, a South African newspaper, published on 30 January 1943. The article titled 'Twenty-five Native Strikes in Six Months' shows the tremendous increase in strikes involving black workers.*

**Questions**

1 How useful is **Source A** for finding out about the impact of the 1913 Land Act?

2 Does **Source B** provide sufficient information to explain why many whites were worried about developments during the Second World War?

# The apartheid state

## Malan and the creation of apartheid

The 1948 general election was won by the (Purified) National Party, even though it received only 39% of the vote. This was because the 1910 Constitution gave the votes in rural areas greater weight. The leader of this National Party was Dr. D.F. Malan and he immediately began to put into operation his party's plans for extending and maintaining white supremacy by creating an apartheid state. From 1949 to 1956, his government passed a series of apartheid laws. These included Acts which made sex between different racial groups illegal and a law which made protests against any law illegal. J.G. Strijdom, his successor as Prime Minister, was particularly concerned to remove the voting rights of the Cape Coloureds, which had been guaranteed by the 1910 Constitution. Malan had previously tried to do this, but had failed to get the necessary two-thirds majority in Parliament, which, according to the Constitution, was necessary. Strijdom simply appointed enough members to the Appeal Court and the Senate to get it pushed through. He then filled the Civil Service with Afrikaners to ensure all apartheid laws were fully carried out.

## The importance of education

Under apartheid, the education of black children was designed to ensure that their qualifications would always be inferior to those of white children. The Bantu Education Act of 1953 abolished all missionary schools which had given good instruction in English and encouraged black children to study for qualifications. Instead, responsibility for the education of blacks was transferred from the Department of Education to the Department of Native Affairs.

Under the Act, black children were to follow a different syllabus from that taught to whites. In fact, black children were only given enough education to enable them to be unskilled workers in factories and mines, or on the land, or to be servants in the homes of white people. They were taught their own language, but only enough English to communicate with their white employers. Virtually all black secondary schools were built in their homelands so that blacks could be kept out of white areas. In 1954, Verwoerd said that those who believed in equality were 'not desirable teachers for natives'. Many such teachers were then sacked or left in protest, and the number of high school teachers in black schools with university degrees declined dramatically.

## The extension of apartheid, 1958-1967

In 1958, Dr. H.F. Verwoerd became Prime Minister. He had been Minister of Native Affairs under Malan since 1950 and was a firm believer in apartheid. He was determined to begin a second phase of apartheid laws. In 1959, he pushed through the Bantu Self-Government Act, which involved the forcible removal of over 3.5

---

## (Purified) National Party

*This had been formed in 1934 by Dr. D. F. Malan, a member of the Nationalist Party, along with 19 other MPs who had been against Hertzog's decision to join forces with the South African Party. Malan was a minister in the Dutch Reformed Church, and was a strong believer in white supremacy. His aims of uniting all Afrikaners in a strongly nationalist campaign to defend white Christian 'civilisation' was supported by the Dutch Reformed Church. He was also supported by the Broederbond (Brotherhood), a secret but powerful society of white male Afrikaners. This new National Party won the support of those worried about the relaxation of segregation during the Second World War.*

## Apartheid

*This term means 'separateness', and was first developed by some Afrikaner intellectuals in the 1930s. Their ideas were strongly influenced by fascist ideas, and especially the racist doctrines which were put forward by the Nazis in Germany. They wanted a complete separation of all racial groups, with blacks only allowed to come into towns to work. For the 1948 election, they set up a special Committee, under P. O. Sauer, to draw up a programme for establishing apartheid which they hoped would win them the majority of Afrikaner votes. Although the Sauer Report helped them win 39% of the vote, the United Party and the Labour Party won 53%. However, the extra weighting given to rural votes allowed Malan to become Prime Minister. Malan's type of apartheid became known as 'baaskap' or 'white supremacy' apartheid.*

### Source A

The Natives will be taught from childhood to realise that equality with Europeans is not for them... What is the use of teaching the bantu mathematics when he cannot use it in practice...? There is no place for the Bantu child above the level of certain forms of labour.

*An extract from a speech made by Verwoerd to the South African Senate in 1953.*

million people from urban and rural areas which were declared to be white-only areas. The Act set up eight (later ten) Bantu 'homelands' and gave extra powers to the government-approved chiefs. All blacks were then attached to a particular 'homeland' area, known as a Bantustan, to which they had to move. However, although black South Africans were 70% of the population, they were only given 13% of the land.

In theory, Verwoerd claimed that these 'separate nations' would be given full political control and had been set up to allow the Africans to protect their language and culture. This was known as 'separate development' and was an attempt to make apartheid seem more acceptable. In fact, most of these Bantustans were in poor areas, with no amenities or industries. This forced people to seek work in white areas as 'migrants', where they had no rights. Verwoerd rejected the findings of the Tomlinson Report which, in 1955, had said that a large amount of central funding would be necessary if the policy was to work. Despite many protests, this forced removal was carried through - often with great violence. In 1964, the Bantu Labour Act made it illegal for black workers to seek work in the towns, and a State Labour Bureau was set up to administer it. This was followed in 1967 (a year after Verwoerd was assassinated) by regulations which forced blacks to live in their 'homelands' when they were not needed for work in white areas.

**Source B**

**Apartheid Laws, 1949-57**

**1949** Prohibition of Mixed Marriages banned marriages between different races

**1950** Population Registration Act classified the population into four categories

**1950** Group Areas Act set aside different residential areas according to race

**1951** Bantu Authorities Act set up local self-government areas for blacks, but under government-approved chiefs

**1952** Abolition of Passes Act replaced old pass documents for blacks with a new pass book

**1953** Separate Amenities Act segregated all public facilities

**1953** Bantu Education Act restricted education for blacks

**1956** Separate Representation of Voters Act deprived Cape Coloureds of the vote

**1957** Job Reservation Act, which further limited jobs which blacks could do

**Source C**

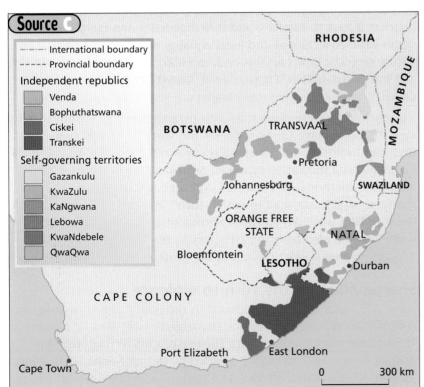

- - - - - International boundary
- - - - Provincial boundary

Independent republics
- Venda
- Bophuthatswana
- Ciskei
- Transkei

Self-governing territories
- Gazankulu
- KwaZulu
- KaNgwana
- Lebowa
- KwaNdebele
- QwaQwa

RHODESIA
MOZAMBIQUE
BOTSWANA
TRANSVAAL
• Pretoria
Johannesburg
SWAZILAND
ORANGE FREE STATE
NATAL
Bloemfontein
LESOTHO
• Durban
CAPE COLONY
Port Elizabeth
East London
Cape Town
0        300 km

*The Bantustans 'homelands' set up by the South African government for blacks.*

HUURMOTOR STAANPLEK VIR BLANKES.
TAXI RANK FOR WHITES.
TAXI WHITE PERSONS

**Source D**

*A photograph, taken on 15 November 1967, showing an example of segregation under apartheid.*

**Questions**

1 What were the two types of apartheid associated with, respectively, Malan and Verwoerd?

2 What do **Sources A** and **C** tell us about the aims of apartheid under Verwoerd?

# Growing opposition 1910-1977

## Early resistance to apartheid

Even before 1910, some Africans had tried to oppose the segregationist policies of both the Boers and the British. In 1912, after the formation of the Union of South Africa, the South African Native National Congress was set up. This became the African National Congress (ANC) in 1923. However, the ANC failed to stop the racist laws of the 1920s and 1930s. In part, this was because each African group was a distinct nation and they were unused to co-operating. In addition, white governments increasingly made sure that there were not many educated Africans capable of becoming leaders. Although there was some opposition to segregation from white liberals, and from the South African Communist Party (SACP) which was set up in 1921, the mainly middle-class ANC leaders were suspicious of the SACP. Furthermore, police violence meant that before the 1940s, the ANC had little success.

The Second World War provided an opportunity to organise opposition more easily, as so many more African workers were brought together to work in the towns and factories.

## The Freedom Charter

In 1952, Chief Luthuli became leader of the ANC and, under him, the ANC continued its policy of peaceful protest. He began what was known as the Defiance Campaign and, in 1955, a Congress of the People, made up of all anti-apartheid groups, drew up the Freedom Charter. It had 10 Clauses, and it demanded a non-racial and democratic government and legal equality for all. The government decide to crack-down on this and, in 1956, 156 people were arrested and put on trial. This 'Treason Trial' lasted for five years, so depriving the ANC of its main leaders.

Black women were particularly hit by apartheid, as the absence of men forced to leave the homelands and work in white areas meant they had to bring families up on their own for most of the time. Consequently, they also organised protests. One of the most important methods were the bus boycotts against the high cost of bus fares which they had to pay to travel into the white areas in order to find work. When the government announced that black women would also have to carry passes, the Federation of South African Women (FSAW) organised big protests in 1955 and 1956.

## Sharpeville and the turn to violence

Some ANC members were opposed to the policy of co-operating with non-African groups and became frustrated by the lack of success. In 1959, these more militant 'Africanists' split off to form the Pan-African Congress (PAC) which was led by Robert Sobukwe. In 1960, the PAC held a demonstration at Sharpeville. Police opened fire, and 69 protestors were killed. There was worldwide condemnation of this Sharpeville Massacre, but the South African government simply

### Source A

Early the next morning we set off. We proceeded in groups of twos and threes, silently. We could not sing or shout slogans because that would constitute a gathering and a march and we would open ourselves to police action... the Prime Minister was not there to receive the petition. They left their petition outside his empty office... and dispersed singing 'Now you have been touched by the women, you have struck a rock, you will be crushed'.

*An extract from an account of a 20 000-strong protest against the Pass Laws by women on 9 August 1956. The account was by Frances Board, one of its leaders. The protest and petition were organised by the Federation of South African Women, a multi-racial group. Its President was Lilian Ngoyi (a black woman); other leaders included Rahima Moosa, Sophie Williams and Helen Joseph.*

### Source B

*South African police checking the bodies of protestors killed at Sharpeville, 1960.*

responded by arresting thousands of people. It then decided to ban the ANC, the PAC and the SACP.

This event caused Nelson Mandela and some other ANC members to believe that non-violence had failed, so they formed Umkhonto we Sizwe (Spear of the Nation) to sabotage State property. In 1961, they blew up power lines in several places. At the same time, white students set up the African Resistance Movement, while the PAC formed a terrorist group known as Poqo.

## The Rivonia Trials

However, the police arrested Mandela in 1962 and eight other leaders in 1963. In 1964, they were brought to trial in what became known as the Rivonia Trials. They were sentenced to life imprisonment on Robben Island. Many ANC leaders who had escaped arrest, then went into exile to build support for the ANC, while others trained as ANC guerrillas.

Resistance also began to grow amongst young people. In 1969, Steve Biko set up the South African Students' Organisation (SASO). In 1972, he began a Black Consciousness Movement amongst black students, but his activities led to his expulsion from university.

## The Soweto Riots

Youth protests increased in 1976, when the government ordered that at least half the lessons (including Maths and Science) in black schools should be taught in Afrikaans, which was seen as the language of their oppressors. This came on top of the continued unequal funding of black schools. Many black students blamed their unemployment on the inadequate education they received. In Soweto, on 16 June, black school students organised a peaceful demonstration in protest. However, when the police opened fire and killed a 13 year-old boy, the protest turned into a riot. When white students heard of the killing, they organised their own protests in defiance of the government. Despite police and army attempts to suppress these protests, they continued to grow. It took several weeks before the government was back in control.

In 1977, Biko was arrested, tortured and eventually murdered by the police. The government also banned 17 organisations and two newspapers in an attempt to prevent further unrest.

### Questions

1 Why did some ANC members set up Umkhonto we Sizwe?
2 What caused the protests by school students in Soweto, referred to in **Source C**?
3 How reliable is **Source D** for finding out about the police response to the protests and riots in Soweto?

### Nelson Mandela

*Mandela was the son of a chief, and was educated at a mission school and then Fort Hare University. He was training to be a lawyer, but also worked for a time in the mines. He became involved in active politics in 1947, with the Youth League which had been set up by the ANC in 1944. In 1961, he was acquitted of treason, despite being an ANC organiser. But his leadership of Umkhonto we Sizwe led to his arrest in 1962. He was sentenced to solitary confinement for life in 1964, and was not released until 1990.*

### Source C

Twice the group of police tried to stop the procession. One policeman shot a boy who fell. I think he was dead. At that moment the children spread out and picked up stones. They started throwing stones at the police. Then the other policemen fired with revolvers at the children and seven more were hit by bullets. The dead boy was Hector Peterson.

*An eyewitness account of the events in Soweto on 16 June 1976, published in the Rand Daily Mail the following day.*

### Source D

There was a knock on the door. My husband opened the door and saw the riot police who then allowed a group of migrant [black workers] to come in, and they beat my husband until he was half-dead. One riot policeman remarked, 'You are lucky he is not stone dead'. Minutes later my husband died of head injuries.

*A description, by a young black South African wife, of what happened to her husband in their home near Cape Town. She is describing a police response to the Soweto Riots. In many places, the police encouraged older black migrant workers to attack and kill those they thought had been involved with the riots. In all, almost 6000 were arrested between June 1976 and February 1977, and over 700 blacks were killed - most of them by the police or those working for them. Hundreds of pupils were caned for demonstrating, and over 14 000 students fled from South Africa - many then joined the ANC.*

# Growing isolation and crisis

### External pressure

The response of the South African government to the increasing internal opposition to apartheid led to its growing isolation in the rest of the world. This began in the 1960s, after the Sharpeville Massacre. In 1962, the UN imposed sanctions against South Africa and, in 1974, expelled it. In 1961, South Africa left the British Commonwealth because of strong criticism of its policies. In 1969, the Organisation for African Unity (OAU) issued the Lusaka Manifesto, which called for the overthrow of apartheid by force if necessary. Across the world, including in Britain, anti-apartheid groups demonstrated against South Africa and organised boycotts of its goods and sports teams.

### Survival

However, despite this hostility, South Africa prospered in the 1970s. This was because it possessed many important resources (such as gold, diamonds and chromium) which were needed by many important countries, such as the USA and Britain. Because of the Cold War, Western governments supported South Africa (which was fiercely anti-communist) to make sure these resources, and the important oil-supply routes from the Middle East, did not come under the control of a pro-Soviet government. Also, because of the low wages paid to non-whites, foreign companies which invested heavily in South Africa were able to make huge profits. Many of these large firms put pressure on their governments to keep trading with South Africa. In 1966, Vorster became Prime Minister, and tried to assure the world that conditions for blacks would eventually improve.

**Source A**

*Supporters of the British anti-apartheid movement protesting in Trafalgar Square, London in 1977. They are outside the South African Embassy.*

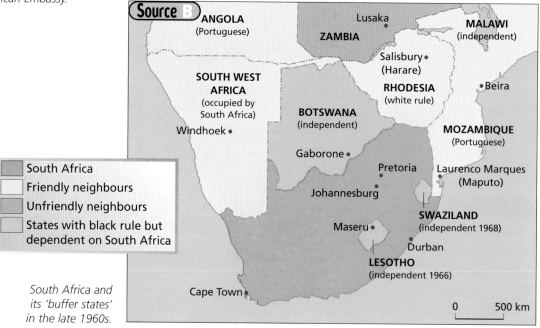

**Source B**

*South Africa and its 'buffer states' in the late 1960s.*

South Africa was also helped by the fact that in the 1960s and early 1970s, it was surrounded by many friendly countries, which acted as buffer states between South Africa and black African states.

## Increased control

The extra wealth resulting from increased prosperity was then used to make South Africa more self-sufficient and so overcome the effects of sanctions. This money also allowed the government to build up the armed forces (including the secret development of nuclear weapons). Government censorship of the mass media was also increased. Television remained completely banned until 1976. Finally, the minority white population remained contented as they were able to enjoy a very high standard of living with servants, big houses and swimming pools. As a result, many whites emigrated from Europe in order to share in this prosperous life-style.

## The collapse begins

During the 1980s, however, the situation began to change. By 1980, blacks made up 76% of the population (compared to 69% in 1948), and many were moving into urban areas. Yet the restrictions and inequalities of apartheid made it increasingly difficult for foreign firms to get the number of skilled workers required by modern technology. Then, in 1975, the Portuguese colonies in Africa became independent. In 1980, Rhodesia also became independent and changed its name to Zimbabwe. These new black African governments were opposed to apartheid, and allowed ANC and PAC guerrillas to operate across their borders.

As a result, South Africa decided to take military action to destroy these guerrilla bases. It sent troops into Angola in October 1975 to attack the ANC bases, and to destroy guerrilla bases belonging to the South-West African People's Organisation (SWAPO) which was struggling against South Africa's continued occupation of South-West Africa (declared illegal by the United Nations in 1966). However, the South African forces met strong opposition from Cuban forces which had been sent to help Angola. South Africa was soon involved in an expensive campaign which produced few results but which needed more and more troops.

### Buffer states

*These were the Portuguese colonies of Angola and Mozambique; Rhodesia (ruled by an illegal white government since 1965); and South-West Africa, which South Africa formally took over in 1969. Botswana, which had become independent in 1966 and had a black government, was too poor and dependent on trade with South Africa to offer resistance.*

### Source C

There is no case in history that I know where punitive general economic sanctions have been effective in bringing about internal changes.

*An extract from a speech made by the British Conservative Prime Minister, Margaret Thatcher, in 1986. She was commenting on the question of sanctions against South Africa. At the time, her husband had investments in South Africa.*

### Source D

Sustained international pressure and economic sanctions played a very important role in ensuring that it became impossible to continue with apartheid.

*An extract from a speech made in 1994, by Nelson Mandela, who became President of South Africa that year.*

### Questions

1 Why were the buffer states, shown in **Source B**, so important to South Africa in the 1960s and 1970s?

2 What do **Sources C** and **D** tell us about the issue of sanctions against South Africa?

# The collapse of apartheid 1978-1994

## 'Total Onslaught, Total Strategy'

In 1978, P.W. Botha became Prime Minister. He developed a new policy to deal with these problems, in an attempt to strengthen the links between his National Party, big business and the army. 'Total Onslaught' referred to the ANC guerrilla attacks, and Botha's policy involved increasing the army, attacking ANC and PAC guerrilla bases in the surrounding countries, and conducting a secret 'dirty' war against its opponents (this included assassinating ANC and PAC leaders). However, Botha also believed some reforms were necessary. So his 'Total Strategy' tried to win some support from Asians, Coloureds and Blacks by offering some limited improvements.

## The growth of opposition

Despite Botha's efforts, resistance to apartheid continued to grow. In particular, trade unions became stronger, and put pressure on international companies not to invest in South Africa. As well as organising political strikes and marches, they also began to form federations. As a result, some of the job restrictions were removed, the Pass Laws were relaxed and more money was spent on black education. Although these reforms did not alter the forced removals and segregation of the races, right-wing Nationalists split away in disgust and set up two rival parties: the Conservative Party and the even more extreme Afrikaner Resistance Movement (AWB).

Black secondary school students also increased their protests, while ANC guerrillas used the easing of the Pass Laws to enter South Africa and carry out attacks. In 1983, the multi-racial United Democratic Front (UDF) was set up to campaign for the Freedom Charter, while ANC leaders such as Oliver Tambo called on their supporters to make South Africa ungovernable. From 1984 onwards, outbreaks of violence took place in the black townships and, in 1986, the government declared a state of emergency in most of the country. The police violence used to suppress this opposition was broadcast across the world and made it increasingly difficult for companies to defend their decision to invest in South Africa.

> ### Source A
>
> The world does not remain the same, and if we as a government want to act in the best interest of the country in a changing world, then we have to be prepared to adapt our policy to those things that make adjustment necessary, otherwise we die.

*An extract from a speech made by P. W. Botha to a conference of the National Party in 1979.*

### Source B

*A South African policeman after riots in Soweto in 1986.*

### Source C

*A demonstration by young black South Africans in Middelburg, 1986. Note the UDF banner.*

# The end of apartheid

In 1989, F. W. de Klerk became Prime Minister, and immediately announced a new reform package. He continued the secret talks which Botha had been having with ANC leaders and, in 1990, Mandela was released. This ended the guerrilla war and de Klerk repealed most of the apartheid laws. Talks to draw up a new Constitution began in 1991 but important differences meant progress was slow, so the violence continued. Some of this violence was between ANC supporters and the Inkatha Freedom Party, formed in 1990 and led by Chief Buthelezi. However, in 1992, whites voted in a referendum for complete change. Despite this, negotiations broke down again in the middle of 1992, and serious violence broke out between the ANC and other black African organisations. Some believed the police had encouraged these attacks on the ANC. With the country close to total chaos, Joe Slovo, the leader of the SACP, suggested that the National Party and the ANC should agree to share power for five years. This resulted in the signing of the Record of Understanding in September 1992, which was an agreement to re-open discussions. Further violence failed to prevent progress, and a new Constitution was agreed in 1993. Free elections were held in 1994, which the ANC won. Nelson Mandela then became President on 10 May 1994.

**Source D**

Let me remind you of three little words... The first word is 'all'. We want all our rights, not just a few token handouts which the government sees fit to give... And we want all of South Africa's people to have their rights...not just 'Coloureds' or 'Indians'... The second word is...'here'. We want all our rights here in a united, undivided South Africa. We do not want them in [poor] homelands,...in separate little group areas. The third word is... 'now'. We want all our rights, we want them here, and we want them now...

*An extract from a speech made by Dr. Allan Boesak, a black South African Church leader, in 1983.*

**Source E**

*Winnie Mandela with some of her supporters, They wanted a more radical transformation than the official ANC leadership.*

*The results of the first democratic elections held in South Africa, April 1994.*

**Source F**

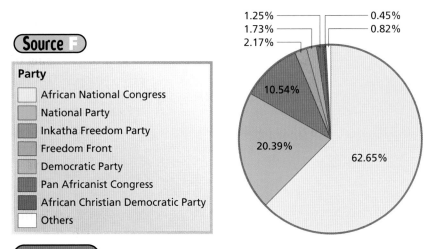

**Party**

- African National Congress
- National Party
- Inkatha Freedom Party
- Freedom Front
- Democratic Party
- Pan Africanist Congress
- African Christian Democratic Party
- Others

1.25%  0.45%
1.73%  0.82%
2.17%
10.54%
20.39%
62.65%

**Questions**

1. What led Botha to decide on making changes in South Africa, as indicated in **Source A**?
2. According to **Source D**, why were many black South Africans unhappy with the reforms carried through by Botha?
3. Why did violence continue even after de Klerk had repealed most of the anti-apartheid laws?
4. What do you think were the main problems that Mandela's new government faced when they finally took power in 1994?

# SUMMARY

## 1902–1948

- After the Boer Wars, the Afrikaner republics of the Transvaal and the Orange Free State came under British rule.
- In order to appease the Boers, the new Constitution gave them extra voting rights and allowed them to keep their racial policies. From 1910 onwards, many new segregationist laws were passed.
- Racial segregation and discrimination was undermined during the Second World War, when large numbers of black factory workers were needed.

## 1948–1966

- In 1948, the (Purified) National Party won the elections. Under its leader, Malan, the National Party began to create a system of apartheid (separateness). In 1958, Verwoerd became Prime Minister and began a second phase of apartheid laws.
- Resistance to this racial segregation was led by the ANC, and other organisations such as the South African Communist Party. In 1952, there was the Defiance Campaign and, in 1955, several groups drew up the Freedom Charter.
- Peaceful protest became difficult after the Treason Trial. Some left the ANC to form the PAC and the ANC set up Umkhonto we Sizwe to carry out sabotage. After the Rivonia Trials in 1964, Mandela and other leaders were jailed.
- International opposition began to grow after 1960. In 1961, South Africa left the Commonwealth and in 1962 the UN imposed economic sanctions.

## 1966–1977

- In 1966, Verwoerd was assassinated and was replaced by Vorster. Under him, South Africa became increasingly wealthy, and many international firms invested there because of the low wages paid to blacks.
- Surrounded by friendly countries, South Africa could ignore international condemnation of apartheid. The USA also gave support because South Africa was strongly anti-communist.
- Despite increased suppression, resistance continued to grow - especially amongst young black people. Steve Biko set up the Black Consciousness Movement and, in 1976, there were the Soweto Riots.

## 1978–1989

- In 1978, Botha became Prime Minister and adopted a policy of 'Total Onslaught, Total Strategy' to deal with growing sanctions and ANC guerrilla activities. Despite this, resistance grew, especially from the trade unions. Increased police violence led to more international condemnation.
- From 1975-80, South Africa was weakened by the loss of its buffer states. After the formation of the UDF in 1983, Botha began to make some limited reforms.

## 1989–1994

- In 1989, de Klerk took over as Prime Minister and immediately announced significant reforms. In 1990, Mandela was released.
- In 1992, whites voted for complete change in a referendum and Mandela and the ANC won the 1994 elections.

# Exam Question Practice

## Comprehension in context

Study Source A below, which is a poem about resistance to, and supporters of, apartheid in the 1980s.

Explain what Source A is telling us about the situation in South Africa in the 1980s.

*'A tough tale' by Mongane Serote, quoted in Beyond the Barricades.*

## Examiner's Tips

**When answering questions like this:**

◎ Try to extract as much information as possible from the source itself (such as names) and/or from the information about the source provided by the Principal Examiner.

◎ Try to comment on the impression the writer of the poem is trying to create or suggest.

◎ Remember to use your own knowledge to explain what is in the source, and to explain what is being referred to/what perspective is shown etc.

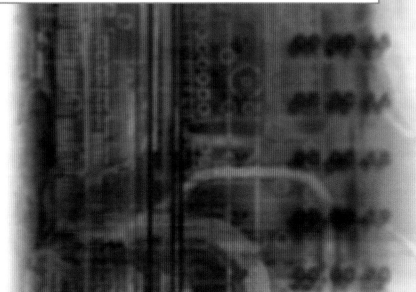

# CHAPTER 16

## THE RISE OF COMMUNIST CHINA

**Source A**

Mao Zedong (on the horse), and other Chinese Communists, escaping from Guomindang government forces on the Long March, 1934-35.

**Source B**

Troops of the Communist Eighth Army on the Great Wall of China. They are preparing to fight the Japanese invaders in 1937.

**Source C**

A woodcut of a Communist parade in Beijing in 1951, displaying the military power of the Communists. The Communists took power in China in 1949.

*A lone protestor confronts government tanks as they move towards Tienanmen Square to crush the pro-democracy protests there in 1989.*

*A huge Communist rally during the Cultural Revolution in the 1960s. The people in the front are all holding their copies of Mao's 'Little Red Book'.*

## Key Questions

**Why** was there a civil war in China for most of the 1930s and 1940s, a scene from which is shown in **Source A**?

**How** did the revolutionary leader shown in **Source A** come to achieve the power and adoration shown in **Source D**?

**How** did life change for the Chinese people under Communist rule?

**Why** has China continued to be the scene of political upheaval and violence, as shown in **Source E**?

These are some of the issues we will cover in this chapter. The main focus of this chapter on China will be:

* Why conflict broke out between the Nationalists and the Communists in the 1920s

* The civil war and the effect of Japanese aggression in the 1930s

* Why the Communists were able to come to power in 1949

* How Mao Zedong tried to modernise the Chinese economy in the 1950s and 1960s

* The political and economic turmoil which began in the late 1960s

* How China developed in the last part of the twentieth century.

# The rise of the Communists

## Mao becomes leader

In January 1935, in the town of Zunyi, a Conference of the Chinese Communist Party (CCP) elected a new leader. This new leader was Mao Zedong, and he took over at a critical time for the CCP which, since 1927, had been involved in a bitter civil war with the Guomindang (GMD) government of China. The head of this government was Jiang Jieshi, who had a fanatical hatred of communism. In 1930, Jiang had launched the first of five 'extermination campaigns' which were designed to wipe out the CCP and their Red Army, which were based in some provinces in the south and west of China. In the autumn of 1933, with the help of two military advisers from Nazi Germany, Jiang began the fifth extermination campaign, involving a GMD army of over 500 000 troops. This forced the CCP to decide on an attempt to escape to other areas. Their journey became known as the Long March. Eventually, the survivors reached Yan'an, a town in Shaanxi province, and began to carry out the reforms which had made them popular in Jiangxi. This won them new recruits, and they were also reinforced by other Communist forces which had escaped from the south. This gave them an army over 80 000 strong.

## Japanese aggression

The Communists were helped by Jiang's response to the increasing Japanese aggression against China. In 1931, Japan had conquered Manchuria and, from 1933, had begun to move into some of China's northern provinces. Since 1935, the Communists had been putting forward the slogan 'Chinese do not fight Chinese', but Jiang would not fight the Japanese until he had crushed the Communists. This made him very unpopular, especially as the Communists' move to the north had put them in a good position to organise resistance against the Japanese armies.

Despite this, in 1936 Jiang ordered another extermination campaign against the Communists and their base in Yan'an. His army in the area was commanded by the ex-ruler of Manchuria, and he and his troops wanted to fight the Japanese, not the Communists. As a result, they agreed unofficially not to fight each other. When Jiang heard of this, he flew up to his army's HQ in Xian in December. On arrival, he was taken prisoner by his own troops and forced to agree to form a 'United Front' with the Communists against the Japanese. He was released and Stalin then recognised him as the overall commander of all Chinese forces and provided him with weapons to fight the Japanese.

### Mao Zedong

*Mao was born in 1893 and became a librarian at Beijing University. In 1911, while he was still a school student, the last Emperor of China was overthrown in a nationalist revolution, led by Sun Zhongshan who then formed the People's National Party (Guomindang - GMD). Sun based the GMD on his 'Three People's Principles' of democracy, welfare and nationalism. Although the GMD won a majority in elections to a new National Assembly in 1913, a military dictator then took over and, after 1916, central government collapsed as China fell into chaos. Rival warlords carved out small empires for themselves, while the GMD tried to re-establish control. During this confusion, Mao helped found the CCP in 1921. In 1922, the GMD and the CCP formed an alliance to defeat the warlords. In 1924, Mao was elected to the Central Committee of the CCP. In 1925, Sun (who since 1922 had been receiving help from Communist Russia) died. He was replaced by Jiang Jieshi who, at first, continued the GMD-CCP alliance. However, in April 1927, Jiang turned on the Communists and massacred many in Shanghai and other important towns. Mao and several other leading Communists escaped and fled to rural provinces in the south and west of China, such as Jiangxi. Meanwhile, in 1928, Jiang became ruler of China after defeating the last of the warlords, although gangs of bandits and warlord rebellions still kept parts of China in chaos.*

### Source A

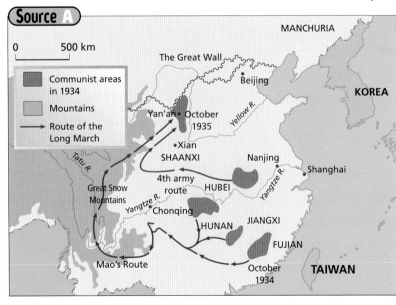

*The route of the Long March.*

## The Japanese invasion

In July 1937, Japan launched a full-scale invasion of China. By December, they had pushed so far south that they were able to capture Jiang's capital in Nanjing. Jiang and the GMD forces retreated before the Japanese and formed a new capital in Chonqing. However, even though the USA, after 1941, began to send massive supplies to Jiang, he tended to keep them for later use against the Communists. In fact, the United Front did not last long. As early as 1938, fighting between the two sides broke out near Beijing and, in 1941, the GMD launched a massive attack on the Red Army as the first step in another extermination campaign. The Communists, on the other hand, remained in the north to offer resistance to the brutal tactics often used by Japanese troops against Chinese civilians. As the Japanese army moved south, the Communist Red Army took control of many parts of the north and east in the years 1937-40. In 1940, they began their 'Hundred Regiments' offensive against the Japanese. The Japanese army's brutal response, designed to stop the peasants from supporting the Communists, had the opposite effect. In 1945, the Japanese began to withdraw from China, and the Red Army was able to establish many 'liberated areas' under its control.

## The role of the USA

Jiang had hoped that the Communists would be weakened by their battles against the Japanese. Yet, in fact, their resistance and their reforms brought them many new recruits. By 1945, the Communists controlled 18 'liberated areas' in rural China, while the GMD were restricted to a few coastal areas and towns. In August 1945, the US atomic bombs led to Japan's surrender and both the Communists and the GMD rushed to occupy the areas vacated by the Japanese armies.

Initially, the USA had been angered by Jiang's reluctance to fight the Japanese but had continued to send him supplies. Because the GMD had retreated so far inland, by August 1945, the Communists were best placed to take over most of the areas left by the Japanese. However, the USA did not want this to happen. As they wanted to prevent a Communist presence in Asia, they organised a massive airlift of GMD troops to the major cities and ports. In December, the Marshall Mission tried to prevent an immediate resumption of civil war between the CCP and the GMD by setting up a coalition government and by getting Jiang to agree to some democratic and social reforms. At the same time, Stalin put pressure on Mao to agree, as Stalin's main concerns were about Germany and eastern Europe. The USSR and the USA were both prepared to recognise Jiang as the head of the coalition government.

## The Long March

*Once established in the rural province ⌐ Mao decided that the CCP, defeated in the⌐ should set up a 'Soviet Republic'. In 1930, the⌐ introduced a Land 'Law' which took the land of rich landowners and divided it up between the peasants, abolished rents, reduced taxes, set up schools and intoduced other social reforms. They also set up Peasants' Councils which gave the villagers a say in running local affairs. The Communists also set up their own Red Army, under the control of Zhu De. It had a strict code of discipline and was well-behaved, and so won the support of the peasants. When Jiang launched the first of his extermination campaigns in 1930, Mao and Zhu adopted guerrilla tactics to avoid destruction. But, by October 1934, the Communists had lost over half their territory and over 60 000 soldiers, and were totally surrounded by the GMD armies. The leaders of the CCP, under Stalin's instructions, then decided that the Red Army should fight the GMD in pitched battles, and Mao and Zhu were removed from their positions as they were against this idea. After a serious defeat, which reduced the Red Army to 87 000 soldiers, Otto Braun (the Soviet adviser sent by Stalin) decided that the Red Army should attempt to break through the GMD lines, to join Communist forces in the Hunan and Hubei provinces. Though they succeeded in doing so, the Communists were reduced to just over 40 000 troops. It was these dreadful losses which saw Mao and Zhu returned to their positions in 1935. Mao decided that the Red Army should move to the more remote provinces in the north. They fought many battles on the way. In all, they covered over 9000 kms and did not reach the north until October 1935. Although they lost over 70 000 troops, they had built up good relations with many peasants on the way, and had been able to spread their ideas. They soon set up another soviet in Shaanxi.*

## Questions

1 Why, in the late 1930s, did Jiang Jieshi decide to fight the Communists rather than the Japanese?

2 Why, despite attempts to exterminate the Communists, did they in fact gain more support and influence?

# CHAPTER 16

# The birth of Communist China

PLA soldiers in the final stages of capturing the GMD-held town of Chinchow, in the autumn of 1948.

## The civil war, 1946-49

However, the truce soon broke down and fighting between the two sides began again in early 1946. At the start of this last phase of the Civil War (which had first begun in 1927), the GMD seemed likely to win as they outnumbered the Communists by 3:1. Their 3-million strong army was also well-equipped with American weapons. In addition, all the main towns, ports, and railways were under GMD control. The Communists, in the main, only controlled rural areas and had no airforce or navy. Much to their annoyance, they did not even have the support of the Soviet Union. However, their one-million strong Red Army, renamed the People's Liberation Army (PLA) in 1946, had a lot of popular backing and was led by Lin Biao, a skilful commander.

By June, the GMD began to launch major attacks on the PLA, and secured several victories. In March 1947, they captured the Communist HQ in Yan'an. Despite these setbacks, Lin Biao concentrated on guerrilla warfare and slowly built up his armies. By the end of 1947, the GMD had again lost control of most of central and northern China to the Communists. Jiang's position was further undermined by his failure to cope with rapid inflation and by the corruption of his regime. The USA had tried to set up and encourage a new party, the Democratic League, in order to build a popular non-communist alternative. But during 1947, Jiang's secret police, the Blueshirts, had wiped it out. By then, the USA had already given Jiang aid worth over $200 million. His corruption, his refusal to carry out promised reforms and the growing ineffectiveness of his armies finally led the USA to end its aid to Jiang, in case it fell into the hands of the Communists.

## The Communist victory

In 1948, the Communists were strong enough to begin direct attacks on Jiang's armies. Large numbers of Jiang's troops began to desert, bringing with them valuable military supplies. Gradually, the PLA moved south and north and began to capture the important cities. By the end of 1948, Jiang had even lost control of Nanjing. In January 1949, the GMD suffered a massive defeat which allowed the PLA to take Beijing in April. Further Communist successes led Jiang to flee to the Chinese island of Taiwan, taking with him the remnants of his

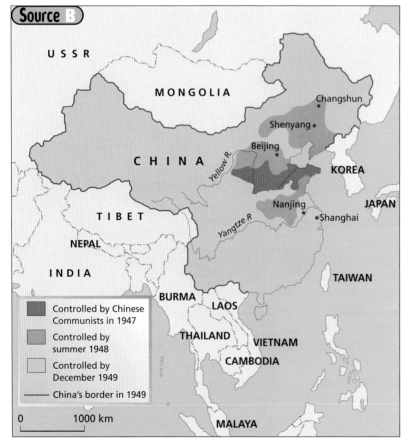

USSR
MONGOLIA
Changshun
Shenyang
Beijing
CHINA
Yellow R.
KOREA
TIBET
Nanjing
JAPAN
Shanghai
Yangtze R
NEPAL
INDIA
TAIWAN
BURMA
LAOS
THAILAND
VIETNAM
CAMBODIA

Controlled by Chinese Communists in 1947
Controlled by summer 1948
Controlled by December 1949
China's border in 1949

0       1000 km

MALAYA

The Communist takeover of China from 1947-49.

army and China's entire gold reserves. On 1 October, Mao and the Communists held a massive rally in Beijing at which 300 000 heard them announce the creation of the People's Republic of China. Jiang, who still claimed to be the real leader of China, then called Taiwan the 'Republic of China' and threatened to overthrow the Communists in the near future.

## Early policies

In September 1949, the CCP drew up the Common Programme which was to be the basis of its early policies. At first, the government was a coalition between the CCP and several smaller parties. The biggest problem was to provide sufficient food for China's rapidly-growing population which, by 1949, stood at over 450 million and was increasing by 15 million a year. However, the many years of civil war and war had greatly disrupted agriculture and communications. In the cities, there was high inflation and unemployment. At first, China's administrative system was reorganised to ensure central control. China's eighteen provinces were merged to form six large regions, each made up of smaller units ranging from towns as the smallest ones, through districts, cities, counties and provinces. At each of these levels there were Communist committees which, among other things, had to ensure that each unit carried out government decisions.

The five-million strong PLA was used to rebuild the damaged economy, and did much to repair the railway lines, bridges, ports and roads which had been destroyed in almost 40 years of civil war and invasion. But the PLA also played an important administrative role, as its top commanders shared power with the six regional councils.

## Equality for women

One of the government's first acts was to introduce a Marriage Law in April 1950, which gave equal rights to women, as well and made illegal things such as arranged marriages, child marriages and the killing of unwanted girl babies. Women were given equal ownership of family property, and the right to apply for divorce. In February 1951, expectant mothers were given maternity benefits equivalent to two months' wages after the birth of their child. The government also set up nurseries so that women could play an important part in the reconstruction and development of China's economy.

Plans were drawn up for a National People's Congress to act as a parliament, and to elect a Chairman of the Republic and a State Council to run the country. This met for the first time in 1954. Mao became Chairman, and Zhou Enlai - another founder-member of the CCP and an important leader - became Prime Minister and Foreign Minister.

**Source C**

The People's Republic of China strives for independence, democracy, peace, unity,... prosperity, and the strength of China... It must ... transform the land.... into a system of peasant landownership... It must steadily transform the country from an agricultural into an industrial one... The People's Republic of China shall abolish the feudal system which holds women in bondage. Women shall enjoy equal rights with men...

*Extracts from the CCP's Common Programme of September 1949.*

**women**

*For centuries, women had had very few rights in China. Female babies could be drowned at birth, while girls could be sold as servants or concubines (prostitutes) to wealthy men. Marriages were usually arranged, only men could demand a divorce, and women could be beaten by their fathers, husbands and mother-in-laws. Women were also not allowed to own property, which was solely in the hands of their husbands. The Communists were determined to end all these inequalities.*

**Questions**

1 Why did the USA finally stop its aid to the GMD during the closing stages of the Civil War?

2 To what practices before 1949 was **Source C** referring when it said that women were held in 'bondage'?

# CHAPTER 16

# Communist transformation 1950-1957

### Source A

In 1951 we set up a Mutual Aid Team. The work went well, but there were lots of quarrels about whose land should be worked on first. It was difficult to resolve all these problems. Some said 'Why should his field be taken first? I've got a bigger crop. It ought to be my turn now.' Whatever we did this went on. So we then began to talk about forming a peasants' co-operative.

*A Chinese peasant talking in 1953 about the move towards creating cooperative farms.*

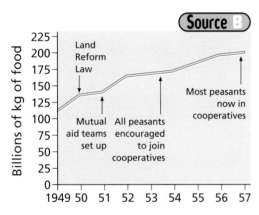

### Source B

*The increase in agricultural production achieved before 1958.*

*A painting showing a meeting between Stalin and Mao in Moscow in 1951.*

## Agriculture and industry, 1950-52

The main priority was agriculture, and the Communists simply extended many of the policies they had adopted in their soviets and 'liberated' areas. Especially important was taking land from the wealthy landowners and sharing it amongst the peasants. Many peasants either had to pay high rents or were too poor to rent any land at all. In June 1950, the Land Reform Law encouraged peasants to decide who were landlords or 'rich' peasants and which ones had treated people harshly. Those who it was decided had more land than they needed had their surplus land confiscated. This was then given to those who had none. Around 40% of all farmland was taken away and given to over 300 million peasants from 1950-53. However, because most peasants had no equipment, and their farms were very small, many formed mutual aid teams which were made up of about 10 cooperating families. A new Land Reform Law in 1952 organised peasant farms into larger collectives (lower-stage cooperatives), each involving about 30 to 100 families, in order to improve efficiency and output. Under this system, the land still belonged to the peasants, who received a rent from the cooperatives in return for the use of their land.

China had had very little industry, most of it foreign-owned. Although the banks, largest firms and those owned by foreign companies and GMD supporters were nationalised, the Communists at first cooperated with small-scale Chinese capitalists in order to avoid disrupting the economy. As a result, small firms were left in the hands of their private owners. According to Mao, it would be necessary to use elements of urban and rural capitalism to improve the national economy and that, therefore, the policy of the Communists would be to 'control not eliminate capitalism'. Instead, the Communists concentrated on dealing with unemployment by placing large State contracts, and improving workers' pay and rights by insisting that firms paid a minimum wage and gave paid holidays to their workers. In 1951, a People's Bank was set up which, by 1955, had ended inflation by taking control of all financial transactions and by limiting the issue of banknotes.

## The Five-Year Plan

Stalin had at first been opposed to the CCP taking power in China, in case it led the USA to change its mind over Soviet influence in eastern Europe. However, by 1949, the development of the Cold War persuaded Stalin to help the new Communist government in China. In January 1950, the USSR and China signed a Treaty of Friendship, Alliance and Mutual Assistance. Its main aspects were to provide China with Soviet financial and technical assistance over the next 15 years. This mainly consisted of credits rather than loans, but also included over 10 000 engineers and 300 modern industrial plants. Acting on the advice of Soviet experts, Mao set up a State Planning Commission to design a Five-Year Plan which would expand and modernise China's economy. However, at first, China's involvement in the Korean War meant there was little surplus funding available. Eventually, a Five-Year Plan was introduced in 1953, designed to build up heavy industry over the period 1953-57.

Because the Five-Year Plan required many more industrial workers, it was decided to further improve agricultural output by merging the lower-stage cooperatives into bigger higher-stage ones, involving 200 to 300 families. The idea was to increase agricultural efficiency, so that more food could be grown by fewer peasants. This would release many peasants for work in factories. This change began in 1954. However, in 1956, the peasants had to give up the ownership of most of their land. They were no longer paid rent for their land, which became the property of the cooperative. Instead, they were paid wages out of the profits of the cooperative. Many peasants were angry at having lost all but about 5% of their land, while the concentration on heavy industry and rapid industrialisation was causing shortages of goods and housing in the towns.

## Campaign of the Hundred Flowers

As well as carrying out a series of social reforms, the Communists also took steps to strengthen their position. During 1950-51, mass rallies had been organised at which people were encouraged to bring 'enemies' and 'reactionaries' to account. These were mostly collaborators with the Japanese or GMD soldiers. In all, such People's Courts condemned almost 1 million 'reactionaries' to death. Later in 1951, the Communists began a movement for 'thought reform', based on the study of Mao's writings. There were also various 'mass campaigns' to stamp out corruption, theft of government property and waste.

By 1956, Mao decided enough reforms had been carried out to allow people greater freedom to express their views. So he announced that the government would allow 'a hundred flowers [to] bloom and a hundred schools of thought [to] contend'. However, the changes and problems associated with the Five-Year Plan had caused much discontent, and many people began to criticise Mao, government policies and even the goal of socialism itself. As a result, in June 1957, Mao ordered a clampdown in which many critics were sacked or sent off to 'thought reform' camps.

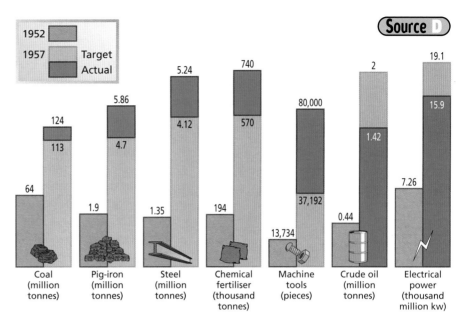

Source D

Legend: 1952; 1957 Target; Actual

- Coal (million tonnes): 64, 113, 124
- Pig-iron (million tonnes): 1.9, 4.7, 5.86
- Steel (million tonnes): 1.35, 4.12, 5.24
- Chemical fertiliser (thousand tonnes): 194, 570, 740
- Machine tools (pieces): 13,734, 37,192, 80,000
- Crude oil (million tonnes): 0.44, 1.42, 2
- Electrical power (thousand million kw): 7.26, 15.9, 19.1

*Official Chinese government statistics showing the increased industrial production achieved under the Five-Year Plan begun in 1953. Although the accuracy of these statistics is questioned, historians are agreed that tremendous increases were nonetheless achieved.*

### social reforms

*These included making all healthcare free and trying to improve the level of medical treatment. There was also a strong emphasis on the prevention of illness and disease. For instance, there were campaigns to clean up the cities and control the number of rats and flies. Basic education became a high priority, and a literacy campaign was launched as the vast majority of the population had had no education and were illiterate. By 1965, over 90% of Chinese people had achieved basic literacy and numeracy.*

### Questions

1 Who benefitted from the early reforms of the Communists in agriculture and industry? Explain how.

2 In what way did the closer relationship between the USSR and China, as shown in **Source C**, help Mao in his plans to modernise China's economy?

3 What aspects of the Five Year Plan, launched in 1953, upset many peasants?

# The Great Leap Forward

## The 'Great Leap Forward'

Despite the discontent revealed by the 'Hundred Flowers Campaign', Mao decided in 1958 that a Second Five-Year Plan was needed to deal with some of the problems which had emerged during the First Plan. In particular, he wanted to spend more on agriculture and on producing agricultural machinery, as well as developing light industry. He also wanted to establish or move industrial centres into rural areas. He hoped that 'the work of 20 years' could be done in just a short time by taking a 'Great Leap Forward'. In 15 years, he hoped China would have an economy superior to Britain's.

## The communes

To do this, Mao decided that China should be divided into communes, made up of groups of villages. Each commune was given a certain degree of self-government and was encouraged to be as self-sufficient as possible. The average commune had about 5000 families which decided together what work needed to be done and who was to do it. The local Communist Party formed a part of each commune and tried to ensure that Party policies were carried out. By the end of 1958, the vast majority (about 700 million people) were organised into just over 26 000 communes. Particular emphasis was placed on the production of steel in what was called the 'backyard steel campaign'. This involved setting up over 600 000 furnaces in towns and villages all over China. Most were so small they could only produce a few tonnes of steel.

## The 'Three Bitter Years'

However, although steel production in 1958 was over 50% higher than it had been in 1957, much of the steel was of very poor quality. In addition, although the communes had carried out the construction of many dams and irrigation systems using very basic technology, this had led to a neglect of agriculture as more time was spent on building projects than on growing food and fertilising the soil. In all, about 70% of all new spending in this period went towards industry, with only 7% going to agriculture. Bad weather in 1959 led to a massive shortfall in food production and to starvation in some areas. As a result, food rationing had to be introduced in 1959. The weather, and thus the harvest, was even worse in 1960, and serious food shortages lasted until 1961. Some estimates claim as many as 20 million Chinese may have died from starvation or diseases related to malnutrition.

One result of these 'three bitter years' was that, in 1959, Mao and his supporters were removed from some of their positions of power. Mao was allowed to remain as Chairman of the Party, but

### Source A

A propaganda poster produced for the Great Leap Forward, showing Mao.

### Source B

Coal and iron cannot walk by themselves... I and the Premier [Zhou Enlai] did not concern ourselves with this point.... I understand nothing about industrial planning. Comrades, in 1958 and 1959, the main responsibility was mine, and you should take me to task... The chaos caused was on a grand scale, and I take responsibility. Comrades, you must all analyse your own responsibility...

Extracts from a speech made by Mao in 1959, to senior members of the CCP. He is admitting that his plans for a Great Leap Forward have failed.

was replaced as Head of State by Liu Shaoqi. Zhou Enlai remained as Prime Minister and Deng Xiaoping became Party Secretary. These last three leaders were associated with the centre-right of the CCP, and were often referred to as the 'moderates'.

## Power struggle

The centre-right of the CCP began to make significant changes to Mao's economic policies. At the end of 1960, the Great Leap Forward was abandoned. Communes were made smaller, and the size of peasants' private plots was greatly increased. The 'backyard' steel furnaces were run down, and more reliance was placed on technicians and experts. The wages of factory workers were increased, and peasants returned to working on the land.

However, although Mao had lost control of economic affairs, he was still Party Chairman and an important member of the leading group of Communists and continued to have much political influence over ordinary Chinese people. He had always been suspicious of experts, fearing they might put their interests above those of the people and the revolution. He also believed that the Soviet model of industrialisation was not appropriate for a country like China. As a result, Mao began to use his position and influence to find a way to regain control of the CCP.

A serious debate soon developed within the leadership of the CCP over future economic policy. Liu Shaoqi and Deng Xiaoping argued for more incentives - including even larger private plots - for peasants, and for a return to the methods of the First Five-Year Plan, which had been drawn up with the advice of Soviet experts. Mao disagreed with these ideas and, in 1962, he launched a 'Socialist Education Movement', which attacked these ideas as taking China along a 'capitalist road' and attacked those administrators and peasants who showed signs of becoming 'capitalists'. At first, Mao's ideas had little support but, in 1965, he won over Lin Biao, the Minister of Defence responsible for the army. As a first step towards greater equality, Lin Biao abolished all ranks in the PLA, and issued each soldier with a copy of a book entitled 'Quotations from the Thoughts of Chairman Mao Zedong'. This small red book soon became known as the 'Little Red Book', and the 4 million soldiers of the PLA were instructed to study Mao's ideas.

### Questions

**1** What were the main problems associated with the Great Leap Forward?

**2** Study **Sources B** and **C**. Which source do you think is more useful as an explanation of why the Great Leap Forward failed?

### Source C

The disaster [of the Great Leap Forward] was seventy per cent man-made and thirty per cent due to natural causes.

*Comments made by Liu Shaoqi, a deputy leader of the CCP, on the problems associated with Mao's Great Leap Forward. After Mao was forced to resign as Head of State, Liu took his place.*

### Socialist Education Movement

*Mao had come to the conclusion that the Russian Revolution had been undermined by the reliance on experts and administrators. He believed this had led to a new class of bureaucrats who gave themselves privileges and, under Khrushchev, had begun to restore aspects of capitalism in the USSR. He believed that 'moderates' such as Deng and Liu were trying to do the same in China. To stop them, he concentrated on influencing school and college students to take action in a new revolution. He saw young people as being particularly important, as most had been born after 1949 and so had no real idea of what China had been like before. If they saw nothing wrong with current policies, then Mao believed that capitalism would soon re-emerge in China.*

# Mao and the Cultural Revolution

## The Cultural Revolution

Strengthened by Lin Biao's support, Mao launched the 'Great Proletarian Cultural Revolution' in the summer of 1966 against the centre-right and the administrative elite which he said was emerging in China. School and university students in Beijing formed themselves into units of Red Guards and began to put up large posters which criticised 'capitalist roaders' (those accused of following capitalist ideas) and those displaying 'bourgeois tendencies'. Schools and colleges were then closed down for six months while a new curriculum was drawn up which would place more emphasis on Communist education and values. This long holiday enabled the students to concentrate on the political campaign in support of Mao and his ideas. Large demonstrations took place, and some of them resulted in violence against those being criticised. Mao then gave the students free travel so that they could extend their campaign to the rest of the country. The PLA also provided transport and support. Between 1966 and 1969, almost 750 million copies of the Little Red Book were printed and distributed.

The Red Guards conducted a 'Four Olds' campaign against 'old ideas, old culture, old customs and old habits'. 'Counter-revolutionary' teachers and university principals were sometimes forced to do manual work such as cleaning toilets or working in the fields. Then the Red Guards began to get out of control and go on the rampage. Factories, offices, homes, and even the local headquarters of the Communist Party were broken into. Books, works of art - and even technology and machinery - which were considered 'bourgeois', were destroyed. Thousands of innocent people were accused of being 'capitalist roaders', and many were beaten, imprisoned and even killed. Many others were driven to commit suicide as a result of the accusations and ill-treatment they suffered.

However, the violence began to escalate in 1967, with rival groups of Red Guards fighting each other about which one was closer to the thoughts of Mao. Initially, Mao ignored this and a 'cult of Mao' was deliberately encouraged, with posters and statues of him appearing all over China. The Red Guards' growing criticisms of Liu Shaoqi and Deng Xiaoping enabled Mao to get both of them expelled from their government jobs and from the Party. Liu died in prison, three years later, in 1969.

**Source A**

*Chairman Mao with a group of school students.*

**Source B**

Although the bourgeois [capitalist] class has been overthrown, it is still trying to use the old ideas, culture, customs and habits of the exploiting classes to corrupt the masses, capture their minds and endeavour to stage a comeback.

*An announcement made by the Central Committee of the CCP in 1966. This then became the basis for the 'Four Olds' campaign conducted by the Red Guards.*

# China after the Cultural Revolution

By September 1967, some parts of China were in a state of virtual civil war as different Red Guard factions fought each other, so Mao began to reassert control. At the same time, the constant disruptions and accusations were seriously affecting industrial output. The Red Guards were told to go into the countryside to work with the peasants, and the PLA was used to disarm Red Guard units. Where disorder was most widespread, the PLA set up Revolutionary Committees made up of peasants, soldiers and Red Guards, as a way of forcing the students to be more practical. After concerns expressed by Zhou Enlai about the disruption of production and education (even government statistics showed an increase in illiteracy amongst the under-30 age group), schools and colleges were reopened. In all, some historians estimate that as many as 3 million people were dismissed or imprisoned during the Cultural Revolution, of whom about 400 000 lost their lives. However, by 1969, the upheavals came to an end. Although the political campaign continued, this was done by propaganda rather than by demonstrations.

Mao's position had been greatly strengthened as a result of the Cultural Revolution. Most of the centre-right had lost their Party and government positions and, in 1969, Lin Biao was named as Mao's 'successor' and 'closest comrade in arms'. However, Mao and Lin soon fell out. Lin, who had originally supported Mao's Cultural Revolution, had begun to have doubts by 1968 and, from 1970, seemed to think that Mao was power-mad. Mao, on the other hand, came to believe Lin was too impatient to wait for his death (Mao was 77) before becoming the next leader of the Communist Party. So, during 1970, Mao began to remove Lin's supporters from important Party positions. In 1971, Lin appears to have attempted the overthrow of Mao after drawing up a plan codenamed 'Project 571'. Though the circumstances are still not clear, it was later announced that Lin and his co-conspirators had been killed in a plane crash while attempting to escape. Some historians, however, argue that the tensions between Mao and Lin were deliberately created by the centre-right in order to prevent Lin from taking over when Mao eventually died.

**Source** C

Every letter in Chairman Mao's words is gold and every sentence is truth. Mao Zedong's thought is the red sun in the hearts of the entire Chinese people and of the revolutionary people the world over; it is their life line and their treasure. Fish cannot live without water and without Mao Zedong's thought how can people make revolution?

A Red Guard chant used during the Cultural Revolution. It shows the influence of the 'cult of Mao'.

**Source** D

In the 1950s, the Chinese were very simple. They believed in the Communists - like my mother. She's a teacher... Then in the Cultural Revolution they locked her up for a year and a half because her father was a well-known scholar whom they said was a 'capitalist'. Some Red Guards in her school made her kneel on broken glass in front of all the students...

Extracts from an account of her experiences during the Cultural Revolution, by a 16-year-old Chinese girl. The comments were made several years after the Cultural Revolution had ended. Forcing people to kneel on broken glass was a common punishment used by some Red Guards.

## Questions

1 Why do you think Mao decided to use sudents and even children to drive his 'Cultural Revolution' forward?

2 What were the effects of this decision?

3 According to **Source B**, what were the four methods being used by 'the exploiting classes' to regain their wealth and power?

4 How reliable is **Source D** as evidence of what happened in China during the Cultural Revolution?

# CHAPTER 16

# Right against left

## New power struggles

Whatever the truth about whether or not the centre-right might have helped 'engineer' differences between Mao and Lin in order to help their own return to power, a power struggle broke out after Lin's death. The debate about what policies China should follow was reopened, and the Party was soon split again between right and left. The right were now led by Zhou Enlai who, during the Cultural Revolution, had used his position to give protection to Deng Xiaoping after his dismissal. The left was led by Jiang Qing, Mao's wife, and by three radicals from Shanghai. Together, they were known as the 'Gang of Four'. The left had the support of the trade unions, the Communist Youth League and of many of the militias in the larger cities. They also controlled the press and the radio. In 1973, elections to the Politburo - the highest ruling body of the CCP - took place. These elections produced a fairly even balance between the left and the right.

By 1974, the main differences were over whether to concentrate on modernising China's economy or to continue the political campaign. Zhou Enlai and the right put forward the 'Four Modernisations', calling for changes in industry, agriculture, science and technology, and the army. The Gang of Four, however, believed the most important thing was to continue with the political struggle and campaign, in order to prevent officials in the Party and the State becoming conservative and so slowing - or even reversing - the revolutionary process.

## The death of Mao

In January 1976, Zhou Enlai died. He was a popular leader and thousands of Chinese people laid flowers in Tienanmen Square as a mark of respect. His place as Prime Minister was at first taken by Deng Xiaoping, who had recently been readmitted to the Party. But, in April, over 10 000 people rioted in the Square when police began to remove the flowers. The crowd also shouted slogans in support of Zhou and Deng. The 'Gang of Four' were able to use this riot as a way of removing Deng by accusing him of organising the riot in order to strengthen his position. The left were able to get him expelled from the Party, and replaced as Prime Minister by an obscure Communist, Hua Kuofeng, who seemed to be neither pro-left nor pro-right. The left hoped to manipulate him.

The influence of the left, however, was eventually undermined by Mao's death on 9 September 1976. Although they thought they were now secure, they were outmanoeuvred by Hua and the Politburo of the CCP. Hua quickly moved to make himself Party Chairman, which meant he also controlled the armed forces - as well as keeping his position as Prime Minister. As a result, Hua ended up with more power than Mao had ever had, as he now controlled the Party, the government and the army.

### Source A

In the days after Mao's death I did a lot of thinking... I tried to think what his philosophy was. It seemed to me that the central principle was the need - or the desire? - for perpetual conflict.... He was, it seemed to me, a restless fight promoterby nature and good at it. He understood ugly human instincts such as envy and resentment and knew how to use them for his ends. He ruled by getting people to hate each other.

*An extract from Wild Swans, a book written by a woman who had been a Red Guard at the age of 14, and whose parents (both members of the CCP) had been persecuted and imprisoned during the Cultural Revolution. She later left China and wrote her book in Britain.*

## The arrest of the Gang of Four

In October, Hua had the 'Gang of Four' arrested. He immediately launched a massive political campaign in the newspapers, on the radio and via wall posters, against the Gang of Four and their actions during the Cultural Revolution. Many of the wall posters demanded harsh punishments for the four, as well as attacking their ideas. However, it was soon clear that many of the attacks were really on Mao's policies rather than on just the Gang of Four. Yet, despite arresting the Gang of Four, Hua did not pursue the economic policies wanted by the right and, instead, continued with the broad outlines of Mao's economic strategy. In fact, because Hua said that whatever decisions Mao had made should be followed, the right soon began to call Hua and his supporters the 'Whateverists'. At this stage, though, the right were not strong enough to do more than criticise, as Deng was still without a position. Soon, however, wall posters began to appear with slogans calling for his return.

## Return of the right

In 1977, Hua brought back Deng as Deputy Prime Minister and Deputy Chairman of the Party. Deng then got Hua to appoint other members of the right to important positions. Soon the right were pushing Hua into going forward with Zhou Enlai's Four Modernisations. The CCP began to say that, following the death of Mao, China was now entering a 'New Historical Period', in which the economy would be quickly modernised. At the same time, Deng was associated with a campaign calling for the 'Fifth Modernisation' - democracy. In 1978, posters began to appear on what became known as 'Democracy Wall' in Beijing. These posters called for greater freedom, and many praised Deng. Some even began to criticise Mao's policies. Criticisms also began to appear in the official newspapers, and a number of unofficial papers began to appear. The fact that these criticisms were tolerated increased the popularity of Deng and his supporters. By 1980, Deng was strong enough to remove or demote Hua and his supporters, and to replace them with his own. Zhao Ziyang became Prime Minister and, the following year, Hu Yaobang became Party Chairman.

**Source B**

A Shanghai wall poster attacking the Gang of Four before their trial. Behind them, on the wall, can be seen pictures of Khrushchev, Hitler and Lin Biao.

**Source C**

Without democracy, the Fifth Modernisation, the other Four Modernisations are only a lie.

A wall poster from 1978, which appeared on Democracy Wall in Beijing. It was entitled: 'Democracy - the Fifth Modernisation'.

## Questions

1 Explain the meaning behind the numbers '571' which can be seen on the picture of Lin Biao in **Source B**.

2 What were the other 'Four Modernisations' in **Source C**?

3 Draw up a timeline covering the years 1973-1980 and mark on the main events (changes of leadership, deaths, arrests) outlined in this chapter. Use a system of colour-coding to indicate whether these events were a shift to the left or the right - or a combination! Explain the reasons for each of your coding decisions.

# Developments in China since 1980

The people are very clear that Chairman Mao was responsible, so far as his leadership was concerned, for their plight during the Cultural Revolution... However, they will never forget or obliterate his great contributions to ... founding the People's Republic of China and pioneering the socialist cause in China. Chairman Mao's great achievements are primary, while his mistakes are secondary.

*Comments made about Mao during the trial of the Gang of Four in 1981.*

**market forces**

*This means economic planning based on demand and supply rather than politics. Many in China were worried about the collapse of the Soviet Union in 1991, which seemed to underline the dangers faced when introducing 'socialist' market forces. Despite these fears, the number of Special Economic Zones increased and, in 1993, a Socialist Market Economic Structure (SMES) was set up. Although SMES had at its centre publically-owned sectors, it was intended to replace a centrally-planned national economy. As economic efficency was given greater emphasis, unemployment and food prices rose so much that the government had to introduce a new social security system to provide relief, though those in rural areas often had to rely on their families for support. Under the new Party Secretary, Jiang Zemin, there have been attempts to get the CCP to concentrate more on politics and less on economic efficiency.*

## Political repression and economic liberalisation

Once Deng and the right were in control, however, they began to clamp down on free speech. Wall posters were banned, the leading poster-writers were arrested and then Democracy Wall was closed to the public. At the end of 1980, Deng had the Gang of Four put on trial. In 1981, they were found guilty of various offences and sentenced to death - though Jiang Qing was spared. Deng and the right used the trial as an opportunity to attack Mao's policies, and to isolate Hua and the centre.

With all his main opponents defeated, Deng began to concentrate on China's economic problems. These were made especially clear during 1980 and 1981 when serious droughts and floods in some areas increased the general poverty existing in many parts of China. Deng's answer was to achieve modernisation by decentralising economic decision-making and opening up China to 'market forces' and foreign trade with capitalist countries. This process began in 1981, and he claimed it would allow the creation of 'socialism with Chinese characteristics'.

## Economic transformation

As early as 1979, Deng had influenced the drawing up of a new Ten-Year Plan to increase industrial production. Many new factories were built and workers were encouraged to produce more by being given bonuses. They were even allowed to open up their own small businesses. The Plan also allowed for an increase in the production of consumer goods. In agriculture, Deng again increased the size of peasants' private plots, while a 'responsibility system' (first tried in 1978) was developed in the communes. Peasants signed contracts to work an area of commune land and produce a set amount of food to be sold to the State. Any surplus could then be sold privately. This soon led to a significant increase in food production and the more efficient agriculture finally removed the fear of starvation. While industrial production did not increase as rapidly, the Chinese economy was soon experiencing a growth rate in excess of 10% a year.

Deng also set about tackling the problem of China's population which, according to the 1982 census, was increasing by about 12 million each year. In particular, the figures showed that if each family had the average three children, starvation would be a serious threat in the 21st century (see Source B). So the planners developed the One Child Policy as a way of combatting what was called 'the enemy in the womb'. The age for marriage was raised, and couples had to get the consent of the commune and pass a written family planning test before they could marry. Those who kept to one child were given bigger family allowances and better housing, as well as easier access for that child into higher education.

However, in some remote parts of the country this policy was ignored and couples continued to have more than one child. In other areas which did follow the policy, if the first child was a girl, she might be murdered by the parents, so they could try again for a boy. This was because Chinese society valued boys more than girls. As a result, thousands of baby girls were killed.

## The demand for political freedom

Although Deng's policies resulted in economic growth, they also increased unemployment in many areas, and widened the gap between rich and poor. Some Communists were concerned at these developments, and the encouragement given to foreign firms to build factories in China in 'special economic zones', as they believed Deng was deviating too far from Mao's egalitarian policies. Some of these Communists also seemed to be wanting some return to the mass participatory politics which at times had existed under Mao. Deng sacked or demoted several such critics and would-be reformers.

In 1986, university students began to demonstrate for political freedoms and human rights and, on 1 January 1987, many occupied Tienanmen Square in Beijing. Deng wanted to crush this unrest but was opposed by CCP leaders such as Hu Yaobang, who was Party secretary and was seen as Deng's successor. Hu was therefore sacked and was replaced by Zhao Ziyang.

## Tienanmen Square

In the spring of 1989, Hu died and student protests were soon joined by workers. The unrest continued to grow and, in May, a rally involving 1 million protestors took place. As in 1987, many of the protestors then occupied Tienanmen Square. The timing was highly embarrassing for Deng, as it coincided with a visit to China by Gorbachev (the leader of the Soviet Union who had been reforming the political and economic systems of the USSR since 1985). Deng, and the hard-line Prime Minister, Li Peng, wanted to use force to end the protest, but Zhao favoured discussions over the possibility of political reforms. At first, a compromise seemed likely, and Zhao obtained a promise of no punishments if the students ended their hunger-strike and occupation. But then the leadership of the students passed to Chai Ling, who was against any compromise.

Zhao and the reformers were dismissed and, on the night of 3 June, Deng ordered in the PLA. Over 50 000 troops, supported by tanks, were involved in the suppression. In all, about 1000 students and workers were killed before the occupation was ended. In the weeks which followed, many thousands were arrested and beaten, and some of the main leaders of the protest and occupation were eventualy tried and executed. While Deng was in favour of opening up China to world trade, he was clearly opposed to any political liberalisation. However, the discontents and the protests continued, as did the Democracy Movement.

**Source B**

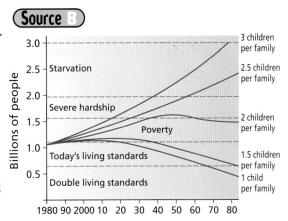

A chart drawn up by Chinese planners to predict the likely effects of China's growing population. These statistics became the basis for the 'One Child' Policy.

## Questions

1 How reliable is **Source A** as evidence of the extent to which Deng intended to follow Mao's economic policies?

2 What was meant by the phrase 'the enemy in the womb'?

# China and the world

## Friendship with the Soviet Union

Before the Communist victory in China in 1949, Communist Russia had given help to both the GMD and the small Chinese Communist Party. This continued under Stalin, even though he believed China was too backward - culturally and economically - to have a socialist revolution for decades to come. In fact, he urged the CCP to continue the alliance with the GMD, and even continued to give aid to Jiang Jieshi after his massacre of Chinese Communists in 1927.

In 1945, Stalin put pressure on Mao to form a coalition with Jiang and not renew the Civil War. However, with the start of the Cold War, Stalin began to change his attitude to Communist China. The first evidence of this was the Treaty of Friendship, Alliance and Mutual Assistance signed between these two countries in 1950. Later that year, Stalin and Mao cooperated to a limited extent over the war in Korea.

## Differences between the two Communist states

However, there had been several differences between Mao and Stalin. As well as thinking that the aid given by the USSR in 1950 was not enough, Mao was particularly angry that the USSR refused to help China develop its own atomic bomb. Communist China felt especially threatened during the Korean War, when US/UN forces came right up to its borders and General MacArthur hinted at the possibility of using nuclear bombs to end China's support of the North Koreans. In addition, throughout the 1950s, the USA gave strong support to Jiang Jieshi who had taken over the Chinese island of Formosa (Taiwan) after his defeat in 1949. At this time, Jiang was constantly threatening to launch an invasion against the new Communist regime in Beijing.

## The Sino-Soviet split

The relationship between the USSR and China began to cool even further after the death of Stalin in 1953. This was especially true after 1956, when Khrushchev emerged as the dominant leader of the USSR. Mao felt his economic policies were likely to lead to the restoration of capitalism in the Soviet Union. More importantly, he did not like Khrushchev's policy of 'peaceful coexistence' with the USA and its western bloc. According to Mao, such a policy was impossible and he became increasingly suspicious of Khrushchev's motives. The relationship deteriorated further as a result of border clashes along the Amur River which ran between the two countries.

There was also a serious dispute with the USA, in 1954-55, over some off-shore islands which the Communist government tried to re-possess. Tensions over these islands flared up again in 1957, and China asked the USSR for its support in re-taking the islands. Khrushchev refused and said he would only provide assistance if the USA invaded mainland China. Once again, the USA threatened

**Source A**

*A poster produced by the Soviet Union in the 1930s, showing its support for China. The poster says: 'China's path - the fight against imperialism'.*

**Source B**

n 1945 Stalin refused to permit China to carry out a revolution. However, we did not obey him and the revolution succeeded. Even after the success of the revolution Stalin feared that China might try to be too independent of the USSR. I went to Moscow and we signed the Treaty of Friendship. This was also the result of a struggle. Stalin did not wish to sign the Treaty, he only signed it in the end after two months of negotiating.

*A comment written by Mao in 1962 about his relationship with Stalin.*

China with nuclear weapons, and Mao was forced to back down. In September 1959, Mao was angered by Khrushchev's refusal to support China in a border dispute with India. The tensions between these two Communist countries came into the open at the Congress of the Romanian Communist Party in June 1960, when the Chinese delegate bitterly attacked Soviet policy. Khrushchev then abruptly ended all Soviet aid to China, just at the time when, as a result of the failure of the Great Leap Forward, China needed such help more than ever. The worldwide communist movement soon split into pro-Moscow and pro-Beijing parties. Although Khrushchev fell from power in 1964, relations between the USSR and China did not improve. Tensions were increased when, in 1964, without Soviet help, China was able to explode its first atomic weapon. In fact, in 1969, there were more serious border clashes along the Ussuri River, which ran along the border between Manchuria and the USSR.

## Relations with the USA

Since 1949, the USA had refused to allow Communist China representation at the UN. Instead, the USA insisted that the true representative of China was Jiang's tiny state of Taiwan. During the 1950s, the USA deliberately took a hard line with Communist China over the off-shore islands, partly in the hope that it might cause a split between the USSR and China and so destroy the alliance established by their Treaty of 1950. However, as the USA began to realise that it was losing in Vietnam, it saw closer relations with China as a way of putting pressure on the USSR and North Vietnam to reach an agreement. Finally, in 1971, the USA allowed Communist China a seat in the UN and, in 1972, US President Nixon visited China.

## China and Asia

When Mao died in 1976, China's foreign policy towards the West became closer, but relations with the Soviet Union remained cool. From the late 1970s, China also began to adopt a more active foreign policy in the Asian region. In the 1950s, China had encouraged Communist guerrillas in Malaya and the Philippines but, after the end of the Vietnam War, it was prepared to use force in key areas. In January 1979, after the newly-reunited Vietnam had invaded its ally Kampuchea (Cambodia), China sent an army into the northern provinces of Vietnam. After inflicting a lot of destruction, Chinese forces withdrew in March 1979. The main reason for this invasion was that, in the previous year, Vietnam had signed a treaty of friendship with the Soviet Union. China did not want to see the USSR establish a stronger position to the south of China in south-east Asia. Since the collapse of the USSR in 1991, China has been keen to establish close trading links with the West.

**Source C**

*The historic meeting between Mao and Nixon in Beijing, during Nixon's visit to China in 1972.*

**Source D**

Let me suggest something about the Chinese visit that the President can't say. The President, knowing of the quarrel between China and Russia, visits China, butters up the warlords and lets them be. Russia, therefore, has to keep 40 divisions of troops on the Chinese border.

*Comments made in 1972 by Ronald Reagan, a staunch Republican and anti-communist, about Nixon's visit to China in that year. Reagan later became President of the USA himself.*

**Questions**

1 How adequate is **Source B** as an explanation of why Stalin was initially hostile to the Chinese Communist movement?

2 Why, according to **Source D**, did the USA change its policy towards Communist China in the early 1970s?

3 Draw a line graph to summarise China's changing relationship with

a the USSR

b the USA

GOOD

POOR

1949          1996

# SUMMARY

## 1935–1949

- By the end of 1935, the Communists under Mao had completed their Long March and the survivors had established the new Shaanxi Soviet, based at Yan'an in north China.

- Despite growing Japanese aggression in the 1930s, Jiang continued to concentrate on trying to destroy the Communists. Although his troops forced him to make a United Front with the CCP in 1936, this was soon broken.

- Communist reforms and their resistance against Japan (which invaded China in 1937) made them popular with most peasants. Although a truce was arranged in 1945, following the defeat of Japan, civil war broke out again in 1946. By 1949, the GMD had been defeated and the Communists were in control.

## 1949–1976

- Under Mao, the CCP tried to modernise Chinese agriculture and industry, as well as carry out social reforms. At first, there was help from the USSR and, in 1953, China began its First Five-Year Plan. Its success led Mao to launch his Great Leap Forward in 1958. However, serious problems arose and, in 1960, he was forced to give up his government post. By then, a split had taken place between the USSR and China.

- By 1965, Mao felt strong enough to attack his centre-right opponents and, in 1966, began the Cultural Revolution. The Red Guards eventually got out of control and, in 1969, with most of his opponents defeated, Mao called off the Cultural Revolution.

- Although Mao had defeated his rivals, another power struggle began between right and left, which resulted in the defeat of Lin Biao in 1971. In that year, the USA allowed China to join the UN, and relations between the two states began to improve. Mao died in 1976 and the left (known as the Gang of Four) managed to get Hua Kuofeng appointed as Chairman. However, Hua then had the Gang of Four arrested.

## 1976–1996

- By 1977, the right (led by Deng Xiaoping) had begun to dominate the Party and, in 1980, Hua and his supporters were demoted or removed from power. Deng and his supporters wanted to modernise China's economy by introducing 'market' incentives and by 'opening up' China to foreign investment. In 1979, a new Ten-Year Plan was begun. Chinese forces also briefly invaded Vietnam.

- However, the modernisation programme caused unemployment in many areas, and created a widening gap between rich and poor. Growing protests against these economic effects began to combine with demands for democracy. In 1989, Deng ordered the PLA to use force to crush a student-led occupation of Tiananmen Square.

- Since then, the new 'socialist market' policy has continued, and the CCP continues to oppose any serious extension of democracy. But trade links with capitalist countries have continued to improve.

# Exam Question Practice

## Cross-referencing of sources

Study Sources A, B and C, which are about the Great Leap Forward.

How far do these sources agree about the reasons for the failure of the Great Leap Forward and the extent to which Mao was to blame?

### Source A

Coal and iron cannot walk by themselves. They need vehicles to transport them. This I did not forsee. I and the Premier did not concern ourselves with this point.... Comrades, in 1958 and 1959, the main responsibility was mine, and you should take me to task... The chaos caused was on a grand scale, and I take responsibility. Comrades, you must all analyse your own responsibility....

*Extract from a speech made by Mao Zedong to Communist Party leaders in 1959, about the failures of the Great Leap Forward.*

### Source B

The disaster was seventy per cent man-made and thirty per cent due to natural causes.

*The views of Liu Shaqui on the reasons for the failure of the Great Leap Forward.*

### Source C

However, the Great Leap Forward was actually a disasterous failure. In 1960, Mao quarelled with the new Soviet leader Khrushchev who then withdrew his advisers from China. The Chinese people were willing but they did not have the technical expertise to make the plan work...

This failure damaged and humiliated Mao. Deng Xiaoping and Liu Shaoqi edged him out of control of China. Mao remained Chairman of the Party but Deng and Liu were now in control.

*From a school history textbook, published, in 1996.*

### Examiner's Tips

**When answering questions like this:**

◎ Remember that comparing sources does not mean just describing, copying out or re-phrasing what the sources say or show - you must compare and contrast the sources.

◎ Remember that 'how far' means you must look for both agreements and disagreements, or similarities and differences, between the sources mentioned. For example, does one source contain extra information compared to the other?

◎ Make sure that you make detailed, precise and clear references to all the sources mentioned. However, the references do not have to be long - a brief quotation or example (or even a reference to specific lines in written sources) will be enough.

◎ It is a good idea to get in to the habit of writing answers to such questions which contain sentences like these: 'Sources A and B are similar/agree/support each other because Source A says... and Source B says...However, though Sopurce A says...this is not supported by Source B which says.../gives a different figure'.

# CHAPTER 17

## RACE RELATIONS IN THE USA, 1945-1980

**Source A**

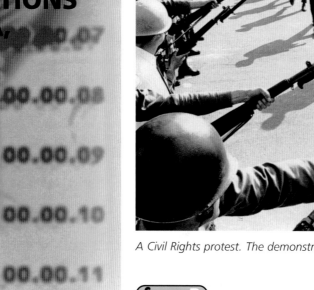

*A Civil Rights protest. The demonstrators are asking to be treated equally.*

**Source B**

*The Civil Rights leader, Martin Luther King, addressing over 250 000 people who joined a march to Washington on 28 August 1963. They were demanding that Congress pass a Civil Rights Act. It was at this meeting that King made his famous 'I have a dream' speech.*

A scene from the riots which broke out in Los Angeles after the Rodney King verdict in 1992. Rodney King was an African-American motorist whose vicious beating by white policemen was caught on camera. The policemen were acquitted.

The Black Power protest made by African-American US athletes at the Olympic Games in Mexico in 1968.

## Key Questions

**Why** were African-Americans in the USA, like those seen in **Sources A** and **B** - still having to demand equal rights over 20 years after the Second World War?

**What** led some African-Americans, like those shown in **Source C**, to make such a public protest about the situation in the USA in the late 1960s?

**Why** is there still such a problem over race relations in the USA that scenes like the one in **Source D** still take place today?

These are just some of the issues we will cover in this chapter. The main focus of this chapter on race relations in the USA will be:

- The impact of the Second World War on race relations
- The growing struggle against segregation in the 1950s
- The civil rights movement in the 1960s
- The emergence of more militant groups and their campaigns for equal rights
- Developments in race relations during the 1970s and 1980s

# CHAPTER 17

# The stuggle against segregation begins

## Four Freedoms

*These were: freedom of speech and expression; freedom of worship; freedom from want; and freedom from fear. On 6 January 1941, Roosevelt had said these four freedoms were to apply 'everywhere in the world'.*

## Source A

The British population lacks the racial consciousness which is so strong in the United States. The small-town British girl would go to a movie or a dance with a Negro quite as readily as she would go with anyone else, a practice that our white soldiers could not understand. Brawls often resulted and our white soldiers were further bewildered when they found that the British press took a firm stand on the side of the Negro.

*Comments made by General Eisenhower, US Commander-in-Chief of Allied Forces in Western Europe during the Second World War. In 1954, he became President of the USA.*

## Source B

I have personally seen the American trops kick, and I mean kick, coloured soldiers off the pavements, and when asked why, reply 'stinking black pigs' or 'black trash' or 'uppity niggers'.

*Comments made by an Englishman living in Birmingham during the war.*

## The situation in 1941

The USA's decision in December 1941, after the Japanese attack on Pearl Harbor, to fight in the Second World War was based in part on the 'Four Freedoms' which Roosevelt had mentioned in January 1941. By then, the USA was already giving aid to Britain in its struggle against Nazi Germany. However, some of these freedoms did not even apply to all US citizens, even though the USA was now involved in a war against the racist Nazi regime in Germany. In 1941, segregation and discrimination in the USA against black people was still widespread. They were treated as second-class citizens. Many were denied the vote, and there was discrimination against them in education and employment. This was despite the abolition of slavery in the USA nearly 80 years earlier.

Discrimination even existed in the US armed forces. Over 1.1 million blacks fought in the war, but they were kept in segregated units, with white officers. In 1941, there were only twelve black officers in the US armed forces, and no black pilots. In fact, segregation in the US armed forces was not ended until 1948. Very often, black servicemen were given menial labouring jobs in special labour battalions, rather than being allowed to use weapons in combat. They also suffered from racial taunts and abuse, even from their white officers. There was often trouble in Britain where white soldiers from the southern states of the USA were outraged that the lack of segregation meant black American servicemen could drink in the same pubs as them.

## The impact of the Second World War

However, under the impact of the war, things began to change. General Eisenhower supported the creation of racially-mixed units, and the number of such units - and of black officers - increased. By 1945, there were also several units of black pilots.

In the USA itself, over 2 million black workers were doing crucial war production work. Many migrated from the southern states, where segregation was strongest, to work in factories in the north. In 1941, Roosevelt was pressured by black campaigners into stating that all government agencies and defence contractors should end discrimination, and the Fair Employment Practices Committee was set up to check that this was happening. In 1942, the Congress of Racial Equality (CORE) was set up by black civil rights organisers and, in May 1943, Roosevelt announced that no government war-contracts would be given to firms which practised racial discrimination. Such developments, however, angered white racists and there were outbreaks of racial violence in several parts of the USA, such as Detroit and Harlem, in New York.

Whether they were in the armed forces or in factories, such African-Americans received much better wages than they had been used to. In particular, their wartime contributions led many to believe that, after the war, things would be different. During the war, the membership of the National Association for the Advancement of Colored People (NAACP) - the main black organisation campaigning for equal rights - rose from 50 000 to over 450 000. Black newspapers organised the 'Double V' campaign, which said that as well as victory in the war, there should be victory at home in the struggle for equality and black civil rights.

## Early attempts at desegregation

In 1945, despite some improvements under Roosevelt, black Americans were still clearly treated as second-class citizens. Under President Truman, some limited attempts were made by the Democrats to alter the situation. In 1946, he set up a Committee on Civil Rights to draft a programme to achieve greater equality. In 1948, on the basis of the Committee's work, he drew up a civil rights plan which proposed, among other things, an anti-lynching bill and a bill to outlaw the prevention of poor blacks voting. However, little progress was made as Truman faced opposition from southern Congressmen in his own party, as well as from the Republicans, and many of his proposals were dropped. However, segregation in the armed forces was ended, and government agencies were told to employ more black Americans.

## Education

It was not until the early 1950s that racial segregation in the USA was first seriously challenged by the government. This challenge came in relation to education, which was a highly-contentious area. Although segregation still existed in public facilities such as restaurants and transport, the harmful effects of segregation were greatest in education. In 1950, the Supreme Court made two decisions which encouraged groups such as the NAACP and CORE to step up their campaigns for greater equality. The first decision was that black children could not be segregated within a school attended by whites. The second was that when comparing the education provided for black and white Americans, all aspects - including the quality of teaching - should be examined.

**Questions**

1 How did the Second World War change the hopes of black Americans?

2 What does **Source C** tell us about the educational opportunities for young black Americans in the USA before 1950?

**Source C**

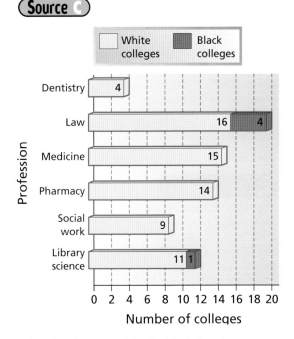

*Educational opportunities for black Americans before 1950.*

# CHAPTER 17

# Segregation and civil rights

## Segregation in schools and the US Constitution

In 1954, when Eisenhower became President, only sixteen states had laws which said that all children must be educated in integrated schools. Many of the local school districts also ignored these laws. On the other hand, twenty US states - and Washington DC itself - had laws which enforced segregated education in schools which were said to be 'separate but equal'. This segregation had been upheld by the Supreme Court which, in 1896, had ruled that provided there was 'equal provision', segregation was legal. However, these schools had never been equal. Instead, much less money was made available for black schools which, as a result, had larger classes and fewer resources. This meant that black children were denied equal educational opportunity. The black civil rights organisations were determined to change this.

## Brown v. Topeka Board of Education

The NAACP decided to challenge the legality of segregation by taking a test case to court, against the school board of Topeka in Kansas. The NAACP argued that Linda Brown, who was seven years old, should be allowed to go to her nearest school (just a few streets away) rather than be forced to go to an all-black school several miles away.

On 17 May 1954, the Chief Justice of the Supreme Court, Earl Warren, announced that the Supreme Court had unanimously agreed that segregation in schools was illegal. The court also said that all states should set up schools which educated black and white children together. Although Eisenhower had, as one of his first acts on becoming President, appointed Warren, he was not happy about the ruling. This was because, though he supported racial desegregation, he knew many whites - especially in the South - would react violently against such a decision. Eisenhower had hoped instead to end segregation by a series of small reforms spread over a number of years. However, he accepted the ruling and promised to enforce it. In 1955, the Supreme Court ruled that all states had to comply with the 1954 ruling and integrate their schools.

## Little Rock, Arkansas

However, many schools resisted the order to desgregate their schools. This was particularly so in the South where, by the end of 1956, six states were still keeping all black pupils in separate schools. In many other states, very little had been done to achieve integration. In part, this was the result of a massive resistance campaign organisd by white racists. The Ku Klux Klan experienced a revival among poor whites, and beatings and even lynchings began to occur once again. Middle-class whites, meanwhile, organised 'White Citizens' Councils' to prevent integration.

### Source A

To separate [Negro children] from others of similar age and qualifications, solely because of their race, generates a feeling of inferiority as to their status in the community that may affect their hearts and minds in a way never to be undone...We conclude that in the field of public education the doctrine of 'separate but equal' has no place. Separate educational facilities are inherently unequal.

*An extract from Chief Justice Warren's ruling on 17 May 1954 on the Brown v. Topeka case in the Supreme Court. It said segregation in education was against the US Constitution.*

### Ku Klux Klan

*This racist organisation had been very active in the 1920s and 1930s, but had then begun to decline until the controversy surrounding the de-segregation of schools in the 1950s. In 1955, a 14 year-old black boy, Emmett Till, was brutally murdered in Mississippi for having said 'Bye, baby' to a white woman. Emmett, who was from Chicago and was visiting relatives, was not used to the racist ways of the South. Those believed to have been responsible for his death were acquitted by an all-white jury. However, Emmett's murder, and the failure to punish his killers, did much to raise awareness of the problems of racial intolerance in the South. Many liberal whites then joined blacks in the civil rights campaigns.*

One of the most famous incidents connected to the desegregation of schools took place at the Central High School in Little Rock, the capital town of the state of Arkansas. In September 1957, nine black students were supposed to enrol in the school which, until then, had always been an all-white school. The Governor of Arkansas, Orval Faubus, used the state's National Guard to prevent the black students from entering the school. When a court ruled against this action, he withdrew the National Guard, even though a crowd of over 1000 whites then gathered outside the school to prevent the attendance of these students. Eisenhower responded by sending in 1000 federal army paratroopers to protect the children and to allow them to attend the school. Faubus was then ordered to use the National Guard to protect the students for the rest of the year, once the federal troops had left in October. The following year, Faubus tried to prevent integration by closing all schools in Little Rock, but he was forced to open them up by the Supreme Court.

## The Montgomery bus boycott

The successful use of the law to end segrgation in schools encouraged other attempts to end all aspects of segregation in the USA. One aspect of segregation which affected many blacks in the South on a daily basis was the segregation on buses. Blacks were only allowed to sit at the back of buses, and had to give up their seats if whites had nowhere to sit. On 1 December 1955, in Montgomery in Alabama, a black woman called Rosa Parks sparked off an important protest. She was tired after a hard day's work and refused to give up her seat to a white man. She was arrested and fined $10 but, within 48 hours, her friends had organised a boycott of the bus company in protest. After one day, they extended the boycott and demanded that the company should seat all passengers on a first-come basis.

## The start of the civil rights movement

One of the main organisers of this protest was a young Baptist minister, Martin Luther King, who had been inspired by the peaceful protests organised by Mahatma Gandhi in India against British rule. He was against violence and instead urged blacks to adopt civil disobedience to obtain their civil rights. He persisted in his calls for peaceful protest, even when the homes of the organisers were attacked and even bombed by white racists. The bus boycott lasted for over a year, and cost the bus company a lot of money, as blacks were 75% of their customers. Eventually, in November 1956, the Supreme Court ruled that segregation on buses was illegal. On 20 December, the bus company gave in. Many blacks then decided to organise sit-down protests and demonstrations against segregation in other areas of life, such as hotels, restaurants and libraries. Black Americans were further encouraged by the passing of the Civil Rights Act in 1957. This was an attempt by Eisenhower to stop black people being prevented from voting.

**Source B**

The mob was jeering and spitting. It had to be the most frightening thing, because she had a large crowd of white peole threatening to kill her. And she had nobody. There wasn't a black face anywhere. Then this whitw womwn came out of the crowd and guided her on to the bus and got her home safely. Elizabeth was in tears.

*One of the 'Little Rock Nine' describing the experience of Elizabeth Eckford (another of the nine black students) when she tried to gain entry to the Litle Rock Central School in September 1957.*

**Source C**

*Some civil rights protestors carrying out a 'lie down' protest in front of the White House in Washington DC. This was typical of the non-violent civil disobedience methods favoured by Martin Luther King.*

**Questions**

1  What was the significance of the Brown v. Topeka judgement made by the Supreme Court in 1954?

2  What methods did King adopt in the struggle by blacks for civil rights?

# Civil rights or black power?

*An extract from Martin Luther King's famous speech made in Washington in August 1963. He was awarded the Nobel Peace Prize in 1964 for his efforts to achieve equal treatment for everyone.*

## Civil rights under Kennedy

In 1960, the USA elected J F Kennedy as President. Although he supported sit-ins and promised civil rights, his first official statement made no mention of these things. So black organisations decided to increase their protests, and take more direct action. Some members of CORE organised 'Freedom Rides' in an attempt to get integration on all buses and in all bus stations. Many of these 'Freedom Riders' were arrsted, but this only gave their cause more publicity. In April 1960, the Student Non-violent Co-ordinating Committee (SNCC) was set up to join the fight against segregation which still operated in many southern states. Many of these campaigners were beaten up and some were even murdered. However, in September 1961, the government ruled that all segregation in bus stations and terminals should end. Meanwhile, talks had begun between the government and the main civil rights organisations. One result was the Voter Education Project, which was an attempt to get black people to register as voters. But this too often resulted in violence from white racists.

## Events in Birmingham, Alabama

In 1962, the authorities in Birmingham, Alabama, closed all public facilities in order to avoid having to open them up to blacks. So, Martin Luther King organised huge but peaceful protests which were suppoted by many whites as well as blacks. During a peaceful demonstration in April 1963, the Chief of Police, 'Bull' Connor, ordered his men to attack the demonstrators with tear gas, fire hoses, dogs and electric cattle prods. Many were injured, and over 3000 - including King - were thrown in jail. This received much TV coverage and shocked many white Americans in the North. In August 1963, King organised a huge demonstration in Washington to demand civil rights. Over 250 000 demonstrators were present, including over 60 000 whites. Spurred on by these events, Kennedy at last decided to take action to end racial discrimination. However, although he drew up a Civil Rights Act, opposition from southern Congressman meant it had not become law before he was assassinated in November 1963.

**Source B**

*A meeting between Martin Luther King (left) and Malcolm X.*

## Civil Rights legislation in the 1960s

Vice-President Johnson, who took over in 1963, was able to get Kennedy's Civil Rights Act through Congress and the Senate in 1964. This made discrimination in employment, public facilities and all public bodies, including schools, illegal. Further acts followed: in 1965, the Voting Rights Act outlawed racial discrimination over the right to vote and, in 1967, the Supreme Court declared illegal all laws in the southern states which prevented inter-racial marriages. Then, in 1968, the Civil Rights (Fair Housing) Act made racial discrimination in housing illegal.

## The emergence of the Black Power movement

However, although the laws had been passed, it was often still extremely difficult to get them enforced. Violence against blacks still took place, especially in the South. In addition, the Civil Rights Acts did nothing to tackle the great poverty experienced by many blacks in the North as well as the South. This led some black leaders to split away from King's leadership. Younger leaders, such as Malcolm X and Stokely Carmichael, argued that whites would not give blacks equal rights unless they met violence with violence. Malcolm X set up the Nation of Islam and, as well as calling for self-defence, began to argue for black separatism, but was assassinated in 1965. Tensions built up in poor black communities and serious riots broke out in many US cities. The worst riot was in the Watts district of Los Angeles in August 1965. This lasted for six days and 34 people died, as well as much property being destroyed. During the summers of 1966-67, such riots became a common feature. In the 1967 riots, 83 people died.

In 1966, Stokely Carmichael was elected leader of the SNCC. He believed in 'Black Power' and also supported the idea of blacks separating from white society which he said was inherently racist and violent towards blacks. The most militant Black Power group set up, in 1966, was the Black Panthers, whose members openly carried guns as protection against the police. Violence increased again after April 1968, when King was assassinated by a white man while he was in Memphis.

## Race relations in the 1970s

The serious riots in the late 1960s forced the government to take a closer look at the situation of blacks in the USA. President Johnson set up a Commission of Inquiry, headed by Governor Kerner of Illinois, to discover the reasons behind these riots. The Kerner Report identified the many frustrations experienced by black Americans, including their relative poverty as a result of low pay and substandard housing. Gradually, however, the various civil rights laws were enforced, while many blacks were determined to exercise their rights. After the riots and the death of King, many black Americans began to use their vote to elect black politicians who they hoped would improve their conditions. As early as 1967, the first ever black Mayor was elected, when Carl Stokes became Mayor of Cleveland. By 1985, over 10% of all elected officials in the USA were black. However, racial inequality and prejudice are still major problems in the USA.

Source C

A demonstration by members of the Black Panthers in New York in protest at the arrest of one of their leaders.

Source D

An armed policeman standing over the body of a black American shot during the race riots in Watts, Los Angeles, in August 1965.

### Questions

1 Why did some black leaders, such as Malcolm X shown in **Source B**, reject the methods of Martin Luther King?

2 How important was Martin Luther King's role in achieving civil rights legislation?

3 How did the US government react to the outbreak of riots in the late 1960s, such as the one referred to in **Source D**?

# SUMMARY

## 1945–1959

- As a result of developments during the Second World War and growing pressure from black organisations, the US government began to make attempts to improve the civil rights of black Americans.
- In 1946, Truman set up a Committee on Civil Rights. But, although his plans were blocked by Congress in 1948, he was able to end segregation in the armed forces. He also ordered government agencies to employ more blacks.
- In 1950, the Supreme Court made two rulings about segregation in education. In 1954, the Brown v. Topeka case saw the Supreme Court rule that all segregation in schools was illegal.
- in 1955, the Montgomery bus boycott began against segregation on buses. But change was slow to come in the South. In 1957, the government had to send troops to Little Rock in Arkansas to protect nine black school children who were trying to attend a school which had previously been white-only. Later that year, Eisenhower was able to get a Civil Rights Act through Congress.

## 1960–1969

- Despite earlier promises, reforms were slow to come from Kennedy, so some black organisations began to take direct action - such as sit-ins, and the 'Freedom Rides' to enforce desegregation on buses.
- After great police violence in Birmingham Alabama in April 1963, against a peaceful protest led by Martin Luther King, a huge demonstration took place in Washington in August. Kennedy finally decided to take action against racial discrimination, but his proposals for a new Civil Rights Act were blocked by Congress.
- However, in 1964, Johnson was able to get the Act through. In 1965, he pushed through the Voting Rights Act and, in 1968, another act outlawed racial discrimination in housing.
- By then, though, some blacks had become impatient at the slowness with which these laws were implemented. Leaders such as Malcolm X and Stokely Carmichael, and organisations like the Black Panthers, rejected King's non-violent methods. Instead, they called for Black Power and black separation. During the late 1960s, there were riots against discrimination, police violence and poverty in many American cities. In 1968, King was assassinated.

## 1970–1980

- Although racial discrimination and violence continued, more blacks were able to obtain a better education.
- At the same time, the growing number of black voters began to use their vote to bring about change by electing black officials to positions of power.

# Exam Question Practice

## Judgement or interpretation questions

Study Sources A and B below, and then answer the following question:

'Racial discrimination was so strong throughout the USA in the 1950s and 1960s that only violent methods stood any chance of succeeding in getting reforms'. Do you agree with this statement? Use the sources and your own knowledge to explain your answer.

### Source A

It ought to be possible for American citizens of any color to register and to vote in a free election without interference or fear of reprisal... in short, every American ought to have the right to be treated as he would wish to be treated. But this is not the case.

*An extract from a TV speech on racial discrimination in the USA, made by President Kennedy in June 1963.*

### Source B

I don't go along with any kind of non-violence unless everybody's going to be non-violent. If they make the Ku Klux Klan non-violent, I'll be non-violent. If they make the White Citizens' Council non-violent, I'll be non-violent. But as long as you've got somebody else not being non-violent, I don't want anybody coming to me talking any non-violent talk...

You get freedom by letting your enemy know that you'll do anything to get your freedom; then you'll get it. It's the only way you'll get it... fight them, and you'll get your freedom...

*Comments made by Malcolm X on Martin Luther King's call for non-violent protest against racial inequality and discrimination.*

## Examiner's Tips

**When answering questions like this:**

◎ Make sure you do the two things the question asks you - use your own knowledge AND the sources.

◎ Don't just say 'Yes' or 'No' - the Principal Examiner will be expecting a balanced answer which tries to look at both sides of the question ( 'Yes'- violent methods were needed and 'No'- other non-violent methods were effective). You should try to spend roughly the same amount of time on putting both sides, even if you have a strong view one way or the other.

◎ Make sure you give reasons for your conclusions - don't just give different arguments and then simply identify the one you prefer.

◎ Make sure you deal with a range of issues/factors - you will not score high marks if you only comment on one aspect.

◎ When you are using your own knowledge, try to give detailed and precise bits of information, e.g. don't just say non-violent methods did achieve results, try and refer to particular examples, such as the bus boycott campaign.

◎ If you can't make a decision one way or the other, say so and show why (e.g. that while changes in the law were achieved by non-violent means, in many instances it was force - or the threat of force - which finally got the reforms fully implemented).

# INDEX

# INDEX